Taxation: Policy and Practice

17th Edition

2010/11

Taxation
Policy and Practice

17th edition
2010/2011

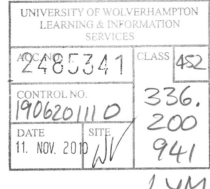
Andy Lymer
Professor of Accounting & Taxation
University of Birmingham

Lynne Oats
Professor of Taxation & Accounting
University of Exeter

FISCAL
PUBLICATIONS

Taxation: policy and practice – 17ᵗʰ Edition 2010/2011

Copyright © Andy Lymer & Lynne Oats

For more information, contact Fiscal Publications, Unit 100, The Guildhall Edgbaston Park Road, Birmingham, B15 2TU, UK or visit: http://www.fiscalpublications.com

ISBN 978-1906201111

First edition	1993	Tenth edition	2003
Second edition	1994	Eleventh edition	2004
Third edition	1995	Twelfth edition	2005
Fourth edition	1996	Thirteenth edition	2006
Fifth edition	1997	Fourteenth edition	2007
Sixth edition	1999	Fifteenth edition	2008
Seventh edition	2000	Sixteenth edition	2009
Eighth edition	2001	Seventeenth edition	2010
Ninth edition	2002		

Cover design by Filter Design Ltd
Printed in Great Britain by Antony Rowe Ltd., Chippenham, Wiltshire
Typesetting and production by Mac Bride.

You will also find a number of quick quizzes, longer self-test and full exam level questions at the end of each chapter that cover the material explained in the chapter. Some of these have answers provided in the back of the book but for others you will have to obtain the answers from your lecturer or teacher, as they will only be provided to them via their section of the website.

As you read the text you will regularly meet new tax terms. You will find all the terms you will need to be familiar with in the glossary at the back of the book. Use this resource as you come across the terms so you can gradually build up your tax vocabulary as you learn new tax ideas and techniques. To help you in this process we put words in italics when we introduce new terms that so you can easily spot you need to take special note and make sure you are aware of their meaning.

Website

A comprehensive website is available to all purchasers of this book to support your use of this text (**http://www.taxstudent.com/uk**). This site is enhanced each year and you should consider it as a direct extension to the book. It contains a range of materials and resources that will help you gain the most from your studying of the UK's taxation system. The site includes:

- extensive multiple choice based self-test questions for each chapter,
- extensions to many areas of the text to allow you to go deeper into particular topics if you need to (watch out for the pointers to this as you work through the text – these are marked with the computer symbol in the left hand margin), and
- a range of links and other resources to help with your wider reading for this subject and any assignments/dissertations you may need to undertake associated with a course you may be taking.

The website is frequently updated throughout the year so check it from time to time for changes.

Acknowledgements

We acknowledge the permission granted us by CIMA, ICAS and ACCA to use past examination questions in this text, and on the website. The Fiscal Facts notes added throughout the text were sourced from various public online resources including the Institute for Fiscal Studies, HM Treasury and HMRC websites.

Please note, however, that whilst every attempt has been made in writing this text to be accurate and true to the current UK tax system it should not be solely relied upon as a definitive source of information on current tax rules. Readers are advised to seek specific professional advice in their tax planning affairs. Neither the authors nor the publishers accepts any legal responsibility for any loss related to actions taken based on material contained in this book.

Any comments on this book, or suggestions for future development of this book, or the associated website, would be appreciated. The authors can be contacted for this purpose at:

lymer&oats@taxstudent.com

Andrew Lymer and Lynne Oats
July 2010

Taxation: Policy & Practice – website

http://www.taxstudent.com/uk

Fiscal Publications, and the authors of this text, have created a website to be used in conjunction with this text book.

Visit the above address to find:

1. Answers to questions at the end of each chapter (note – some are reserved for lecturer use only as teaching aids – if you want copies of these please ask your lecturer).
2. Extension materials for many parts of the text allowing you to go deeper into these topics than are covered in the book.
3. Multiple choice questions – self test questions for each chapter.
4. Large extra question and answer bank for self or classroom managed extra practice and illustration of tax computations.
5. A large list of tax related links for further reading, dissertation etc.
6. Easy to print rates and allowance pages.

Whilst the lecturer area of the website is only available to bona fide teachers, the student area is open to all purchasers of this book. Basic registration will be required for this access.

Please use your unique user ID and password, as listed below, to gain access to this part of the site.

User ID: 2010student
Password: 2010qw12e

Fiscal Publications

Other useful books to aid your study of UK and international taxation

This text is produced by a UK-based publishing house that specialises in taxation and public economics texts. See below for some of their other books that will enhance your understanding of UK and international taxation.

Taxation: incorporating the 2010 Finance Act

by Richard Andrews, Alan Combs and Peter Rowes

ISBN 9781906201128

This is the companion text for Taxation: Policy and Practice. It provides many further examples and 100s of questions and answers for additional explanation and practice of all the topics covered in this book.

Economics of Taxation – 10th edition

by S. James and C. Nobes

ISBN 9781906201135

For over 30 years this textbook has been the leader in its field. Now updated annually, the 10th (2010/11) edition provides a clear and authoritative introduction to the economic theory of taxation and to its practical operations in the UK. Part 1 of the text examines the principles of taxation, whilst Part 2 gives abroad-based description and evaluation of the policy and practice so the UK's tax system, highlighting international comparisons.

Why tax systems differ

by Cedric Sandford

ISBN 9780951515785

This book analyses and compares taxation in different countries. It looks at what tax systems have in common, how they differ and seeks to explain the similarities and the differences. The book seeks to answer questions such as: why has VAT become the dominant sales tax world-wide? why are there so many differences in the way countries tax corporate income and capital gains? and why is income tax the dominant tax in advanced countries?

For further details see – **http://www.fiscalpublications.com**
Student discounts available for many titles – see website for details.

1 The framework of UK taxation

Introduction

Taxation has played an important role in civilised societies since their birth thousands of years ago. The earliest written records we have of how such societies formed and were organised illustrate the importance of taxation in their successes, but also in their downfalls on occasions. Taxation continues to play an important role in modern societies, as we will see throughout this chapter.

Ever since people began to gather together in groups and share resources as communities, taxes have had to be raised to pay for services that can be used by the community as a whole, rather than just to the benefit of specific individuals or groups. This included, for example, provision of defence for the group. In the early part of the 21st century taxes are now used to achieve a number of government objectives as well as to raise revenue to fund its public spending and to repay its rapidly rising borrowing. In modern Britain taxation has become completely embedded in our society. Without taxation the country would cease to operate. Whilst few people would say they like to pay taxes, their presence provides the foundation for an orderly, well managed, country.

At the end of this chapter you will be able to:

- outline the need for tax in a civilised society;
- discuss the historical background of taxation, particularly in the UK;
- describe the main features of the UK tax system today, including the systems for collecting taxes, the legal framework of taxation and the administration of taxation;
- identify progressive and regressive taxes and discuss their characteristics; and
- understand the different ways in which tax is raised in the UK at present.

Objectives of taxation

Taxation is used as a tool by the UK government to support and pay for its basic functions. These basic functions include:

- Managing the economy – including employment levels, the nature, type and location of business activity, levels of inflation, the balance of payments and relationships with our trading partners overseas;
- Regulation – protection of the environment, the public generally or of groups within society who might otherwise be exploited;
- Developing society – providing a social welfare and health system to improve the standards of living for the whole society;
- Providing public goods – provision of products and services for common consumption that would be unlikely to be adequately provided by the market if the Government did not organise it. These include defence and education systems for example.

The primary purpose of imposing a tax on society is to raise money to pay for public (government) spending in undertaking the basic functions listed above. However, taxes are also used to influence the behaviour of taxpayers directly in ways that will support achieving these functions for society's benefit. For example, taxes are charged on petrol, alcohol and tobacco (in part at least) to increase their cost in the attempt to discourage their consumption in order to improve the environment and health of the country.

Tax reductions can also be offered by a government to encourage activity that might not otherwise occur but that is considered beneficial for society in some way. For example, creating enterprise zones which have lower than normal taxes to persuade businesses to locate in particular areas.

Taxation, therefore, is a very important feature of a modern society and the nature of a particular tax system reflects the views of its society, and government, at a point in time. Tax systems change regularly as society changes its views on how best to balance the various aspects of the basic functions of government we listed above. They also change as society's views of the balance of the importance of particular issues in the society, such as environmental protection, change over time. Key changes in the tax system often therefore occur when government philosophies change, such as when power in the Government shifts from one political party to another after an election as we are seeing happen in the UK resulting from the 2010 General Election.

What is a tax?

Before we study the history of tax and examine the current UK rules for taxation in detail, we must understand what a tax is. All taxes have some features in common. They are a compulsory levy, imposed by government or other tax raising body, on income, expenditure or capital assets, for which the taxpayer receives nothing specific in return.

Not all payments to a government are taxes however. Charges, tolls and other levies could be paid to a government, but where they are paid simply to cover the cost of provision of something specific received in return then this is not strictly a tax.

The collection of all the taxes in operation in an economy and the rules related to these taxes is called a 'tax system'.

A brief history of taxation

Throughout history tax has been a sensitive issue between rulers or governments and their subjects or citizens. Significant civil unrest, even wars, have resulted from tax disputes. This section reviews some of these events both in ancient history, and in the case of more recent British history, illustrating the dynamic nature of tax systems over time and how methods and mechanisms for taxing people have changed. As you will see in this section, governments and rulers have used a wide variety of methods to raise money from their citizens and subjects. These include taxes on purchases and sales of goods and services, ownership and transfers of property and on receipts of income and wealth. As you read this section note how the complexity of the tax system generally can be said to be developing over time but that many of the basic features of taxation have in fact remained fairly constant.

Taxation in ancient times

Taxes have been levied on societies for just about as far back in history as we have records (e.g. taxes feature in ancient Egyptian, Chinese and Central American societies). We will use the example of taxes in the Roman Republic (and then Empire) to illustrate how many taxes raised now have their roots in ancient tax practices.

Taxation in the Roman Republic and Empire

In the times of Julius Caesar (c100 – 44BC) Roman citizens did not pay tax. All the revenue required by the Empire, including the cost of the military operations, was requisitioned from the people who lived in territories which had been occupied by the Romans. Only *indirect taxes** such as taxes on the sale of goods were raised in Rome itself, as direct taxes were seen to be humiliating and undignified because of the need to reveal details of personal circumstances (e.g. income levels) to enable such taxes to be levied.

Whilst the requisition system raised resources for the state, it had a number of serious disadvantages as a source of funding public expenditure, principally its lack of certainty. This led to tax demands being levied in an unpredictable and arbitrary way (which taxpayers did not like) and made planning for state expenditures difficult.

Occasionally (e.g. to fund a larger than normal war) it was considered necessary to raise a *direct tax*, called a tributum, on the citizens of Rome and it's dependent, controlled territories, leading to the necessity of a census. Often the tributum was repaid by the state after the need for it passed. In addition, some indirect taxes were raised by charging import and export duties.

The Romans introduced a system of collective responsibility so that members of the taxpayer's family, neighbours and community could be called upon to pay any taxes which the taxpayer could not pay. Tax collection was undertaken by publican companies under contract to the Republic and there was a considerable amount of corruption by both the various rulers of the Republic and the publican companies.

When he became Rome's first Emperor, Augustus (Julius Caesar's great nephew 63BC – AD14 and First Citizen of Rome 27BC – AD14) realised that a fairer system of tax would have to be introduced to improve the stability of the newly created Empire, and created a civil service to administer the tax. He introduced a 5% inheritance tax, which was payable on the death of a taxpayer from their estate, a 1% sales tax on public auctions and a 4% tax on the sale of slaves.

Tiberius (42BC – AD37 and Roman Emperor AD14 – 37), when encouraged to increase the direct taxation from the provinces, refused saying 'A good shepherd should shear his flock, not skin it.'

---

* Where you meet a technical tax term like this for the first time you may want to check its meaning in the glossary at the back. All the technical terms you need throughout this book are defined for you there so you can refer back to their definitions as you need them.

Fiscal Fact

This offered wisdom from Tiberius is hung prominently inside No 11 Downing Street (the official residence of the UK's Chancellor of the Exchequer – the person ultimately responsible for tax policy and its implementation in the UK). Chancellors today could be said to agree with Tiberius, operating with rates of income tax between 0 – 50%, but in the 1970s some taxpayers paid tax at rates as high as 98% on some income types – which most people would consider to be skinning and not shearing!

The Romans also introduced a rudimentary system of social security as part of their public expenditure return to society. This was in the form of a type of family allowance.

Between the 2nd and 3rd centuries AD inflation was extremely high and many of the taxes described above were allowed to lapse. Instead taxes were raised in the form of goods rather than money.

At the beginning of the 4th century AD, Diocletian introduced *capitatio*, (a poll tax), and *jugatio*, (a tax on land). The land was divided into four classes: vines, olive trees, arable land and pasture land, each class with further sub-classes. Land of a higher quality fell into a higher class leading to greater taxes than land of a lower quality, regardless of the way in which the land was actually used. This is an early example of taxing the capacity to generate wealth, rather than taxing the wealth generated, a trend used in some taxes today as we will see later.

An individual paid poll tax for himself and all his employees. The fraction to be paid varied across the Empire. A man was taken as being a unit of tax with all taxes, including land taxes, expressed as a fraction of a man. Rome decided how much tax should be raised in total and allocated this to regions, which then calculated the tax which must be levied on a 'man'.

From this process all tax liabilities were calculated and collected from the citizens. Taxes were still largely based on payment in kind rather than cash and the majority of the taxes were collected at their source. Hence landowners with tenants were required to pay taxes for themselves and their tenants. Individuals, who were not wealthy landowners or tenants, paid their taxes directly to the local municipal council. In practice the land tax system tied citizens to their land, limiting prospects for advancement, and was extremely progressive.

Under a *progressive tax system* a taxpayer who is better off pays a higher proportion of his or her income or wealth in tax than a less well off individual. In contrast, in a *regressive tax system* the 'burden of tax' falls more heavily on the poorest, who pay higher proportions of their incomes or wealth in tax.

The income tax system in operation in the UK now is largely progressive because taxpayers on lower incomes pay a relatively smaller proportion of their income in income tax while better off taxpayers pay a higher proportion (0% or 20% compared to up to 50% as we will see in Chapter 4). For a tax system to be progressive, better off taxpayers do not just pay more tax than the less well off: the better off must pay *proportionately* more (i.e. a higher proportion) in tax than the less well off.

Parts of the tax system in Diocletian's time in Rome were so progressive that the tax paid on an extra 'unit' of income was greater than 100%. This tax system was blamed for the decline in both economic prosperity and personal freedom and ultimately contributed significantly to the downfall of the Roman Empire by undermining its ongoing stability.

The development of taxation in the UK

What about the history of the UK tax system? England was, of course, part of the Roman Empire and some traces of Roman tax principles remain in the UK's tax system. In this section we review some of the key parts of UK tax history after the Norman Conquest (1066), to help you understand further how the current tax system evolved.

Medieval taxation

In medieval times kings (via their Treasuries) had access to revenue from three sources. Firstly, they received income from Crown property – that is property owned by the ruling King rather than personal property owned before becoming King – and secondly from feudal rights where kings received income (in various forms) from the land owners (who in turn extracted it from their tenants). These together were considered to provide the kings with sufficient revenue to meet their normal expenditure. In addition, kings could raise customs duties and other levies in times of emergency, provided that King's Counsel or Parliament approved this extra levy being charged.

Feudal services, or payments made in lieu of such services called scutage, are examples of direct taxes, while customs duties are indirect taxes. Indirect taxes prove to be both easier and more economical to collect while the direct taxes were generally more difficult and expensive to collect. For example, citizens were able to challenge an assessment of a direct tax in the courts which often delayed payment and therefore also increased the cost of collecting taxes. There were, (and still are) a number of advantages of customs duties as a means of raising revenue for the Government compared to direct taxes. Firstly, during this time there was a large volume of overseas trade, primarily with Europe, so that a relatively large amount of tax could be raised from a relatively low rate of tax. Secondly, the tax was relatively cheap and easy to collect via customs officials at the docks (although tax evasion, through smuggling, was widespread).

Fiscal Fact

King John levied scutage, the payment in lieu of feudal knight's service, eleven times in his sixteen year reign at rates varying from 2 marks (26s 8d.) to 3 marks (40s.) per knight.

Taxation in the Middle Ages

In times of war the King was often unable to raise enough revenue from his usual sources to fund the military effort. The King had no absolute right to raise additional funds and so had to negotiate with his wealthier subjects to raise extra sums if needed. These subjects usually insisted that the King follow the formal procedures which meant that Parliament had to be convened for the King to request either increases in customs duties or to raise a 'lay subsidy', such as the system of the 'fifteenths and tenths', which was a tax on all movable property and some income. This system operated by taxing a fraction of the assessed value of goods such as livestock, corn and other produce, household goods and stock-in-trade. The tax fraction applied was one fifteenth in country areas and one tenth in cities and boroughs. Some personal goods however, such as clothes and armour, were exempt from this tax.

The members of Parliament at the time were the country's wealthiest citizens, and were therefore the people most likely to be affected by an increase in the King's tax raising power. The role of Parliament was to act as a brake on public expenditure. (Ironically today, it is more likely to be Parliament which is restrained by the Treasury than the other way round). On the other hand, these members were also the people with the most to lose if the King was unsuccessful in the war, and so Parliament usually granted the King his request, in part, if not in its entirety.

Perhaps ironically, increases in these taxes raised to fight wars had the effect of redistributing wealth from the King's wealthier subjects (who paid the taxes) to the peasants who became soldiers (and therefore received wages and other 'benefits' like food and clothing from the taxes paid). Taxes are still regularly used to produce economic redistribution in this way.

In 1377, Parliament gave the new King permission to levy a poll tax of four old pence on all his adult male subjects. Two years later the King was granted permission to raise a graduated poll tax. Peasants still paid four old pence but subjects with positions were taxed at higher rates depending on their status: up to £4 for barons, earls and mayors. In real terms the poll tax represented about 2% of the King's income. On both occasions when this poll tax was used, the general populace rebelled and evasion was widespread.

Two years later Parliament once again, and with reluctance, granted the King the right to levy a poll tax, this time at one shilling (12 old pennies) a head. Because the tax was not graduated by reference to the taxpayer's wealth it was effective regressive, that is the burden of tax fell most heavily on the poorest members of society, and was once again widely evaded. Once again the peasants revolted and nearly brought about the downfall of the King and the feudal rights system, by then increasingly outmoded. (Perhaps if Margaret Thatcher had taken more notice of tax history she might have survived the challenge to her leadership in 1990 which was due, in part, to the unpopular poll tax, called the community charge, she had reintroduced in the UK in the late 1980s and that followed similar principles to these earlier taxes!).

By Henry VIII's reign (1509 – 1547) a mixture of the two systems of taxing the population was operating. Individuals whose income could easily be ascertained, such as the clergy, wage-earners and landowners, were subject to a form of income tax while individuals whose income fluctuated, such as merchants, professionals and tenant farmers, were subject to tax on their movable property.

During the reign of Elizabeth I (1558 – 1603) the income tax rate was 20% while movables were taxed at a rate of two-fifteenths. Movables included coins, plate, merchandise, household goods and debts owing less debts owed to the taxpayer. Even the poor were subject to these taxes as exemption limits were set very low. As before both these taxes were only raised during times of financial urgency. By the middle of the 16th century the exemption limits had been raised somewhat so that only the upper classes paid taxes.

The struggle between King and Parliament

Taxation became a particularly contentious issue between the King and Parliament during the first reign of the Stuarts (1603 - 1649) primarily because, as is now generally agreed by historians, the Stuarts had insufficient revenue to fulfil their royal functions. This led to King James (1603-1625) applying to Parliament for further financing for the ordinary expenses of government causing bitter quarrels. King Charles I (1625-1649), James's son, also suffered from this problem (although by the later 1630s the King's income had risen to £1,000,000 a year) and Parliament refused to grant him the right to raise revenue through customs duties for life, as had been done in the past, but granted the duties for only 12 months at a time. As customs duties at this time made up the bulk of Charles' revenue (only 8% of his income came from direct tax sources), eventually in 1629, Charles began levying the duties without the consent of Parliament.

The differences (both tax related and others) between the monarch and Parliament became insurmountable and finally there was a civil war which ended with Charles' execution in 1649. From that day until the present, Parliament has effectively ruled in the UK, although a limited monarchy, as we have it today, was restored with Charles II in 1660.

One interesting result of this struggle is that the Board of Her Majesty's Revenue and Customs (HMRC) receive their commission to act from the Crown rather than from Parliament. Thus the Board is deemed to have inherited some of the qualities of the Crown, in particular justice, equity and mercy. (We will not have the opportunity to evaluate the performance of HMRC against these criteria in this book, but you might like to consider this question during your working life of dealing with the Revenue).

Excise duties on food, drink and other essentials were introduced by Parliament in 1643 during the English Civil Wars. They were unpopular because the burden of the tax fell on everyone including the poor, but they had the administrative advantage of being easy to collect. Like the poll taxes before them, excise duties on the necessities of life are regressive, that is, the poor pay a larger proportion of their income in duty than the better off (because a large percentage of their incomes have to be spent on these excise bearing necessities).

Parliament attempted to reform the personal tax system after Charles' execution in 1649 but was largely unsuccessful. The country was divided into regions which were each then required to raise a set amount of revenue, with little guidance about the way in which the tax should be levied, and little central supervision. The tax system under this structure became dominated by taxes on land rather than on income or other assets.

Unusual taxes

Over the UK's history some unusual things have been taxed. In 1662 for example, a hearth tax was introduced (a tax charge on the number of hearths/fireplaces you had in your house). This was a crude attempt at a progressive tax on the basis that people who have more fireplaces probably have bigger houses (and therefore probably are richer), would have to pay more of this tax than those with fewer hearths (and therefore probably relatively poorer). This was a relatively easy tax to avoid, however, by the simple practice of blocking up hearths.

A similar attempt at developing progressivity by using taxes linked to property was made in 1696 when a window tax was introduced. In a similar way to the hearth tax it was argued that the rich had larger houses and therefore more windows and so would pay more tax than poorer citizens. Like the hearth tax before, it was fairly simple to avoid the tax by bricking up a window. Also lying about the number of windows in the house was widespread. In 1851 the window tax was abolished on the grounds of public health.

Fiscal Fact

In 1792-3 the Government earned 23% of its total taxation revenue from direct taxes on land and property, 53% from excise duties on food, drink and tobacco, 18% from excise duties on other items such as coal, iron, cloth, soap, candles and 6% from stamp duties.

The modern era of taxation

Modern-day income tax has its roots in 1799 in the tax introduced by William Pitt (The Younger), the UK Prime Minister at the time. When the Napoleonic Wars started Pitt borrowed money against future excise revenue in order to finance the war, a practice first developed at the start of the eighteenth century (a system called 'deficit financing'). However, it became apparent that the war was going to last too long to enable this method of financing to be sustained. Pitt needed to find a new way to raise taxes. He introduced an income tax at a rate of 10% which was targeted on the rich middle and upper classes, the people with the most to lose if the war was lost. However, there was widespread evasion of the tax and only £6m was raised in the first year, rather than the £10m anticipated.

Although the poorest people were not subject to direct tax in the form of income tax, it is estimated that by 1810 a labourer earning £22 a year paid £11 in indirect tax. Given how high indirect tax already was, it did not seem possible to fund the war by further increasing this form of taxation. Instead taxpayers earning over £60 per annum were required to make a return listing all their sources of income and calculating the amount of tax which was due on it.

The law bringing this new tax into force did not allow for any control over enforcing the correctness of the return. In an attempt to reduce the widespread evasion that this brought about, *withholding taxes* were introduced by the Bank of England, by paying its dividends net of tax.

Pitt resigned in 1801 and his income tax was repealed in 1802 by Addington (Prime Minister after Pitt) because it was seen as a wartime tax only. In 1803 however, Addington re-introduced a new income tax based on five Schedules, named using the first five letters of the alphabet, which largely continue to be used as the structure for the UK's income tax rules today, although as we will see later, the names of these Schedules have been changed in recent years.

Addington was also responsible for more widespread taxation at the source. This means that the payer of certain amounts, such as rent, salaries, pensions and interest had to deduct tax and pay the recipient net of a suitable rate of tax. Because of these innovations it is probably fair to say that Addington is the truer father of UK income tax rather than Pitt, who has generally been awarded the dubious honour of this title. Addington's income tax was progressive and ranged from 1% on an income of £60 to 10% on an income of over £200. Income tax was repealed once again in 1816.

Income tax reintroduced

In 1842 Peel (Prime Minister from 1841–1846) reintroduced income tax, again as a temporary measure, at a very low level, this time to try to deal with the budget deficit the country faced at the time of £5million. Peel drew on Addington's Act of 1803 for his legislation, making only minor amendments. Peel rejected proposals to impose high rates of tax on the wealthy, arguing that it would lead to them closing their businesses or even leaving the country. A major criticism of the use of any income tax is the need to undertake an annual investigation of income, or as Peel put it: 'A certain degree of inquisitorial scrutiny is, therefore, inseparable from an income tax.' As in Roman times, it was this need to disclose their income, rather than the actual rate of the tax, which was generally opposed by those who disliked this form of taxation.

Under Peel's income tax system, income below £150 was exempted. Income above this figure was taxed at 3% regardless of the amount of the income. This fairly high minimum threshold level excluded a large proportion of the population from needing to pay the tax.

At the same time indirect taxes were reduced as part of the free trade movement in order to help the country's manufacturing, trading and commercial sectors. The appropriate balance between the use of direct taxes, like income tax, and indirect tax is a key decision for any government now, just as it was in Peel's time.

Peel's income tax was supported, despite its drawbacks, because it was seen to be a temporary solution to resolve a particular public finance problem, and set at a relatively low level. In addition, industrialists were supportive of this tax as they believed that if the Government were to raise all the revenue they needed by means of further indirect taxation, it would cut consumer spending and increase inflation.

Fiscal Fact

The administration of the new income tax, like many existing taxes, was largely in the hands of Commissioners who 'ought to be persons of a respectable situation in life, as far as possible removed from any suspicion of partiality or any kind of undue influence, men of integrity and independence.' In 1798, however, (the famous 'Coventry scandal') the list of Land Tax Commissioners was found to include journeymen, weavers, scavengers, dealers in dead horse flesh and cat meat, dealers in dung, paupers receiving parish relief, two fiddlers and two idiots.

Under Peel's rules, income was not all taxed in full, for example, farmers were taxed on the rental value of their land rather than their farming profits. Farmers were not taxed on their income until 1941.

In order to ease the concerns of taxpayers about making personal income declarations, Peel created a system of Special Commissioners, (who were experts in taxation), with whom businessmen could deal rather than the General Commissioners (who were local businessmen), from whom the taxpayer might want privacy. In addition, if the taxpayer disputed the amount of tax which was deemed to be payable he could choose to appeal to either the Special Commissioners or the General Commissioners. Like much of the rest of Peel's system, this process of appeals to expert Special Commissioners remained in operation for many years and only ceased to operate like this in April 2009 when a new tribunals system was introduced in the tax area as we will see later in this Chapter.

Peel also introduced penalties into his income tax system. For example, a fixed penalty of £50 was created for any taxpayer who was found to be 'neglectful' in connection with his return of income. This specific penalty was abolished in 1923 but today penalties are still a key part of the administration of the tax system and HMRC can impose interest charges as well as penalties on taxpayers who fail to pay the full amount of tax due and provide their tax returns on time.

William Gladstone, UK Chancellor who then became Prime Minister from 1868-74 (and again at various points between 1880 – 1894), introduced 13 budgets during the last half of the 19th century. At the time of his first budget in 1853 public expenditure was over £50 million a year and nearly £30 million of the total was used to pay interest on the National Debt. Gladstone claimed that the cause of the deficit was the prevailing level of income tax. Less tax was raised in 1853 from income tax than was collected in each of the years from 1806 to 1815.

Gladstone was aware of the limitations of the system of income tax, especially self-assessment, which led to widespread fraud. To start to redress the balance Gladstone extended the legacy duty so that land and also businesses were subject to tax on the death of their owner. He reduced the rates of indirect taxation, believing that this would stimulate consumption and thus not actually reduce the net receipts to the Government. This, together with the reforms introduced by Peel, helped to free the restrictions on trade by encouraging imports and enabling exports to be sold as cheaply as possible.

Gladstone intended to phase income tax out by 1860, but for a number of reasons this did not prove to be possible and instead the rate of income tax actually rose. Public expenditure was growing rapidly, much to Gladstone's regret, and this made it impossible ever again to consider abolishing income tax.

Harcourt, as UK Chancellor of the Exchequer at the time, introduced Estate Duty, referred to as Death Duties, in 1894. The Estate Duty removed many of the injustices of the old legacy duties which had evolved over many centuries and so suffered from many inconsistencies. The origin of the present-day inheritance tax can in fact be traced back to at least 1694 and the development of probate duties. This new Estate Duty fell most heavily on the landowners. Harcourt justified this bias by claiming that property values had been greatly increased since the railways were built. The duty was at the rate of 1% on estates worth between £100 and £500, with estates worth more than £1 million taxed at 8%.

The new tax was highly unpopular with the families who were affected by it. They argued that an individual who chose to spend his money during his life could avoid paying the tax which would be levied on the estate of the careful person who accumulated assets to pass on to the next generation. The question of tax avoidance was also raised by commentators at the time who argued that by simply giving the estate away during the lifetime of the testator the tax could be completely avoided. Harcourt defended his tax, arguing that estate duty was the only viable opportunity to tax non-income-generating assets such as the taxpayer's main residence. This debate about the fairness of inheritance taxation continues today.

Fiscal Fact

In 1855 the tax on newspapers, which had been introduced in 1712, was finally repealed. At its highest rate in 1815, the tax was 4d per sheet of paper so that most newspapers were printed on a single sheet folded in half and sold for 7d. This is why 'broad sheets' began to be printed as they are today – to get as much text on as little paper as possible to minimise the tax to be paid.

Harcourt next turned his attention to income tax, in particular seeking to make it more progressive. Harcourt was strongly in favour of the system of deduction of tax at source, which could be applied to about three-quarters of all income tax collected, arguing that it meant that there was limited inquisitorial prying into the affairs of individuals this way (one of the key problems of using income tax if you remember from earlier in this chapter). The Revenue supported this strongly and argued that if the system of deduction at source was not widened, the investigations that they would have to make and the penalties which they would have to impose for mis-declarations as the income tax system continued to grow would render the collection of the income tax so 'odious' as to 'imperil' its existence and in all probability make it impossible to maintain the tax.

Taxation in the 20th century

At the beginning of the 20th century tax was paid on earned income by fewer than a million people. Hence income tax was a tax paid only by the better off in UK society. However, during the 20th century (and of course particularly now in the 21st century as a result of the financial crisis) public expenditure increased phenomenally and today income tax in the UK is paid by the majority of working adults.

In 1907 Asquith, the UK Chancellor at the time, introduced a system of personal allowances, which exempted a proportion of earned income from income tax. In 1908 old-age pensions were introduced. This, together with a need to increase spending on the Navy, necessitated an increase in taxation to pay for this increased public expenditure. In 1909 Lloyd George introduced the first progressive tax on income in the so-called 'People's Budget'. The budget was not generally accepted and was rejected by the House of Lords in November 1909, but it eventually became law in 1910. As a result of this problem, the power of the House of Lords to veto budgets was removed in 1911 (and is still the case in the UK now). Lloyd George believed that the tax system should ensure that everyone contributes taxes to the country no matter how poor they were. He also believed that taxes should be so constructed that they did not inflict injury on trade and commerce – a concept called *tax neutrality*. This is an idea which we will consider later in this chapter and in more detail in Chapters 2 and 3.

The First World War led to increases in income tax including a top rate of 15%. However, the tax raised was insufficient to fund the war and the deficit was funded by borrowing from the population at large, using War Bonds, etc. The new top rate of income tax was called 'supertax' and its introduction doubled the rate of tax on incomes. In 1928 supertax was renamed surtax and income over £5,000 (around £150,000 in today's values) was taxed at 8%. In addition, car licences were introduced and a new tax on petrol was imposed.

Fiscal Fact

By 1939 less than one in five of the working population was liable to income tax and so people on average earnings did not pay tax. However, the Second World War tripled the number of taxpayers to 12 million as well as tripling the amount of tax raised. One of the reasons for this increase was a substantial increase in inflation during the Second World War.

A new income tax payment system called *pay-as-you-earn* (PAYE) was introduced in 1944, where tax is deducted from individuals' wages and salaries before they received it. Until the introduction of PAYE only individuals paid by central or local government had tax deducted at source from their salaries. Everyone else paid any income tax due by *direct assessment* that is, were billed for the tax owed on their income at some stage after they received it, and after declaring it to the tax authority.

The PAYE system has a number of advantages over a direct assessment system. Primarily, the Government's cash flow was improved as they no longer have to wait until the end of the tax year for the collection of tax. Their bad debts are also reduced as the Government made themselves the ultimate preferential creditor both in the case of business failures and personal bankruptcy, receiving its cut of any remaining business assets even before the individual employees got their final wages and requiring bankrupt individuals to pay of sums owed to them before paying off other creditors. It was also believed that it was easier for individuals to pay tax weekly or monthly rather than facing a large bill at the end of the tax year.

After the Second World War ended there was an explosion in government expenditure and this was inevitably matched by the increase in taxes raised to pay for this, with the top rate of tax on incomes of over £20,000 per annum standing at 52.5% in 1946.

By 1946 the exemption limit for estate duty purposes had increased from £100 to £3,000, the first increase in this area of taxation for 50 years. The increase had the effect of exempting many smaller estates from the duty. However, the highest rates of tax to be paid on non-exempted estates were also increased to a maximum of 75% on estates of over £2 million.

After the Second World War, the National Health Service was formed and national insurance contributions were introduced to provide for health care, retirement pensions and sickness benefit. Although these payments are not strictly taxes because of their direct association with returns received for their payment (remember the definition of 'tax' at the start of this chapter), all national insurance contributions now are added to the general taxation 'pot' that the Government receives. They are no longer earmarked (called in tax terms *hypothecated*) specifically for expenditure in the areas they are traditionally paying for, and therefore are effectively an additional tax on income in practice.

Purchase tax was used to tax spending for a large part of the 20th century. There were a large number of rates of tax and many inconsistencies in the rates applied to various expenditure. For example, pianos and organs were exempt but other musical instruments were taxed at 27.5%; records were taxed at 50% while books were exempt from the tax. Purchase tax was replaced in 1973 by VAT, which is now the primary tax on expenditure in the UK (we will discuss UK VAT in Chapter 10).

In 1965 two new taxes were introduced, corporation tax and capital gains tax. Until 1965 companies were subject to income tax as if they were individuals and there are still many similarities between the two systems because of this common history they share (we will discuss corporation tax in Chapter 9). Capital gains tax was originally intended to reduce tax avoidance and increase the equity of the tax system rather than primarily to raise significant revenue. This tax helps reduce the opportunities for people to earn capital growth untaxed instead of receiving income which is taxed (we will discuss capital gains tax in Chapter 8).

In 1975 capital transfer tax was introduced as a new taxation on estates but was itself replaced by inheritance tax in 1984 (we will discuss inheritance tax in Chapter 8). The pre 1975 estate duty only taxed the value of the taxpayer's estate at death. Lifetime gifts were completely exempt. Capital transfer tax introduced tax on lifetime transfers of wealth for the first time.

In 1979 the top rate of tax on earned income in the UK was 83% and unearned income over £5,500, such as rents received and dividends, was subject to an investment income surcharge of 15%, giving a top rate of tax of 98% for some taxpayers.

Tax administration today

Until April 2005, the UK tax system was mostly managed by two Government departments, the Inland Revenue and H.M. Customs and Excise.

The Inland Revenue administered all of the following parts of the tax system:

- Income tax
- Corporation tax
- Capital gains tax
- Inheritance tax
- National insurance contributions
- Stamp duties
- Working tax credit and child tax credit
- Child benefit
- Other smaller duties including overseeing the national minimum wage rules and student loan repayments.

HM Customs and Excise were tasked with managing customs duties and excise charges (such as on petrol), and other taxes not managed by the Inland Revenue, including the landfill tax, the climate change levy, and insurance and air passenger duties. They also looked after the VAT system.

Customs and Excise was in fact one of the oldest Government departments (although they were only combined into one department in 1909) with a history dating back to the 13th century as a formal body working for the King to collect duties and prevent smuggling.

Fiscal Fact

Losses due to VAT evasion (e.g. fraud) accounts for approximately 12% of the theoretical UK liability to VAT. This would amount to approximately £9billion.

Following a lengthy consultation process, the Inland Revenue and H.M Customs and Excise merged into one body with effect from 18 April 2005 and are now called Her Majesty's Revenue and Customs (HMRC). While the two former departments continue to operate in part independently of one another, they now have a common management structure and some joint or merged HMRC departments (e.g. research). This was an important development in UK tax administration as it brought the UK into line with most other developed countries in having one main government department in charge of the tax system.

This new administrative body is primarily focussed on tax policy maintenance and delivery for both customs and revenue services. The setting of tax policy is the sole remit of the UK's Treasury.

The tax year

Until the mid-18th century the Government used an accounting year which ended on Lady Day, which was 25 March, the first quarter day in the calendar year (and the date of the start of the church year as the Feast of the Annunciation of the Virgin Mary – exactly nine months before Christmas Day). In 1752 the Government adopted the Gregorian calendar which required the loss of 11 days between the 2 and 14 of September to bring the calendar year back into line with the solar year. However, the Government was unwilling to have an accounting period which did not run for 365 days and so moved their year-end forward by 11 days to 5 April. Hence today a tax year (for an individual) runs from 6 April to the following 5 April: the tax year 2010/11 runs from 6 April 2010 to 5 April 2011.

The self assessment system

Self assessment is a system under which the taxpayer is responsible for working out his or her own tax liability and reporting it to the revenue authority – the HMRC in the UK's case. During the 1990's the Government switched a number of UK taxes over from an official (direct) assessment system, where the revenue authority works out the tax liability, to self assessment. For example, individual taxpayers are now required to use self assessment in the case of income tax and capital gains tax, as are companies for corporation tax. The key advantage of self assessment from the Government's point of view is that the tax authority doesn't have to produce assessments for taxpayers. By putting the responsibility on the taxpayer to work out his or her own tax liability (i.e. to 'self' assess), HMRC can devote more of its resources to following up cases that might be inaccurate, providing more advice and offer other services to help taxpayers rather than having to check every tax return that is filed to assess the tax liability as previously was the case. So self assessment may reduce the cost to the Government of administering the tax system, but on the other hand, increases the cost to the taxpayer of complying with the system as they can no longer rely on the tax authority to do the work for them.

Time limits apply to the operation of various parts of the tax system and penalties are possible if those time limits are not adhered to. For example, a taxpayer may find that they have forgotten to include something in their self assessment for income tax, perhaps an expense that qualifies as an allowable deduction, and need to ask for an amendment to be made. Another possibility is that HMRC may discover something about the taxpayer's affairs, perhaps some omitted income, that means that the self assessment is incorrect, and need to issue a new assessment. From 2008, the time limits have been harmonised across the different taxes and they are as follows:

For taxpayer claims	4 years
For ordinary assessments	4 years
Assessments where the loss of tax is due to carelessness	6 years
Assessments where the loss of tax is deliberate	20 years

This is a change from the previous regime where, for example, income taxpayers used to have up to 6 years to go back with claims they had missed, but now as you can see, it is only 4.

Another important feature of the UK's self assessment system is online filing. The Government have for some years been encouraging taxpayers to file their annual tax returns online and provides free software to allow many taxpayers to do so. Online filing, or e-filing, has a number of advantages for both HMRC and taxpayers. For example, the online filing system has a number of checks so that as a taxpayer completes his or her return form online, the system ensures that figures are put in the correct place and calculates the amount of tax due. For both parties the key advantage is speeding up the filing process. This includes for taxpayers getting any tax refunds due to them as soon as possible.

Table 1.1 summaries details of the number of UK taxpayers over the last 35 years. It shows the number of people or entities paying the key four UK taxes assessed by self assessment. It illustrates how, after a steady rise for much of this period, the economic problems of the last few years has reduced the number of those paying all of the taxes (particularly dramatically in the case of capital gains tax).

Table 1.1: Estimated number of UK taxpayers
(Source: HMRC website - Tax receipts and Taxpayers section, Numbers: thousands)

	Income Tax	Corporation Tax	Capital Gains Tax[3]	Inheritance Tax[4]
2010/11[1]	30,600	NA	NA	15[1]
2009/10[1]	30,200	NA	NA	15[5]
2008/09[1]	31,300	NA	130[1]	16[5,6]
2007/08[1]	32,500	940	270[5]	25[5,6]
2006/07[2]	31,800	885	265[5]	34
2005/06	31,100	875	225[5]	33
2004/05	30,300	830	195[5]	32
2003/04	28,500	715	175[5]	30
2002/03	28,900	580	145	27
2001/02	28,600	525	140	23
2000/01	29,300	520	200	22
1999/00	27,200	505	210	20
:	:	:	:	:
1988/99	25,200	355	150	23
:	:	:	:	:
1983/84	24,000	230	115	23
:	:	:	:	:
1978/79	25,900	185	225	38
:	:	:	:	:
1973/74	23,100	175	285	47

[1] Projected in line with the April 2010 Budget Report

[2] Latest survey

[3] After 1990/91 married couples count as two if both have CGT liabilities as a result of independent taxation. Prior to this they only counted as one.

[4] Transfers on death only figures given.

[5] Provisional

[6] The transferable nil rate band introduced in October 2007 led to a significant reduction in the number of inheritance tax payers during 2007-08 and 2008-09

Tax payments

The process for actually paying tax due varies for the different types of taxes. For income tax, as we will see in more detail in Chapter 4, tax that is not collected throughout the year through deduction at source is paid in instalments with a final payment on 31 January following the end of the relevant tax year. Companies' tax payments vary depending on their size; large companies pay tax in quarterly instalments (two during the course of the tax year and two after it has ended) whereas small companies pay their entire tax bill 9 months after the end of the tax year (see Chapter 9 for more details). VAT for most traders is payable on a quarterly basis, although there are some variations for both very small and very large taxpayers (see Chapter 10).

Compliance Checks

The merger of the former two revenue departments into HMRC has led to a number of new procedures that now apply to all the different types of tax that they administer. Under the self assessment system, taxpayers file their tax returns and do their own tax computation. HMRC accepts this information (and the payment of tax) at face value in the first instance, but then has the right to check that the information and calculations provided are correct.

Compliance checks were introduced in 2008 and apply to income tax, capital gains tax, national insurance contributions, VAT and PAYE, as well as student loans. HMRC have produced a series of leaflets explaining how the new compliance check system works. HMRC can ask for information or documents by sending what is known as an 'information notice'. There are penalties for not supplying the information requested in such a notice. HMRC can also ask for information about a taxpayer's affairs from other people and if necessary, can visit the taxpayer either with a pre-arranged visit or sometimes unannounced.

If the result of a check is that the taxpayer has to pay additional tax, he or she will also have to pay interest on the additional tax not paid at the right time and may be subject to penalties.

Penalties

Another recent development in tax administration in the UK is the introduction of a new penalty regime that also applies to all the taxes under the control of HMRC. The new penalty regime applies to tax periods commencing on or after 1 April 2008 for returns that are due to be filed on or after 1 April 2009. The new penalties are charged as an additional percentage of the tax involved (i.e. in addition to paying the tax due) and are linked to taxpayer behaviour. There are three levels of culpability as follows:

- Careless – where the taxpayer has failed to take reasonable care (maximum penalty 30%).
- Deliberate but not concealed – where the inaccuracy is deliberate but the taxpayer has not tried to hide it from HMRC (maximum penalty 70%); and
- Deliberate and concealed – where not only has the taxpayer made a deliberate mistake, but they have also made arrangements to hide it from HMRC (maximum penalty 100%).

In deciding whether a taxpayer has taken reasonable care, the penalty system considers the particular situation of that taxpayer, so, for example, HMRC will expect a different standard of care from a large company than from a low income salary and wage earner.

There is provision for the penalty to be discounted if the taxpayer tells HMRC about the mistake before they find out, i.e. unprompted disclosure. In this situation the three levels of penalty become 0%, 20% and 30% for the three levels of culpability listed above. Even where the disclosure of the mistake is prompted by HMRC, the maximum penalty may also be reduced under some circumstances, but not as much as for an unprompted disclosure.

Disputing tax liabilities

What happens if the taxpayer and HMRC disagree about the amount of tax payable? Prior to 2009, there were four separate tax tribunals that handled tax disputes. For income tax and corporation tax, for example, the Lord Chancellor appointed Special and General Commissioner to hear taxpayers' appeals against HMRC's assessments. General Commissioners were part of the income tax system since its inception in 1799, and were part time and unpaid. They were appointed for a division with a focus on a particular area of the tax system. They were aided by a clerk, usually an accountant or a lawyer, who were paid by the Board of Revenue and Customs. There were around 2,000 General Commissioners in the UK at the point they ceased to exist in April 2009.

Special Commissioners were full time and were paid for their services. They had to have been legally qualified for at least ten years. Generally they heard more complex appeals than those reviewed by the General Commissioners.

Fiscal Fact

A number of famous historical figures have worked for Customs and Excise including Geoffrey Chaucer (Controller of Customs, London 1374-1380), Robert Burns (joined Excise in 1789) and Adam Smith (appointed a Commissioner in 1778 and whose picture is now on the back of new £20 notes!).

There were separate tribunals which dealt with VAT and stamp duty appeals.

This situation changed from April 2009 as part of a new tribunals system being rolled out across many areas of the tax system in the UK. The new tax chamber is headed up by Lord Justice Carnwath as senior president and has its own specialist judiciary and rules of procedure. Importantly it is independent of HMRC and appeal notices are sent directly to the Tribunals Service (they used to be sent to HMRC under the previous system). If a taxpayer disputes an assessment of tax, he or she has 30 days in which to appeal. There are two tiers of tax tribunal; a first tier tribunal that will hear the less complex cases, and an upper tribunal that will hear more complex cases, and also appeals from decisions of the first tier tribunal. One consequence of this change is that the new system may be more expensive for taxpayers than using the old general commissioners system, since there are fewer first tier tribunals than there were general commissioners, so taxpayers may have to travel further afield to have their dispute with HMRC resolved.

The upper tribunal can hear appeals from the first tier tribunal. Appeals from the upper tribunal are to the Court of Appeal and then the Supreme Court (formerly the House of Lords until October 2009), but only on points of law, not questions of fact (as was the case under the old system).

As part of the change, HMRC are also setting up a new internal review procedure, so that as far as possible, disputes can be settled without taxpayers having to go to the new tribunal.

In a number of other countries, there is a dedicated tax court, and there is some suggestion that in the longer term, the new tribunal system will evolve into such a court.

A Taxpayers' Charter

Many countries have charters, or bills of rights, for taxpayers, which help to clarify the relationship between taxpayers and the tax authority.

In the UK, the old Inland Revenue and HM Customs and Excise both had taxpayers' charters which set out the rights and obligations of both taxpayers and the respective tax authorities. These fell into disuse, however, during the early 1990s. Recently, there has been a push to reinvigorate the idea of a taxpayer's charter, and consultation has been ongoing for some time about what form this document should take.

Most of those involved in the current UK debate agree that the charter should be clearly written and set out the rights and obligations of both the tax authority and the taxpayer. It has also been suggested that it is important that the right to a charter be enshrined in statute, if not the charter itself. Both the Chartered Institute of Taxation and the Institute of Chartered Accountants in England and Wales are concerned that that the charter be more than just a list of service standards for HMRC. A draft proposal has been criticised for being too short and confused. A dedicated website has been set up (http://www.taxpayerscharter.co.uk) which you may want to visit to find out the latest developments in this area.

The UK budget

The most critical event of the annual taxation calendar in the UK (most years) is the annual Budget Statement made by the Chancellor of the Exchequer. This is usually made during March each year, although the 2009 Budget was presented to Parliament on 22 April 2009 – the latest it has been for many years. This statement outlines the Government's budget plans for the year, which correspondingly have to be balanced with how they will raise the money to finance these plans. It is in this statement each year that most tax changes for the year are therefore to be found.

The Treasury is in fact legally bound to provide two economic forecasts each year. Between 1993 and 1997 this was done in the Budget in November and the Summer Economic Forecast (given late June or early July). However, under the Labour Government, elected in May 1997, the system changed back to a Spring Budget with the addition of a Pre-Budget report in the previous autumn. For example, the 2009 Pre-Budget Report was made on 9 December, 2009. This Pre-Budget statement gives an update on the state of the economy. It also outlines ideas and plans for the main Budget the next year.

This Pre-Budget pattern allows for much wider debate on the proposals for tax changes than previously had been the case and also results in fewer surprises on Budget day. (Summary details of this year's Budget, and summaries of those of the last few years, can be found in Appendix B.)

Income and corporation tax categories and schedules

Income was for many years taxed according to a number of different Schedules and Cases. These were the same broad categories as introduced by Addington in 1803 and in recent times directly refer to parts of the Income and Corporation Taxes Act 1988. These classifications disappeared for individual taxpayers however, in April 2005 (although continued for corporate taxpayers until 2009, as we will see in Chapter 9) and, although the tax rules themselves haven't changed, their names have. Previously each source of income received by a taxpayer was assessed under a Schedule and some of these Schedules were further sub-divided into "Cases". Income from a trade or profession was taxed under Schedule D Case I and II. Schedule A was used to describe the rules for taxing income from UK property. Schedule F outlined the rules for taxing dividends from UK companies (having been introduced in 1965 in conjunction with the introduction of corporation tax). Schedule D Case VI was used to tax annual profits or gains not falling under any other Case of Schedule D and not charged under either Schedule A or ITEPA 2003.

Income from employment, including pensions, used to be taxed under rules outlined in Schedule E. In March 2003 however, Schedule E rules were replaced by the Income Tax (Earnings and Pensions) Act 2003 (ITEPA 2003), which is a re-write of the relevant parts of the 1988 Act and subsequent amendments to this Act found in places such as various Finance Acts resulting from Budget changes over the years since 1988. This process consolidates the rules in this area into one place.

The other schedules of the 1988 Act still applied for both individuals and companies until 5 April 2005 when a new Act came into force, the Income Tax (Trading and Other Income) Act 2005 which re-classified Schedules A, D and F into new headings for income tax. Each category of income has its own rules which determine how much income should be assessed, what deductions are allowed and when the tax should be paid. The final Act needed to rewrite all the relevant income tax rules into new legislation came into force on 6 April, 2007 as the Income Tax Act (ITA) 2007. For corporation tax, the Corporation Tax Act 2009 removed the

Schedule names and corporation tax is now largely consistent with income tax in the categories. We will study these rules for each category in detail in later chapters.

Current tax legislation and regulation

Tax rules are currently created in the UK by a combination of law, regulation and cases, and to a lesser degree rulings and best practice guidance from HMRC. There are a number of sources of tax law today. The table below lists the key tax laws that contain the rules we will examine in this book.

Table 1.2: UK Tax Legislation

Source	Key Relevant Act
Income Tax	
Earned income/pensions	Income Tax (Earnings and Pensions) Act 2003 (ITEPA)
Other sources	Income Tax (Trading and Other Income) Act 2005 (ITTOI) and Income Tax Act 2007 (ITA)
Corporation tax	Income and Corporation Taxes Act 1998 (ICTA), Corporation Tax Act 2009 (CTA) and Corporation Tax Act 2010.
Capital Allowances	Capital Allowances Act 2001 (CAA)
National Insurance Contributions	Social Security & Benefits Act 1992, National Insurance Contributions Act 2006
Capital Gains	Taxation of Chargeable Gains Act 1992 (TCGA)
Value Added Tax	Value Added Tax Act 1994 (VATA)
Inheritance Tax	Inheritance Tax Act 1984 (IHTA)
Stamp Duty	Stamp Act 1891/Electronic Communications Act 2000 (ECA)
Administration of direct tax	Taxes Management Act 1970 (TMA) and Commissioners for Revenue and Customs Act 2005 (CRCA)

In each of the above cases the rules may subsequently be changed or amended by the annual Finance Acts that bring into UK law the plans of the Chancellor announced in the Budget each year (for example, significant new stamp duty rules were contained in the Finance Act 2003). In most years only one Finance Act is created and it is given the date of that year – i.e. this year it would become the Finance Act 2010. However, in some years (2010 being one of them) there can be more than one Finance Act if this proves necessary. The different Acts in the same year are given a number to differentiate them from each other i.e. the second Finance Act in 2010 will become Finance (No. 2) Act 2010. Other regulations and laws (such as Statutory Instruments) can also be used by the Government to amend or extend these various Acts as thought necessary.

Some tax aspects can also be found in more general, non-tax specific, Acts. For example, in November 2006 an Act on charity regulation came into force. This Act included various details about the taxation of charities.

Whilst we look at the current law as we examine each tax issue, this text does not include a detailed consideration of these laws and therefore does not make reference to particular parts of these Acts or regulations. This is a deliberate policy to reduce the complexity of our explanation. However, it is very important that you remember that law underpins all the detail we describe and you may need to refer to this at some point to fully understand how the tax rules work for a particular issue.

In addition to UK tax law, the UK's tax system is determined by a number of other laws, cases and guidance statements from HMRC. This can make for a complex web of rules in many areas of tax but is a factor of the UK's detailed tax system.

Because the UK is a member of the European Union, EU law must also be adhered to in the UK and EU law in fact takes priority over UK law where they disagree.

The UK's tax system is a case law system. This means that specific tax related laws created by Parliament are interpreted by judges in courts as disputes are brought before them to be settled. Throughout this book you will meet a number of legal cases that determine how the more general legal principles should be applied to specific circumstances.

The UK's tax authority (HMRC) also periodically issues guidance of various types for taxpayers and their advisors. Whilst this is not legally binding on taxpayers and can be challenged, it does provide useful advice on the tax authority's view on how specific tax issues should be handled. Taking a look at HMRC's website for example, you will find guidance in the form of Statements of Practice (their interpretation of the law), Extra statutory concessions (specific relaxations of the law allowed by HMRC), Press Releases (various statements on tax issues), Internal Manuals (publicly published internal manuals to illustrate how tax issues are to be handled) and leaflets (general advice that usually provides over-views for taxpayers). However, the boundaries between these forms of guidance are disappearing with the growth of the Internet where technologies, such as search engines, make it easier for taxpayers to discover information they need in a timely fashion.

National v local taxation

Like many other countries, the UK suffers from 'vertical fiscal imbalance'. This means that lower levels of government, which in the UK is local (e.g. city, district or county councils) or regional government (e.g. Welsh or Northern Irish Assemblies and the Scottish Parliament), don't raise enough money of their own to meet their spending obligations and instead need to rely on central government for extra funds, usually paid in the form of grants. In the UK, local government currently only raises about 25% of its own revenue needs and has to get the rest from central government. This balance of funding between the two levels of government hasn't always been this way. Before 1992, local government used to raise between 45% and 60% of its own revenue, mainly from taxes. After this date however, capping systems imposed on local governments by central government have prevented local governments raising higher percentages of their spending from taxation.

Fiscal Fact

Despite local government having legal powers to use council tax to raise some of their funding, the only regional government with legal rights to raise taxes in the UK is the Scottish Parliament. They can vary income tax by increasing or decreasing it up to 3% in either direction from the national levels for taxpayers in Scotland. To date however, they have not used this power but it is often referred to as 'the tartan tax' when the possibilities of using these powers to raise the income tax levels are periodically discussed.

The current degree of vertical fiscal imbalance is considered to be a problem, and the Government set up a Balance of Funding Review in 2003 to consider options for change. Following on from this Review, which concluded that further research was needed, in 2004 the Government commissioned Sir Michael Lyons to examine the issue. He produced an interim report, and a consultation paper in December 2005 and his final report was published with the 2007 Budget. However, the fallout from these new proposals will take some time to affect what is currently happening. The change of Government in 2010 may hasten these changes.

The main tax levied by local government is *council tax*, which was introduced in 1993. Before considering how this tax works, we will briefly review the local taxes that existed before 1993.

For many years, the main local tax in the UK was *domestic rates*. This was based on a percentage of the value of property (both residential and non-residential) located in the area of control of the local government. In the 1980s there was growing concern that domestic rates were unfair. In part this was because the people who had to pay them were not always the same people who voted for, and benefited from, local government spending; only property owning members of the community paid rates, but everyone who lived in the area, whether you owned property or not there, voted for local government plans.

In 1990, the rates system was abolished and replaced with a new tax, the *community charge*, sometimes referred to as the *poll tax*. The community charge was organised very differently to domestic rates because it wasn't linked to property values and ownership, but rather paid by all adults resident in the area irrespective of whether they owned property or not. The community charge was extremely unpopular (as we will see in Chapter 2) and so in 1993 the Government was forced to abolish it and replace it with yet another form of local tax, the council tax.

The council tax is made up of two elements, which makes it a 'hybrid tax'. Half of the tax bill relates to the value of the property, and the other half is based on a charge of 25% for each of the first two adults living in the property. This means that a single adult household will only pay 75% of the usual bill, although a three or more adult household won't pay more than the usual bill.

Council tax is set locally and therefore it is the only tax in the UK that varies according to where you live. Property values are placed into 8 bands and the local government sets the rate for one of them, the others then are a proportion of that rate.

Recently large increases in the rate of council tax have caused a lot of dissatisfaction, which is one of the reasons why local government funding is currently under review.

Money raised and spent by the UK Government

Income tax has for a long time been the biggest revenue raiser for the UK government, as it is for many other similar countries. To give some idea of how many people pay income tax, Table 1.3 gives details of the number of UK income tax payers over the last thirty years.

Table 1.3: Number of income taxpayers (in thousands)

Year	Number of individuals paying tax	Number of lower, starting or saver rate taxpayers	Number of basic rate taxpayers	Number of higher rate taxpayers
1979/80	25,900	25,226[a]		
1984/85	23,800	22,870[a]		
1989/90	25,000	24,040[a]		
1994/95	25,300	5,180	18,200	2,000
1999/00	27,200	3,234[b]	21,400	2,510
2000/01	29,300	3,830[b]	22,600	2,880
2001/02	28,600	3,887[b]	21,700	3,000
2002/03	28,900	3,830[b]	22,000	3,040
2003/04	28,500	3,950[b]	21,600	2,960
2004/05	30,300	4,403[b]	22,500	3,330
2005/06	31,100	4,360[b]	23,100	3,590
2006/07	31,800	4,380[b]	23,700	3,770
2007/08[c]	32,500	4,510[b]	24,100	3,870
2008/09[d]	31,300	964[b]	26,500	3,800
2009/10[d]	30,200	711[b]	26,300	3,220
2010/11[d]	30,600	727[b]	26,400	3,412[e]

Notes: [a] includes both lower-rate and basic rate taxpayers,
[b] includes savings rate taxpayers i.e. those whose only income is from either savings or dividends,
[c] latest survey year,
[d] projected estimates based upon 2007/08 Survey of Personal Incomes, in line with Budget 2010
[e] includes additional rate taxpayers (282,000 in 2010/11)

Sources: HMRC Statistics updated April 2010
(http://www.hmrc.gov.uk/stats/index.htm – Table 2.1)

Table 1.4 shows the current taxes in operation in the UK for 2010/11 and how much each tax contributes to the total revenue raised by the Government each year. You will see that the most important UK taxes, in terms of the revenue they raise for the Government, are income tax, VAT, corporation tax and social security contributions.

Table 1.4: UK Tax Receipts

From Table C11: Current Receipts, Office of Budget Responsibility, Budget Forecast, June 2010. Crown copyright is produced with the permission of the Controller of Her Majesty's Stationery Office (for full notes to this table please see the full report available on the HM Treasury website).

	£ billion		
	Outturn 2008/09	Estimate 2009/10	Forecast 2010/11
HM Revenue and Customs			
Income tax (gross of tax credits)	153.4	145.6	150.2
Income tax credits	-5.6	-5.6	-5.8
Corporation tax (net of tax credits)	43.7	36.5	43.3
Petroleum revenue tax	2.6	0.9	1.7
Capital gains tax	7.8	2.5	2.6
Inheritance tax	2.8	2.4	2.2
Stamp duties (SDLT & on shares)	8.0	7.8	8.9
National insurance contributions	96.9	95.6	98.9
Value added tax	78.4	70.1	80.7
Fuel duties	24.6	26.2	27.3
Tobacco duties	8.2	8.8	9.4
Spirits duties	2.4	2.6	2.6
Wine duties	2.7	2.9	3.2
Beer and cider duties	3.4	3.5	3.7
Air passenger duty	1.9	1.9	2.3
Insurance premium tax	2.3	2.3	2.3
Temporary bank payroll tax	0.0	0.0	2.5
Other HMRC receipts[1]	6.1	5.9	6.4
Total HMRC	439.1	409.1	441.7
Vehicle excise duties	5.6	5.6	5.9
Business rates	22.9	24.3	24.9
Council Tax	24.4	25.0	25.3
VAT refunds	12.0	11.2	13.5
Other taxes and royalties	4.0	4.5	4.3
Net taxes and national insurance contributions	508.0	479.7	515.5
Accrual adjustments on taxes	-4.7	6.7	2.7
less own resources contribution to EC budget	-5.1	-3.8	-4.8
Interest and dividends	7.7	3.5	4.5
Gross operating surplus	23.3	23.9	24.7
Other receipts	4.6	4.5	5.1
Current receipts	533.8	514.6	547.7
Memo:			
North Sea revenues	12.9	6.5	9.4

[1] consists of landfill tax, climate change levy, aggregates levy, betting and gaming duties and customs duties and levies

How does the UK Government spend its money?

The next table shows how the Government is planning to spend the revenue it raises in 2010/11. To give you a comparison we have also given you the figures for 2008/09 out-turns and 2009/10's estimated expenditure. We have not shown all the expenditure plans of the Government here, but all the key costs are given. The revised plans for 2010/11 and beyond will be announced in the Autumn Spending Review 2010 and will be available on the HM Treasury website after October 20th 2010.

Table 1.5: UK Government Expenditure

Selected from Table 2.2 – Departmental Expenditure Limits – resource and capital budgets, Budget 2010 Report, June 2010. Selected resource budgets only. (Detailed capital budgets not shown). Crown copyright is reproduced with the permission of the Controller of Her Majesty's Stationery Office. For the full table and associated notes to this table please see the full report.

	£ billion		
	2008/09	2009/10	2010/11
	(Outturn)	(Estimate)	(Plans)
Education	46.8	49.6	50.9
Health	90.3	97.6	101.5
(NHS part)	(88.8)	(96.0)	(99.5)
Transport	5.8	7.0	6.4
Business, Innovation & Skills	17.9	19.2	19.2
CLG Local Government	24.7	25.5	26.0
Home Office	9.2	9.5	9.4
Justice	9.2	9.6	9.1
Defence	32.6	35.2	36.0
Foreign and Commonwealth Office	2.0	2.2	2.0
International Development	4.8	5.3	6.1
Environment, Food & Rural Affairs	2.4	2.	2.4
Culture, Media & Sport	1.5	1.6	1.5
Work and Pensions	7.9	9.1	8.8
Scotland	24.1	25.1	25.7
Wales	12.8	13.6	13.9
Northern Ireland (Executive and office)	9.1	9.9	9.8
:			
:			
Total Resource Budget	313.5	334.8	342.7
Total Capital Budget	48.5	56.6	51.6

(Note: Social Security benefits expenditure for same periods £b149.7, £b163.7 and £b169.3
Source: Table C13, Total Managed Expenditure – Budget Report, June 2010)

Summary

In this chapter we have laid the foundations that you will need to study taxation from this textbook, and beyond. We have drawn on the lessons of history to try to illustrate how taxation affects all of us today. You are now able to trace the history of taxation over more than 2,000 years. The difficulties facing Parliament today have been faced by leaders throughout the centuries. Governments must raise revenues in ways which are seen by the electorate as being fair and equitable if they can reasonably expect them to be paid.

A modern Chancellor has to consider many conflicting objectives when setting out tax proposals in the annual budget. He (or she – although there is yet to be a female Chancellor in the UK) must decide how much tax he wishes to raise and then determine exactly how that tax should be raised from the different taxes available. To do this a Chancellor must be aware of the potential consequences of the legislation on individuals and businesses.

In this chapter we have been able to introduce the complex relationship between legislation and case law and understand the limitations of each. We have also looked at some of the procedures that apply in the administration of the UK tax system. Finally we illustrated how the Government uses the current tax system to raise revenue, and briefly how they spend this revenue.

In Chapters 2 and 3 we will consider in more detail the nature of a good tax – if indeed any tax can be considered to be good – addressing firstly the principles of the design of tax systems in Chapter 2, and then some impacts of the specific design of the UK tax system in Chapter 3.

Project areas

There are a number of areas covered in this chapter which would provide good material for projects. These include the following:

- a comparison of the progressive nature of the tax systems of a number of countries,
- exploring the effectiveness of a self-assessment system for income tax assessment,
- assessing the effectiveness of the new Tribunals Service compared to the previous dual roles of the General and Special Commissioners,
- exploring the history of UK taxation,
- examining the implications of tax harmonisation in Europe,
- assessing the relative use of different taxes in the UK tax system and the corresponding spending activity of the UK government,
- reviewing local v central government taxation following the publication of the Lyons review in March 2007,

- comparing the balance of local v national (federal) taxation in the UK with other countries. Why might these balances be different?

Discussion questions

1   Do you think that people will be more likely to work if they receive support through the tax system rather than the benefits system?

2   Is it right (and fair) that the UK is so dependent on income taxation? What risks are involved in such a policy? Why might these risks be acceptable to assume?

3   What are the implications of having a tax system which is governed by tax law, interpretation of law in the form of cases and guidance for the Revenue Authority? Could this system be streamlined?

4   What other unusual taxes can you discover that have existed in some point in history? How effective are they?

5   How is Lady Godiva connected with taxation? What other interesting events in history have been influenced by tax policy issues?

Further reading

History

HMRC website on the history of income tax and current administration procedures; http://www.hmrc.gov.uk

Beckett, J.V., Land Tax & Excise: The levying of taxation in seventeenth and eighteenth-century England *100 English Historical Review*, 285, 1985.

Daunton, M. J., *Trusting Leviathan: the politics of taxation in Britain, 1799 – 1914*, Cambridge University Press: Cambridge, 2001.

Daunton, M. J., *Just Taxes: the politics of taxation in Britain 1914 – 1979*, Cambridge University Press: Cambridge, 2002.

Dowell, S., *A History of Taxation in England* (4 volumes), Frank Cass & Co. Ltd: London, (1965 - 3rd Edition, first published in 1884).

Ezzamel, M., Accounting Working for the State: Tax Assessment and Collection During the New Kingdom, Ancient Egypt *Accounting and Business Research*, 32/1:17-39, 2002.

Farnsworth, A., *Addington: Author of the Modern Income Tax*, Stevens & Sons Ltd: London 1951.

Harris, P. *Income Tax in Common Law Jurisdictions: from the origins to 1820*, Cambridge University Press, Cambridge, 2006.

Kennedy, W., *English Taxation 1640-1799*, G. Bell & Sons Ltd: London, 1913.

Monroe, H.H., *Intolerable Inquisition? Reflections on the Law of Tax*, Stevens & Sons: London, 1981.

Sabine, B.E.V., A *History of Income Tax*, George Allen & Unwin: London, 1966.

Soos, P., *The Origins of Taxation at Source in England*. IBFD Publications: Amsterdam, 1997.

Tax Reform

Sandford, C., *Successful Tax Reform: Lessons from an analysis of Tax Reform in six countries*. Fiscal Publications: Birmingham, 1993.

Steinmo, S., The Politics of Tax Reform, in Sandford, C. (ed.) *More Key Issues in Tax Reform*, Fiscal Publications: Birmingham, 1995.

Progressivity

James, S. and Nobes, C. (2010) *The Economics of Taxation: 10th Edition*, Chapter 2, Fiscal Publications: Birmingham.

Dilnot, A., The Income Tax Rate Structure, in Sandford, C. (ed.) *Key Issues in Tax Reform*, Fiscal Publications: Birmingham 1993.

Dates in UK Tax System

J. Jeffrey-Cook "A year beginning on 6 April", *Taxation*, 5 April, 2001, p8.

Tax Administration

Sandford, C., M. Godwin & P. Hardwick, *Administrative and Compliance Costs of Taxation*. Fiscal Publications: Birmingham, 1989.

For more details of the administration of UK tax see the HMRC website (http://www.hmrc.gov.uk).

Scottish Taxation

Cooper, C., Danson, M., Whittam, G. & Sheridan, T. "The neoliberal project—Local taxation intervention in Scotland" *Critical Perspectives on Accounting*, Volume 21, Issue 3, March 2010, Pages 195-210

For more information about local taxation see the Department for Communities and Local Government (CLG)'s website (http://www.communities.gov.uk) which contains a section on local government including links to the Lyons Review and the plans of the new Government for local taxation changes as they unfold.

2 Principles of tax system design

Introduction

In the previous chapter we considered the objectives of a tax system and determined that taxation is a tool used by government to manage the economy, regulate and develop society and provide public goods. We also noted that the nature of a particular tax system, which consists of a number of different types of tax, is constantly changing with the changing views of society as a whole.

In this chapter we will first discuss a number of ideas and concepts which are relevant to understanding how to design a tax system. We will then identify and explore the desirable characteristics of a tax system that underpin its design. These principles apply to any tax system – not just the UK's. Once we have done this we will evaluate various bases of taxation to illustrate the application of this theory in practice.

At the end of this chapter you will be able to:

- outline the key issues of tax system design;
- state and discuss the five desirable characteristics of a tax system;
- state the range of tax bases which may be used to build a tax system from; and
- discuss the merits and limitations of each of these tax bases.

Key issues in taxation design

In this section we will explore the key issues of tax system design that all tax systems must keep in balance to function properly: what to tax?, what kind of rate structure?, the distribution of the tax burden and the effect taxes have on taxpayer behaviour.

What to tax?

We saw in the historical review of taxation in Chapter 1 that taxes have been imposed on all kinds of activities, goods and services throughout history.

The classification of taxes, however, comes down to three broad groups of taxes:

1. Income Taxes – taxes on a taxpayer's income earned or received between specific points in time;
2. Wealth/Capital Taxes – taxes on a taxpayer's accumulated wealth;
3. Consumption Taxes – taxes on a taxpayer's spending of their income or wealth.

The primary current UK taxes under each of these categories are:

1.	Income Taxes	For individuals: Income Tax
		For companies: Corporation Tax
2.	Wealth/Capital Taxes	Capital Gains Tax
		Inheritance Tax
		Stamp Duty
		Council Tax
3.	Consumption Taxes	Value Added Tax
		Excise Duties (e.g. on alcohol, petrol or tobacco)

The rules used to decide what is taxed, and what is not, under each of these categories is called the *tax base*. For example, what income a taxpayer is taxed on will form the income tax base, and so on. A tax base can change over time, for example, as new income types, in the case of income taxes, are included in the tax rules and become subject to taxation. This also applies to each of the taxes listed above, their tax base may also change over time as their rules of application are developed.

Balancing the rules of the three tax bases to form the whole tax system is an important task carried out by the Government. Later in this chapter we will look at how the Government goes about deciding how this balance should be set, and how it changes over time.

Distribution of the tax burden

The tax burden is the degree to which a tax, specific collection of taxes, or a tax system viewed in its entirety, affects a taxpayer or group of taxpayers. We look at the question of tax burden in more detail in the next chapter, but for now, let's think about the way in which the tax rate structure might work. When examining either the tax system as a whole, or an individual tax within the system, the burden taxation places on a taxpayer will either be:

- *proportional* – the amount of tax to be paid increases directly in line with increases in the tax base;
- *progressive* – the amount of tax to be paid increases faster than the increase in the tax base; or
- *regressive* – the amount of tax to be paid increases more slowly than increases in the tax base.

In most tax systems, including the UK's, there is a generally accepted principle that income tax should be progressive, i.e. taxpayers with larger incomes should pay a higher proportion of their income in tax than taxpayers with smaller incomes.

Progressivity

To be a progressive tax it does not necessarily mean that there is a steadily rising tax rate as the tax base rises. A tax can still be progressive even if it only has two rates of tax. To illustrate this, consider two taxpayers, one earning £10,000 per annum and the other earning twice that, i.e. £20,000 per annum. Assume both taxpayers have personal allowances for income tax of £5,000. This means that the first £5,000 of income is not subject to income tax. The rest of the income is taxed at 20%. The taxpayer earning £10,000 per annum will pay £1,000 ((£10,000 – 5,000) × 20%) tax. This equates to 10% of their income. The higher earning taxpayer will pay £3,000 ((£20,000 – 5,000) × 20%) tax or 15% of their income. The higher income earner pays a higher overall percentage of their income in tax because both have a fixed level of tax-free income (£5,000) before starting to pay tax. In this case the tax they have to pay increases three times when the income only doubles (i.e. the tax rate is rising faster than the income). This simple tax system is therefore a progressive one even with only two rates (0% and 20%).

A good rule of thumb for assessing whether a tax system is progressive, proportionate or regressive is to compare the *average rate of tax (ART)* with the *marginal rate of tax (MRT)* faced by the taxpayer. The average rate is found by dividing the amount of tax payable by the amount of the tax base. The marginal rate of tax is the rate the taxpayer would have to pay on an extra £1 of the tax base.

If the average rate of tax is less than the marginal rate of tax the system is progressive (for that taxpayer at that point). If the average rate of tax equals the marginal rate of tax the tax system is proportional, and if the average rate of tax is greater than the marginal rate of tax it is regressive.

In this case, for the first taxpayer (with £1,000 income), the average rate of tax is 10%, and the marginal rate of tax is 20% (as they would pay 20p extra in tax if they earned £1 more in income) so the system is progressive for them (10% < 20%) at the point they are currently. The same applies for the second taxpayer (15% < 20%). We will develop these ideas further in Chapter 3.

This example is simplified from reality, of course, to illustrate the point about how progressivity works. When other tax factors are taken into account, for example tax relief on particular payments made by the taxpayer, or when combined with the effects of other taxes, a fuller analysis of the UK tax system may not give the same distribution effects.

An exercise illustrating the relationship between personal allowances and progressivity can be found on the website. You could now attempt it to further develop this idea of tax burdens.

Regressivity

A regressive tax is one that places a heavier burden on poorer taxpayers than wealthy taxpayers. For example, unlike most income taxes, VAT is a regressive tax as it is usually imposed predominantly using a flat rate. Wealthy individuals generally spend proportionally less of their incomes each period than poorer taxpayers. Consequently, because VAT is charged at a fixed rate (17.5% on most items rising to 20% from 4 January 2011), poorer taxpayers will spend a higher proportion of their income on VAT than their richer counterparts. In the UK, this problem is balanced to some extent by policies to reduce VAT on some essential goods, such as the zero rate (i.e. 0%) of VAT on most food. However, this zero rate taxing does not apply to all basic items and therefore VAT is generally considered a regressive tax.

Taxpayer behaviour

It might seem strange, but we actually know very little about how taxpayers behave in response to the introduction of new taxes, or changes to the tax system. There are academic studies that attempt to match taxpayer behaviour with tax changes, but few are conclusive. This is perhaps to be expected because modern society is so complex. Creating even a moderately complex tax system within such a society will then make it very difficult to map the correlation between changes in taxes and taxpayer responses.

A recent example of the use of the tax system to influence taxpayers' behaviour in a positive way is the switch to taxing company cars by reference their level of CO_2 emissions (rather than business miles driven as was previously the case). This made it more expensive to drive higher polluting cars relative to lower polluting cars for the same mileage.

When the Government introduced this new approach in 2002, it hoped that companies providing cars for their employees to drive would switch to using lower emission cars, which would be beneficial for the environment. Recent statistics suggest that this has been successful to some extent. In 2006/7 65% of company cars had CO_2 emissions of 165 gm/km or less. This compares to only 41% in 2002/03, so it certainly seems that the change in rules could have had the desired impact of encouraging employers to provide greener vehicles for their employees. (You can find out more detail on company car taxation in Chapter 5)

Unfortunately, taxpayers don't always behave in the way the Government expects them to. One recent example in the UK of an unexpected change in taxpayer behaviour was the increased use of companies as the trading structure for a business to take advantage of the lower tax rates that apply to corporations as compared to individuals. Following the introduction of a new 10% rate (later reduced to 0%) for companies with low profits, there was a significant increase in the number of businesses that switched to trading as companies. In the 2006 Budget the then Chancellor, Gordon Brown, reacted by increasing the rate of tax on corporations with taxable profits of less than £50,000 to the full tax rate that companies earning between £50,000 and £300,000 previously paid. In the 2007 Budget he went further and announced future rate rises for these low profit companies, again citing tax avoidance as his excuse for hitting these smaller companies hard. This action was assumed to make the use of corporate structures solely for tax avoidance somewhat less attractive.

Also, as we saw in the discussion of tax history in Chapter 1, people have found imaginative ways of circumventing a liability to tax for as long as taxes have been used. Some evade tax, for instance by smuggling goods into the country from abroad rather than paying the correct import tax on those goods. Others will under-declare their incomes, or overstate their expenses, to reduce their income tax bill.

Fiscal Fact

The number of higher rate income taxpayers increased from 1.7 million in 1990/91 to 2.1 million in 1996/97 and is estimated to rise to 3.13 million in 2010/11, paying an average total income tax bill of £16,000 each.

Tax evasion is illegal and is punishable by fines and/or imprisonment. Tax avoidance on the other hand is legal and involves arranging your activities in ways that will reduce your tax bill. Some acceptable tax avoidance, or tax planning, is simple. For instance, saving money in an ISA rather than an ordinary building society account has the result that income from the account is paid without being subject to tax (subject to certain limits as we will see later). This, therefore, is a (perfectly legal) arrangement which enables taxpayers to avoid paying tax on investment interest received.

Attitudes to tax avoidance have changed over the years, and vary even at the same point in time depending on the perspective from which the question is considered. Indeed the boundary between acceptable and unacceptable tax avoidance is an issue of constant debate (we will explore this further in Chapter 11). Some tax avoidance schemes are highly artificial and involve changing the nature of transactions or creating artificial transactions so as to take advantage of concessions in the tax law. These are generally considered to fall into the unacceptable tax avoidance category (i.e. are not legal). Others are not so clearly on the wrong side of the boundary, and will be viewed differently as to whether or not they are acceptable by taxpayers and the tax administrators.

Another topical example is exploiting the different tax rules that apply to employees and consultants (who are self employed or use a small company structure with themselves as the main/only employee). In the early part of 1993 it became public knowledge that John Birt, the then new Director General of the BBC, was not on the payroll as an employee of the BBC but was employed, through his own company, as a consultant to the organisation. In this capacity John

Birt was able to arrange his affairs so that his tax liability was less than it would have been if he had been an employee. The details of his financial arrangements were published in virtually all the national newspapers and widely discussed on television and radio.

Although there was no suggestion that such an arrangement was illegal, indeed it was claimed that for some groups of staff within the BBC it was normal, there was widespread condemnation of the situation. It was soon announced that John Birt would become an employee of the BBC and pay tax under the PAYE system, as normal employees do. This use of what are called 'personal service' companies, continues to be a tax avoidance issue of concern to HMRC, which we look at in more detail in Chapter 11.

In the next section we will review in more detail the foundation principles of tax system design that help us to find solutions to some of the problems faced in creating a working tax system.

The desirable characteristics of a tax system

Prior to the late eighteenth century, taxation was used mainly to raise revenue to fund military campaigns and defend the nation state against their enemies, whoever they happened to be at the time. Taxation was viewed as being the price paid for the protection of the state. Thomas Hobbes wrote in his famous book 'Leviathan' in 1651:

> "For the impositions that are laid on the people by the
> sovereign power are nothing else but the wages due to them
> that hold the public sword, to defend private men in the
> exercise of their several trades and callings."

By the late eighteenth century, at the start of the industrial revolution, more consideration was being given to the ways in which taxes were raised and the most appropriate forms of tax to create effective tax systems.

Adam Smith was one of a number of early thinkers on this topic who considered the principles of how to design an effective tax system, and in his book, *The Wealth of Nations*, published in 1776, he outlined four desirable characteristics for a tax system:

1. "The subjects of every state ought to contribute to the support of the Government, in proportion to their respective abilities; that is in proportion to the revenue which they respectively enjoy under the protection of the state."

2. "The tax which each individual is bound to pay ought to be certain, and not arbitrary."

3. "Every tax ought to be levied at the time, or in the manner, most convenient for the contributor to pay it."

4. "Every tax ought to be so contrived as both to take out, and keep out, of the pockets of the people, as little as possible over and above what it brings in to the public treasury of the state. A tax may either take out or keep out of the pockets of the people a great deal more than it brings into the public treasury, and in four ways: a) by the number of officers who levy it; b) by obstructing the industry of the people; c) by penalties incurred in attempting to evade the tax; d) by subjecting the people to the frequent visits and examinations of the tax-gatherers."

It must be remembered, however, that at the time Adam Smith was writing, there was no income tax in Britain, indeed the idea of a tax on income was considered to be abhorrent so his comments are largely made in the context of a tax system made up predominately of capital/wealth and expenditure taxes. In more modern terms these 'Canons of Taxation', as they became known, can be re-stated as:

1. Equity: a tax should be seen to be fair in its impact on all individuals. Taxes should be levied according to people's taxable capacity.

2. Certainty: taxes should not be arbitrary, the taxpayer should know his or her tax liability and when and where to pay it.

3. Convenience: it should be easy for the taxpayer to pay what they owe.

4. Efficiency: the tax system should not have an impact on the allocation of resources and it should be cheap to administer. Taxes which are too costly for the tax authority to administer should be avoided as much as possible. Costs to governments include administration costs, the cost of chasing up delinquent taxpayers through audits and the like, and the costs of considering disputes with taxpayers over the way in which the tax laws operate.

Other writers have subsequently proposed further characteristics to add to this list. Two common additions are *simplicity* and *flexibility*. Designing for simplicity would suggest that, where possible, the tax system should have as few complications as possible (e.g. not having elaborate or large numbers of exceptions for particular activities or income types). It is important for a tax to be simple to understand so that a taxpayer can easily calculate his or her liability.

Aiming for flexibility suggests that a tax system should be established in such a way as to be able to cope with changing economic circumstances over time without requiring substantial changes.

A problem with desirable characteristic lists, as given above, is that their authors usually do not order the desirable characteristics in any practically useful way. Should each of the characteristics be allocated equal weight in the design of the tax system, or are some more important than others? Are some of the characteristics so important that any successful system of tax must have them? What happens when two desirable characteristics conflict with each other? We need to consider each of these characteristics in more detail before attempting to answer these questions.

Equity

A tax which is not seen to be fair is usually resented by the individuals asked to pay it and therefore equity is an important constituent of any tax system – as a government clearly needs people to pay the taxes they charge them with or the whole system will grind to a halt.

There are two aspects to the fairness of a tax system – *horizontal equity* and *vertical equity*:

- a tax system is horizontally equitable if taxpayers with equal taxable capacity bear the same tax burden;
- a tax system has vertical equity if those with greater capacity to pay tax bear a higher tax burden.

We have two problems of definition when considering horizontal equity. Firstly, how will we identify taxpayers with equal taxable capacity? Two individuals doing the same job for the same money with the same personal circumstances are likely to have the same taxable capacity in most tax systems, but how do you compare the taxable capacity of an individual who has earned income with another, who is not working but has substantial wealth? Equally, an individual who prefers to spend his leisure time drinking incurs a greater tax liability (because alcohol attracts VAT and excise duty) than an individual who spends the same amount of money on trips to the theatre, as this isn't as heavily taxed (only VAT, not excise duty, is charged on theatre tickets), regardless of their relative taxable capacities.

45

The second problem of definition relates to ensuring that in practice equal amounts of tax are paid by individuals with the same taxable capacity. Suppose we consider two individuals with the same lifetime income, one of whom earns the average UK income for each year of his working life of 40 years while the other earns 20 times as much as the average for only two years of her working life. Under a progressive income tax system, like the one in operation in the UK at present, the first taxpayer will pay less tax than the second. For a tax to have full horizontal equity it would need to be based on the lifetime income of the taxpayer not on incomes from year to year. This approach is likely to prove difficult, if not impossible, to operate in practice. Even if this could be arranged it would, in turn, raise further knock-on difficulties. For example, how should individuals with different life spans be taxed? Women generally have a longer life expectancy than men. If income is to be spread over a taxpayer's lifetime should women pay less tax than men on their taxable capacity because they will need to support themselves for more years?

What about vertical equity? Achieving this is also difficult in reality. There are at least three layers to this problem. To implement a tax system with vertical equity we must first decide who, in principle, should pay tax at higher rates. Then we must decide how much higher that rate should be than the rates paid by other taxpayers, and finally we must devise a tax system which achieves these objectives for the full variety of taxpayers.

An individual may be considered to have a greater taxable capacity or to have a higher level of economic well-being or to receive more benefits from government spending. Any of these criteria might be used to identify individuals who should pay the higher rate of taxation. However, which, or which combination, of these criteria should be used? So far, we have assumed that it is easy to determine what a person's taxable capacity is, so that we can make judgements about horizontal and vertical equity. In practice, however, it is extremely difficult to decide what factors should be taken into account in working out a person's taxable capacity. Most often we use the notion of 'ability to pay', which ties in with Adam Smith's notion of 'respective abilities'.

Ability to pay

There are a number of practical difficulties involved in measuring ability to pay.

Activity

What factors should be taken into account when measuring a person's ability to pay taxes?

Feedback

The most obvious factor is the person's income level. But then this raises further questions about how people earn their income. For example, suppose two individuals undertake the same job but the first chooses to work only the basic hours and spends more leisure time in their garden while the second chooses to work overtime each week instead. If income alone is used to determine 'ability to pay' then the second individual will pay more tax than the first. But both employees had the same opportunity to earn extra money so is it really fair that one of them should pay more tax than the other? If we could assess the ability to earn an income, instead of simply taxing what is actually earned, then both could be made to pay the same amount of tax.

If we want to use the ability to pay as our criteria for assessing how much tax someone should pay we must first decide whether we will use actual income or some measure of potential income. In practice, of course, it is actual income that is taxed because of the practical difficulties of reliably measuring potential income. But even if we settle for only being able to tax the actual income of taxpayers we will have still further problems with achieving vertical equity. Suppose two individuals have the same income but the first saves money in order to provide for retirement while the second spends money as it is earned and depends on the state for support in their old age. The first individual will pay tax on the returns earned on their savings and so could well pay more tax in total than the second individual, while the second receives more benefits from the state if given extra help in their old age. Can this be considered to be equitable? It is unlikely that, put this way, the first individual will agree.

You may also have considered a person's stock of wealth as part of ability to pay. Some people are known to be asset rich, but income poor, which raises the question of whether wealth holdings should be counted in deciding what ability to pay is.

What about family circumstances? There is an argument that a single person with no dependents has a larger capacity to pay tax than one who has numerous dependents, maybe a non-working partner and several children for example. There may be an argument that this should be factored into decisions about how much tax burden he or she should bear.

As a result of these difficulties in working out how to assess people's taxable capacity using a concept of ability to pay, both horizontal and vertical equity are therefore difficult to achieve in practice – even if in theory they sound appropriate.

Fiscal Fact

According to the Taxpayers' Alliance (using 2008/2009 data), over a 40 year working life plus a 15 year retirement, the average sum of income tax paid in the UK will be £233,000 in today's prices (plus a further £109,000 in VAT, £78,000 in National Insurance Contributions and £46,000 in Council Tax). This rises to £621,000 (plus a further £165,000, £146,000 and £46,000 respectively) for the highest quintile of earners but falls to £26,000 (plus a further £67,000, £16,000 and £30,000) for the lowest quintile.

The benefit principle

An alternative approach to the use of 'ability to pay' to achieve equity is to try to relate tax charged to the benefit received from the state. This implies creating a tax system where those who benefit most from the services provided by a government should pay the most tax. This might sound fair in principle but proves difficult to achieve practically.

In practice there are relatively few activities which can be effectively taxed using the benefit approach. For example, many services provided by a government cannot be opted out of if someone does not want to receive the benefit. Defence or law and order are, for example, benefits which are impossible for a citizen to choose whether to consume or not (these types of services or goods are referred to as *public goods*).

On the other hand, it may be undesirable for some services to be withheld from citizens who do not contribute to their cost, even if it were feasible. For example, there was a time when homeowners and businesses could subscribe to the fire service in the same way as a motorist can choose to join the roadside assistance agencies (like the AA or the RAC) today. While on the surface it seems this could work – the fire service would only show up for subscribers – however, if a non-subscriber suffered a fire and the fire services did not put the fire out it was possible that the fire would spread to neighbours who had paid to have their property protected. A public service to put out fires that is common for all makes more sense practically. In addition, it is likely to be unacceptable to the community as a whole that some members of society are not helped by the fire services when they are in need, for example, those who cannot otherwise afford to make a private contribution. Nowadays, this service is therefore provided largely as a public good.

Another example of this situation is education. The imposition by the Government of minimum education standards for all citizens produces a benefit for the whole of society whether the individual would want to, or be able to, pay for these benefits directly or not. Therefore education to at least the age of 16 is provided free of charge to all children in the UK.

Further problems with achieving equity via a benefit approach includes issues with how to value benefits received, over what time scale do you try to measure the benefit (e.g. over their whole life or only part of it?) and also what does this do to the redistribution objective of a government (an important element of the objectives for a tax system as we discussed in Chapter 1).

It therefore seems difficult to imagine that a significant part of the tax system could be organised on the basis of assessing, and taxing, benefit received. Taxes which are raised to pay for specific (usually predefined) activities are termed *earmarked* or *hypothecated* taxes. In the past they have been unpopular with the Treasury as it limits how they can use tax revenues received. We therefore have seen little use of such taxes in recent tax history.

However, there are a number of examples of hypothecated taxes that have been raised in the UK. For example, vehicle excise duties were originally intended to fund highway construction and maintenance. In practice, the receipts from vehicle excise duties are now used for general expenditure from which highway construction and maintenance will come, but not in a way that is directly related to the revenue raised from these taxes (i.e. they are no longer really hypothecated).

Another example is the TV licence fee. Only those individuals who have a television are required to contribute to the cost of the BBC by way of the licence fee – a sort of tax as it is a compulsory levy on owning a TV (and not really directly related to the benefit received as the tax must be paid even if you never actually turn the TV on). However, this is a crude measure of benefit. There is no way of evaluating how much benefit a taxpayer derives from watching BBC programmes. In addition, the tax is difficult to collect and necessitates the use of a database of all addresses in the UK and detector vans to ensure compliance with the tax to collect a relatively small sum per taxpayer. The charge also is levied on the unit of a 'household; with no differentiation as to how many people share the benefit of the single licence just because they happen to live in the same house.

The television licence fee, however, is still used exclusively to finance the BBC as a hypothecated tax, although there are increasing calls for this to change too, so that the licence fee can be shared more widely (e.g. shared with commercial TV channels).

In the past proposals have been outlined for the National Health Service (NHS) to be funded by way of a hypothecated tax on the basis that taxpayers would be willing to pay more taxes if a clear link between the tax and health care could be established. A new hypothecated tax of this kind was proposed by the then Chancellor, Kenneth Clarke, in his November 1993 budget but this was never implemented. The 2002 Budget, however, picked up on this idea, and announced a rise from April 2003 in National Insurance Contributions to pay for some of the growth in the NHS. This may be an indication that we will see more hypothecation of this type in the future – although the subsequent budgets since this change have not brought any further direct hypothecation so perhaps this was a one off.

The congestion charge now in operation in London is yet another example of a hypothecated tax as money raised from car users in the centre of London from this charge, over and above the cost of providing the collection service itself, is spent directly on improvements to the city's infrastructure and public transport system rather than paying for other services the Greater London Authority is responsible for.

The concept of equity is complex and we have done little more than introduce the subject in this section, however, you should now be able to see that it is an important concept that should be considered when examining the effectiveness of any tax system.

Certainty

Having explored the desirable characteristic of equity, and the difficulties that arise in putting it into practice, we will next examine the nature of certainty as a feature of good tax system design.

A country's citizens need to be fully informed about who will have to pay the taxes in the tax system and when they will have to be paid (called the *incidence of tax*). Taxes where the incidence is clear are to be preferred over taxes where there is disagreement and uncertainty over the ultimate payer of the tax and when the tax must be paid. Under this criterion, as we will see in Chapter 9, corporation tax could be considered to be a poor tax, for example, because it is unclear whether the shareholders, consumers or others bear the ultimate burden of the tax. It is also argued by some that individuals are more aware of how much income tax they pay than how much VAT they pay, making income taxes more certain than VAT. We will consider the question of incidence more fully in the next chapter.

To achieve full certainty, the complete tax consequences of any financial transaction should be known in advance of the transaction being undertaken. In practice this is not always the case in the UK's tax system. This is due to both problems with interpreting the rules (particularly grey areas of the law), but also as rules need to change from time to time (e.g. because the ideas of how to tax develop or economic conditions alter and so on) so perfect certainty can't be assured.

This characteristic has an important impact on how tax systems evolve over time. In part, because of the need to consider certainty when designing tax systems, tax rule changes are only rarely made retrospectively. Tax policy makers typically only change how the tax system will be applied in the future, not how it was applied to past events or activities that have already been undertaken, or are difficult to undo now they have been done. They will very rarely seek to collect different taxes on past events to those that have already been paid.

If imposing taxes retrospectively regularly occurred in a tax system then a taxpayer's certainty would be significantly decreased. When they made a particular choice that affected how much tax they pay (e.g. accepting a new job or taking out a particular investment) they could not be certain the tax cost of doing this would not change. A good example of how retrospective taxes can upset taxpayers is the suggestion to increase Vehicle Excise Duties on the most polluting cars that was announced in the 2007 Pre-Budget. As these plans were to impose increased duties on all cars over a certain engine capacity obviously people who have already made the choice to own such cars are going to have to pay extra taxes they were not expecting to have to pay when they bought them. This rarely meets with taxpayer approval.

As another example, in recent years there has been growing unrest among large corporate taxpayers about the uncertainty surrounding changes proposed to the way the UK taxes foreign income in the hands of companies. Some large companies have even threatened to leave the UK and move to other jurisdictions because of the uncertainty about how the new rules would operate. We look at some of these changes in Chapter 12.

Certainty is therefore an important characteristic that affects how tax system changes are usually brought about. However, no tax system can remain the same forever or it will rapidly lose its other characteristics. Tax systems do have to change from time to time and will often affect at least some previous decisions people have made (e.g. income tax rates may go up meaning you have to pay more tax on the same job you do for the same wages). A government therefore has a difficult task balancing these often conflicting characteristics,

Convenience

The third 'Canon of taxation' is convenience which relates to how people pay their taxes, or otherwise engage with the tax system. For example, it is usually more convenient for people to have tax deducted at source (before it is received, like income taxes), or at the time they pay for something (like a VAT) than having to pay a lump sum periodically on something already received.

This raises the question of whether tax should be paid at source (as you receive it) rather than directly assessed (paid some time after receipt). This is a particularly important feature of the income tax part of the UK's tax system. For example, if an individual taxpayer receives income in the form of interest from a bank account, income tax will usually have already been deducted by the payer of the interest before the net interest is then given to the recipient.

Tax deducted at source is normally calculated independently of the taxpayer's personal circumstances and so does not always represent the correct amount of tax due. An individual who is not liable to income tax can sometimes reclaim any tax deducted at its source by contacting HMRC, or can even prevent its automatic deduction in the first place (for example, in the case of bank interest, by signing a form for the bank to say they do not receive enough income to pay income tax so the bank will then pay the interest gross instead of deducting tax).

An individual may also sometimes need to pay more tax on income they receive than is deducted at source. We will review how this extra payment is collected in practice in Chapter 4.

Taxpayers who are employed pay income tax on their earnings from employment under the Pay As You Earn (PAYE) scheme. Although this tax is deducted at its source (i.e. by the employer on behalf of the employees) it is different to the other examples of income taxed at source because the amount of tax deducted is partially dependent on the taxpayer's personal circumstances to try and improve the accuracy of the tax deducted. This, however, involves a complex process that is difficult to administer to get right. We'll review further how PAYE works in practice in Chapter 4.

Income tax collected via the self assessment system is an example of direct assessment – the alternative to taxing at source. In the UK, any income subject to taxation which has not been fully taxed at source already will need to be directly assessed. Each year, if you have any such income, you are required to declare it to HMRC (i.e. self-assess – hence the name) by filling out a tax return. Tax due on this income can then be paid directly to the Government. Capital taxes are mostly paid by direct declaration and assessment in this way, and some categories of income are also taxed in this way for some taxpayers. Look back to Chapter 1 to be reminded of who has to file tax returns as they need to be directly assessed.

You can see that the way in which tax is collected is an important consideration and taxation at source would seem to meet the criteria of 'convenience', at least for the taxpayer. It is not so convenient, however, for the person having to deduct the tax, for example in the case of PAYE, the employer incurs considerable cost in making sure the correct amount of tax is deducted from employees' wages and paid to HMRC on time.

The costs of administering a tax system include not only the direct costs incurred by government in operating the system itself, but also the difficulties the tax rules create for the taxpayer (i.e. how inconvenient they are). These difficulties are given a numeric value to give what is known as the *compliance costs* of the taxpayer. Compliance costs are the costs which are imposed on a taxpayer when he or she attempts to comply with a given tax or set of taxes. These will include any costs related to the need to keep records for tax purposes, costs of employing tax related staff, costs of collating data to complete the tax returns and so on. Compliance costs can be significant as part of the total cost of taxation – in some cases they can as much as five times as big as the direct costs for some types of tax.

There is a welcome current trend from the UK Government towards measuring and planning for the full costs of tax imposition (direct and indirect) as they review new taxes or changes to the tax system. This includes changes to tax rules in the last few years directly aiming to reduce some of the compliance costs on sole traders and partnerships. These assessments of impact costs are called Tax Impact Assessments or TIAs (were called Regulatory Impact Assessments or

RIAs before June 2010). A TIA will be associated with each non-minor change to the tax system and they are usually published on the HMRC website to make them easy to access.

The burden of complying with rules for PAYE, VAT and capital gains tax should not be underestimated when you are thinking about ways in which a tax system could be developed.

Efficiency

There are two separate aspects to efficiency derived from Adam Smith's Canons of taxation: economic efficiency and administrative efficiency.

Economic efficiency

A tax system is seen to be *economically efficient* if it does not distort the economic and commercial decisions which are made by individuals. Economic efficiency is sometimes referred to as *fiscal neutrality*, and the key idea is that taxes should, as far as possible, not interfere with the workings of the market. We will be considering economic efficiency in more detail in the next chapter where we discuss the impact of the UK tax system on decision making. Here, however, we will consider the way in which the tax system affects people's behaviour more generally, referred to as "distortions", and therefore the extent to which a tax system is economically efficient by its design.

As we noted earlier in this chapter, tax can affect peoples' behaviour in many ways. For example, take planning for retirement. An individual who invests funds in an approved pension fund obtains tax relief on contributions and the pension fund itself is exempt from both income and capital gains tax. This contrasts with an individual who proposes to finance retirement in some other way, perhaps by investing in a valuable asset such as a painting or perhaps property – with the aim of selling the items for a profit in the future to provide a source wealth to fund their retirement. For these assets, the tax situation may be very different to the approved pension fund asset. No relief is available in the current UK tax system for funds initially invested in the valuable asset that is being purchased to fund retirement and capital gains tax will probably be levied when the asset is sold. This means the tax system, distorts how people choose to invest to provide for their retirement. This means there is not economic efficiency between these choices.

Sometimes distortions resulting from particular taxes are deliberately intended by a government in order to affect individuals' behaviour. Such taxes are termed *corrective taxes*. The example above of giving tax advantages to pension funds may be considered a corrective tax as investing in a pension, rather than other assets, will encourage people to save for their old age where they might not otherwise make such arrangements, or may spend the money they would have otherwise invested before they reach retirement age.

Other examples of planned distortions might include a *tax break* or *tax concession* (a reduction in taxes normally due) given to employers who provide jobs to individuals who have been unemployed for a long time, or the tax reductions given to businesses for locating in a particular area the Government is seeking to regenerate or develop.

We also have a number of examples of the impact that tax related announcements have on people's behaviour. For example, if people believe that the duty on cigarettes will be increased in the budget they may purchase more cigarettes in the days before the budget in anticipation of an increase in tax.

Apart from the immediate effect of a tax change on taxpayer behaviour, there is also the problem of subsequent effects over time that is even more difficult to control. For example, there is currently discussion about road-pricing for motorways that may encourage at least some drivers to use other roads instead. A problem of pricing some roads and not others is that some drivers will change how they use different roads to avoid paying the taxes. The accident rate per mile driven is higher on roads which are not motorways, leading to fears of an overall increase in road traffic accidents if such a scheme was introduced. It also seems likely that congestion will increase on roads which do not carry a charge as road users switch to them more. This might increase journey times and fuel consumption for all road users and the accident rate might rise still further. To minimise these effects the Chancellor would have to set carefully the cost per mile travelled to a level that would deter enough road users from motorways but not simply to transfer too many journeys onto other roads.

Knock-on effects like this, caused by the presence of taxes or resulting from changes in the tax system, are a common feature of many taxes and a constant headache for tax policy creators. Tax system changes which do not have a knock-on effect will not distort the decisions made by individuals and companies and are therefore referred to as 'fiscally neutral'.

The extent to which tax changes create behavioural changes depends in part on how heavy the tax burden is to start with. The 1980s and early 1990s was an active period of tax reform throughout many parts of the world. In particular, the major trend was a move to limit (usually meaning reduce) the level of public expenditure (and hence the amount of tax revenue needed to sustain this expenditure was able to fall). This was followed by the reform of the assessment of taxation. Many tax rates were reduced throughout the world but correspondingly the tax base was broadened in many countries at the same time. That is, a wider range of taxpayer's income sources were taxed but the tax rate applied per pound was lower. In 1979 the highest rate of tax in the UK was 98% (on some types of income from investments). This was (probably rightly) seen as undesirable, if only because the incentives to avoid (legal) or even evade (illegal) tax were so large given that the potential savings that could be made were such a large percentage of the income. Today the highest rate of personal income tax in the UK is 50%, and in other countries can be even less, for example, in the US it is only 35%. The lower the rate of tax, the more the taxpayer keeps of their income and so (theoretically at least) the less incentive there is to avoid or evade tax. This makes further changes to the tax system more fiscally neutral – i.e. have less effect on changing people's behaviour due to the tax change.

Since 1979, although the rates of tax in the UK have generally fallen, the tax base has been broadened by decreasing the range of allowances which taxpayers can use to reduce their taxable income and adding taxes to more things that previously were not taxed. The removal of a tax deduction (generally termed a *tax relief*) available for interest paid on mortgages and the benefit of the married couple's allowances are recent examples of this practice.

While the goal of fiscal neutrality can be important in tax policy development, it would not be right to say that the UK Government is committed to fiscal neutrality to the extent of never introducing policies which are intended to distort the economic decisions made by individuals and businesses. As we discussed in Chapter 1, taxation is an important tool for a government to use explicitly to affect how people make decisions. The Government will therefore sometimes use non-fiscally neutral taxes in a targeted way where they consider the knock-on impacts to be desirable (and manageable). For example, tax advantageous treatment has been given to new forms of investments, particularly pensions, but also ISAs (Individual Savings Accounts) and on items of expenditure like the reduction in the vehicle licence fee for the cleanest and smallest cars. These were all done deliberately to affect taxpayers' behaviour towards using these saving schemes, or buying these cars, over alternative choices.

The reverse can also, of course, be true. Taxes can be explicitly used in a non-fiscally neutral way to dissuade particular behaviour. For example, heavy increases to the Vehicle Excise Duty on the most polluting cars in the 2007 Budget was an attempt by the Government to use the tax system to reduce the environmental impacts of cars by making it more expensive to use some cars (the more polluting ones) compared to others (less polluting ones).

Taxes therefore regularly have distortionary effects on peoples' decisions – some planned and some not. Examining economic efficiency, or fiscal neutrality, provides a measure of the extent to which these distortions are created by the tax system, or changes to the tax system. Some distortions improve the system, but controlling these impacts can prove difficult in practice. The use of taxation as a behaviour influencing tool by governments is one of the key reasons the tax system is constantly changing. We will return to the subject of fiscal neutrality again in Chapter 3 when we look in more detail at how tax systems are designed.

Administrative efficiency

A second aspect of efficiency as a characteristic of a good tax system relates to the administration of taxation. The more a tax costs to administer (creating returns, checking returns, chasing non payment etc.) the less of the money raised by the tax is available to the Government for their expenditure plans. It is not possible to have a 100% efficient collection system where some non-compliance is likely to occur (to achieve the equity aim at least – some administrative effort must be incurred to ensure everyone pays who should pay) but this administration cost should be as small as possible to achieve desirable economic efficiency.

An example of seeking to apply this characteristic in practice is the move to a self-assessment system for income and corporation taxes in the UK. This move aims, in part, to reduce administrative costs of these taxes for the tax authority. Unfortunately it shifts the burden of some of these costs to taxpayers in the form of higher compliance costs so that the overall efficiency gains for society associated with self-assessment (i.e. both the direct government costs savings plus the extra 'cost' placed on taxpayers) are difficult to measure.

Simplicity

Simplicity was not specifically mentioned as one of Adam Smith's Canons of taxation, but this is not surprising since, at the time he was writing, the tax system was relatively simple. There was no income tax for example, only a variety of wealth and consumption taxes. The idea of simplicity as a goal for tax and tax system design is linked to certainty and convenience, and really only began to become popular as an explicit goal in the last part of the twentieth century. The rationale for stating that a good tax is a simple tax is that the more complex a tax or tax system is, the more difficult it is for everyone concerned, both taxpayers and tax administrators, to operate and use it. It is also a commonly held view that too much complexity allows opportunities for more unacceptable tax avoidance activity and that if the system were more simple and easy to understand, tax avoidance opportunities would be reduced.

The aim of simplifying the tax system has quite a long history in the UK, and the last Conservative government initiated a rewrite of the tax legislation trying to make it easier to understand. This rewrite has made some progress and we have seen several pieces of tax legislation rewritten in recent years, as we noted in Chapter 1. Arguably, however, rewriting the legislation is not enough by itself, because the legislation still has to deal with the underlying complexity of the detailed rules governing the different types of taxes levied in the UK.

The Brown Government reiterated a commitment to simplification of the tax laws in the Pre-Budget Report of 2007 and announced several reviews aiming to simplify specific aspects of the tax system. Some progress has been made, for example with capital gains tax where recently a complex system to remove the inflation component of capital gains so that it is not taxed has been replaced by a low flat rate of tax, at least for individual taxpayers.

In July 2008, the Conservative opposition published proposals designed to lead not only to simplification of the tax system but also a reduction in the size of tax legislation. One recommendation is to establish an Office of Tax Simplification (OTS) to examine the existing rules and make proposals for simplification. With the recent Government change these plans now appear to be in the process of implementation. A new Joint Parliamentary Select Committee on Taxation is also proposed to have oversight over tax legislation and to whom the OTS would report.

Simplification is therefore becoming a more prominent issue, as concerns about the costs of complexity, including lack of certainty, increase. One of the difficulties, however, is that in order to simplify the tax system, or individual taxes within the tax system, policy makers have to be able to identify the causes of the complexity that needs to be removed.

Flexibility

A flexible tax is one which changes, or can be changed, easily in response to changes in the economic environment. A key aim of government is to reduce the fluctuations in economic activities caused by the economic cycle (the so called 'boom/bust' cycle) as this is often seem as good for an economy in the longer term. A flexible tax, designed properly, can have a stabilising effect on the economy to assist with this goal. For example, it can cause money to be taken out of a growing economy to keep its growth at a manageable level, and reduce the amount of money that is taken out of the economy when it enters a 'slow down' or a recession to soften any downward spiral effect.

Therefore, in times of recession a government might be content to see its tax receipts fall and increase its borrowing (as an alternative way to fund its expenditure plans) in order to give the economy a boost while during boom years a government might be happy to see its tax receipts increase, thus moderating the boom.

The modern UK income and corporation tax systems are good examples of relatively flexible tax systems. When incomes and business profits rise, the amount of tax raised increases without any direct action from the Government and equally when income or business profits fall, the amount of tax collected also falls. Because of the stepped progressive nature of the UK income tax system the percentage change in the tax collected is greater than the percentage change in wages or profits. If wages increase by, say, 10% in a year income taxes will increase by more than 10% over the same period without a need for a change in the legislation. Taxes will increase by a greater percentage than wages because marginal rates of tax (the amount of tax you must pay if you earn an extra pound of income) are higher than average rates of tax for most income taxpayers on the UK (a feature of a progressive tax system).

Another example of a tax which changes automatically and flexibly is stamp duty on houses. On all house purchases over £125,000 a stamp duty tax is due on the transfer of the property as part of its sale (currently set at 1%), although this doesn't apply to first time buyers. If the the house value exceeds £250,000 this stamp duty of 3% is payable regardless of whether the purchaser is a first time buyer or not. It rises again to 4% for values over £500,000. So this is a progressive tax rate, and importantly, the amount of this tax collected increases both as the number of houses sold increases and as the value of houses sold increases.

Fiscal Fact

In 2008/09, total revenue from stamp duty land tax on property and land was around £4.8billion. While this has grown from a total of only £2.1 billion in 1998/99, it is a significant decrease on 2007/08 when this amounted to £9.9 billion.

In practice, there is often a time lag between the decision by the Government to take some fiscal action, the implementation of the policy and the full impact of the tax on the economy. For example, during the 1980s there was great pressure from environmentalists to reduce the lead emissions from petrol. In the late 1980s the duty on unleaded petrol was reduced to make it more attractive to use than leaded petrol. Demand for unleaded petrol increased as a result of the changes but there was a time delay while information about unleaded petrol was disseminated throughout the population and car owners arranged to have their engines modified or changed the type of car they drove. Ultimately, however, this has now resulted in almost no new cars being sold which (if petrol driven) do not use unleaded fuel.

This same trend is being seen in the gradual move to more environmentally friendly bio-fuels as extra tax concessions are again being used by the Government to encourage, albeit slowly, their wider use.

Smith's canons revisited

Now that we have spent some time discussing each of Smith's desirable tax system characteristics (plus simplicity and flexibility) we can return to the question we asked at the start of this section – can we rank the factors by importance to make them more useful for tax system designers to use in practice? To do this we can use the examples of two particular taxes proposed and supported by the Government at the time, to illustrate the importance of understanding the different characteristics and considering their relative ranking: first the community charge (or poll tax) and then the proposed increase in VAT on domestic fuel from 8% to the then full rate of 17.5%.

Community Charge (Poll Tax)

As was introduced in Chapter 1, the Community Charge replaced Domestic Rates in April 1990. The Rates had been a long-established, but unpopular, tax used as the primary form of local taxation for provision of many local services (like schools, roads, police, fire service etc.). Rather than levy local tax solely on homeowners as the rates system did, the Community Charge was instead levied on virtually all individuals over 18 years of age i.e. changed from being a property tax to an individual, personal, tax. The supporters of the Community Charge argued that it increased certainty (at least political accountability) by making the individuals who were eligible to vote in local government elections responsible for paying for their elected council's expenditure proposals – not just those individuals in the community who owned property there.

Opponents of the Community Charge, however, claimed that the tax was unfair because the majority of individuals were required to pay the same amount of tax regardless of their personal circumstances (i.e. was regressive) It was considered vertically inequitable as it was less 'ability to pay' focused than the rates system had been and instead tried to focus more on a benefits approach to tax setting – i.e. everyone benefited from good local services so all should contribute to their cost. Some individuals, including students and the unemployed, were able to pay a reduced amount but little relief was available for the majority of individuals.

In practice the tax proved to be difficult to collect (i.e. administrative inefficient) with significant numbers of people simply disappearing from official records, like electoral rolls, to avoid having to pay the tax. With many missing taxpayers equity was therefore compromised. In addition to the administrative problems, protests about the unfairness of the Community Charge (leading ultimately to the Poll Tax riots in March 1990) escalated until the Government backed down on the tax's imposition and it was replaced with the current system of Council Tax which, ironically, took us back to a property related, 'ability to pay' style, local tax system as the previous Rates system had been, despite its apparent faults and flaws.

VAT on domestic fuel

An increase in VAT on domestic fuel was proposed in the Spring Budget of 1993. In April 1994 VAT was levied on domestic fuel at 8% and towards the end of 1994 the then Chancellor attempted to introduce the legislation needed to increase the rate from 8% to 17.5%. In the event the House of Commons defeated the motion and the Chancellor was forced to abandon his proposal. The defeat occurred despite measures announced in the Budget to protect many of the less well off in society from the increase in VAT. These measures included substantial increases in the state pension as well as increases above inflation to a number of other state benefits.

The opponents of this proposed tax argued that heating and lighting were essential for everybody, and not a luxury, and so should not be taxed at the full rate despite the presence of any compensatory benefits. They successfully argued that, in general, people on lower incomes spend proportionately more of their income on gas and electricity and so the increase in price would affect the poorest people in society disproportionately (again an issue of equity).

The importance of equity

It would appear then that the Community Charge failed because it was difficult to collect once taxpayers considered it to be unfair (i.e was regressive). The increase in VAT on domestic fuel was also seen to be regressive and therefore unfair. While only two taxes are used here to illustrate the case, there is also other evidence that the most important characteristic of a good tax system, (in the UK at least), is that it should be seen to be (and ideally should actually be) fair, making equity important to get right in planning tax reform. These two cases illustrate that the most effective way of achieving acceptable equity is likely to use an ability to pay approach. They also illustrate the importance of perceptions of equity, taxpayers will be unhappy if they think a tax is unfair, even if a closer analysis shows that it is, in fact, equitable.

However, other characteristics should not entirely be ignored just to improve equity. Some consideration must at least be given to these other characteristics if the tax system is not to become unbalanced. What is clear from our examination of the desirable characteristics of the tax system is that there are overlaps between them, but also considerable tensions, or even conflicts, between them and it is not possible to design a system that contains all characteristics at the same time. Over time, priorities change, and also different countries will have different priorities depending on social, cultural and economic conditions.

Alternative tax bases

We started this chapter by asking the question what should be taxed? We now return to that question with a more detailed look at the three main possible tax bases. A considerable amount of debate has been generated by the question of the tax base, or other method, which should be used to determine an individual's contribution to public funds. The above discussion of six desirable characteristics of a good tax system should now equip you to evaluate the relative merits of each of these tax bases. We have already discussed two ways of allocating the tax burden; the ability to pay and the benefit approaches. In this section we will consider the nature of the three possible tax bases to which these approaches can then be applied i.e.:

- wealth (or capital)
- income
- consumption.

In particular, we need to ask ourselves, if we were designing a tax system, should we use one, two or three tax bases in our tax system design to enable the six desirable characteristics of good tax system design to be delivered optimally?

Wealth

First, could we create a tax system just using a wealth tax (or taxes)? Wealth can be held in various forms so a tax system only using wealth taxes would need to include a focus on various forms of wealth to work effectively. These would include probably both what you have earned yourself (your accumulated income) and what you have been given (inheritances or gifts).

Chapter 1 provided a history of wealth taxes. These types of taxes are among the oldest forms of taxation. This is because wealth can, under some circumstances, be easier to tax than income, where wealth is held in forms you can see (e.g. tangible property).

A comprehensive wealth tax could perhaps therefore be used to replace separate wealth related taxes such as those on unearned income (savings or dividends) and capital gains and could be a tax based on wealth ownership, which reflects the ability to pay of the taxpayer. At present, the few wealth taxes in the UK are imposed on a 'realisations' basis, that is they are applied when the taxpayer disposes of the wealth, not throughout the period of ownership.

A tax on wealth is also useful as a tool for redistributing wealth, often a key goal of a government. However, there are a number of difficulties which arise when trying to fairly value wealth which can make wealth taxes costly to administer.

Activity

List some of the things that may contribute to an individual's wealth.

Feedback

You have probably included some tangible assets in your list like land and buildings. Other assets include shares and securities and the market value of a business run by the individual. However, for many people the present value of their future earnings and the present value of their pension fund are probably their most valuable assets. Did you include these? Wouldn't these need to be included in any comprehensive wealth tax?

The present value of an individual's future earnings is the estimated positive cash flows arising from employment throughout their working life, restated in present value terms. However, we live in a rapidly changing world in which an individual may be faced with redundancy, retraining and second or even third careers during his or her working life. In practice it does not seem feasible to value the future earnings of every citizen for taxation purposes. Since future pension rights are generally dependent on earned income it would also be difficult to value the future pension of every citizen regularly – at least in a way taxpayers are likely to accept as appropriate given it would then affect how much tax they have to pay.

In practice a wealth tax is usually a tax on (capital) assets. However, individuals who do not use a pension fund, for whatever reason, may accumulate other assets in order to provide for old age (e.g. property) and a wealth tax which is levied on these assets but not pension rights will therefore be inequitable to some people.

In addition, some capital assets may provide additional benefits to their owner such as power and influence. For example, a wealthy individual is likely to be able to borrow money at a lower rate than is available to other people because they can influence the lending decision in ways others may not be able to. However, it would be extremely difficult to ascribe a value to these economic benefits to determine a comprehensive measure of wealth.

So, while some wealth taxes (for example, property based taxes like Council tax) have proven relatively cheap to collect in practice, a general wealth tax as the primary tax base for the country is likely to be expensive to administer compared to other tax bases because of the difficulties of assessing current values of assets not currently available for sale (i.e. for which there is no market that will reveal their true value). The difficulties of a general wealth tax are probably too great to enable it to be used as the main national tax base in the more developed economies, where people's wealth can be held in complex forms. They could, however, be useful as a, or the, key tax in less developed countries where more wealth is held in assets that can be more easily valued (land, buildings, physical property etc.).

Although a full wealth tax may be impractical for the reasons we have just examined it is probably a good idea to have at least some way of taxing stocks of wealth in a tax system. In the UK at present, there are two taxes which fit into the category of wealth taxes; capital gains tax and inheritance tax. Together these taxes provide the Exchequer with less than 2% of its total tax revenue and are predicted to only contribute £4.8billion in 2010/11. This is only about half of the average proportion of total revenue which is raised by wealth taxes in other OECD countries, suggesting the UK makes proportionally little use of wealth taxes in its tax system when compared to other countries.

Fiscal Fact

For 2008/09, around 130,000 individuals are expected to have paid capital gains tax totally approximately £7.8billion. In 2007/08, around 2,000 individuals had gains of more than £1,000,000 on which they paid tax totally almost £3billion.

Do wealth taxes then have any place in a tax system? One of the purposes of having wealth taxes in your tax system, such as a capital gains tax, is to reduce tax avoidance. Without some kind of wealth tax as part of the tax system some tax otherwise due could be avoided if a taxpayer was able to increase their total wealth in a form that is not then captured by the other tax bases you choose to use, for example, by owning shares or owning property either of which may grow in value over time, but aren't easily captured by income or expenditure taxes.

To illustrate this idea, imagine you owned your own company. To take money out of the business you could either pay yourself a wage from the profits of your business or you could instead issue new shares to yourself each year and then sell them periodically to achieve the same increase in your total wealth but in a different form – wealth gains rather than income. Without a tax on the sale of shares, you would be able to keep more of the increase in value of the company than if you pay yourself a wage, on which an income tax would probably have to be paid. This would provide an incentive (i.e. create tax induced distortion) to receive capital (new shares) instead of income (wages). In the UK until 2008/09, taxpayers had to pay tax on their realised capital gains at the same rates of tax as for income (i.e. at their marginal rate of income tax). As a result of having both an income tax and a similar wealth tax therefore, there was relatively little incentive to realise capital gains in the UK rather than taxable income. Between April 2008 and June 2010 however, the capital gains tax system changed, in the interests of simplicity as we noted earlier. Capital gains tax was charged at a flat rate of 18% (for individuals) irrespective of their income level. Basic analysis suggests that as the marginal rate of income tax for many people was 20% in that period (with others paying a marginal rate of income tax at either 40% or 50% for the last 3 months of that period) this is likely to create a tax incentive to receive wealth gains in capital forms rather than as income if taxpayers can (as 18% is less than 20%, 40% or 50% obviously).

This incentive to receive gains via the capital tax base instead of the income tax base was partly reduced in the Emergency Budget in June 2010. Higher and additional rate (50%) tax payers will have to pay 28% on any gains over their allowance instead of 18%. However, this isn't a full return to the use of marginal income tax rates as in the pre-April 2008 system, which could be argued to be a more equitable rate perhaps and many were expecting.

Other measures may now have to be introduced to restrict the scope for converting income into capital gains in order to limit the potential loss of income tax revenues or to create inequity between different citizens who earn wealth gains in different ways.

Inheritance tax, although a wealth tax, does not serve the same purpose as a capital gains tax as it is currently used in the UK. This is because it is almost entirely avoidable by most taxpayers who undertake effective tax planning and are not unfortunate enough to die unexpectedly. However, there are a number of other arguments in favour of keeping inheritance tax as a part of the UK's tax system even though it affects relatively few people. Firstly, there is no evidence that a tax on inheritance affects individuals' incentives to work so its distortive effects in this area are less of an issue than other taxes (we'll talk about this more in Chapter 3). Secondly, it is argued that one role of the tax system is to facilitate a fair balance of wealth between the better off and the poorer in society (see Chapter 1's discussion of redistribution). An inheritance tax is probably one of the best ways of achieving a redistribution of wealth, as at least once in a lifetime money is taken from richer people so that the Government can pass it on to others.

We will explore the details of the current system of capital gains tax and inheritance tax further in Chapter 8.

Activity

Could a comprehensive wealth tax be used to replace all other taxes? What would be the advantages or disadvantages of such an approach to taxation?

Feedback

It could be argued that a comprehensive wealth tax is most in keeping with the concept of using ability to pay to design a tax system and is therefore likely to lead to a more equitable tax system overall than other taxes alone may be able to achieve. On the other hand, it is unlikely to raise enough revenue alone because of the levels of the UK Government's expenditure plans. It would need a rate so high that it would force taxpayers to sell off assets each time it is due in order to pay the tax, which may not be in the best interests of either the taxpayer concerned, or wider society. There are also considerable measurement and assessment problems. For example, it is relatively easy for some items of wealth to be concealed from the tax authorities. Finally, as we have discussed, wealth is difficult to accurately value.

Income

If wealth isn't a perfect tax base to use by itself, what about just taxing income? Income is used as a major tax base throughout the world and in many countries, including the UK, is the most important tax base in the tax system (at least in terms of revenue raised for the Government). However, this does not mean that the application of an income tax is without difficulties or that it is the best tax base to use in all cases. Our first problem arises when we try to define what we mean by "income".

Problem of definition

On the surface income might seem an easy concept – isn't it just what we earn between two dates? In reality it isn't as simple as that, at least when it comes to writing rules for a workable tax system. If you have studied any accounting, for example, you will know that profit for a business (their 'income') can be measured in various ways resulting in different 'profit' figures. Which one should we pick for tax purposes? The same applies to individuals' income measures. How comprehensive should it be? Should it include more than your wages or salary? What if you aren't paid in just cash but also receive goods or services as part payment for your labour? Should they also be included in your taxable income? If so, at what value? Also, when should they be included? When you are given them or when you use them? Writing a set of rules that will work out the income to be taxed for a period of time is therefore not easy.

Hicks (1939) defined income as the maximum value which "a man can consume during a period and still expect to be as well off at the end of the period as he was at the beginning". Hence, if a tax system which taxes income is to be equitable it must allow for the inflation impacts i.e. some value will be lost from the tax base each year just because of price increases. In times of inflation some of the income generated therefore must be retained within a business just in order to cover the loss in value of assets over the year due to inflation. Perhaps this inflation component shouldn't be included in income for tax purposes therefore? This sounds very reasonable but there are a number of difficulties which have probably deterred HMRC from implementing such a system. These problems include:

- Determining how the value of the capital base should be measured.
- The use of the word 'expect' in Hick's definition. It does not tell us how much an individual can consume with certainty, only what he can consume and expect to maintain his capital base. It does not help us, therefore, to determine how to tax unpredicted profits, or losses.

Governments are generally reluctant to allow inflation to become an integral part of the tax system. One area of the tax system you will find this, however, is for some personal allowances and tax limits which are usually increased in line with the increase in the retail price index, unless the Chancellor elects to either freeze them (as he did for the basic personal allowance between 2002/03 and 2003/04, and again between 2009/10 and 2010/11) or increase them by some other amount (as was the case for age allowances in 2008/09 when they were increased by more than inflation and as is proposed for 2011/12 for the extra £1,000 to be added to basic personal allowances). Governments are perhaps reluctant to cater for inflation impacts for fear that it will fuel further inflation.

Comprehensive Income Tax

At the same time as Hicks was coming up with a definition of income, in the US, the economists Simons and Haig were considering this same issue in relation to income tax. Concerned with equity, they recommended a broad tax base. Simons' classic book *Personal Income Taxation* recommended accrual taxation with a definition of income that didn't contain any exceptions and deductions. Under this system, income is the sum of the increases in a person's net wealth over a period of time plus the amount of that person's consumption during the period. This can be restated in terms of real events so that comprehensive income would be equal to the amount which is consumed plus/(less) any increase/(decrease) in the value of the individual's wealth. By using such a definition for the tax base, we have a clear picture of a person's taxable capacity, but don't need to be concerned with how that capacity came into being.

Like many theoretical approaches to tax, however, the idea of a comprehensive income tax sounds good, but is almost impossible to put into practice. The use of this type of comprehensive income tax would result in creating all the difficulties described in the section on a wealth tax above, as it links income measures to measures of wealth.

In 1978 a group of tax experts, called the Meade Committee, was set up to evaluate the UK's tax system. The report they produced was entitled *The Structure and Reform of Direct Taxation*. Among the assessments and proposals for change they examined, the Committee considered the possibility of using a comprehensive income tax – i.e. one that could exist as the only form of taxation in the UK removing the need for capital and expenditure taxes.

The Meade Committee rejected the possibility of using a comprehensive income tax of this kind, claiming that it was impracticable to introduce all the measures which would be necessary to adjust for inflation. Instead they supported the introduction of an extended expenditure tax, which we consider in the next section.

Activity

Explain why the use of a comprehensive income tax might result in undesirable impacts on the economy of the country that introduces it.

Expenditure

Having found problems with taxes on wealth and income as sole tax bases, let us finally consider the possible use of consumption taxes as the key tax base in a tax system. A consumption, or expenditure, tax taxes what an individual takes out of the economy, unlike an income tax which can really be said to tax what is contributed to society. When using an expenditure tax there is no need to value wealth, which we have already concluded is difficult to do equitably in all circumstances. This problem is avoided as expenditure tax is only levied when the taxpayer spends money, not on the wealth they hold on to in whatever form.

Income receipts would also be free of expenditure tax. Importantly, not only would wages, salaries and profits be tax free on receipt, but since an expenditure tax does not tax the return on an investment until it is spent, there is a significant encouragement to save rather than spend with this type of tax system. As many governments see increasing savings as good for the economy, this would arguably be a good feature of this kind of tax system.

An expenditure tax can be designed to incorporate personal allowances and varying rates of tax exactly as an income tax typically does. This would probably require some kind of tax return being filed to obtain refunds of overpaid tax, but is probably possible to achieve with reasonable administrative efficiency. Hence, it is possible for an expenditure tax to be progressive and to take account of a taxpayer's personal circumstances – if that is considered desirable.

However, because savings are not taxed directly under an expenditure tax, the tax base will be narrower than for income tax and so the expenditure tax rate will have to be set at a suitably high rate to compensate for this narrowing in order to raise the same revenue for the Government.

There are a number of ways of operating a comprehensive expenditure tax system. The Meade Committee offered four alternatives. In each case the main problem is how to trace actual expenditure. The Committee proposed that this was to be resolved largely by measuring expenditure as a residual from gains in income or wealth (i.e. increase in wealth in a period = income received – expenditure) to avoid the impracticality of needing to track actual expenditure.

The Committee considered two forms of expenditure tax: a universal expenditure tax which is described below, and a two-tier expenditure tax which would collect a basic rate of tax through a system of VAT at the point of purchase and higher rates of tax directly from taxpayers periodically under a separate collection/ repayment system such as an annual return detailing what you have spent in a period.

Under a universal expenditure tax, a taxpayer's consumption expenditure would be calculated by adding the taxpayer's total realised income to any capital receipts, including the sale of capital assets and any amounts borrowed, and deducting any expenditure which is not for the purposes of consumption, including expenditure on capital assets and amounts repaid. Then tax could be levied on consumption expenditure at a number of rates if desired.

Expenditure taxes, particularly in the form of value added taxes as the first of the Meade Committee's options above, have become popular with governments everywhere in recent years but only a few countries have used this tax as their primary tax base. We'll review why this might be the case in the next section.

Growth of the expenditure tax base

Income is used as a tax base in almost all countries around the world but expenditure or consumption taxes have become more popular as a way of raising revenue in recent years. There are a number of reasons for preferring an expenditure tax to an income tax as a way of increasing tax revenue or as part of a general reform of a tax system which may explain this trend back towards expenditure taxes and away from income taxes as the core of a tax system design:

- It can be argued that it is fairer to tax consumption, that is, the value of goods and services which an individual takes out of society, than to tax the contribution that he or she makes to a society in the form of either work effort or capital supplied (i.e. expenditure tax tries to take a greater account of benefits received as a motivation for the tax system design). The difference between income and consumption is equal to savings. However, even the individual who saves will eventually use savings for consumption and therefore has just really deferred the expenditure tax rather than avoided it. Of course, it may be that the beneficiaries of an individual's estate who use these savings for consumption at a later stage pay the tax rather than the individual who earned the income in the first place, but eventually the expenditure tax will be paid by someone.

- An expenditure tax does not discriminate against individuals who defer their expenditure by saving. An income tax discriminates against individuals who save in order to undertake consumption in the future, by taxing the return on savings as part of their measure of income, having already taxed the money they put into the savings once when it was received as income (i.e. saved income gets taxed twice but an expenditure tax instead only taxes income once; when it is spent).

- The evidence suggests that savings are relatively inelastic. That is, the amount that is saved is not entirely dependent on the return available (people save for reasons others than just the level of return e.g. to provide future security or spending power). Hence an expenditure tax would perhaps not seriously distort the savings decision whereas income taxes probably do (as evidenced by all the adverts each year for tax free savings schemes like ISAs).

However, there are a number of potential disadvantages of an expenditure tax which make an income tax look more attractive in practice than may otherwise be the case. For example:

- Because the return on savings is not subject to an expenditure tax it seems likely that the level of an expenditure tax will have to be higher than its equivalent income tax. This may prove to be a disincentive to work. People are generally good at valuing their work effort in terms of goods and services rather than money. This is important in times of inflation when people know that a certain increase in salary is necessary simply to maintain a given standard of living (and hence why workers ask for at least inflation levels of salary increases every year). Prices can be thought of in terms of how many hours an individual on average wages must work in order to earn enough to buy the goods or services. If this is indeed how individuals think about the relationship between work and consumption then an increase in an expenditure tax will have a similar effect to an increase in an income tax. Hence an expenditure tax can still distort the decision to undertake extra work and does not resolve this distortion.

- Individuals who save in order to consume later are subject to higher levels of uncertainty than those who spend their income immediately because they cannot be sure of the tax they must pay when they spend their savings.

- Individuals usually have a changing pattern of income and expenditure over their lifetime. Many individuals spend more than they earn in the early years of their adult life and save in the middle years in order for expenditure to exceed income once again in retirement. This pattern may mean that individuals incur the greatest tax burden in years when their income is least able to provide for their needs.

Therefore, as none of the tax bases are adequate in their own right to form the sole tax base for a balanced tax system, it is more commonly found that a combination of the bases are used. In most cases these will usually involve all three bases being used to enable the advantages and limitations of each base to offset each other to the extent this is possible. This doesn't have to always be the case however, and some countries will sacrifice a rounded tax system design to focus on one or two tax bases. This may be found, for example, in a tax haven country.

The UK taxation system

To conclude this chapter we will briefly review how the theory of tax bases that we have just discussed in the previous section is directly translated into the UK's current tax system. In reality, because the use of any one tax base alone creates practical difficulties for the effectiveness of tax systems (as we have seen) a mixture of income, wealth and expenditure taxes are often used to try and minimise their individual limitations, create maximum flexibility in the system and address each of the other desirable characteristics of a good tax system, (to the degree this is possible in practice).

As we saw in the section on how the UK raises its revenue in Chapter 1, the key taxes in operation in the UK at present are:

1. Income tax – direct tax on income base payable by individuals
2. Corporation tax – direct tax on income base payable by companies
3. VAT – indirect tax on expenditure base payable by all
4. Capital Gains tax – direct tax on capital asset disposals/wealth payable by all
5. Inheritance tax – direct tax on wealth/capital asset transfers on death payable by individuals
6. Stamp Duty – direct tax on certain capital/wealth transfers payable by all

7. Customs and Excise Duties (Various) – indirect taxes on expenditure payable either by all or on a selective basis on some purchases.

The rest of this book, in conjunction with the web site, presents a review of most of the above taxes in detail. It illustrates how the detailed rules for each tax, and the interaction of these taxes, are applied in practice at the present time.

As we examine the detail of the current rules for each tax, consider what we have learned so far about the desirable characteristics of a good tax system and ask yourself to what degree the UK's current tax system is effective in achieving these goals. You will see we are good in some areas and not so good in others, and hence the need for constant reappraisal of the tax system and regular adjustments to its operation.

Summary

In this chapter we explored what to tax and how to design a suitable tax system to tax it. This included thinking about issues such as: whether we should tax at source or to directly assess tax due, the role of hypothecated taxes, tax neutrality, distribution of the tax burden and issues of tax avoidance and evasion in tax system design.

We have also spent some time discussing desirable characteristics of taxation as the foundation principles for how a tax system should be designed. We then evaluated the feasibility of using wealth, income and expenditure as a dominant tax base for the tax system before concluding with a brief summary of how the theory of tax bases is applied in current UK practice.

In this chapter we may have raised as many questions for you as we have given answers. We will attempt to answer many of these questions as we review the detail of the current UK tax system throughout the remainder of this book.

Project areas

There are many interesting questions which are inspired by the material dealt with in this chapter. For example,

- the potential role for hypothecated taxes;
- the impact on the UK economy of avoidance activity and corresponding anti- avoidance strategies;
- is progressivity always desirable in a tax?
- what is the appropriate mix of tax bases for the UK's tax system?

You may consider for a project the extent to which a particular tax, or tax system, achieves one or more of Adam Smith's desirable characteristics, or how some countries can operate without a balance of income, wealth and expenditure taxes.

The question of the funding of higher education is topical. An interesting question is 'Should a graduate tax be used to fund higher education?' Would this comply with the characteristics of a good tax system?

Using the tax system as a way of influencing transport policy has been a recent focus of the current UK Government. For example;

- congestion charges have been introduced for vehicle traffic in London (and proposed for other UK cities),
- a number of new roads have been built in a way that allows for them to pay for themselves using tolls,
- the Government is considering replacing the Vehicle Excise Duty (VED) with a charge based on road use (and the 2006 Budget introduced more graduation to the levels of this duty in favour of low emissions producing vehicles and in 2008 increased Vehicle Excise Duty on higher polluting cars).

Why do you think taxes, and related charges, have become some popular as a way of influencing transport policy?

Discussion questions

1   Road fund licences were originally introduced to pay for road building and maintenance. This is a tax based not on an ability to pay but according to use. In practice much of the road fund licence is now used for other purposes. Is this a good way to raise taxes?

2   Would increased hypothecation be a better way to organise the Government's revenue and expenditure systems?

3   What corrective taxes, if any, might you introduce in the UK at present?

4   Do you think parents should pay more or less tax than childless individuals?

5   If a government wished to provide funding to increase the level of fitness of the population would it be better to provide subsidised facilities such as leisure centres or to give tax relief on the cost of getting and keeping fit, such as health club memberships?

6   To what degree does the current UK tax system fulfil the characteristics of a desirable tax system?

7   Is an expenditure, income or wealth tax inherently fairer than the others?

8   Not all countries use all tax bases. Why might this be the case and what features of a country allow different mixes of tax bases to operate?

Further reading

Hicks J.R. (1939), *Value and Capital*, Oxford University Press: Oxford, UK (2nd Edition, 1974).

James, S. and Nobes, C. (2010), *The Economics of Taxation, 10th edition*, Fiscal Publications, Birmingham, UK.

Meade Committee Report (1978), *The Structure and Reform of Direct Taxation*, IFS/Allen and Unwin: London.

Mutén, L. (1998), "Minimising the Tax Effects of Inflation" in Sandford, C. (ed) *Further Key Issues in Tax Reform*, Fiscal Publications: Birmingham.

Smith, A (1776), *An Inquiry in the Nature and Causes of the Wealth of Nations* Ward, Lock & Co. Ltd: London, UK. (The World Library 1812 reprint).

Sandford, C. (1995), "Taxing Wealth" in *More Key Issues in Tax Reform*, Fiscal Publications: Birmingham.

Sandford, C. (1995), "Minimising Administrative and Compliance Costs" in *More Key Issues in Tax Reform*, Fiscal Publications: Birmingham.

For detailed discussions of alternative tax bases and their application see Sandford, C. (2000), *Why Tax Systems Differ*, Fiscal Publications: Birmingham, UK

3 Impacts of the UK tax system

Introduction

In Chapters 1 and 2 we saw how tax can affect the economic decisions made by taxpayers. When a tax on windows was introduced in 1747 homeowners blocked them up to reduce their tax bills, even though this led to health problems. Today the Government uses this same eagerness of taxpayers to avoid tax to influence their behaviour. For example, fairly generous tax deductions are available for those who are willing to put aside income into a private pension scheme. This tax deduction makes the cost of providing a private pension relatively cheaper than it would be otherwise. Therefore the Government hopes this will change taxpayers' behaviour and encourage take up of greater private pension provision than might otherwise have occurred without the tax break. This will then, in turn, reduce the reliance on the state benefits system for those taxpayers in the future.

When making a relief available, such as the one above, the Chancellor will have undertaken some sort of cost/benefit analysis. For example, if the only people who took advantage of the scheme were those who were already subscribers to a private pension scheme the Chancellor would have lost some tax revenue he would otherwise have collected without encouraging anyone else to help to reduce the costs of the benefits system by investing in their own pension provision. Although using taxes to affect people's behaviour is common, determining exactly how a tax change will affect behaviour is very difficult to predict reliably and governments can sometimes get it wrong.

In this chapter we will expand on some of the concepts we looked at in Chapter 2 to help us understand the effects of taxation on the economy generally (i.e. macro effects). We will then look at a number of other ways in which the tax system in the UK affects the decisions made by individual taxpayers (i.e. micro effects). We will introduce some new economic concepts that help us understand the effect of taxation on society.

At the end of this chapter you will be able to discuss the:

- concepts of tax incidence, compliance costs and excess burden;
- distorting effects of UK taxation on the decisions made by individuals, businesses and companies;
- impact of tax on personal and business investment decisions;
- the use of taxation to affect decision making, e.g. environmental taxation; and
- problems of moving towards fiscal neutrality.

The incidence of taxation

In the previous chapter, we looked at the burden of taxation in terms of the tax rate structure. Here we extend that analysis by looking more closely at a wider range of issues relating to the incidence of taxation. The tax system affects many people – both directly and indirectly. The *formal incidence* of a tax falls on those who must actually pay the tax while the *effective incidence* of tax falls on everyone whose wealth or income is reduced, or purchase opportunities changed, in any way by the tax. This will often include people other than those who directly pay the tax.

While it is often easier to identify where most of the *formal* incidence of tax will fall, it is, in practice, often impossible to identify the full effective incidence of tax. However, to plan for the effects of tax changes this wider incidence should ideally be taken into account.

To illustrate this problem consider the example of a newspaper purchase. Currently VAT is not levied on the sale of newspapers. If, however, the Chancellor decided he wanted to reform VAT and introduce such a tax, he would want to assess the incidence of this tax change. The formal incidence of the new VAT cost would fall on the people who buy newspapers. That impact would be relatively easy to track and measure. The effective incidence is, however, likely to fall not only on the buyers but also on the newspaper sellers and their distributors. This is because, other things being equal, it is likely that the increase in price of a newspaper the tax will bring will result in a fall in the volume of sales of newspapers leading to reduced profits for the newspaper owners, their distributors and the retailers. In addition, in order to reduce the impact of the tax on the volume of sales, the newspaper proprietors, their distributors and retailers may decide not pass on the full amount of the VAT to their readers but may choose to reduce their profit margins instead. These 'ripple' effects may then spread further still, for example, creating reduced profitability for newspaper proprietors that may mean lower wage increases can be funded for their workers or lower dividends paid to their investors so these groups could also be affected – and so on as the ripples of tax incidence spread.

For the Chancellor to fully understand the likely impact of this tax change he would therefore need to review both the formal and, as far as possible, the likely effective incidence of the tax changes or he may introduce undesirable changes into the economy. This same principle applies to any tax change not just for VAT.

Tax wedges

The impact of the incidence of taxation can be assessed by looking at what is called the *tax wedge*. This is the difference between what the purchasers pay for a good or service and what suppliers get of this payment (i.e. after tax). As demand and supply levels are changed as prices of goods or services change, e.g. by imposing a tax or changing tax rates, a tax wedge is created by the interaction of the new demand and supply levels caused by the tax inclusive/exclusive price.

In the case of indirect taxes, such as VAT, the tax wedge is the difference between the marginal cost of producing and selling a good and the marginal benefit from consumption. In the UK then the tax wedge is equal to the VAT (and any customs duty levied if applicable on a sale). An item which is sold for £100 before VAT has a marginal benefit from consumption of £117.50 (£100 plus VAT at the usual standard UK rate of 17.5%) or after 4 January 2011 this would be £120 (£100 plus VAT at the new VAT rate of 20%), because this is what the purchaser is prepared to pay for it, and a marginal cost of producing and selling the good of £100 since this is the price at which the seller is prepared to produce and sell the good. Hence the tax wedge is £17.50 or £20, the amount of VAT which is due from the consumer.

In the case of a direct tax, such as income tax, the tax wedge can be said to be the difference between the marginal value of leisure sacrificed by a worker and the marginal value to society of another hour of work.

In the case of taxes on unearned income the tax wedge is the difference between the gross and net after-tax rates of return.

Activity

Determine the variables which make up the tax wedge when a trader employs a new worker.

Feedback

The tax wedge will be equal to the difference between the total cost of the worker to the employer and the after-tax salary of the employee.

This difference will be made up of four elements: the income tax which is levied on the employee's salary, the employee's national insurance contributions, the employer's national insurance contribution and finally the value of any business tax relief which will be available to the employer related to the cost of employing the extra member of staff.

The distorting effects of taxation are not just dependent on the formal incidence of tax; rather it is dependent on the size of the tax wedge. For example, in understanding the full distortion effects of employing a new worker, it is not as important to draw a distinction between employer and employee national insurance but the total amount of national insurance which must be paid. The total payment will determine the distortion effect.

The larger the tax wedge the greater the potential for distortions. We will be exploring these in more detail in the next section.

The ultimate payer of tax

The concept of the incidence of taxation is concerned with the question of who ultimately pays the tax.

In theory the burden of indirect taxes, like VAT, falls on the final consumer. Yet there is evidence that sometimes manufacturers absorb some of the burden of VAT, rather than passing it on in full to their customers, either by not charging as much as they should with the tax included or by offering special sales deals. For example, many traders offered to fit double glazing free of VAT for some time after VAT was extended to double glazing. They, of course, aren't actually selling it free of VAT – but are paying it on their customers' behalf as a sales discount, thus absorbing the burden of taxation themselves in the form of lower profit margins.

In many cases, at least some of the burden of an indirect tax will fall on the supplier – not just the intended consumer – as whenever a price is adjusted (e.g. by applying or changing a tax like VAT) both the levels of demand and supply are likely to be affected. For example, normally as prices increase because of a tax change, demand will correspondingly fall, therefore suppliers have to either lower their price to attract back lost demand, or accept lower sales levels at the price they previously charged; Either way, their profits are likely to be affected even though the tax is supposed to fall only on the consumer.

Compliance costs

The incidence of taxation will also create secondary costs that must be considered in determining the full impact of tax on a taxpayer. You will recall we defined compliance costs briefly in Chapter 2 as the costs resulting from the need to comply with the tax rules such as paying for tax advice, employing someone to keep records for tax computations, time spent completing tax forms if you do it yourself or costs for paying someone else to do it for you, and so on. Such costs would not have been incurred if there was no tax to pay and so should be considered as part of the effective incidence of taxation.

In 2005 the accounting firm KPMG undertook a study of compliance costs in the UK tax system. They discovered that these costs amount to around 0.45% of UK GDP (i.e. approximately £5 billion!). While this is a large amount of money, the situation in the UK is comparable to other developed countries where these costs are of a similar scale. Compliance costs are a problem for any tax system.

There are regular calls for these costs to be reduced. One possible way to do this is to make the tax system less complicated; therefore, hopefully, costing people less to comply with it. The KPMG report highlighted around 2,600 obligations in the UK tax system in force at the time, most of which only impact on a small numbers of businesses but, they argued, could be rationalised, or even done away with, to reduce the extra complexity in the tax system. HMRC responded to this KPMG study, and other calls, in the 2006 Budget by suggesting they have an aim to reduce the compliance cost burden on businesses of the current UK tax system by 10% over the following five years. In the 2009 Budget, HMRC reported that they had reduced the burden by £540million since the KPMG study as evidence they were taking these promises seriously. To achieve this they created a new Board within the Revenue, called the Administrative Burden Advisory Board, to look at, then implement, the best ways of achieving these cost savings.

Distortions and the excess burden of taxation

The burden of taxation is the amount by which a taxpayer's economic wellbeing is reduced because of taxation. However, direct burdens (i.e. actual costs of tax directly affecting investments or wealth) are only part of the impact we must consider from the presence of taxation. Further, secondary, impacts can occur when taxes are charged. For example, as we noted earlier, consumers may change their purchasing patterns if VAT changes, resulting in a secondary impact on consumption. When organising or planning for tax system changes policy makers must not only take into account the direct impacts or distortions they expect to create – but also look for the wider (excess) burdens that may be created elsewhere that may need to be mitigated if the knock on, or ripple, effects of a tax change is to be controlled. Managing these wider changes is a key headache for all tax policy makers as you can never be sure exactly how people will react to changes in the tax system. However, two economic principles of possible behaviour can help us better understand what may happen as a result of a tax change. The first is the substitution effect, the second the income effect. In this section we will review each of these and illustrate how they are useful to tax system designers in understanding the distortions to 'normal' behaviours they may create because of the presence of, or changes to, tax.

The substitution distortion

Tax induced substitution distortions arises when individuals consume more of one item rather than another because of the effect of taxation i.e. tax affects their relative levels of consumption or use of something.

This substitution distortion is also called the *excess burden of taxation*. The burden of tax caused by a government transferring spending power from the taxpayer to the state when they collect tax from them is not, in itself, inefficient but if it is done in a way that affects the economic choices of the taxpayer, the cost to the taxpayer is the excess burden of taxation. For example, as the then Chancellor, Norman Lamont, explained in his first budget of 1993; VAT was not at that time charged on domestic fuel but was levied on the costs of insulating a home. This distortion might have been influencing taxpayers to consume more energy to heat their homes rather than spending money on insulating their property as it was relatively more expensive to pay for insulation (because it was taxed) than to pay your domestic fuel bills (with no tax included). In an effort to remove this distortion, the then Chancellor subsequently extended the scope of VAT to domestic fuel, thus taxing both commodities on a more similar basis. In the 2000 Budget this reversal was then extended further. New measures were introduced to extend the reduced rate of VAT to installation of energy saving materials in the home. The tax substitution distortion bias was now in the favour of energy saving activity rather than energy consuming activity i.e. the excess burden of tax fell on energy consumption rather than energy saving choices –

producing a distortion that most would agree is a 'better' one towards saving rather than consuming energy.

There are other examples of taxes that cause a distortion in the economic decisions made by a country's citizens. For a number of historical examples, look again at Chapter 1. You could also include perhaps brewing your own alcohol to avoid excise duties on purchased drinks, so called 'booze cruises' to France to buy drinks at a lower VAT rate, or even emigrating for tax reasons, and so on.

We will see later in this chapter that taxes can also distort the capital investment decisions of businesses. Investment projects which have a positive net present value before tax can have a negative net present value after tax. If this happens a company may choose to use its money in some other way than would have been the case without the effect of taxation. Suppose that the company decides to distribute the funds they would have used for the investment to its shareholders. The shareholders then suffer a loss equal to the before-tax net present value of the project. The community more generally could also be said to have lost the benefit of the expenditure planned by the company that will now not happen because of the distortion tax has created. This may have been for the consumption of goods or services from other businesses, causing other businesses to lose potential orders, with the knock-on impact to their profitability also. The total number of jobs may also fall (or at least not rise, as may have resulted from the new investment). Finally the Government has lost tax because the project was not undertaken. The 'ripple effect' of substitution distortions can be significant.

The income distortion

A second tax related distortion to consider is the *income distortion*. This is when there is a transfer of wealth from the taxpayer to the Government caused by taxation. The income distortion describes the reduction in the amount that the taxpayer can consume out of the money they earn resulting from having to pay taxes on their income. Of course, all taxation creates at least some income distortion when viewed in isolation from the rest of the tax, benefits and public expenditure systems as the imposition of a new, or extra, tax will always move wealth from the taxpayer to the Government. Taxpayers may respond in different ways to this distortion – but it will usually encourage them to put in more effort, work harder, seek better investments and so on to cover the loss to their returns the cost of tax creates. However, if they believe taxation is becoming excessive they are likely either to give up the effort entirely (e.g. stop work and retire) or switch to another activity or investment type where lower taxes are found (e.g. substitution distortions drive a change of behaviour as outlined in the previous section).

Later in this chapter we will look at these possible responses in more detail to assess their possible impact on work versus leisure decisions, personal and business investment choices (where the presence of a tax affects returns earned, and therefore the investments that may be made) in more detail. Understanding the likely responses at a micro level to tax changes through these two distortions is a critical part of effective tax policy making by a government.

A lump-sum tax

The degree of income distortion resulting from a tax will be dependent on the average rate of tax applicable to the taxpayer. The greater the average rate of tax, the greater the income distortion. However, the degree of the substitution distortion will be dependent on the marginal rate of tax (the amount of tax paid on the next pound of the tax base being examined). It is argued by economists that a *lump-sum tax*, where an individual pays a given amount of income tax regardless of the amount of work which he or she undertakes, would eliminate the substitution distortion when individuals decide whether to work harder or enjoy more leisure time.

If a lump-sum tax were to be introduced then a taxpayer's marginal rate of tax would be zero (once the lump sum is paid there is no further tax to pay).

A lump-sum tax would be less likely to affect the behaviour of individuals compared with variable taxes that change with changes in the tax base. The benefit of working for an extra hour will increase because there is no corresponding increase in taxation and so more work is likely to be undertaken by rational taxpayers. This does not mean that the lump-sum tax is not distortionary; any tax will introduce a cost which will change the taxpayer's behaviour, however, lump sum taxes will not have further distortionary effects after their fixed payments have been met as further activity then is tax free.

To achieve this reduction in the distortionary affect by a lump-sum tax the amount of a lump-sum tax paid by an individual must be independent of characteristics which the individual can influence. For example, a tax which increases with the educational and vocational qualifications of the individual is not a lump-sum tax because it may have a distortionary effect on the decisions made by individuals about their education and training. The same principle would apply if the lump sum was differentiated on other characteristics such as wealth, geography, etc.

While the lump-sum tax approach has some advantageous impacts, its use would not be without knock-on effects. For example, if only members of the workforce paid the lump-sum tax, there may be a distortionary effect as low paid individuals may be deterred from joining or remaining in the workforce.

The excess burden of taxation, and the distortions to economic decisions that result from the incidence of taxation, are therefore important considerations for the Government in making choices on the best way to develop the tax system.

Flat taxes

In the previous chapter, we looked at some of the implications of using income as the sole tax base. Many of the problems with income tax arise because of the use of a progressive tax rate, in the interests of vertical equity. There is currently considerable debate around the world, however, about the benefits of using a 'flat tax'. The premise for this tax is that a progressive system of income tax rates is a disincentive to extra work, savings and reinvestment, whereas if a tax was imposed at a low, flat rate, people would have more incentive to work and invest which would then benefit the whole economy. This can be demonstrated using the Laffer curve, developed by Dr Arthur Laffer in the US, which shows the relationship between tax revenue and the tax rate as follows:

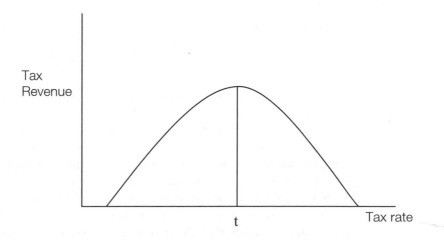

The graph shows that tax revenues will increase at a steeper rate when the tax rate is low as the low rates encourage growth of economic activities. A point is then reached (tax rate t) where a government is obtaining the maximum possible revenue. After this point, if the tax rate increases, a government gets a decreasing amount of revenue, because there is less incentive to work harder or invest, and more incentive to avoid paying taxes.

In a 1985 book by Hall and Rabushka called *The Flat Tax*, published in the US, a new system of flat taxes was proposed. Under this system, wages and salaries would be taxed at a low flat rate after a personal allowance. Business income would be taxed on:

- Total revenue from sales
- Less inputs purchased from other businesses (which are taxed in the hands of those other businesses)
- Less wages and pensions paid to workers (which are taxed in the hands of the employees)
- Less purchases of plant and equipment (so that investment is not discouraged by the tax system)

Notice that savings and investment income is not taxed at all under this model.

There is some evidence that a flat tax works well as an incentive to economic activity, but so far it has only been tried in either tax haven countries such as Hong Kong and Jersey, or transitional economies such as Estonia and Russia. No other developed country has yet tried a flat tax of the type described here, despite its potential attractions.

Fiscal neutrality

We introduced the idea of fiscal neutrality briefly in Chapter 2 under the heading of economic efficiency. We can now explore this idea further as it is important in helping us understand and assess tax impacts.

You will recall that a tax system, or a sub-set of the tax system, can be said to be *fiscally neutral* if it does not cause a taxpayer to discriminate between economic choices. In practice this implies that the introduction of changes to the tax system does not change the economic choices made by taxpayers. Hence a fiscally neutral system seeks to raise revenue in ways which avoid distortionary effects.

A tax has a distortionary effect if it changes the relative cost of goods and services. If tax changes are made in one part of the tax system, and not in another, the changes could result in a distortion to the relative costs of goods or services. If such goods or services are substitutes of one another, this can create a distortion (termed therefore a substitution distortion) in their consumption patterns.

Consider, for example, how VAT is levied when you purchase a product. VAT of 17.5% (20% from January 2011) is added to the purchase price of chocolate biscuits, like Hobnobs, because they are classed as a luxury good, but not to Jaffa Cakes which are deemed to be cakes and therefore as an item of food are a zero rated supply (we will discuss VAT further in Chapter 10). The laws of supply and demand tell us that the increase in the price of Hobnobs due to the tax, will lead to a decline in the number of packets of Hobnobs sold as purchasers will choose to buy other products instead (or maybe just go on a diet!). Some individuals may purchase Jaffa Cakes rather than Hobnobs because of the price differential the increase in Hobnobs' price has created (i.e. Jaffa cakes are now relatively cheaper than Hobnobs as their price does not need to include VAT). This switch from one product to another, because of taxation, is an example of the *distortionary substitution effect* as we discussed earlier in the Chapter. (Of course some people just prefer Hobnobs and will continue to buy them – but there are always exceptions to the rule!)

Until the autumn of 1993 there was a similar distortion between freshly squeezed fruit juice, which was not subject to VAT, and long-life fruit juice which was taxed at the full rate of VAT as a luxury good. This tax treatment had the effect of making freshly squeezed juice relatively more attractive to buy than long-life juice. In the autumn of 1993 the Government announced that freshly squeezed juice would also in the future be taxed at the full rate of VAT, thus removing the odd substitution distortion between the two products.

Other such anomalies in the tax treatment of similar products can be found throughout the UK tax system, as you will discover as you study tax in more detail.

VAT would be a fiscally neutral tax if all goods and services were taxed at the same rate. If this was so, the marginal rate of substitution of one product for another will be the same including and excluding VAT. As this is not the case in the UK, then VAT cannot be said to be entirely fiscally neutral. However, as the majority of products are taxed at one general rate (17.5% until 4 January 2011 and 20% thereafter) VAT can be said to be fairly neutral in practice. Fiscal neutrality only becomes an issue for VAT therefore when the Government changes the VAT tax base (which products are taxed at different rates) which it does periodically.

If a tax system is not fiscally neutral it is possible that the economic loss to the community because of the impact of the tax may be greater than the revenue raised by the tax. The difference between the economic loss and the revenue raised is termed the economic, or excess, burden of taxation as we discussed earlier in this Chapter.

Since VAT is charged only when goods or services are purchased, VAT in effect makes saving relatively more attractive than spending money. This is another example of the inefficiencies introduced into our economy by our tax system and explains why expenditure taxes are considered by some people to be recessionary – because they encourage saving at the expense of consumption, thereby artificially reducing expenditure in the economy. This was illustrated in 2008/09 with the temporary reduction in the general rate of VAT (17.5% to 15%). The claimed reason for this reduction was to help stimulate spending as part of the Governments' anti-recessionary policies.

What about the taxing of investment? If investments are to be taxed neutrally, the amount of tax paid will need to be related to the returns earned and will need to be independent of the particular investment vehicle used. This implies that in a fiscally neutral environment all forms of saving and investment income would need to be subject to the same taxation. This is not how the system in the UK works at present. Some products receive better tax treatment than others i.e. they are not fiscally neutral.

Is this a useful economic concept in tax therefore if tax systems aren't likely to achieve fiscal neutrality in practice? In fact, yes it is useful if we want to assess the impact of relatively small changes to tax systems rather than as a goal in its own right for larger scale tax reform. Also, as we have been discussing throughout this chapter, the fact that the presence of tax may affect economic decisions is an important feature of the tax system which can then be used to achieve political, social and economic goals that may otherwise be difficult to make possible.

Decisions about work and leisure activities

For most of the first part of this book so far our perspective has been at a macro level – how does the Government make tax decisions and how do its citizens respond as a group. Of course, taxpayers do not really respond to the tax system as groups, they respond as individuals, and so it is not appropriate to only focus on impacts of taxation at a macro level. We also need to consider micro level responses to get a fuller picture of what effects the presence of tax has. To show how difficult this can be in practice, however, we will use the illustration of tax impacts on work versus leisure decisions.

While not always the case, in most jobs there is generally a relationship between how hard you work and how well you are paid (premiership footballers aside!). Many individuals therefore have the opportunity to choose whether to earn more money by working harder. Some people may be able to work overtime, others may choose to do jobs which have longer basic working hours in order to earn more money and still others may work many unpaid extra hours in the hope of gaining promotion and higher pay in the longer term. Of course, many people also make decisions which reduce their income, for instance taking early retirement, working part time or taking unpaid holidays.

In this section we will consider the tax factors which influence an individual when making a decision about how hard to work and then briefly consider the effect of their decisions on wealth creation and the revenues collected by governments.

Marginal rates of taxation

When considering the role that tax plays in the decision to work harder or not it is the *marginal rate* of tax (MRT) which is important, rather than the *average rate* of tax (ART). We briefly introduced these in Chapter 2; the marginal rate of tax is the rate of tax which is due if the taxpayer earns £1 more than their current income. The average rate of tax is the total amount of tax paid as a proportion of their total income.

MRT (on income) = amount of tax paid on next £1 of income

$$\text{ART (on income)} = \frac{\text{total tax due on income}}{\text{total income}}$$

The role of marginal rates of tax in work/leisure decisions was one of the reasons given by the Government to explain their overall policy of the last thirty or so years of systematically reducing the top rate of income tax (Budget 2010 reversing this trend with the introduction of a new 50% top rate of income tax for very high earners). Their argument had been that lower marginal rates of tax can encourage individuals to work harder and that is a good thing for the economy generally as it generates more tax revenues, creates wealth and helps produce economic growth for the country.

Full details of the current rules for national insurance contributions and details of income tax rates are contained in Chapter 4. However, in order to better understand this section you need to know a few basic facts about the current UK tax system, namely that:

- individuals are entitled to a personal allowance (the first £6,475 of their income is free of income tax.)
- employees' national insurance contributions (primary) are a percentage of earnings between £110 and £844 per week. Income over this limit attracts a reduced percentage.
- income tax is levied at up to five marginal rates, depending on the type of the income, which increase at certain points as the taxpayer's income increases.

Firstly, if marginal rates of tax are so important to people's work/leisure decisions, what are the marginal rates of tax which are in force in the UK at the current time? The *effective rate of tax* on earned income can be considered to be the combined rate of income tax and national insurance contributions, since they are both compulsory. National insurance contributions are a contribution 'insurance' paid to earn the rights to certain benefits – however, as they are a compulsory levy on an employee's income, and contributions made only partly determine what benefits might be received in return, they are effectively a tax in all but name.

It is not possible to simply list all possible marginal rates because they depend, in part, on the personal circumstances of the taxpayer. Let us consider a single employed person, without investment income (i.e. no dividends or savings), who does not contribute to a pension scheme. Their marginal rates of income tax and national insurance contributions combined (assuming only non-savings income) are:

Annual income	Income tax rate %	NIC rate %	Effective MRT %
0–5,715	0	0	0
5,716–6,475	0	11	11
6,476–43,875	20	11	31
43,876–156,475	40	1	41
156,476+	50	1	51

The UK currently has an income tax system which, when combined with national insurance contributions, levies a marginal rate of tax of 31% on an individual with non-savings income of

£10,000 per annum and 41% on an individual with non-savings income of £41,000 (assuming their income is earned evenly over the year as this can affect their national insurance contributions).

The section on national insurance contributions in Chapter 4 explains how this system has evolved to become as it is today and why these calculations apply as they do.

Prior to April 2003, an upper limit on incomes subject to national insurance contributions applied so that incomes above a certain level did not attract the charge. From April 1, 2003, however, the Labour Government introduced a 1% levy to apply to all incomes without a ceiling. This may not seem to be a large amount, but nevertheless marks the breaking of a barrier that has existed for a number of years and may lead to further increases in the future.

To work or play?

As already suggested, many taxpayers are able to decide whether or not to increase their income by increasing their work effort. Let us take a simple example, an employee is offered the opportunity to work for an extra hour one evening. When making the decision whether or not to accept this overtime, an individual is likely to weigh the benefit of any extra money they might earn against the costs of working an extra hour.

Some individuals will be offered pay at a higher hourly rate to encourage them to work overtime. This may help persuade an employee to work the extra time offered as it increases the gap between their marginal benefit and cost of working or not working overtime (their marginal cost). Of course, employers usually offer their employees the opportunity to work overtime because they believe that the marginal cost to them, even at a higher rate of pay offered to the employees, is less than the marginal benefit to be gained from the work which the employee will do (i.e. they'll still make a profit).

In addition to the extra money being earned, an employee should also consider the tax consequences of the decision. An employee who undertakes overtime will, of course, pay tax at his or her marginal rate on their overtime income.

Activity

What are the costs and benefits to an individual of deciding to work overtime?

Feedback

On the benefit side, of course there is their overtime pay. There may also be some cost savings associated with working these longer hours; for example, the employee might have socialised with friends otherwise and they will therefore save the cost of the drinks etc. they would have bought.

There may also be some benefits from working overtime which are difficult to express in monetary terms. For example, if some kind of emergency has created the need for overtime, there may be an enjoyable sense of camaraderie among the individuals who undertake extra work to help fix the problem.

What about the direct costs of working overtime? These may be zero, but some employees may incur significant costs if they work for an extra hour including any of the following:

- extra child care costs
- transport costs
- additional eating out, and so on.

In addition, there may be many other costs which cannot easily be assigned a monetary value, for example, missing spending time with their family.

Now that we have identified some of the costs and benefits of making the decision to work overtime we can consider the marginal utility (i.e. value to the employee) of an extra £1 to a taxpayer. This may seem an odd thing to suggest at first; surely £1 is £1? However, value, as a comparison of relative costs versus benefits, can in fact change over time. For example, individuals may be willing to work more overtime in the month before they go on holiday than at other times as their need for this money (called by economists their *expected utility*) may be greater at that time than other times in the year. This is just one example of a complex set of circumstances which combine to determine whether an individual employee would rather work more hours at one time than another or one employee might choose to work overtime and another might decline the offer.

We identified one reason for the employer to offer extra work: the marginal benefit to them (e.g. profit earned from extra work produced) is greater than the marginal cost to them (i.e. over-time wages). For the employee therefore the decision is effectively the same one. That is, the collective marginal benefit is greater than the collective marginal cost. In practice, of course, identifying the marginal benefits and the marginal costs is likely to be difficult sometimes but, as employees, most people can make this rational decision even if we cannot fully justify why in monetary terms.

Activity

What effect does a change in the rate of taxation have on the decision to work overtime?

Feedback

Once again we only need to consider marginal rates of taxation faced by a particular employee rather than the total tax paid or the average rates of tax. Suppose an employee habitually works overtime. If their marginal rate of tax is increased they may choose to work more hours to maintain their net (after tax) income. Alternatively they may decline to work overtime because their net income per hour is such that the marginal costs exceed the marginal benefits.

We can illustrate these two possible situations with two examples. The first is an individual with a large mortgage who has to earn a given amount in overtime each month to sustain his/her lifestyle. The second is an individual with children who has to pay a childminder an hourly rate to look after the children. The first taxpayer may choose to increase his hours of overtime to maintain his level of income because his marginal rate of tax has increased. The second may conclude that the net benefit of working overtime, that is the extra gross income less the tax and the costs of childcare, is too low to be worthwhile.

Similarly a drop in the marginal rate of tax may provide an incentive to some taxpayers to work extra hours so as to maintain their previous net income while others may lower the number of hours they work as the marginal benefits gained perhaps then no longer exceed the marginal costs.

However, if we return to our original hypothesis, that the extra work would be undertaken so long as the marginal costs are less than the marginal benefits, then the lower the marginal rate of tax is, the higher the marginal benefits will become relative to the marginal costs associated with the extra work, and it is reasonable to expect that most individuals will undertake the extra work.

So far we have only considered individuals who are already working and are deciding whether or not to accept overtime. We could also consider the situation of those who do not currently work but may be able to obtain work if they chose to. This category may include, for example, single-parent families, who may have to rely on the state benefit system instead of any earned income they would otherwise be able to receive because marginal tax rates trap them into this position. If benefit dependent people start to work often their benefits are reduced once they earn over a relatively low limit of income. Once they start to work, therefore, their effective marginal rate of tax can be extremely high. Not only do they pay tax and national insurance contributions now on their new income, but they lose state benefits and may incur other direct costs such as extra travelling and child care costs they otherwise would not have to bear. This can mean the overall effective cost impact to them is prohibitive – much more than others on similar incomes may be bearing. This may make it difficult in practice for some people, particularly those reliant on benefits, to get into work when they want to.

Previous Chancellors went some way towards addressing these problems when providing parents with some relief for the cost of child care and substantial additional help for low income families in the March 1998 budget. This was helped further by the introduction in 2001/02 of the Children's Tax Credit Scheme and was further developed by the provision of the Child Tax Credit from April 2003. We will discuss how this system works in practice in Chapter 4.

There are many other important issues in judging the decision to work or play which are beyond the scope of this text, but we can generally conclude that the lower the marginal rate of tax the more likely it is that individuals will choose to work harder.

Do-it-yourself or subcontract?

So far we have considered the marginal costs and benefits of work versus leisure decisions without looking at the impact on this decision caused by the varying alternatives to working over-time. This section looks at some of these alternatives and how they may affect this decision.

Activity

Suppose that Joe can choose to work overtime regularly on Saturday mornings. If the overtime is worked Joe will employ a self employed person to maintain his garden. Assume that Joe does not enjoy gardening any more than he enjoys work and that he works less efficiently in the garden than in his normal job. We will also assume that the gardener, who has special skills and equipment, works more efficiently in the garden than Joe. List the tax implications of the work or not work overtime options for both Joe and the gardener. (You may assume that all the transactions are recorded and tax is not evaded.)

Feedback

If Joe chooses to reject the opportunity of overtime and maintains his own garden, there are, at least, the following tax related consequences:

- his direct income taxation is unchanged
- his employer does not benefit from his extra work and so his profits are not increased and the corporation tax payable is unchanged
- Joe is likely to be working less efficiently than an experienced gardener and the economic value of the work he produces to society is likely to be less valuable than the economic value of the work which he would have undertaken during the period of overtime he has declined.

If Joe chooses to work the overtime and employ a gardener there are the following tax consequences:

- his direct income taxation increases as his earnings increase
- his employer's profits (should) increase and so the corporation tax payable increases
- the gardener receives an income
- the amount of direct income tax paid by the gardener increases
- the gardener may also charge VAT on his supply of labour.
- all three people have increased their net income which potentially enables them to spend more money and thus potentially pay more tax in the future, perhaps in the form of VAT on their expenditures.

As you can see, from a government's point of view, there is an increase in tax revenues and an increase in the income generating activity of the economy if Joe chooses to work overtime and employ a gardener compared to gardening himself.

Now what about the monetary factors which would increase an employee's desire to undertake additional hours at work and employ others to work for him?

The gardener will probably decide how much to charge for his services by deciding how much money he wants for himself and then adding on the cost of any tax, direct and indirect, which he must pay.

Other things being equal, the greater the difference between the after-tax income which the employee can earn and the gross cost of employing the gardener the more likely it is that the employee will undertake the overtime.

The after-tax income of the employee will also be increased if his marginal rate of tax is reduced. Similarly the gross cost of employing the gardener will be reduced if either his marginal rate of tax is reduced or the rate of VAT he must charge is reduced.

Activity

In reality, a whole series of non-monetary factors will also affect this decision. You may wish to make a second list, like the one above, of these other factors to have a more complete picture of how decisions are really made in practice.

Feedback

Your list may have included items such as enjoyment of work/gardening, opportunity cost of spending time away from friends/family, pressure to work overtime as normal work practice, desire for promotion and so on. Each of these factors may influence the decision (i.e. affect the marginal benefit part of the calculation).

In conclusion then:

- the lower the rate of corporation tax the more likely the employer is to increase his level of economic activity and therefore offer overtime to the employee
- the lower the rate of income tax the more likely it is that the employee will undertake extra work and employ others to do the jobs he does not now do for himself
- the lower the level of VAT the more likely it is that an individual will purchase services from registered traders.

The personal investment decision

Having reviewed micro level 'work versus leisure' decisions in the previous section, this section provides a discussion of personal investment decisions as another micro level subject where the tax system can have significant impacts.

The financial services sector has proven to be very creative and there is a huge choice of investment types for individuals who wish to save money they receive rather than spending it. In this section we will consider the way the tax system impacts on individual's savings choices. In particular, we will consider ISAs, pensions and investments in housing.

Individual Savings Accounts (ISAs)

ISAs are an investment type that were first made available to investors in April, 1999. The Chancellor's stated objective for ISAs when they were introduced was to maintain the total tax relief given for two prior schemes that offered similar tax efficient savings opportunities (called TESSAs and PEPs) but use it to encourage people who are not currently savers to start saving. In 1999 only half of the population had savings in excess of £200, so there was clearly scope for increasing the number of savers.

These savings accounts became available from a much wider range of suppliers – even from supermarkets – as well as the usual financial institutions such as banks and building societies.

The accounts initially had a guaranteed life of ten years – but this was extended and became permanent in the 2007 Budget as they have proven effective in increasing savings in at least some parts of the population. There is no lifetime limit on how much can be saved in the scheme in total, however, the maximum which can be saved in a particular fiscal year is currently £10,200 per annum

An ISA can be made up of cash life insurance and stocks and shares. The account can either be of one single investment in equities (up to the full £10,200) or split between cash, shares and life insurance products. Up to £5,100 can be held as cash and the rest, up to the £10,200 limit, can then be in stocks and shares.

The 2010 Emergency Budget announced that, from April 2011, these limits will increase in line with inflation (using the RPI) each year to keep them in step with average price rises (to maintain their level in real terms).

Fiscal Fact

By September 2009 a total of £275billion is expected to have been invested in ISAs since their launch in 1999 (of this sum £158billion was held in cash assets, the rest in a mixture of stocks and shares). This total was spread between more than 37million individual accounts.

The key tax aspect of these accounts is that, unlike most other forms of savings, qualifying schemes are completely free of income tax and capital gains tax on their investments.

ISAs are therefore a good example of how the tax system is used to affect the decisions people make about their financial position. Their tax free status is used to influence the level, and type, of savings people undertake.

Personal pensions

Saving via a personal pension plan, particularly if it is a scheme to which a taxpayer's employer contributes, has historically been extremely tax efficient. Contributions to a HMRC approved pension fund are eligible for tax relief (i.e. a reduction in the payer's tax bill) at the taxpayer's marginal rate of tax (at least up to what are practically very high rates of contribution for most people in practice). Employer contributions, if they make any for their employees, are also eligible for tax relief through their tax calculation (see details in Chapter 5). Investment returns in a pension fund are also free of income tax and capital gains tax. However, apart from a tax-free lump sum that is usually paid when the pension is eventually taken by the taxpayer, other income from a pension once you start to draw on it is taxed as earned income (i.e. is treated as part of your non-savings income in your personal tax computations). All inputs into approved pension funds therefore get tax relief and you only pay tax on the income the fund generates once you start getting back these funds as your pension.

The significant tax benefits attached to private pensions is a key way the Government encourages people to save for their own retirement. The benefit for society of them doing this will be the decrease in their reliance on the state for income when they stop working. The new UK Government is currently reviewing tax relief on pensions however, to ensure it continues to act as an adequate incentive to save for retirement while at the same time doing so cost effectively in terms of tax revenues foregone from these reliefs.

Further consideration of taxation and pension schemes can be found in Chapter 5.

Home ownership

Finally, we can consider the tax incentives that are, or have been, available for home owners.

Prior to April 2000, the interest paid on the first £30,000 borrowed to buy the taxpayer's main residence attracted tax relief as part of a scheme called MIRAS (Mortgage Interest Relief at Source). In 1998/99 and 1999/2000 this was at a rate of 10%. This scheme provided a significant tax advantage to owning the house you lived in rather than renting it as tax deductions did not apply to rental costs. During the 1980s homeowners could obtain this relief at their marginal rate of tax. This tax relief is no longer available so this particular tax incentive to own property rather than renting no longer exists (although the culture of owning your own home that this tax break helped create is now well established in the UK).

The real tax advantage of buying your own home now, however, is that capital growth does not give rise to a capital gains tax liability, unlike most other assets you may own. Imagine the attitude of home owners to increases in house prices if 18% (or worse, 28% now as a higher or additional rate taxpayer) of any increase in their house values had to be paid in tax – clearly not likely to be a vote winner, which is perhaps why this key personal asset remains largely untaxed compared to other personal assets.

Activity

Could taxation be used to reduce the volatility we experience in housing markets? How should this be done? What knock-on impacts might taxing homeowners have?

Because of the privileged tax position of housing, people have often been persuaded to commit more of their wealth to their main residence than might otherwise be the case. Remember the case of Hobnobs and Jaffa Cakes in the section on fiscal neutrality? The distorting effects of taxing Hobnobs and not Jaffa Cakes made buying Jaffa Cakes relatively more attractive. Likewise, the tax advantages of owning a house over other forms of investment create a propensity to hold wealth in property rather than in other forms. As we have seen in recent years, holding wealth in property isn't always guaranteed to be a safe investment however, (house prices can go down as well as up) so tax-induced bias to hold assets this way may have added to the current housing pricing problems even if this tax policy was useful in other ways (another example of the difficulty of controlling tax incidence).

We will examine capital gains tax on houses in more detail in Chapter 8. We also consider stamp duty in that chapter – a tax home-owners do have to pay when they buy property.

Tax and the business investment decision

Having reviewed some tax induced impacts on personal investment decisions, what about businesses and the investment decisions they make? Does the tax system also impact on these?

Businesses grow by incurring expenditure now in order to increase revenue in the future. There are often a number of ways in which this investment can be undertaken and the business must decide what is the optimal allocation of its resources to these opportunities to achieve its goals – including improving its long term profitability. For example, a business might invest in fixed assets or could instead incur training costs to prepare its workforce for new technologies. One of the features that marks a successful business from an unsuccessful one is the ability to determine which of these expenditures will lead to the best, or most sustainable, future revenue.

When businesses undertake investment appraisal analysis they are encouraged to evaluate the cash flows associated with the project options. Cash flows are however, influenced by tax, and, as we will see, the tax treatment of the cash flows depends on their nature.

In this section we discuss the distortions that the tax system creates when a company is evaluating investment options with a life of several years.

Investment in long-term projects and fiscal neutrality

There are a number of techniques used by companies to evaluate a potential capital project. We will just consider discounted cash flow (DCF) techniques using the net present value (NPV) method as just one example of a widely used technique, as the impact of the tax system is similar on all evaluation techniques. There are a large number of books which explain this method very well, however, the basic principle is that all future cash flows resulting from the investment are stated at their value today, i.e. their present value, by discounting them using the company's cost of capital (i.e. what it would cost them to fund this investment). If the sum of all these present values of predicted future cash flows is positive, the investment is considered to be financially worthwhile. A simple example will help to explain the technique.

Activity

A Ltd., is considering investing £10,000 in a project which will generate a cash flow of £6,000 for two years starting one year after the initial investment. The company's after-tax cost of capital is 12%. (A company's cost of capital might be the company's cost of debt. The after-tax rate is used because interest payments are tax deductible and that should be included in the evaluation calculation).

Feedback

You need to undertake the following calculation in order to calculate the net present value:

Year	Cash flow £	Discount factor 12%	Present value £
0	(10,000)		(10,000)
1	6,000	0.8929	5,357
2	6,000	0.7972	4,783
		Net present value	140

Because the net present value of this scheme is positive, other things being equal, the theory tells us that the investment should be undertaken. Projects which generate a negative net present value should normally be rejected unless there are other, secondary, reasons to do them.

Notes on above example:
- payments of cash are cash outflows and are shown as negative numbers
- the discount factor for each year is calculated by using the formula: $\dfrac{1}{(1+r)^t}$
- where r is the discount factor expressed as a decimal, that is 12% is written as 0.12, and t is the number of the year in which the cash flow arose
- the first cash flow, usually a cash outflow, is deemed to take place immediately and hence is recorded as occurring in year 0 and is already stated at its present value
- cash flows are deemed to arise at the end of the year in which they are recorded and so need to be discounted in full for that year.

From this example we can generate a simple test for fiscal neutrality. A business tax is fiscally neutral if the decision about whether to undertake the investment is the same using the before-tax and after-tax cash flows.

The only way for a tax system to be fiscally neutral for business investment is if tax is charged on positive cash flows at the same time as the cash flow arises, and tax relief should be available for cash outflows at the time the cash payment is made. If this situation exists, the rate of tax is 'T' and if the before-tax net present value is £B then the after-tax cash flows will be £B(1 − T). Provided the rate of tax is less than 100% and if B is positive, then B(1 − T) will also be positive. Equally if B is negative then B(1 − T) will be negative. This means that so long as projects which give a positive net present value are accepted regardless of the numerical value of the net present value, the before-tax decision will be the same as the after-tax decision and the system is fiscally neutral.

The impact of the UK corporation tax system on investment appraisal

In practice, the UK corporation tax system does not tax cash flows, but neither does it simply tax accounting profits (those you will see in a company's annual reports and accounts). The system is instead something of a hybrid with some accounting adjustments, such as depreciation, being ignored for tax purposes and other expenses taxed on the accruals basis. In addition, there is a nine-month gap for all but large companies between the end of the accounting period and the payment of tax on that period's profits. (We will examine the operation of corporation tax in more detail in Chapter 9.)

Expenditure on a new project may include any, or all, of the following items:

- land and buildings
- plant and machinery
- working capital
- advertising
- staff training.

You can probably think of more examples but let us consider the tax treatment of each of these types of expenditure.

In some cases, tax relief is available for expenditures related to business activities. In assessing the impacts of the corporation tax system on investment appraisal, we need to take any reliefs into account. There is no tax relief for expenditure on land and buildings except for industrial buildings such as factories and warehouses which are eligible for industrial buildings allowances (although the 2007 Budget announced this is to be phased out progressively by 2011/12). We will consider the industrial buildings allowance in some detail in Chapter 7.

Expenditure on plant and machinery is likely to qualify for a writing down allowance of at least 20% of the reducing balance each year. Again we will consider the allowances available for expenditure on plant and machinery in detail in Chapter 7.

Expenditure on working capital, that is unsold stock and money invested in debtors which has yet to be realised, is not eligible for any tax relief (although a stock relief of this kind used to be given in the UK on changes in stock holdings over a year, but was scrapped in the 1980s because of its significant impact on business activity).

The costs of advertising and staff training are likely to be considered expenditure 'wholly and exclusively' for the purpose of trade and so are fully deductible for tax purposes. (Once again we will consider allowable expenses in Chapter 6.) Which expenses can or cannot be deducted from our profits in practice will, of course, affect how much tax we then have to pay.

Even before we have looked at the details we will cover later in the book you can already see that there is a wide variety of tax treatments of expenditure incurred to set up and operate a new project. This makes assessing the full impact of tax on a business investment decision very difficult in practice.

In the light of the different tax treatments of different items of expenditure it seems unlikely that any move towards fiscal neutrality is feasible. However, the lower the rate of business tax the smaller the distortions caused by the tax system, but the tax system clearly has important impacts on business investment decisions.

Environmental taxation

A further interesting use of taxes by a government to influence behaviour is in relation to the environment, often referred to as "green taxes". There are a wide range of different green taxes that can be used by a government to influence businesses or individual taxpayers. This section considers some of these options briefly.

There are a number of possible ways of making businesses pay for their polluting activities, including voluntary agreements, tradable permits and regulation. There is an argument, however, that the tax system is a more effective way of encouraging firms to become cleaner. In the UK there are currently two main forms of green tax paid by businesses; the *climate change levy* and the *landfill tax*. Both are part of the UK's Climate Change Programme which was published by the Government on 17 November 2000.

The climate change levy was introduced on 1 April 2001 and is a tax on the use of energy in industry, commerce and the public sector. It doesn't apply to fuels used by the domestic or transport sectors and there are varying rates of levy depending on the type of energy used. It is possible to enter into a "climate change agreement", where an 80% discount on the levy is available to a business in return for agreeing challenging targets for improving energy efficiency or reducing carbon emissions. As further encouragement to businesses, there are 100% capital allowances available for investment in certain energy efficient equipment (see Chapter 7 for more information about the UK system of capital allowances).

Fiscal Fact

The number of traders registered to pay these environmental taxes in 2009/10 is: landfill tax 294, climate change levy 235 and aggregates levy 705. Combined, these three taxes were expected to raise nearly £2billion in 2008/09.

The landfill tax was introduced in 1996 and affects a wide range of businesses from landfill site operators to waste carriers, local authorities and every commercial producer of waste that is disposed of at a landfill site. Landfill is currently the main method of waste disposal in the UK and the tax is designed to encourage businesses from using landfill and finding alternative ways of disposing of waste. The rate of tax depends on the type and volume of wasted disposed of, and there are exemptions for certain types of waste disposal, including pet cemeteries. The tax operates in a similar way to VAT (see Chapter 10 for a discussion of how VAT works in the UK). It is currently charged at £48/tonne (£40/tonne 2009/10) of waste landfilled (and is to continue to increase £8/tonne each year until 2011 according to the 2007 Budget). Provision is made for 'tax free areas' where a landfill operator also recycles, composts or incinerates waste. In this way, the tax ultimately falls on waste that is landfilled. This tax, and particularly its above inflation increases, explicitly aim to increase the cost of landfilling waste with the hope that businesses will look for more environmentally friendly ways to dispose of waste .

For non-business taxpayers, a key mechanism that the Government uses to encourage 'greener' behaviour is transport policy. Road traffic is a major source of nearly all air pollutants and the amount of CO_2 emissions created by UK transport has doubled in the past 25 years according to DETR (2000). The four most important tax measures affecting road transport are:

- High fuel duty rates
- Discounted duty rates for alternative fuels e.g. electricity and LPG;
- Vehicle excise duties which vary according to CO_2 emissions; and
- Taxation of company cars using CO_2 emissions to determine an additional charge on drivers of such cars to add to their income tax liability.

Fiscal Fact

In 2004, HMRC assessed the impact of the change to CO_2 emissions for cars (introduced in 2002) and found that in the first year of the new system, average CO_2 emissions for new company cars fell from 196g/km in 1999 to 182g/km in 2002. This suggests their tax policy of making emissions levels affect tax bills is having an influence as hoped for by changing behaviour of company car buying taxpayers.

Many countries, including the UK, are now increasingly charging for road usage through bridge, tunnel and road tolls, and through congestion charging (city based charging as now in operation in London

Increases in air passenger duty rates (brought in during 2007), and more recently the change to distance related tariffs (2008 Pre-Budget Report) to take effect from 1 November 2009, are also, at least in part, aimed at affecting the cost of air travel attempting to decrease the number of flights people take. As air transport is a significant polluter, any increases in prices of tickets will have a direct affect on pollution created, it is hoped.

Look out for more taxes being used to impact environmental issues as this seems to be a popular strategy of the UK Government at present.

Summary

In this chapter we began by attempting to identify the individual who actually suffers a loss in his or her wealth because of the requirement to pay tax. We found that the actual incidence of tax was often difficult to determine and that it was often different from the formal incidence. We then spent some time discussing some of the limitations of the existing tax system before considering some of the distortions which exist. We have considered the distortions caused by both income and expenditure taxes for both individuals and companies. We have seen that lower marginal rates of tax are less likely to lead to distortions than higher marginal rates of tax. In order to achieve low marginal rates of tax it will be necessary to levy the tax on a wide range of income or expenditure as possible. For example, if VAT was extended to include food, children's clothing, books and newspapers it would be possible to reduce the rate of VAT and still generate the same amount of revenue for the Government.

We concluded the chapter by then examining a number of micro level impacts of taxation on individuals' work versus leisure choice, on their personal investment decisions, on business investment appraisals and finally on environmental issues.

On the question of managing the impacts of taxation generally, we can conclude that a broad tax base and low marginal rates of tax leads to fewer distortions than a narrow tax base with high marginal rates of tax.

Project areas and discussion questions

There are many interesting projects contained within the material of this chapter. A topical area is that of the disincentive to work shared by many single parents who simply cannot afford to work. An evaluation of the Working Tax Credit systems or the Child Tax Credit systems, combined with the benefits system, would be an interesting project in this area.

An investigation into the impact of ISAs on savings patterns would make a good topic for a dissertation. For example, has their use increased or decreased savings in total? (i.e. have they cost the Government foregone tax revenue they would previously have received on taxed savings products?).

An examination of the impact of marginal tax rates on employee decisions to work or not to work may be an interesting area for a project. What impacts might the introduction of capital gains (or other) tax on profits of sales of houses have on house prices, peoples' desire to see house prices keep rising, and related housing costs?

There has been significant work done over the last twenty years on assessing (as accurately as we can) the compliance costs of taxation. An exploration of how this can be done in practice by looking at this research would be an interesting project or dissertation.

This chapter introduced the potential of a flat tax in for profit and income based taxes. As such a tax has been used in various countries, an interesting project could be undertaken to review how these taxes are working in these countries and considering its potential use in the UK.

Environmental taxation is an area of significant interest for the UK Government at present. A project could explore the use of environmental taxes of different kinds to demonstrate how effective different taxes are at achieving impacts on taxpayer behaviour at both the personal and corporate level.

Further reading

James, S. and Nobes, C. (2010), *The Economics of Taxation* (10th edition), Fiscal Publications, Birmingham – a very useful guide to tax incidence, tax distortions and the subject matter of this chapter.

Brown, C. and Sandford, C. (1993), Tax Reform and Incentives: A Case Study from the United Kingdom, in *More Key Issues in Tax Reform*, Sandford, C. (ed), Fiscal Publications, Birmingham.

Pope, J. (2002), Administrative and compliance costs of international taxation, in *The International Tax System*, Lymer, A. & J. Hasseldine (eds), Springer: Heidelberg.

Potter, S & Parkhurst, G. (2005) Transport Policy and Tax Reform *Public Policy and Management* June, pp 171 – 178.

Sandford, C. (1995), *Tax compliance costs measurement and policy*, Fiscal Publications, Birmingham.

Sandford, C. (2000), *Why tax systems differ*, Fiscal Publications, Birmingham.

Scholes, M., Wolfson, M., Erickson, M., Maydew, E. and Shevlin, T. (2001), *Taxes and Business Strategy: A Planning Approach* (2nd Edition), Prentice Hall: Englewood Cliffs, New Jersey.

Smith, S. (1993), 'Green Taxes' – The Scope for Environmentally friendly Taxes in *More Key Issues in Tax Reform*, Sandford, C. (ed), Fiscal Publications: Birmingham.

4 Personal income taxation

Introduction

In Section 1 of this book we examined the history of the UK tax system, outlined its administration, looked at some of the economics related to taxation and discussed some of the ways taxes affect decisions made by people. This foundation provides us with the background we need to now begin to examine the current UK tax system in detail.

This chapter introduces you to the personal income tax computation and explains the various elements that go into its make-up. Chapters 5, 6 and 7 review the sources of taxable income in more detail and show you how to calculate the correct values to enter into the respective parts of the income tax computation. Chapter 8 then introduces you to capital taxes particularly focusing on capital gains tax, a different tax to income tax, but one that is also paid by individuals. Throughout the chapters in this section the focus is on income taxation of the individual, either as an employed person, or as a self employed person (as a sole trader). We will examine how the direct tax system operates for companies in Chapter 9.

Fiscal Fact

In 1938/39 there were only 3.8 million taxpayers liable for income tax (with married couples counting as one taxpayer); by 2010/11 the number is expected to reach 30.6 million. Of these, 26 million are expected to be aged 65 or less, with 4.54 million therefore aged over 65.

In the UK, individuals pay tax on their income for a *tax year*. The tax year runs from 6 April to the following 5 April (the reason for these odd dates was described in Chapter 1).

A tax system rarely remains the same for long and in recent years there have been a number of major changes to the way in which individuals are taxed in the UK. For example, key changes in the last 30 years have included the introduction of independent taxation at the end of the 1980s (separate taxation of men and women whether they are married or not) while self-assessment for personal taxation was introduced from 6 April, 1996. The more recent key change is the renaming in 2007 of the different income components from names that were largely meaningless to the average taxpayer (Schedule A, Schedule D Case 1 etc.) to more obvious names (property income, trading income etc.) as part of the process of simplifying tax rules. We will consider the effects of these important changes to the UK tax system in more detail later in this chapter.

In this chapter you will learn how to calculate the amount of an individual's income that is subject to income tax and learn how to determine the amount of any reliefs and allowances that are available to reduce the tax due. Once you have deducted the allowances and reliefs from the taxable income you will learn how to compute a taxpayer's tax liability.

At the end of this chapter you will be able to:

- differentiate between income that is taxable and that which is exempt;
- describe the tax rules for the different categories under which individuals pay income tax;
- calculate the allowances and reliefs available to an individual;
- describe the system of national insurance and calculate any national insurance contributions payable by both employers and employees;
- prepare a personal tax computation for an individual;
- outline the system of self-assessment for individuals; and
- offer basic income tax planning advice to individuals and members of a family unit.

The tax computation

A tax computation for an individual can be set out in the following way. This structure is identical to the one used by HMRC when calculating income tax due and follows the computation steps of the Income Tax Act 2007. Laying out your computation this way therefore helps with real tax filing processes. However, doing answers to exam questions in the same way as this proforma will also help ensure you include all the necessary stages in your computations and that you apply the figures in the correct order. You are strongly advised to learn, and then follow, this proforma each time you do a personal tax computation.

We will outline the seven steps in this computation briefly for you first in this section before providing further details on each step of the calculation later in this chapter.

Thomas Lester's income tax computation for 2010/11.

	Non-savings £	Savings £	Dividends £	Total £
Income:				
Property Income	500			500
Trading Income	21,000			21,000
Employment Income	19,000			19,000
Savings Income:				
Bank interest received (gross)		3,500		3,500
Building Society Interest (gross)		3,000		3,000
Dividend Income (gross - UK only)			1,500	1,500
Total Income	40,500	6,500	1,500	48,500
Less reliefs	(500)			(500)
Net Income	40,000	6,500	1,500	48,000
Less Personal Allowances	(6,475)			(6,475)
Total Taxable Income	33,525	6,500	1,500	41,525

Tax Due:				
Non savings income	33,525		@ 20%	6,705.00
Savings income	3,875 (37,400 – 33,525)		@ 20%	775.00
	2,625 (6,500 – 3,875)		@ 40%	1,050.00
Dividend income	1,500		@ 32.5%	487.50
	41,525			
Tax Borne				9,017.50
Less:				
Tax reductions	(none apply for Thomas this year)			(0.00)
Add:				
Additional tax	(none applies for Thomas this year)			0.00
Tax Liability				9,017.50
Less tax already paid:				
Bank and Building Society Interest		6,500 @ 20%		(1,300.00)
Dividends		1,500 @ 10%		(150.00)
PAYE				(2,505.00)
Tax Payable				5,062.50

In this section of the book you will find out how to produce a tax computation like this one, given basic facts about a taxpayer's situation.

As we will see later on, Thomas appears to receive his income from a number of sources (called *components of income*). This includes income from owning property in the UK, income from being partly self-employed, income from employment and some interest and dividends. It is not uncommon to see multiple income sources like this in a tax computation although it is probably more common to see either income from employment or from self employment (trading income) rather than from both sources in the same tax year as Thomas has here.

The income tax computation is really split into seven 'steps'. The first three steps aggregate a taxpayer's taxable income from all sources and then deducts any reliefs and allowances that are due to produce taxable income (i.e. compute the top half of Thomas' tax liability as shown above). The remaining four steps then calculate the tax due on this taxable income (i.e. the bottom half of Thomas' tax computation above). The way in which a particular component of income is taxed depends on the tax rules under which it is assessed. We'll look at the key elements of this computation briefly before going into more detail about the current tax rules.

Computing Taxable Income

Step 1 – Aggregating the components of income

All the taxable income Thomas has received or earned in the year, from all sources, is listed in his tax computation. A few sources of income are exempt from income tax, as we will see later, but most have to be taxed and so must be listed here. For most components of income we include what is due to Thomas, even though he hasn't actually received it yet (i.e. we use an accruals basis).

Note that we split up Thomas' income sources into different components by using different rows and into different types by using four columns. This is important to help us calculate the correct rate of tax at step 4 of the tax computation; note how each of the three (non-total) columns in the first part of the computation becomes a row when computing tax borne – the fourth step in the computation.

Property, trading and employment income
Income from owning property, from being self employed or from employment is listed in Thomas's tax computation first. Usually property and trading income have not had tax deducted at source so

can just be listed here at the value the rules for each category determine (we'll show you how these rules work in Chapter 5, 6 and 7). Income from employment, however, usually has PAYE deducted by the taxpayer's employer so you'll see that Thomas shows the total (gross) he has received from a job he had during this year (£19,000) here in step 1, but then he is able to later deduct the PAYE already paid via his employee at the end of the tax computation when determining what tax may still be payable. PAYE can be thought of as being an advance payment of income tax due.

Savings and investment income

Most income from savings or investments is paid to an individual like Thomas after deduction of tax at source. Chapter 2 explained why this is done. Bank deposit interest and the building society interest usually have had tax deducted at the basic rate of tax, currently 20%. Therefore, if the gross interest is £100, the net interest received is £80 or, looked at the other way, if the interest received is £80 the gross interest must be $80 \times 100/80 = 100$ (this process is called *grossing up* and is an important process in completing the tax computation as all numbers must be shown gross). Take note how this computation is done as we'll be using this process regularly to get from net of tax figures to their pre-tax (gross) equivalents.

The gross income is included in the first part of a tax computation and then a deduction is made equal to the tax already deducted at source at the end of the computation when you calculate how much tax is payable. This process ensures that tax already paid is not paid again as a result of the tax computation, but also that the correct total of taxable income is calculated in the first three steps of the computation. This is necessary to ensure we apply the correct rates of tax in the second part of the computation.

Exempt income

UK legislation specifically exempts certain income from income tax. You should be aware of the most significant exemptions which are:

- the increase in the value of National Savings & Investments savings certificates,
- premium bond prizes, betting winnings and other competition prizes,
- gifts,
- interest from Individual Savings Accounts (ISAs),
- some social security benefits, including child benefit and housing benefit,

- shares allotted to employees under approved profit sharing schemes,
- educational grants and scholarships (for the recipient),
- statutory redundancy pay, pay in lieu of notice and some other payments up to a maximum of £30,000 made when an employment is terminated. (Note: The excess received on termination is taxable as for other employment income),
- payments made by employers to employees for death in service or in respect of disability sustained at work (e.g. personal injury payments),
- lump sums received from approved pension schemes,
- fostering income – qualifying income up to an annual sum is exempt from income tax (the excess is taxable). Currently this sum is £10,000 per residence, plus £200 per week (for a child under 11 years of age) and £250 per week (for a child older than 11). In the June 2010 Emergency Budget this relief was also extended to shared lives carers as well as foster carers – the same rates apply),
- providers of children care under special guardianship and residence orders – exempting payments for income received by these carers up to the rates of £400 a week for the first child and £250 a week for other children laced with the same carer. This is a new exemption from 6 April 2010.

All income which is not specifically exempt is potentially subject to income tax under the UK's tax system. Whether or not tax has to be paid on specific sources of income, and how much, is detailed in the tax legislation. We will review the rules for calculating these amounts throughout the remaining chapters of the book.

Fiscal Fact

Exempting income from tax, of course, costs the UK Government in foregone tax revenue (this is termed 'tax expenditure'). For example, for 2009/10, the estimated cost of exempting ISAs from income tax was £1.6 billion, the cost of allowing redundancy pay up to £30,000 to be tax free income is estimated to be £1.2 billion and exempting premium bond winnings could cost £1.45 billion. (See Table A3.1 in the 2010 Budget for a list of other tax expenditures)

Step 2 – Dealing with reliefs

Reliefs are certain payments made by the taxpayer and other items that are eligible for tax deduction. After you have computed the total income by aggregating all components of taxable income any reliefs that are applicable can be deducted as step 2. In our example, Thomas made £500 of payments that can be treated as reliefs. An example of a relief is a trading loss, which we will cover in Chapter 7.

Total income minus reliefs produces *net income*.

Step 3 – Personal allowances

Most individuals are entitled to receive a certain amount of income each year before they have to start paying income tax. This amount alters most years. It needs to be deducted from the total income figure to arrive at total taxable income. If a blind person's allowance is applicable it is also deducted at this stage. Thomas does not appear to qualify for this extra allowance however, so no deduction is made in his case.

Net income minus personal allowances produces *taxable income*.

On completion of steps 1-3 you will have determined the taxable income of the taxpayer and are now ready for the computation of tax due on this income.

Computing Tax Liability

Step 4 - Income tax rates

The next stage of the tax computation is to calculate what rate of tax is to be paid on the total taxable income. At step 1 stage the income components are classified into one of three types – non-savings, savings and investments income and dividend income. This is necessary as each of these income types has its own tax rate. Later in the chapter we will examine exactly how these different rates are applied to a taxpayer's total income.

Step 5 - Tax borne

Tax borne is the outcome from applying the tax rates to the taxable income, and represents the amount of tax that the taxpayer is liable for on his or her taxable income before any tax reductions (which can reduce the tax borne) or additional tax on their income (that may increase it).

Step 6 – Tax reductions

At this stage there is a deduction from the amount calculated at step 5 for any entitlements the taxpayer has for tax reductions. These are a limited range of special reductions that include married couples' and civil partners' reduction, qualifying maintenance payments and some special schemes for tax deductible investments. Tax relief for any foreign taxes paid at sources (double tax relief) is also given at this point in the computation – see Chapter 12 for more on this topic.

Step 7 – Additional Tax

The final step in computing *tax liability* for the taxpayer is to add in any extra tax that may be due. These are fairly rare events, not typical for many taxpayers but include such things as extra tax where gift aid has been claimed but where insufficient tax has been paid to offset this claim. We will discuss charitable donations later in this chapter. Pension related surcharges are also applied here. We will talk about these in Chapter 5.

Tax payable

The result of completing all seven steps correctly is the computation of the taxpayer's tax liability for the tax year. This is the sum that the taxpayer needs to pay to HMRC to settle their income tax bill for the year. In Chapter 2 we explained that some of this tax may have already been deducted at source, via the taxpayer's employer or is otherwise credited to the taxpayer directly, before this computation is done (after the tax year is over). The final stage in the full computation therefore is to deduct from the tax liability any sums already paid to HMRC during the tax year to compute if the taxpayer still owes any tax which must then be paid to HMRC directly. It is possible that the taxpayer may have paid more during the year through deduction at source than the final tax liability. In this case, the taxpayer will receive a refund from HMRC of the tax overpaid (but not for dividend credit as we will see later).

Determining tax payable typically includes taxes paid at source on savings and investments, the dividend tax credit and any PAYE withheld by the taxpayer's employer.

Important: Note that the *taxable income* part of the calculation (steps 1 to 3) is always rounded down to the nearest pound (i.e. you can effectively chop off the pence in your final computation). For the *tax due* part of the calculation (steps 4 to 7), you should always use round down your figures to the *whole penny*. This is important to ensure you do not get rounding errors in your tax computation.

Basis of assessment

The *basis of assessment* is the way in which income is allocated to tax years for tax purposes. For example, employees are normally taxed on income which is paid to them during the tax year, i.e. the *basis of assessment* is income received during the tax year. This is not the only basis of assessment however. An alternative might be to tax income which is earned during the tax year whether it is actually received or not (i.e. an accruals basis). For most employees this would make little or no difference to their tax bills each year but for those who receive performance-related bonuses, which are often paid in the tax year after the one in which they were earned, the tax on the bonus would then be payable before the bonus was actually received. Most people would not like this idea!

For self-employed people, and for companies, the basis of assessment is linked to their business year (i.e. the period for which they produce accounts). We will see how this operates in practice in later chapters.

The system of income tax rules

There are four primary Acts that contain the main rules for income tax: the Income and Corporation Taxes Act (ICTA) 1988, the Income Tax (Earnings and Pensions) Act (ITEPA) 2003, the Income Tax (Trading and Other Income) Act (ITTOIA) 2005 and the Income Tax Act (ITA) 2007. As we explained in Chapter 1, the Finance Acts produced each year from the annual UK Budget have amended the ICTA (1988), together with more recent Acts, in a number of ways. In this book we will look at the combined rules of the various tax Acts and any changes that have occurred to them as a result of any subsequent Finance Acts.

The ICTA (1988) used to lay out the rules for working out income tax in a series of categories called Schedules. In turn these schedules contained subsections called 'cases' containing the detailed rules. Following the re-write of tax legislation, the income tax rules related to employee earnings which used to be in Schedule E are now contained in the ITEPA (2003). With effect from 6 April 2005, the remaining schedules have been re-written into the ITTOIA (2005). The re-written rules only apply to income tax for individual taxpayers; the rules relating to companies continued to use the old Schedules and cases from ICTA (1988) until the Corporation Tax Act 2009 came into effect (see Chapter 9).

It is important to identify which set of tax rules any particular income stream is taxed under because each has its own specific rules for:

- the income to be taxed;
- allowable deductions, if any, from the income;
- the basis of assessment; and
- the date on which tax should be paid.

The current system for determining UK income tax liability is structured as follows:

Employment income	income from employment or office holding (was Schedule E ICTA 1988 now Part 2 ITEPA 2003);
Pension income	income received from a pension (Part 9 ITEPA 2003);
Property income	income, such as rent, from UK property (was Schedule A ICTA 1988 now Part 3 ITTOIA 2005);
Trading income	income from a trade or profession (was Schedule D Cases I & II ICTA 1988 now Part 2 ITTOIA 2005);
Savings income	interest income for example from banks and building societies (was Schedule D Case III ICTA 1988 now Part 4 ITTOIA 2005);
Foreign income	interest from foreign securities and other foreign possessions (was Schedule D Cases IV & V ICTA 1988);
Dividend income	income from UK dividends and other distributions from UK companies (was Schedule F ICTA 1988 now Part 3 & 4 ITTOIA 2005);
Miscellaneous income	income not dealt with under any of the above categories (was Schedule D case VI ICTA 1988 now Part 5 ITTOIA 2005).

As we go through this section of the book we will look in detail at each of the tax rules for calculating what income is taxable. In this chapter we will determine the aggregated income which is subject to tax, the allowances and reliefs which can be set against the income for tax purposes and the date on which tax must be paid. Chapter 5 will look at income from employment and pensions. In Chapter 6 and Chapter 7 we will examine trading income and deductions for taxpayers who are carrying on business as sole traders, as well as property income.

Throughout this chapter we only discuss income from UK sources. The general rules for income tax payment change when the source of the income comes from outside the UK. We will examine these differences in Chapter 12.

Rates of tax

Having looked in outline at how we aggregate the components of income in the top part of the individual taxpayer's tax computation (steps 1 – 3), let us jump ahead and examine the tax due part of the computation before we return to the top part for a more detailed examination in the next section.

To determine the rate of tax to be paid on the taxable income (i.e. step 4 of the computation), we need to classify the taxable income into three types of income ie non-savings, savings and dividend income.

Non-savings income

Let's look at non-savings income first. This includes any employment, property, trading, foreign and miscellaneous incomes. For most people this is will be their main income type.

For the current tax year rates of tax for non-savings income are:

	Tax Band	Rate	Maximum amount payable in band £
Basic Rate	0 – 37,400	20%	7,480.00
Higher Rate	37,400 – 150,000	40%	45,040.00
Additional rate	>150,000	50%	

Before April 2008, non–savings income was taxed at three different rates; a starting rate of 10%, a basic rate of 22% and a higher rate of 40%. Between April 2008 and April 2010 only two rates applied; 20% (on all taxable incomes up to £37,400) and 40% (for all taxable income over £37,400). A new additional rate of 50% tax applies from April 2010 to any income exceeding £150,000.

Activity

Calculate the income tax due on taxable incomes of:
(a) £2,500
(b) £10,000
(c) £45,000
(d) £175,000
(Assume all of this income is non-savings income only.)

Feedback

	£
(a) 2,500 @ 20%	500.00
(b) 10,000 @ 20%	2,000.00
(c) 37,400 @ 20%	7,480.00
(45,000 – 37,400) @ 40%	3,040.00
	10,520.00
(d) 37,400 @ 20%	7,480.00
(150,000 – 37,400) @ 40%	45,040.00
(175,000 – 150,000) @ 50%	12,500.00
	65,020.00

Note what happened in the third case. Initially the basic rate band (first £37,400 of taxable income) was filled up and taxed at 20%. Any amount falling into the higher rate band (greater than £37,400 of taxable income) is then taxed at 40%.

Savings income

Since 1996/97 a distinction has been drawn between savings and non-savings income for calculating tax due and a lower rate of tax used for savings income to encourage people to save more. Savings income is treated as being the middle part of taxable income for the purposes of determining rates of tax to be applied, so you allocate this income to the tax bands only after you have used up all the non-savings income bands as part of your computation.

Savings income includes:

- interest from a bank account (including from National Savings & Investments accounts);
- interest from a building society;
- interest from gilt edged securities (i.e. Government stocks);
- interest from debentures; and
- income from an annuity.

For savings income only, there is a special starting rate band at 10%. Income falling into the basic rate band is taxed at 20% (as for non-savings income) and income falling into the higher rate band at 40%. For the current tax year rates of tax for savings income are:

	Tax Band	Rate	Maximum amount payable in band* £
Starting Rate	0 – 2,440	10%	244.00
Basic Rate	2,440 – 37,400	20%	6,992.00
Higher Rate	37,400 – 150,000	40%	45,040.00
Additional Rate	>150,000	50%	

* only if all of the taxpayer's income is from savings.

Note that the starting rate for savings of 10% only applies if the non-savings income is less than £2,440. Savings income falling into the starting rate for savings band in this way is taxed at only 10%. Once the starting rate is full however, any further savings income which falls within the basic rate band is then taxed at 20%, as for non-savings income. Also like non-savings income, any savings income falling into the higher rate band is taxed at 40%, and that falling into the additional rate band is taxed at 50%.

Try the following activity to illustrate how the bands, and this time two income types, interact. Look out for the order in which the taxable income is applied to the bands. Getting the order right is essential.

Activity

Calculate the income tax liability for an individual with total taxable income consisting of savings income of £1,500 and non-savings income of:
(a) £1,800
(b) £20,000
(c) £50,000
(d) £160,000

Feedback

	£
(a) Non-savings income	
1,800 @ 20%	360.00
Savings income	
(2,440 – 1,800) @ 10%	64.00
1,500 – (2,440 – 1,800) @ 20%	172.00
	596.00
(b) Non-savings income	£
20,000 @ 20%	4,000.00
Savings income	
1,500 @ 20%	300.00
	4,300.00
(c) Non-savings income	£
37,400 @ 20%	7,480.00
(50,000 – 37,400) @ 40%	5,040.00
Savings income	
1,500 @ 40%	600.00
	13,120.00
(d) Non-savings income	£
37,400 @ 20%	7,480.00
(150,000 – 37,400) @ 40%	45,040.00
(160,000 – 150,000)@ 50%	5,000.00
Savings income	
1,500 @ 50%	750.00
	58,270.00

In the first case some savings income can be taxed at 10% as the starting rate band is not filled by non-savings income. The remainder of the savings income then falls into the basic rate and is taxed at 20%.

In the second case, all of the starting rate for savings, and part of the general basic rate band is used up by non-savings income so the savings income all falls into the basic rate band and is therefore taxed at 20%.

In the third case the non-savings income uses all of the starting and basic rate bands so the savings income must be taxed at the higher rate of 40%.

In the final case the savings income is pushed into the additional rate band of 50% by the high non-savings earnings.

Dividend income

Before 6 April 1999 dividends from UK company shares were treated in the same way as savings income. Since this time however, dividends have been subject to their own special tax rules and so must be treated separately in the tax computation. They are now treated as the third part of a person's taxable income when determining the correct rates of tax to apply at step 4 stage of the tax computation. If you receive any dividend income from UK shares it will be taxed at 10% if it falls into the basic rate band, or 32.5% (called the *dividend income upper rate*) if it falls into the higher rate band. If the dividend falls into the additional rate band, it will be taxed at 42.5%.

The special 10% rate for dividends is sometimes referred to as the *dividend income ordinary rate*. We will look at the rules which describe how dividends from companies are taxed later in more detail.

Fiscal Fact

Collectively, all taxpayers are expected to pay £2,640 million in taxes on dividends at the ordinary rate in 2010/11. Higher rate taxpayers however, are expected to pay an extra £6,080 million in tax on their dividends for 2010/11 and additional rate taxpayers an extra £4,780 million.

For the current tax year rates of tax for dividend income are:

	Tax Band	Rate	Maximum amount payable in band* £
Basic Rate	0 – 37,400	10%	3,740.00
Higher Rate	37,400 – 150,000	32.5%	36,595.00
Additional Rate	>150,000	42.5%	

* only if all of the taxpayer's income is from dividends.

Dividends are included in tax computations at their gross value i.e. in the same way as bank or building society interest. They are treated in the taxpayer's computation as if 10% had been deducted by the company as a tax at source – although no deductions are actually made. This procedure *imputes* the corporation tax the company pays on its profits to the shareholders. The gross dividend that is taxed to the shareholder therefore equals the dividend actually received multiplied by 100/90.

For example, a dividend received of £1,440 will be grossed up and included in a tax computation as £1,600 (£1,440 × 100/90). Part of the corporation tax that is paid by a UK company (which we will examine in Chapter 9) therefore forms part of the income of the recipient of the dividends. The imputed corporation tax is then allowed as a credit in the tax computation (as we saw for Thomas Lester earlier). The tax credit is therefore worth one ninth of the value of the dividend.

Activity

Pat (aged 45) has earned the following income for the tax year:

	£
Taxable income from his business	19,600
UK Dividends	900
Income from UK property	1,000

Calculate Pat's income tax payable.

Feedback

As Pat is less than 65 she will receive a personal allowance of £6,475 which is deducted from her aggregated income before you calculate tax due, just as we saw in the Thomas Lester example earlier. (Personal allowances are discussed in more detail later in this chapter)

	Non-savings £	Dividends £	Total £
Trading income	19,600		19,600
Dividend income (900 × 100/90)		1,000	1,000
Property income	1,000		1,000
Net income	20,600	1,000	21,600
Less: Personal allowance	(6,475)		(6,475)
Taxable income	14,125	1,000	15,125

Tax due:	£
Non-savings income:	
14,125 @ 20%	2,825.00
Dividend income:	
1,000 @ 10%	100.00
Tax liability	2,925.00
Less: tax credit from dividends	
1,000 @ 10%	(100.00)
Tax payable	2,825.00

Activity

How would your answer to the previous activity differ if Pat had earned £42,000 income from her business in the tax year instead of £19,600?

Feedback

	Non-savings £	Dividends £	Total £
Trading income	42,000		42,000
Dividend income (900 × 100/90)		1,000	1,000
Property income	1,000		1,000
Net income	43,000	1,000	44,000
Less: Personal allowance	(6,475)		(6,475)
Taxable income	36,525	1,000	37,525

Tax due:	£
Non-savings income:	
36,525 @ 20%	7,305.00

Dividend income

875 (37,400 – 36,525) @ 10%	87.50
125 (1,000 – 875) @ 32.5%	40.62
Tax liability	7,433.12

Less: tax credit from dividends

1,000 @ 10%	(100.00)
Tax payable	7,333.12

Notice that the first £875 (37,400 – 36,535) of dividend income falls in the basic rate band, because this band has not been fully used up by the non-savings income, and so this is taxed at 10%. The rest of the dividend income, £125 (£1,000 – 875), is then taxed at the dividend income higher rate of 32.5%.

We will return to the taxation of dividends in more detail later in this chapter.

Summary

We have seen that there are six rates of tax that may apply to an individual taxpayer's income: 10% (only for some savings or dividends), 20% (non-savings or savings), 32.5% (only dividends may be taxed at this rate) 40% (for non savings and savings), 42.5% (dividends) or 50% (non-savings and savings). The order in which you include the different incomes in the computation can obviously therefore affect the amount of tax paid because of these various tax rates. You are not allowed to pick the order you want to use unfortunately. You must always calculate the tax due on the taxpayer's particular income types in the following order:

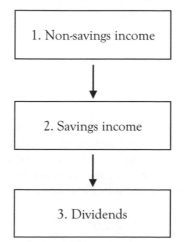

Non-savings income must be included in the computation first (if the taxpayer has any), then savings (if they have any) and finally dividends. Dividends can therefore be considered the top part of anyone's income for their income tax computation as it is almost always included last of the three income tax types when calculating tax due. In practice this mean a taxpayer will only pay 10% on savings income if there is not more than £2,440 of taxable non-savings income as non-savings income must come first in the computation.

Also note that reliefs and personal allowances should be deducted in the same order i.e. from non-savings income first and if not fully used up, next from savings income and finally from dividends. Look back to the example computation at the start of this chapter to review how these rates have been applied to Thomas' income.

Liability to UK income tax

Let's now return to the top part of the personal income tax computation (steps 1 to 3) again to look at how we calculate taxable income in more detail.

The distinctions between the different income tax classifications are important because different rules will apply to a taxpayer having income classified under one category or another. This can have a significant impact on the overall amount of tax they then have to pay and when it is paid.

Income taxed at source

In Chapter 2 we discussed how income can be received in one of two forms:

1. already, at least partly, taxed at source, or
2. not taxed at all yet (to be taxed instead entirely by direct assessment).

Income which is taxed by direct assessment is paid to the recipient gross, while income taxed at source is paid to the recipient after deduction of some tax.

We saw in Chapter 1 that the procedure by which some income is paid to the recipient net of tax was introduced at the beginning of the 19th century as an anti-avoidance measure. This is administratively efficient as the payer of the income can then be made partly responsible for the tax due, not just the recipient.

The following income is taxed at source for individual taxpayers (the rules are different for companies as we will see in Chapter 9):

- interest paid by UK companies to individuals (e.g. interest on loans or debentures);
- interest paid on bank deposit accounts;
- interest paid on building society accounts;
- income from trusts, settlements and the estates of deceased persons;
- patent royalties (but not copyright royalties); and
- annuities.

Most income taxed at source has tax deducted at the basic rate of 20% (i.e. the recipient only gets 80% of the gross amount due to them). Interest on government stocks (gilts) is normally paid gross unless the gilt holder elects (i.e. asks for - usually in writing) to receive the interest net of basic rate tax (i.e. net of 20%).

Fiscal Fact

Tax deductions from interest and other tax deducted at source (i.e. not including PAYE) accounted for £5,980 million (4.3%) of the net total tax receipts to the UK Government in 2008/09.

If individuals who are not liable to income tax (e.g. perhaps because their income is less than the personal allowance) receive income which has been taxed at source, they can usually reclaim the tax which has been deducted directly from the HMRC. However, people who are higher rate taxpayers may have to pay more tax at the end of the tax year to make up the full amount they should have paid on this income. The following activities illustrate these situations for you.

Activity

Linda has £1,000 deposited in a building society account paying 4% interest, credited annually on 31 December each year.

How much interest will be credited to Linda's account in the tax year?

Feedback

Linda's account will be credited with £32 (£1000 × 4% × 80%) made up of £40 gross interest less £8 (£40 × 20%) tax deducted at source.

Activity

As above, Linda has £1,000 deposited in a building society paying 4% interest. We calculated that Linda was credited with £32 interest in the tax year due to having tax deducted at source. Can you now determine how much tax she will have to pay if she is:

(a) a basic rate taxpayer (i.e. her next £1 of income will fall into the basic rate band)

(b) a higher rate taxpayer (i.e. her next £1 of income will fall into the higher rate band)

(c) a non-taxpayer (i.e. she does not have to pay tax as her next £1 does not bring her above the tax free income level for the year).

Feedback

(a) Linda's account will be credited with £32 (£1,000 × 4% × 80%) made up of £40 gross interest less £8 (£40 × 20%) tax deducted at source. The tax withheld by the building society will exactly meet the additional tax of £8 that Linda will suffer as a result of the (gross) interest credited.

(b) Again £32 will be credited to Linda's account but this time Linda will be required to pay additional tax of £8 because she is a higher rate taxpayer so should pay tax at 40% on her savings. The total increase in her tax bill as a result of this interest credited should be £16 (£40 × 40%) and this will be only partly satisfied by the tax deducted at source leaving her £8 (£16 – £8) still to pay.

(c) As a non-taxpayer Linda could have elected to have interest credited to her account without any tax being withheld. This is done by writing to the Building Society to declare she is not a taxpayer. In this case £40 will be credited to her account and there will be no tax consequences. If Linda does not make the necessary election, only £32 will be credited to her account just as for taxpayers because the Building Society must withhold tax for everyone who doesn't tell them they are not taxpayers. She can, however, obtain a tax repayment of the tax deducted at source (£8) by writing to HMRC.

Do remember however, to include income taxed at source in the components of income part of the computation at the *gross* amount and not the *net* amount that is actually received. The tax already paid is then accounted for at the end of the computation (as we saw earlier in the chapter for Thomas).

Income from earnings and pensions

Employment income is taxed using the PAYE (Pay-As-You-Earn), scheme, which means that the tax due on the income of employees is deducted by the employer before the payment is made to the employee. Although this deduction is made at the source, this income is still technically taxed by direct assessment rather than formally considered to be taxed at source because the personal circumstances of the taxpayer are used to determine the amount of tax which should be deducted by the employer for the HMRC. This will mean that for many employees the correct amount of tax is deducted by their employers so they normally won't have to complete a tax computation each year. This feature of the UK tax system means relatively few people file tax returns in the UK each year compared to other countries. Normal tax deductions at source (e.g. building society interest as we have just described above) are made without consideration of the circumstances of the taxpayer and adjustments must then be made via the tax computation after the end of the tax year meaning tax returns will normally have to be completed if you are in that situation (e.g. a higher rate tax payer who has extra tax to pay on savings income).

Remember that income from earnings and pensions must be included in the components of income part of an income tax computation (i.e. step 1) as a *gross* amount. If PAYE has been paid on this income already, the amount paid is then deducted from the tax computation at the very end of the tax due calculation (along with any other tax already paid at source) to determine what tax remains still to be paid by the taxpayer.

Fiscal Fact

Income tax receipts to the UK Government via PAYE were almost £128.5 billion in 2008/09. This represented 87% of non self assessed income tax receipts for that year.

Property income

All income from UK land and property (and some from EEA countries) is taxed using the property income rules. This includes rental income from furnished lettings and letting caravans and houseboats on permanent moorings. Individuals, whether residents of the UK or not in the tax year, are taxed on any annual profits or gains related to UK based land or property. Taxable profits are calculated by deducting total allowable expenses from total income from land and property. The basis of assessment is the accrued income for the tax year. This basis of assessment is usually the *accruals* basis (i.e. as for the accounting for these incomes and expenses in a business) for all items other than short lease premiums.

We will examine the property income rules in more detail in Chapter 6. The following activity illustrates this for you.

Activity

Mary lets a house that she owns in London. Rent was £9,600 a year until 30 September, 2010 when it was increased to £10,200. Rent is payable a month in advance on the first of the month. The rent due on 1 April, 2011 was not received until 10 April, 2011. Mary incurred allowable expenses of £1,000 during the year to 5 April, 2011.
Determine Mary's property income for 2010/11.

Feedback

Income for 2010/11 using the accruals basis is:

$(6 \times £800) + (6 \times £850) = £9,900$

Notice that it does not matter that one payment due in the tax year was actually paid in the following year – that is the point of the accruals basis.

Hence the property income is £8,900 (£9,900 – £1,000). This is the figure you should put in Mary's tax computation. (Note: strictly the income should be calculated on the daily basis but this monthly basis is usually acceptable to the HMRC).

Trading income

The normal basis of assessment for trading profit is the *current year* basis. Under this principle the basis period for a year of assessment is normally the 12 months to the accounting date ending in the tax year. However, there are a number of circumstances in which this simple rule cannot be applied, especially in the early years of trading, the final years of trading or years in which a business changes its accounting date. The rules which apply in most of these circumstances will be discussed in Chapter 6. Expenses which are wholly and exclusively for the purpose of the trade are allowable deductions using the *accruals* basis to create a taxable profit figure to be used in the tax computation.

We will return to examine trading income computations in more detail in Chapters 6 and 7.

Savings and investments income

As discussed in the earlier section of this chapter, interest received, whether or not it has had tax deducted from it at source, is taxed as savings income. Individuals will normally have most savings taxed at source (as we have illustrated earlier with the example of Linda) however, some interest is still received gross. Interest in this category includes:

- National Savings & Investment (NS&I) easy access savings accounts;
- NS&I income bonds; and
- Loans between individuals.

The savings income assessable for income tax in a tax year is the interest arising within the year of assessment without any deductions, which means either paid to the taxpayer or made available, for example, credited to his or her account. Note therefore, that the accruals basis is not used but instead we use a *receipts basis* for savings income.

For individuals, bank interest is usually paid net of tax. This is different for companies who always receive bank interest gross as we will see in Chapter 9.

Activity

Elizabeth opened a National Savings Bank investment account in 1991. Interest is credited on 31 December each year, interest in recent years has been:

	£
31 December, 2008	300
31 December, 2009	360
31 December, 2010	310

Determine Elizabeth's savings income assessment for 2010/11.

Feedback

The assessment is the interest arising in the tax year (i.e. the cash received basis). Hence the savings income assessment for 2010/11 is £310 as that is what was credited in the tax year.

Foreign income

Following the rewrite of the income tax legislation as ITTOIA 2005, foreign income is now generally integrated with UK income and not segregated. For foreign savings and investment income, the basis of assessment is generally the same as for savings income – i.e. it is on an *arising* basis. Where tax has been paid overseas, a credit will be allowed in working out the UK tax liability. We look at these special double tax relief rules in Chapter 12.

Taxpayers who are resident but not ordinarily resident and/or not domiciled in the UK pay tax only on the amount remitted to the UK (although see Chapter 12 for some new rules in relation to non-domiciles).

Dividend income

Dividends and other distributions from UK companies are taxed under this income category. All non-dividend distributions from UK companies (which are not specifically excluded from the general rule) are taxed as if they were a dividend to help reduce an obvious tax avoidance strategy.

As discussed in the 'Rates of tax' section above, income tax is levied on the grossed up dividend (i.e. the aggregate of the distribution received and the related tax credit). Basic rate taxpayers are subject to tax at 10% on their dividends which means that the tax credit exactly equals the tax due on the dividend so that no further tax liability arises (and therefore no tax return will be needed from these people for this income).

Note that, unlike tax on savings income, if the tax credit exceeds the tax liability e.g. if the recipient isn't liable to UK tax as their income is below their personal allowance limit, the excess is not refunded to the taxpayer (under the rules which applied before 1998, refunds of excess dividend credit were available).

Higher rate taxpayers are taxed at 32.5% on the aggregate of their dividends and the related tax credit. Like taxpayers who have had tax deducted at source they are able to use any tax credit received to reduce their total tax liability. However, this will not cover their full tax liability and they will have an extra 22.5% to pay when they do their annual tax computation (32.5% − 10% tax credit). Additional rate taxpayers are taxed at 42.5%, which means they have an extra 32.5% to pay.

Dividends from UK companies are taxed on a paid basis, whereas dividends from foreign companies are taxed on an arising basis. Some changes were made to the rules for foreign dividends from April 2008. From that date some of an individual's income in the form of dividends from foreign companies can be treated just the same as dividends from UK companies (i.e. receive a 10% non-refundable tax credit). For 2008/09 this rule only applied, however, for small shareholdings in foreign businesses (had to be less than 10% of the shares). However, this rule was relaxed from 22 April 2009 so now the level of holding is no longer a restriction and most foreign dividends can be treated this way.

Miscellaneous income

This category is used to tax annual profits or gains not falling under any other category. In particular, income from casual commissions, enterprise allowance payments, some capital sums from the sale of patent rights and post cessation receipts from a business (i.e. business income received after a business has ceased trading) are taxed under this heading. The basis of assessment is the profits or gains arising in the tax year (i.e. the *receipts* basis).

Income tax reliefs and allowances

Individuals may be able to claim tax reliefs and allowances which are deducted from their total income to give their taxable income. Look back at Thomas Lester's tax computation to see where this appears (steps 1 − 3) and the effect it has on his tax computation.

Tax reliefs and allowances can be used to serve a number of purposes. They can help particular individuals, products or services or encourage particular activities. When used in this way they are effectively a replacement to direct public expenditure and therefore can be called *tax expenditures*. Where reliefs or allowances are integral to the tax system they are called *structural reliefs*, for example, the use of personal allowances to support those on the smallest incomes in a system designed to use an ability to pay principle. Structural reliefs

133

typically exist year after year rather than appear and then disappear quickly.

The way in which tax reliefs and allowances have changed in the latter half of the last century, and the beginning of this one, offers an interesting insight into the history of family life in the UK. Tax allowances for personal circumstances (as a tool for economic welfare and redistribution) and the benefits system have intertwined throughout recent UK history to support government policies and objectives. The balance between greater use of allowances and greater use of benefits has changed significantly from benefit focus back to allowances and then back again over this period.

Tax reliefs

An income tax relief is a liability of the taxpayer of a type which income tax law allows as a deduction from the payer's total income to calculate their net income (step 2 of the tax computation).

The following payments are eligible to be treated as reliefs:

- pension contributions (for self employed people or for employed people under net pay arrangements for excess relief – see Chapter 5 for an explanation of these rules)
- loss reliefs that are chargeable against general incomes (these include, for example, trade losses of various types, some property losses if you are running a property business as a landlord, and employment losses)
- payments of eligible interest;
- copyright royalties;
- annual payments and patent royalties
- relief for patent expenses

Relief deductions at this step are only possible if there is sufficient income from which they can be taken. However, the order that is used for deducting reliefs should be one that gives the greatest reduction in the taxpayer's income tax liability where a choice exists.

Tax relief is given on reliefs at the taxpayer's marginal rate of tax. To achieve this all reliefs must be shown gross as they are entered into the tax computation and then relief will automatically be given at the taxpayer's marginal rate of tax.

The following activity illustrates how to include reliefs as step 2 in the tax computation:

Activity

Catherine has non-savings income of £15,000 and is less than 65 years of age. She makes a pension contribution that is eligible for treatment as a tax relief of £500 (gross). Calculate her tax liability for the tax year.

Feedback

	£
Total income	15,000
Less relief: pension contribution	(500)
Net income	14,500
Less: personal allowance	(6,475)
Taxable income	8,025
Tax due/liability 8,025 @ 20%	1,605.00

Payments of eligible interest

Some yearly interest payments can be treated as a relief for tax calculations. The payment of eligible interest is therefore relieved at the taxpayer's marginal rate of tax.

Examples of eligible interest that can be treated as tax reliefs are limited but include:

- *Loans to purchase plant and machinery for use in a partnership or as an employee.* The loan must be used to purchase plant and machinery for which capital allowances are available (these rules will be discussed in Chapter 7). The relief is available to partners or employees only (i.e. not to self-employed people or to corporations directly). The relief is available for a maximum of three years from the end of the tax year in which the loan was taken out. (Note that interest on loans to purchase plant and machinery is an allowable deduction for a self-employed person for tax purposes which is why they are not allowed this treatment. We will meet these taxpayers in Chapter 6 and show you how this applies to them).
- *Loans to invest in an employee-controlled company.* The loan must be used to acquire ordinary shares either before, or within 12 months of, a company first becoming employee-controlled. The

company must be a UK resident, unquoted, trading company or the holding company of a trading group. A company is employee controlled if at least 50% of the issued ordinary share capital and voting power is owned by employees or their spouses (referred to as *beneficial ownership*). If one employee owns more than 10% of the shares he or she is deemed to own 10% when testing to see if the 50% employee-controlled rule is satisfied (i.e. the rest of their shares will be treated as if not in employee ownership). If any capital is repaid the relief will be reduced.

- *Loans to invest in a partnership.* The loan must be used to either purchase a share in a partnership or introduce capital into a partnership or make a loan to a partnership to be used wholly and exclusively for business purposes. The claimant must be a member of the partnership throughout the time the interest relief is claimed. Limited partners are not eligible for this relief.

Annual payments and patent royalties

Tax relief is given at step 2 where a taxpayer makes an annual payment eligible for tax relief (such as a life annuity payment) or a patent royalty payment. Where the payment is a commercial payment, it must be made net of basic rate tax (i.e. net of 20%). Tax relief is given at the tax payer's marginal rate by including the gross sum of the payment a step 2 and adding back the tax actually withheld at step 7 (additional tax stage).

Do note, however, that copyright royalties are not treated in the same way as patent royalties. These payments are always made gross and therefore simply shown at step 2, as illustrated above for other payments eligible for relief.

Activity

How would your answer have differed for Catherine (example above) had the eligible payment she had paid been a patent royalty (i.e. it would have been paid net of basic rate tax)?

Feedback

Catherine will have paid to the patent owner during the year £400 (£500 × 80%) this time (i.e. withholding £100 as the relevant tax due on the charge). The payment must be shown gross in the Total

Income calculation and then, as tax has been withheld which really forms part of the payment, it must be added back to work out the full tax liability for the year.

	£
Total income	15,000
Less: tax relief for patent royalty	
400 × 100/80	(500)
Net income	14,500
Less: personal allowance	(6,475)
Taxable income	8,025
Tax borne (computation as above)	1,605.00
Add tax deducted on patent royalty	
500 × 20%	100.00
Tax liability	1,705.00

In this example, the total of payments eligible for relief actually paid and the income tax liability is £2,105.00 in both cases (i.e. £1,605.00 + £500 or £1,705.00 + £400). Hence Catherine's income after tax and payments is the same regardless of whether the eligible payment is paid net or gross.

While this is case for Catherine as she is a basic rate taxpayer, it is not always the case. A taxpayer actually receives relief for the payment at their marginal tax rate even though they only withhold basic rate tax on a net paid payment like a patent royalty. This means they can save money on the payment if they are a higher rate taxpayer, or have to pay extra if they are not a basic rate taxpayer.

More examples can be found on the website to illustrate the impact of tax relief eligible payments on higher rate taxpayers and taxpayers other than those paying at basic rate.

Tax allowances

Until the Second World War a person on average income did not suffer any income tax because their personal allowances were always greater than their total income. At that time a married man would have been able to claim a married man's allowance, which was substantially higher than the single person's allowance, in order to reflect the costs of supporting a wife who did not work (whether or not she actually worked – a clear tax bias towards marriage). In addition, he received further allowances if he had children. The reverse was largely not however, true for a woman who was married.

A family was seen as a single tax unit until as recently as 1990, and that unit was focused on the husband. A married woman was not entitled to a personal allowance but her husband could claim his wife's earned income relief, which was of the same value as the single personal allowance, against the family's total income. As its name suggests the relief was only available for earned income; a wife's investment income was taxed at her husband's marginal rate of tax even if she did not work. From an equality perspective this, of course, was a ridiculous situation.

Fiscal Fact

It is predicted that for 2009/10 the lowest earning 25% of the UK population will pay only 2.8% of total income tax receipts between them whereas the richest 1% will pay 24.1% between them. 11,000 people are expected to earn over £1,000,000 this year paying an average amount of tax of 36.7% on this income.

Until the 1970s fathers also received tax allowances for any children in the family. However, these allowances were withdrawn in 1979/80 and there was a compensatory increase in child benefit - which was paid each week (usually) to mothers instead. This change was welcomed by almost everyone, especially groups concerned with child poverty. It was believed that this way of making payment was more likely to benefit the children as it was paid to the mother. Child benefit was also paid regardless of the employment status of either partner, thus providing some much needed income in times of unemployment. However, many people appear to have forgotten the reasons for the transfer from allowances to benefit in the 1970s. Now the benefit is not always increased in line with inflation (in fact it has been frozen for at least two years by the Emergency Budget 2010) and there are pressure groups that campaign for the restriction of child benefit to families on relatively low incomes. The innovation of the tax credit systems under the Labour Government (as we outline later in this chapter) in part returns to the principles of the old system.

During the 20th Century there were various other steps taken that reflected the changing role of women, especially professional women, in society. One of these schemes, introduced in the 1960's, was intended to offer women some measure of privacy in their tax affairs. It enabled women to complete their own tax returns and enter into correspondence with the Revenue themselves (where previously the correspondence had been conducted via their husbands even if it had nothing to do with his tax affairs, only hers). The personal allowances available to the couple were also split between the husband and wife in proportion to their income.

From April 2000 a systematic policy of reforming many of the allowances based on personal circumstances in the tax system (including mortgage interest relief, married couples allowance etc.) has rebalanced the overall impact of this aspect of the tax system on society. As we will see, however, significant growth in the use of tax credits has occurred to replace this reduction in allowances. Tax credits have a different impact on taxpayers than tax allowances.

In this section we will now review the allowances and reliefs currently available to UK income taxpayers.

Personal allowance (PA)

Every person (whatever age they are) who is UK resident is entitled to a basic personal allowance of at least £6,475, so long as his or her income is less than £100,000. This includes children and married as well as single people. This amount may be increased if the taxpayer is old enough to get the age allowance, as we discuss in the next section. There is provision in statute for the personal allowance to increase in line with inflation each year, unless Parliament opt to waive the provision for a particular year (as the Chancellor did in fact between 2002/03 and 2003/04, and now 2009/10 and 2010/11). Increases in personal allowances benefit less well off taxpayers proportionately more than better off taxpayers, as these allowances enable a larger percentage of their income to be tax free, lowering their average rate of tax, and are therefore useful as redistribution tools. In effect, the personal allowance is like a tax free threshold, or zero rate band.

Personal allowances are only available to be used by the person who is directly entitled to them (they can't be transferred to anyone else) and they are lost if that person's income is insufficient to use the allowance in full in any particular year. They also can't be rolled forward from year to year – but a new allowance can be claimed each year of course.

The 2009 Budget announced an important change to the longstanding philosophy of everyone getting at least some tax free income, irrespective of their income levels. From April 2010, personal allowances are tapered down to zero for those with an adjusted net income more than £100,000. Adjusted net income starts with "net income" which is the total of the individual's income subject to income tax less certain deductions, for example trading losses and payments made gross to pension schemes. This is then reduced by the grossed-up amounts of any Gift Aid contributions and pension contributions which have received tax relief at source. Relief for payments to trade unions or police organisations deducted in arriving at the individual's net income is then added back to arrive at the adjusted net income.

The tapering of personal allowances for those earning over £100,000 is at the rate of £1 for every £2 earned over £100,000 i.e. you will lose all of their personal allowance when you earn over £112,950 (£100,000 + (2x£6,475)). Note however, you can't end up with a negative personal allowance so for taxable incomes, after reliefs, above this sum the personal allowance just becomes zero.

Activity

Joe's net income for the tax year is £106,728 from various sources (after reliefs but before personal allowances). What will his personal allowance be for 2010/11?

Feedback

Joe's personal allowance will be:

$$£6,475 - (1/2 \times (£106,728 - £100,000)) = £3,111$$

This is the figure you should then use in Joe's tax computation at Step 3 instead of the full £3,111. Had Joe earned over £112,950 this would be zero.

Fiscal Fact

The estimated cost to the Treasury in taxes foregone of allowing personal allowances was £52.4billion for 2009/10.

A quirk of the reduction in the personal allowances for higher earners is that people falling into this high-earning category suffer a higher than normal effective marginal tax rate on this extra income. Examine the following activity to see this illustrated.

Activity

Calculate the marginal rate of tax of a single person aged 50 with net income of £100,000 and compare it with the marginal rate of tax if they earn £8 more in the same period. What is the effective marginal rate on this difference?

Feedback

	£	£
Net income	100,000	100,008
Less personal allowance	(6,475)	
£6,475 – (100,008 – 100,000)/2		(6,471)
Taxable income	93,525	93,537

Hence an increase of £8 in total income leads to an increase of £12 in taxable income. If the marginal rate of tax in both situations is 40% (i.e. assuming the income is non-savings income), the extra £8 of income results in an extra £4.80 (£12 × 40%) of tax which is an effective marginal rate of tax of 60% (£4.80 ÷ £8).

Age allowance (AA)

This allowance is available to a person aged 65 or over at any time during the tax year instead of the ordinary personal allowance. The age allowance is £9,490 for 2010/11 (unchanged from 2009/10). If the person is 75 or over in the tax year then this rate is increased to £9,640 (unchanged from 2009/10).

In much the same way as the adjustment of personal allowance for higher income taxpayers, if the person's adjusted net income exceeds £22,900 (unchanged from 2009/10) the age allowance is reduced by half of the excess (i.e. by £1 for each £2 of income over £22,900). However, unlike the loss of personal allowances for those earning over £100,000 adjusted net income where their personal allowances can be completely eaten away eventually, the age allowance is only lost down to a minimum of the level of the normal personal allowance (i.e. down to £6,475).

This is referred to as the 'age allowance trap', but means that the minimum allowance anyone 65 or over will receive is the same as the regular personal allowance so that no-one receives less than this amount.

Also note that, in computing the age allowance, an individual who dies during the tax year in which they would have reached their

65th or 75th birthday is treated as if they had reached that age during the year.

Activity

Calculate the current personal allowance available to each of the following taxpayers:

Name	Date of birth	Adjusted net income
Paul	10 January, 1946	£14,000
George	1 December, 1939	£30,000
John	18 April, 1935	£23,500

Feedback

Paul

Paul will be 65 on 10 January, 2011, and so will be able to claim the age allowance of £9,490

George

George will be 71 on 1 December, 2010 and so is entitled to a maximum age allowance of £9,490. His total income exceeds £22,900 however, and so the maximum allowance will need to be restricted. The allowance would be restricted to £5,940 (£9,490 –½ (£30,000 – £22,900) however, this would take George below the normal personal allowance so he is only restricted to the normal level of £6,475.

John

John will be 75 on 18 April, 2010. His age allowance will be a maximum of £9,640 however, his total income exceeds £22,900 and so the age allowance is reduced to £9,340 (£9,640 –½ (£23,500 – £22,900).

Fiscal Fact

The estimated cost to the Treasury of giving higher age-related allowances was £2.6billion for 2009/10.

As we saw with the removal of personal allowances for high income taxpayers, a similar quirk of the reduction in the age allowances for higher earners is that people falling into this higher-earning category also suffer a higher than normal effective marginal tax rate on this extra income. Examine the following activity to see this illustrated.

Activity

Calculate the marginal rate of tax of a single person aged 70 with net income of £24,000 and compare it with the marginal rate of tax if they earn £8 more in the same period. What is the effective marginal rate on this difference?

Feedback

	£	£
Net income	24,000	24,008
Less personal allowance		
£9,490 – (24,000 – 22,900)/2	(8,940)	
£9,490 – (24,008 – 22,900)/2		(8,936)
Taxable income	15,060	15,072

Hence an increase of £8 in total income leads to an increase of £12 in taxable income. If the marginal rate of tax in both situations is 20% (i.e. assuming the income is non-savings income), the extra £8 of income results in an extra £2.40 (£12 × 20%) of tax which is an effective marginal rate of tax of 30% (£2.40 ÷ £8).

Like the personal allowance, the age allowance is non-transferable and cannot be rolled forward (or backward) to be used in alternative years.

Fiscal Fact

In 2009/10 it was estimated that 4.04million people aged 65 and over will pay at least some tax on their incomes from a total income tax paying population of 29.3 million people.

Blind person's allowance (BPA)

This allowance is given to taxpayers who are registered as blind under their local government rules. The allowance is £1,890 for this tax year (unchanged from 2009/10) and is available in addition to their personal allowance. Unlike the personal and age allowances however, if the blind person has insufficient income to use the allowance in full the excess may be transferred to their spouse or civil partner so they get a larger tax free allowance than they would otherwise.

Tax reductions

After calculating the tax borne (step 5) a taxpayer may be entitled to various tax reductions that must be then taken into account. These could include:

- tax reduction for married couples and civil partners
- venture capital trust (VCT) reduction
- enterprise investment scheme (EIS) reduction
- community investment tax (CIT) reduction
- relief for interest on a loan to purchase an annuity
- qualifying maintenance payments

Most of the details of computing entitlement to these reductions are beyond the coverage of this book but we will illustrate the first of these for you as one example you may come across. All others are handled in the tax computation in the same way.

Married couples' and civil partners' tax reduction

A tax reduction for married couples (called the Married Couples' Allowance – MCA), along with a number of other tax reducers, ceased for most people from 6 April, 2000. The MCA has now become the Married couples' and civil partners' tax reducer with the addition of the civil partnership legislation. The only people still able to claim this tax reducer are those where at least one partner born before 6 April, 1935. For anyone in this category the reduction is restricted to 10% of the annual amount available for the reduction of £6,965. This can be limited, however, down to the minimum of £2,670 if the husband's total income exceeds £22,900. Note that with the existence since 1990 of independent taxation, the wife's total income is usually not taken into account for limiting this reducer. This situation is only different for marriages or civil partnerships entered into after 5 December 2005 where now the reducer is automatically applied to the higher earning spouse/partner.

This limiting process works in the same way as illustrated above for the Age Allowance with any excess left of the income restriction after reducing the age allowance to be deducted from this tax reducer (subject again to the minimum amount of £2,670 being available irrespective of the individual's total income level).

Any entitlement to this tax reducer can be shared between partners in any way they wish. If one partner earns an income and the other does not it can therefore be beneficial for the total tax they have to pay for the earning partner to receive this reduction.

For all other individuals the MCA was replaced by a new tax credit system from April 2003.

Examples to illustrate the use of this tax reducer, and its limitation, can be found on the student section of the website if you require them for your course, or for other purposes.

Tax credits

As part of a swing back to more benefits focussed policies, the previous Labour Government systematically removed various tax allowances that used to be given to taxpayers as additional taxable income deductions to reflect their personal circumstance and needs.

Initially some of these lost allowances were replaced by a series of tax 'reducers', which were closely related to the tax allowances they replaced (i.e. given to the same people largely) but were used to provide only fixed tax deductions rather than variable deductions. These reducers, as we saw with the married couple's allowance, were deducted from the tax due computation as a fixed sum, rather than from taxable income, as personal and age allowances are. The effect of deductions from taxable income varies depending on the type of income and levels of income of the taxpayer, as lowering taxable income has the effect of lowering the tax due at the highest marginal rate - which varies for each taxpayer based on their personal income profile. Using tax reducers instead of tax allowances therefore means all taxpayers who are awarded the deduction are entitled to the same basic deduction irrespective of their income level and type.

The Labour Government opted to give people tax 'credits' instead of via tax allowances or reducers. These credits are not however, treated the same as tax credits we have already discussed that are associated with dividends from UK companies (the name 'credit' is used in a different way here confusingly). These tax credits are direct tax reductions either received as part of your wages or salary or paid to you directly.

Two main tax credits of this kind now exist in the UK; the Child Tax Credit and the Working Tax Credit. To qualify for these credits you must be over 16 and usually live in the UK. Other restrictions also can apply as we illustrate below.

To see the current rates for each element of these credits see the Allowances table in Appendix A.

We will now look at these credits and how they work in more detail.

Child Tax Credit

The Child Tax Credit is for people who are responsible for at least one child (under 16 or until the first September after that child's 16th birthday) or a young person (aged 16-18 and in full time education for at least 12 hours a week and studying for A levels, NVQ level 3 or below or Scottish Highers).

This credit is paid directly to the person who is the main carer for the child or children. The payment made/reduction the carer is entitled to is made up of two elements; the family element and the child element. The family element is payable to any family responsible for a child. A higher rate applies if at least one of the family's children is aged less than 1. The child element is received for each child within the family. A higher rate is paid for any child with a disability (known as the disability child element).

Fiscal Fact

The estimated cost to the Government in 2008/09 of providing child tax credits and working tax credit was expected to be £5.5 billion. On 1 April 2009, 6.1 million families (representing 10.1 million children) were tax credit recipients of either CTC or WTC or via equivalent child support through benefits.

Working Tax Credit

Working Tax Credit was also introduced from April 2003 to replace the interim tax credits called Working Family's Tax Credit and Disabled Persons Tax Credit. This credit is for people who are either employed or self-employed who:

- usually work 16 or more hours a week;
- are paid for this work; and
- expect to work for at least 4 weeks.

They must also be:

- aged 16 or over and responsible for at least one child ; or
- aged 16 or over and disabled; or
- aged 25 or over and usually working at least 30 hours a week.

If you are in a couple (whether married or not) and both of you are working 16 or more hours week you must choose which one of you will receive the credit – you do not get two credits if you both work.

Extra credit can be available if you, or your partner, are disabled or if one or other of the claimants are over 50 and are returning to work after a period not in employment/self-employment. Further help for child care costs can also be available as part of this credit.

The amount of credit you will receive depends on your annual income. To check the exact amounts that can be received see the HMRC website where a simple entitlement calculator can be found. (http://taxcredits.direct.gov.uk)

Gordon Brown, the then Chancellor, changed the process for receipt of this credit in the 2004 Budget. This payment, previously received via the payroll of the recipient, now is paid directly by HMRC, as the Child Tax Credit is.

Tapering and entitlement

Tax credits taper away (i.e. are reduced) at a rate of 39% (unchanged from 2008/09) for each £1 of income received by the family over an annual threshold level. This threshold is set at £6,420 for 2010/11 (unchanged from 2009/10) or £16,190 (£16,040 for 2009/10) if no working tax credit applies.

The ordering of the elements of the tax credits is important when undertaking a tapering calculation. It is applied first to working tax credit then child care element and then child tax credit.

The family element and baby additions to child tax credit however, are tapered differently using a second threshold (£50,000 for 2010/11 – unchanged from last year) and using a withdrawal rate above the threshold of 1 in 15.

Entitlement to both working tax credit and child tax credit is reviewed annually. By 30 September each year claimants must have lodged their renewal claims or they will lose entitlement to their tax credits. If any personal circumstances affecting the computation of the tax credits change in the year (e.g. a salary change) a claimant must tell HMRC within three months. Any overpayments received by the claimants must be repaid and quite heavy penalties are charged in addition to this to try to ensure people own up to changed circumstances quickly.

Computation of tax credits does not form part of most introductory tax courses however, if you wish to see how this is done an example can be found in the student section of the website.

Donations to charity

Since 6 April, 2000 all gifts to charities by individuals, however small and however regular, have been eligible for tax relief at the basic rate (i.e. 20%) under the Gift Aid rules (i.e. you pay them after deducting tax at the basic rate). All that is necessary to operate this scheme is that the donor gives to the charity a Gift Aid declaration (a simple form, or even an oral statement) saying that they are giving money to the charity, which the charity can then use to get back the tax paid by the taxpayer related to the donations from HMRC. Charities can actually reclaim 22%- even though the taxpayer only pays the donation net of 20%. This is as a result of a transitional agreement between charities and the Government for the three years following the reduction in the basic rate of tax effective on 6 April 2008.

The rules that apply when companies donate to charities are different to the rules for individuals. (We will look at the rules for companies in Chapter 9).

Gift relief is also available for donations to community amateur sports clubs as well as to registered charities. The system for receiving the relief is identical to donations to charities.

The Budget 2010 extended Gift Aid relief to certain EU based charities for gifts made by UK taxpayers. The same computation rules apply as for donations to UK based charities.

To be eligible for tax relief on charitable donations the donor must have paid at least the amount in tax on their taxable income that HMRC will be asked for by the charity. Either income tax or capital gains tax will suffice to cover the tax. Where a taxpayer does not do this HMRC will ask the taxpayer to pay back the money the charity claims from them.

Fiscal Fact

In 1990/91, income tax repayments totalling £474 million were made to charities. In 2007/08 total repayments totalled £918 million (of which £896 million was via gift aid). Budget Report 2010 reported that since 2000 £5.7billion has been reclaimed by charities via the Gift Aid scheme.

Tax relief is given to the taxpayer when making Gift Aid donations by increasing their basic rate band by the gross amount of the gift. This process ensures that relief is given at higher rates to taxpayers who are higher rate taxpayers (as their higher rate band starts at a higher taxable income). To illustrate how this works in practice, if you made a £100 donation to the charity, your payment will actually be worth £125 (£100 × 100/80) to the charity as it is able to reclaim the basic rate tax you will have paid on this donation (£25). They can't however, get back 40% even if you are a higher rate tax payer.

A charitable gift paid under these Gift Aid rules does not in fact need to appear in the taxpayer's tax computation however, adjustments to that computation may need to be made under certain circumstances, such as for higher rate taxpayers. The following activity shows you how this may occur.

Activity

In this tax year Andrew, an employee who is less than 65 years of age, makes a Gift Aid donation of £1,000 (net) to his favourite charity. What would his income tax computation be if his only income was non-savings income of:

a) £29,000
b)   £7,000
c) £48,000

Feedback

Andrew's payment, grosses up to £1,250 (£1,000 × 100/80). The charity collects the extra £250 (plus the extra 2% transitional relief) from HMRC via the Gift Aid scheme. What we need to do is to check that Andrew has paid enough basic rate tax to cover the repayment to the charity.

a)

	£
Earnings from employment	29,000
Less personal allowance	(6,475)
	22,525
Tax due:	
22,525 @ 20%	4,505.00

Nothing else needs to be done in this case as Andrew's income easily covers the reclaiming of the £250 from HMRC. He also is a basic rate taxpayer so no higher rate band adjustment is needed. In such a situation you would not normally need to list this gift aid payment in Andrew's tax computation as it will have no impact on his calculation.

b)

	£
Earnings from employment	7,000
Less personal allowance	(6,475)
	525
Tax due:	
525 @ 20%	105.00

In this case Andrew is not paying enough tax to cover the £250 that the charity reclaims directly (before the extra relief) on his donation. He will therefore need to pay another £145 (£250 – £105) to HMRC as extra income tax.

c)	£
Earnings from employment	48,000
Less personal allowance	(6,475)
	41,525
Tax due:	
(37,400 + 1,250) @ 20%	7,730.00
(41,525 – 38,650) @ 40%	1,150.00
	8,880.00

In this case as Andrew is a higher rate taxpayer his basic rate band needs to be extended by the gross amount of his charitable donation so that he receives relief for this payment at the higher rate. This means £1,250 extra of his income is taxed at 20% instead of at 40% as would normally be the case, saving him £250 (20% × £1,250) in tax. This, added to the tax withheld on this net donation means he gets relief at 40% on the whole donation (£250 + £250 = £500 = 40% × £1,250).

One quirk of this scheme is that, if the donor to the charity is entitled to receive age-related allowances, their net income is deemed to be reduced by any Gift Aid payments they may have made as part of computing their adjusted net income. This deduction is only for determining their age allowance however; it does not actually reduce their total income in the computation (look back to the Age Allowance section above for more on this).

With effect from April 2004 taxpayers can nominate a charity on their self-assessment form to receive any tax repayment they are due from HMRC who will pay these sums directly to the nominated charity on behalf of the taxpayer.

Gift Aid donations made on or after 6 April, 2003, do not necessarily have to be dealt with in the tax year in which the payment is actually made. Provided a claim is made before the tax return for that year is presented to HMRC, a taxpayer can opt to 'carry back' their payment so that it is treated as if it had been paid in the previous tax year. This will then affect the taxpayer's tax computation for that year, not for the current year.

Another form of tax relief for gifts to charities is the *Payroll Giving Scheme*, set up in the Finance Act 1986. The scheme applies to employees who pay tax under the PAYE scheme and whose employer runs a scheme, which is approved by HMRC, which operates by withholding sums from them. Where this scheme operates the taxpayer can instruct their employer to make the donation to the charity of their choice before PAYE deductions meaning tax relief at their marginal rate is automatically applied then.

National insurance contributions

As we saw in Chapter 1, national insurance was introduced in 1948, largely in order to provide for retirement pensions, unemployment and sickness benefit. Much of the UK's social security system continues to be paid for, albeit indirectly now, by these payments made by the working population and by their employers.

Initially national insurance was payable at a flat rate by both employees and employers. The intention was for the payment to represent an insurance payment rather than to tax people on the basis of an ability to pay. Thus the burden of the tax fell heaviest on the lowest paid, hence the tax was regressive.

Over the next few years the amount which each contributor had to pay increased as social security expenditure grew. By 1961 the flat rate contribution was seen to be too great a burden on the lowest paid and earnings-related contributions were introduced. By 1975 the entire national insurance contribution was earnings related. Although national insurance is now assessed on a percentage basis there is an upper limit above which employees only pay 1% extra national insurance instead of the full amount. This arrangement means that the tax is still regressive, i.e. taxpayers on low incomes can pay a greater percentage of their income in national insurance contributions than taxpayers on higher incomes.

Until 2000/01 neither employee nor employer national insurance contributions were payable on most benefits in kind (i.e. benefits received by an employee related to their employment but not paid in cash e.g. goods, use of a company car for private purposes and so on), making provisions of benefits in kind a relatively tax efficient form of remuneration. Now employers (but still not employees at present) are required to pay contributions (called Class 1A) on most benefits in kind they provide to their employees. For example, if an employee has a company car and/or fuel for private motoring the employer must pay Class 1A contributions, at 12.8% of the value of the car and fuel benefits. (We will consider how these values are calculated in Chapter 5.)

National insurance contributions are collected by HMRC (http://www.hmrc.gov.uk/nic). The PAYE system is used to collect these payments for employees, but direct payment to HMRC must be made by those who are self-employed, or others not in employment but making contributions.

A record is kept of an individual's national insurance contributions during their lifetime and gaps in contributions can lead to a reduction, or even loss, of benefits in some circumstances, so National Insurance still has some characteristics of an insurance scheme.

Unlike income tax, which is charged on a taxpayer's expected income for the year and collected as income is received under PAYE, national insurance contributions are calculated according to the employee's income for the payment period only. Hence, if a taxpayer works for a number of months during the year and then has no income for the rest of the year, he or she may be able to reclaim some of the income tax already paid so that the correct amount is paid over the whole year, however, no repayment of national insurance contributions already made in the year is possible. UK income tax is termed a cumulative tax system because unused allowances accumulate; national insurance is a non-cumulative tax because payments are only due in periods when payment thresholds are exceeded, irrespective of other earnings in the year.

There are four main classes of national insurance contributions:

- Class 1 are paid by both employees, (primary contributions), and employers, (secondary contributions);
- Classes 2 and 4 are paid by the self-employed;
- Class 3 payments are made on a voluntary basis, by those who, while in work and earning money, would otherwise not pay enough contributions via other classes to entitle them to a state pension when they retire.

Various personal circumstances can affect contributions paid, for example, you don't pay if you are under 16. If you are in full time education between the ages of 16-18, you get credited these years as if you'd paid them. If you are a full time child carer, and therefore don't work in paid employment, you can claim home responsibilities protection which reduces the number of years needed to pay contributions for to get a full state pension.

Once employees are over pensionable age (currently 60 for women born before 5 April, 1955 and 65 for all men and women born since 6 April 1955) they are not required to make further national insurance contributions. However, the employer's contributions, (at the non-contracted out rate) are still payable.

National insurance contributions for the current year are as follows (rates are unchanged from the previous year, but the thresholds have risen after being fixed last year):

Class 1

Pay per week (per annum)	Employee	Employer
£110.00 (£5,715) or less		
– employee lower earnings threshold	0%	0%
£110.01 – £844.00 (£5,715 – £43,875)		
– employee's lower earnings threshold to upper earnings limit (UEL) main primary percentage	11%	12.8%
Over £844.00 (£43,875)		
– additional primary percentage	1%	12.8%

If the employee is a member of a contracted out occupational pension scheme (either salary related or money purchase type – see the next chapter and the website for more details on various types of pensions and their tax implications) employee contributions on earnings reduces to 9.4% (i.e. a reduction of 1.6%) but only on earnings between the lower earnings threshold and a point called the upper accrual point (or UAP). The UAP is a new threshold introduced in 2009/10 and is set at £770.00 per week. If the employee earns more than the UAP, their contributions rise again to 11% until they reach the UEL (£844.00 per week). £770 per week was the UEL for the 2007/08 year and the UAP is scheduled to stay at this level for future years. The effect is to increase the amount of contributions for contracted out employees without changing the rates of tax payable.

Similarly, the employer's contribution is reduced by 3.7% (i.e. to 9.1%) if the employee has a pension scheme based on their final salary or by 1.4% (to 11.4%) if the pension scheme is a money purchase scheme. The employer's reductions also only apply up to the employees UAP when the normal rate of 12.8% becomes applicable again.

Class 1 contributions are based on the employee's gross pay without deducting pension contributions.

Because directors may be able to influence the timing of their remuneration package, their Class 1 national insurance contributions are always calculated on an annual basis for this class of employee.

Activity

Calculate the primary and secondary Class 1 contributions of:
* Matthew, who earns £90 per week and is not contracted out.
* Mark, who earns £200 per week and is contracted out on a final salary scheme.
* Luke who earns £500 per week and is contracted out on a money purchase scheme.
* John, who is a company director, earns £400 per week, receives an annual bonus of £10,000 in the year and is not contracted out.
* Paul, earns £895 a week and contracted out on a money purchase scheme

Feedback

Matthew

Matthew does not pay primary Class 1 contributions because his earnings are less than the employees' lower earnings threshold of £110. Similarly his employer does not pay secondary Class 1 contributions because his earnings are below the employer's earnings threshold of £110.

Mark

Mark pays (£200 – £110) × 9.4% = £8.46 per week and his employer pays (£200 – £110) × 9.1% = £8.19.

Luke

Luke pays (£500 – £110) × 9.4% = £36.66 per week and his employer pays (£500 – £110) × 11.4% = £44.46.

John

For company directors, the annual earnings threshold is £5,715.
John receives an annual income of £30,800 (£400 × 52 + £10,000) so is below the employee's UEL and only pays annual primary Class 1 contributions of (£30,800 – £5,715) × 11% = £2,759.35.
His employer will pay (£30,800 – £5,715) × 12.8% = £3,210.88.

Paul

Paul's weekly salary exceeds the £844 per week UEL level and the £770 UAP level so he will pay:
(£770 – £110) × 9.4% + (£844 – £770) × 11% + (£895 – £844) × 1%
i.e. £62.04 + £8.14 + £0.51 = £70.69.

His employer will pay:
(£770 – £110) × 11.4% + (£895 – £770) × 12.8%
i.e. £75.24 + £16.00 = £91.24.

If someone has more than one employment, they are liable to pay primary Class 1 contributions for each job, subject to a maximum annual contribution. This maximum contribution is based on formulae that take into account how much was earned in each employment (i.e. to balance how much should be paid at the regular rate and how much at the extra 1% rate). Any overpayments made can be reclaimed at the end of the year. To avoid the need for repayment, a taxpayer can also claim for a deferral of payment on some of their contributions. Any extra due at the end of the year will then need to be settled directly with HMRC.

Class 1A

Benefits in kind (non-cash rewards related to an employment or office) are usually not chargeable to Class 1 contributions for employees; however, they do create a Class 1A contribution for employers (not employees). The value used to determine how much the contribution will be is the same as calculated for the employment income benefit in kind on which the employee pays income tax. We will see how this is determined in the next chapter in more detail. Class 1A contributions are paid at the same rates by employers as for normal Class 1 contributions (i.e. 12.8%).

Class 2

The self-employed pay national insurance contributions of £2.40 (unchanged from 2009/10) per week for the current tax year provided their annual profits are at least £5,075 (unchanged from 2009/10). If it is below this level they are exempted from these contributions.

Class 3

Anyone can pay voluntary contributions of £12.05 per week (unchanged from 2009/10) to maintain rights to some state benefits (particularly the state pension) that they might otherwise lose, for example, because their earnings are too low to pay other contributions.

Class 4

In addition to Class 2 and maybe Class 3 contributions, the self-employed pay 8.0% (unchanged from 2009/10), of their profits between lower and upper limits, which are £5,715 (unchanged from 2009/10) and £43,875 (unchanged from 2009/10) for this tax year. As for employees, profits above the upper limit are subject to a further 1% charge (called the additional Class 4 percentage).

For Class 4 national insurance contribution purposes profits are the taxable profits under the trading income rules less trading losses and any interest or annual payments to do with the business but not already deducted in working out trading profit. Personal allowances are not taken into account for Class 4 contributions. The calculation for this amount due usually forms part of the tax return. Class 4 contributions are normally paid at the same time as the income tax on their business profits. This normally means it is paid in two instalments (on 31 January in the tax year and on 31 July following it) with a third payment due the following 31 January if any balancing payment is due.

Activity

Simon, who is self-employed, has taxable income from his business of £20,000 for this tax year. Calculate his national insurance contributions for the tax year.

Andrew, who is also self-employed, has taxable business income of £45,000 for this tax year. Calculate his national insurance contributions for the tax year.

Feedback

Simon
Simon will pay Class 2 national insurance contributions of £124.80 (£2.40 ×52) as his earnings are over the small earnings exception limit for the year, and Class 4 contributions of £1,142.80 (8% × (£20,000 –£5,715)).

Andrew
Andrew will also pay Class 2 contributions of £124.80. His Class 4 contributions will be £3,064.05 (8% × (£43,875 – £5,715) + 1% × (£45,000 – £43,875)).

Benefits received

A full basic pension is paid to individuals who, for at least nine out of every ten years of their deemed working life, have paid at least the equivalent of the lower earnings limit contribution for the whole year, or 52 Class 2 or Class 3 contributions. The deemed working life is from 16 to 65 for a man and from 16 to 60 for a woman, although the retirement age for men and women will be equalised in due course.

Some credits for contributions are available however, if you are registered as unemployed, are receiving job seekers' allowance, are unable to work through incapacity or disability, are in receipt of a carer's allowance or if you receive maternity allowance. People between 16 and 18 will also automatically receive credits if they do not pay enough contributions but this is not the case for anyone in full time education over the age of 18 (i.e. while you are at University you only get the years of contribution counted if you actually make national insurance payments).

Taxpayers making Class 1 national insurance contributions at the higher rate are eligible to receive job seekers' allowance and earnings related (i.e. second) state pension which Class 2 and Class 4 contributors are ineligible to receive.

Impact of national insurance contributions

We saw in Chapter 3 that national insurance contributions are levied on earned income in addition to income tax. This provides a distortion in the tax system between earned income and investment income. A taxpayer with taxable income of less than £43,875 will have a marginal rate of tax of 33% on earned income but either 10% or 20% on unearned income (depending on whether it is dividend or savings income). This anomaly may encourage shareholder/directors of family businesses to draw relatively low salaries and pay dividends in order to reduce national insurance contributions. This question is discussed more fully in Chapter 11 as it is (at least in the eyes of the current Government) a common tax planning strategy.

Basic income tax planning points for couples

If one married partner's marginal rate of tax is lower than the other's it is tax efficient to shift income from the higher rate payer to the lower rate payer as this will save some of their combined tax bill. There are broadly two ways of doing this. Firstly, investments held in the higher rate payer's name could be transferred to the lower rate payer. (There is no capital gains tax liability arising from a transfer between spouses as we will see in Chapter 8). These investments might include shares in a family business, in which case dividends paid on the shares would be taxed at the lower rate.

The second opportunity for shifting income from the high rate taxpayer to the low rate taxpayer is where a business is being run by one or both of the spouses. For example, it is possible to pay a wage to a spouse who also does work for the business e.g. deals with telephone calls and paperwork (although beware – this must be a fair wage for the work actually done or it may be challenged by HMRC). The alternative is to set up in business as a partnership in which case the other spouse can be allocated a share of the profits. A similar strategy can be adopted with adult children with low marginal rates of tax if they also help run the business. If a partnership is established then it is the responsibility of the partners to agree the profit-sharing ratio and HMRC will not challenge such an agreement. However, if a relative is employed by a sole trader, partnership or company then HMRC may wish to be satisfied that the payment is wholly and exclusively for the purpose of trade. In the case of *Copeman v Flood* (1941) a farmer employed his son and daughter as directors of the company and they each received a salary of £2,600. The son was aged 24 and had some business experience but the daughter was only 17 and unable to carry out the duties of a director. Both did undertake some duties for the company but it was held that the entire salary was not an expense incurred wholly and exclusively for business purposes. The Commissioners were asked to decide how much of the payments should be allowable based on the actual work carried out by the son and daughter. This established the principle still in operation now over 60 years later.

Further discussion of income tax planning can be found in Chapter 11.

Summary

This chapter has provided you with the income tax framework which will enable you to apply the legislation discussed in later chapters.

In order to calculate an individual's tax liability it is necessary to undertake a number of steps:

- Identify each source (component) of income for a taxpayer.
- Use the income tax rules to determine the basis of assessment for each component of income.

- Determine the income tax rules which are used to calculate the taxable income for each component of income.
- Calculate the income which is assessable and determine any reliefs and allowances from that income which are allowed for tax purposes. This will enable you to calculate the taxable income from each component of income.
- Now you can calculate the tax liability of a taxpayer.

You should now be able to review the example personal tax computation for Thomas we presented at the start of this chapter to check that you understand how the figure of Tax Payable has been reached.

Some possibilities for simple tax planning for families were also briefly discussed in this chapter.

You are now able to progress to the next three chapters, which build on the foundations which have been laid in this chapter to provide you with further details of how to perform personal tax computations. In turn they expand on the rules for taxing property income, income from employment and pensions, and income from self-employment (trading income).

Project areas and discussion questions

1. Until April 2005 the various categories of income tax were called Schedules, each of which had sub-sections to them called cases. These names have disappeared now for individuals as part of a process of re-writing the Income tax laws. Check out the role of the Tax Law Rewrite Committee who has been undertaking this work. What is their motivation for doing this work?

2. The addition of 1% extra NIC on earnings of employees over the UEL was controversial as it marked a move away from an upper cap on this charge/tax. Is this a fair way to raise extra money by the Government?

3. Does it make sense continue to have a separate income tax charge and national insurance contributions payment requirement? Review the 2006 Budget consultation for the options outlined by the UK Government.

4. Should unearned income also be subject to National Insurance contributions?

5. Is the tax credit system (e.g. Working Tax Credit and Child Tax Credit) a more or less effective way to give targeted income tax reductions than previous methods?

6. Does having a separate unit of taxation (i.e. everyone pays their own tax liability rather than combining this into family tax bills as was the case before the 1990's) make this a fairer (more equitable) system for all? Are there losers from charging income tax this way?

Quick quiz

(Each of the following taxpayers are under 65 years of age unless otherwise stated.)

1. Benson has pension income of £24,300 for the year and is 65 years of age. What is his tax liability?

2. Candice has saving income of £15,000 (net) and received UK dividend income of £2,500. What is her net tax payable?

3. Angela has non-saving income of £22,500 for the year and pays a patent royalty of £200 (net). What is her tax liability?

4. Dominic has earnings from employment of £20,000 and no other income. He makes a charitable donation of £500 under the Gift Aid scheme during the year. What is his net tax payable?

5. Erica is 76 years of age and has pension income of £10,500 and savings income (net) of £500 for the year. What is her net tax payable?

6. Frank has net trading income of £32,500 for the year and receives UK dividends of £3,000. What is his net tax payable? What national insurance contributions are due on this income?

Questions

Question 1 Sam is under 65 years of age and has the following income:

	£
Salary (PAYE deducted of £4,200)	26,000
Building society interest (net)	1,600
Dividends (from UK company)	2,700
Qualifying charitable donation (gross)	880

Required: : Calculate Sam's income tax payable for the tax year.

Question 2 Janet and Dave, both 35 years old, have lived together for two years. Janet earned £35,000 during 2010/11 on which she already paid £6,500 via PAYE. She also received an annual bonus of £3,000 in August 2010 for the year ended on the previous 31 March. She received income of £3,500 (net) in interest payments from a Building Society account in her own name. She also received £1,000 winnings from her premium bonds. Janet owns a cottage in North Yorkshire which she let from 1 October, 2010 at an annual rent of £8,000 payable quarterly in advance. Her allowable expenses on the property for the year were £1,000.

Dave earned a salary of £34,500 in the tax year 2010/11 from which his employer deducted £5,725 in PAYE. He also had some investment income of £3,000 (net) from a bank deposit account and received dividends of £6,760 from UK shares.

Required: Compute Janet and Dave's income tax payable for 2010/11.

Question 3 Calculate the national insurance contributions due by both the employee listed below, and their employer.

a) Peter earns £550 per week. He is not contracted out.

b) Alan earns £240 per week. He is contracted out using a money purchase scheme.

c) Kath's earnings in the year are as follows (all for the same employer and all earned evenly over the periods given). She is not contracted out.

Jan – April	£1,500 per month
May – Aug	nothing was earned
Sept	£350 only was earned
Oct – Dec	£1,200 per month

d) Chris is self employed. His adjusted profits for tax purposes (i.e. his trading profit) for 2010/11 were £27,600.

(Answer can be found in the lecturers' section of the website.)

Question 4   Zach is employed and has the following income and expenses:

	£
Employment income	45,000
Building society interest (net)	2,000
National Lottery win	5,000
Qualifying charitable donation (gross)	2,000

Required: Calculate Zach's income tax payable for the year.

(Answer can be found in the lecturers' section of the website.)

 Further test questions for this chapter to test your knowledge can be found in the student section of the website at:

http://www.taxstudent.com/uk

Further reading and examples

Andrews, R., Combs, A. & Rowes, P. (2010), *Taxation: incorporating the 2010 Finance Acts*, Fiscal Publications: Birmingham.
   – use this book for many other examples to further develop and test your knowledge of this chapter's contents. See http://www.fiscalpublications.com/rowes/2010

5 Taxing employment and pension income

Introduction

In Chapters 1 and 4 you read about the Schedular system, and new income tax components that we now use in place of Schedules, that had been the foundation of how we tax income for nearly 200 years. You learnt that to calculate the tax liability from the receipt of income it is necessary to identify the tax rules under which the receipt is taxed. In Chapters 6 and 7 you will study the trading income rules, which are used to tax income from trades, vocations and professions (i.e. collectively – trading income) as well as the property income rules.

In this chapter you will learn about the detail of the other key tax rules – namely employment and pension income under Income Tax (Earnings and Pension) Act, 2003 (ITEPA). We will not consider the other categories of the Income Tax (Trading and other Income) Act 2005 (ITTOIA) in any more detail than was given in Chapter 4 as you already know all the basics on these components for the level of knowledge we are aiming to give you in this book.

At the end of this chapter you will be able to:

- understand the tax treatment of employment income, including benefits in kind, and calculate an individual's taxable income from employment:
- outline the rules which relate to pension contributions

Income tax on employment earnings and pensions

This chapter examines the tax rules relating to employees. Since employees form a majority of the UK's working population the regulations which apply to the taxation of employees are clearly very important.

Employment earnings are defined as "any gratuity or other profit or incidental benefit of any kind obtained by the employee if it is in money or money's worth". This will therefore include any bonuses an employee may receive, tips from customers if working in the kind of business where this occurs, and also any non-cash payments received (called *benefits in kind*). In general, earned income is taxed in the year of receipt, i.e. on a receipt, not an accruals basis (although pensions and job-seekers allowance are taxed on an accrued basis).

Employment or self employment

It is not always clear whether an individual taxpayer working in conjunction with someone else is in fact employed by them (working *for* them) or is self-employed (working *with* them). This distinction matters for tax purposes as it will determine whether the taxpayer is taxed using trading income rules or the employment earnings rules. The total tax the taxpayer will pay on their earnings will vary, sometimes significantly, based on how they are classified.

To determine this classification an important consideration is the contract that describes the working relationship. If it is a contract *of* service, this would often indicate employment, and the taxpayer will be taxed under employment income rules as an employee. If it is a contract *for* services then this would often indicate a self employed relationship and the taxpayer will be allowed to pay tax under trading income rules. As the latter usually results in lower income tax and national insurance bills, taxpayers usually try to achieve trading status if they can.

A simple examination of the contract title alone is of course not usually sufficient and the content of the contract will need to be examined to look for the real relationship that is in existence. For example parts of the contract may indicate:

- who has control in the relationship,
- who provides the equipment,
- whether further work must be accepted by the taxpayer,
- whether the "employer" must provide further work,
- who is responsible for providing other staff to help the taxpayer,
- who bears the financial risk involved in the contract,
- who benefits from efficient management of the contract,
- whether the taxpayer can choose when to work on the contract.

This list is illustrative, not exhaustive, and HMRC may be interested in other aspects of a contract in some circumstances. However, these are the key features most used and will give you the idea of how to approach this classification task. If the taxpayer appears to be suitably in control of the relationship, providing their own equipment, hiring their own staff, bearing the risk of the contract but benefiting from managing it well, and so on, then the relationship is a proper self-employed relationship. If the balance favours the grantor of the contract, then it is likely the taxpayer will be classified as an employee instead and taxed as such, irrespective of what those involved might prefer.

In recent years HMRC has examined more closely the range of occupations which are taxed under the employment income rules. For example, many individuals who work in television in the past were able to operate their relationships with their "employers" as if they were self-employed. In many more cases than used to be so they are now considered to be employees and therefore taxed under employment income rules instead of trading income.

The taxation of so called 'personal service companies' has also been caught in this trap. These are where individuals set up companies with themselves as the only employee and with their "employer" as their only client so as to benefit from being taxed as a company rather than as an employee. There are special rules dealing with personal service companies (the IR35 rules) which we consider in Chapter 11.

Activity

While you are reading this chapter and undertaking the activities you might like to try and identify the reasons for HMRC's tactics in wishing to have more people taxed under employment income rules rather allowing anyone who wants it to be taxed under trading income rules.

We will look again in the tax planning chapter (Chapter 11) at the implications for a taxpayer's tax bill of the classification as employee or self employed.

If you want to explore further the various factors HMRC will consider in determining employment versus self-employment status you can now use an Employment Status Indicator tool on HMRC's website. This tool asks you various questions, similar to those we have just been discussing, and then it will give you an indication of what the likely employment status is based on the facts your provide. This is a useful guide as to how HMRC are likely to view you.

Basis of assessment

Pensions and job-seekers allowance are taxed on the accruals basis and benefits in kind are taxed when they are provided. However, in general, employment earnings are taxed on the receipts basis, that is, they are taxed in the tax year in which the date of the receipt falls.

For all employees, other than directors, the date of receipt is deemed to be the earlier of the date on which payment is made and the date on which there is an entitlement to payment. This legislation is intended to prevent employees from transferring earnings, such as bonuses, to a tax year in which their marginal rate of tax is lower.

Activity

When might a taxpayer's marginal rate of tax be likely to fall?

Feedback

There are several possible reasons for a fall in a taxpayer's marginal rate of tax. These are most likely to be related to hours they work, or to changing tax rate bands or allowances. Firstly, he or she might suffer a drop of income, or an increase in allowable deductions, which reduces his or her highest rate of tax by dropping then into a lower income tax band. This might happen if, for example, they change their terms of employment to a part-time basis.

Secondly, since 1979 there has been a generally downward trend in income tax rates (in fact, the new 50% rate introduced in Budget 2010 was one of the first increases to rates of personal income tax in many years). In years where rates fall, anyone in the bands where rates drop will benefit from a lower marginal rate of tax. The same principle applies if tax bands increase while the taxpayer's income doesn't change as much. If the taxpayer is on the bottom edge of a band, increases in that band starting point could move them into the lower band thus dropping their marginal rate of tax to that of the lower band. This would also occur if tax allowances increase for those whose income then falls within the new allowance limits.

There are additional restrictions on the date of a receipt for tax purposes if the employee is a company director who is likely to be in a position to influence when the payment is to be received. Directors' earnings are taxed in the tax year which contains the earliest of the following dates:

- the date of receipt as determined by the above rules for all employees;
- the date when the payment is charged in the company's accounting records;
- the end of the company's period of account in which the amount arose provided that it had been determined by then; or
- the date on which the amount is determined if it is after the end of the company's period of account.

Allowable expenses

Allowable expenses are the deductions that a taxpayer can subtract from their income to compute their taxable income. There are two basic rules:

1. the employee must be obliged to incur and pay the expense as the holder of the employment, which means that it is the job itself that is important, not the preferences of the person doing the job. An expense will therefore only be deductible if every holder of the particular job would have to incur it; and
2. only expenses which are *wholly, exclusively and necessarily* incurred in the performance of the duties of employment will be allowable deductions. 'Wholly and exclusively' means that if an expense has more than one purpose, e.g. partly private, then it will not be deductible.

The second rule includes a 'necessary' element (which is not required for trading income deductions as we will see in Chapter 6). In practice this means it is often difficult to claim expenses as a deduction from employment income because 'necessary' is difficult to prove. Indeed one judge in 1953 described the wholly, exclusively and necessarily requirement as 'notoriously rigid, narrow and restrictive'.

Some trade unions and associations have negotiated special allowances on behalf of their members, to help employees with overcoming this rule in practice. These are typically for specialist equipment, such as safety equipment that is genuinely necessary to carry out their jobs. For example, if you are in the agricultural trade you can claim a fixed deduction of £70 annually for specialist clothing and upkeep of your tools. If you are in the food industry this is £45 (these deductions are, of course, only available to workers who have to buy specialist clothing or upkeep tools to do their jobs – they will not be available to other workers in these trades). However, in other cases you may need to negotiate with HMRC if you wish to get deductions from your employment income.

There is a substantial amount of case law which is used to identify expenditure which is an allowable deduction for the purposes of employment income computations. For example, in *Brown v Bullock* (1961) the employee, a bank manager, was required by his employers to join a London club. Even though a case could perhaps have been made that this expenditure was wholly and exclusively used for business (not private) purposes, his subscription was held not to be an allowable deduction because it was not considered to be necessary for the performance of his duties, despite his employer's wishes. Therefore, all three parts were not satisfied.

In *Lupton v Potts* (1969) a solicitor's articled clerk was not able to claim the costs of his examination fees because the expenditure was held not to be incurred wholly and exclusively in the performance of his duties.

In another case, the House of Lords disallowed the cost of newspapers bought by journalists arguing that buying and reading the newspapers was preparation for work rather than part of the performance of their duties. There are many other examples of similar case law.

Some expenditure is however, specifically allowed as a deduction from employment earnings. This includes:

- contributions to an approved pension scheme;
- subscriptions to professional bodies and learned societies listed by HMRC, provided they are relevant to the duties of the employment;
- payments to charities under a payroll deductions scheme (as we discussed in Chapter 4);
- expenses incurred in performing duties and reimbursed by the employer (within limits) and
- capital allowances on plant and machinery if provided by the employee – rather than, as is more usual, their employer (see Chapter 7).

Fiscal Fact

The estimated cost to the UK Treasury of allowing professional subscriptions to be tax deductible is £80 million for 2009/10. Much more significant however, is the cost of making contributions to approved pension schemes tax deductible – this is estimated to be £19,700 billion for 2009/10

In practice, most of the expenses you incur as an employee that would be 'wholly, exclusively and necessarily' needed for your job will be paid for by an employer. The employer will reimburse these costs to the employee and deduct them as an allowable trading expense as part of their own income tax, or corporation tax computation. In this situation the employee will have to declare this reimbursement as income received and then seek a deduction against their enlarged income for expenses incurred. This prevents abuse of the expenses system through employers reimbursing employees more than actual expenditure incurred. In some cases large employers negotiate a *dispensation* for their employees with HMRC so that reimbursed expenses can just be ignored by the employee. This, of course, involves some checking by HMRC of the appropriateness of the employers' expenses payment rules to ensure there is no abuse.

Travelling expenses

There are special rules dealing with travel expenses, which are sometimes incurred by an employee. These will often be paid for by the employer and where this occurs, the amount of allowance or reimbursement is included as income for the employee and the actual cost of the journey will then be deductible. Travel expenses that are not reimbursed by the employer may be deductible to the employee.

There are two issues here. The first concerns the nature of the journey, and the basic rule is that ordinary commuting (travel to and from your place of work) and private travel (unrelated to your work duties) does not qualify for relief. The second concerns the amount of expense that can be allowed as a deduction. We will look at these two issues in order.

Allowable journeys

It is important to be able to establish where you work (according to the tax rules) to know when you are travelling to get there (not deductible expenses) and when you are travelling 'for' work (usually deductible expenses).

Examples of 'on the job' travel that qualifies for relief include:

- From a permanent place of work to visit a client and back;

- Where the travel is a normal part of the employee's job, for example a service engineer who moves from place to place throughout the day; and

- Travel to a temporary workplace such as a client's office, even if from home, but only so long as it is because of the nature of the job and not just for the employee's convenience.

Because of the complexity of travel related costs as tax deductions, and concerns over potential abuses that may occur, the rules on employees' travel and subsistence expenses were changed in 1998 to distinguish 'ordinary commuting' (which is not deductible) from other deductible travel. Ordinary commuting is defined as travel between home and a permanent place of work. So travel to a temporary place of work will not be ordinary commuting and on the face of it will be eligible for relief.

This raises the question of what is a permanent place of work. As a general rule it will be somewhere where the employee attends regularly to perform the duties of the job. A temporary place of work on the other hand will be where an employee attends for only a limited amount of time.

However, to prevent abuse of the 'temporary' place of work exemption, a rule is needed describing how long a place of work can be temporary for tax purposes before becoming considered a permanent place of work instead. If an employee is required to work to a significant extent at a place for a continuous period of more than 24 months, this place will be considered to be a permanent place of work. HMRC considers 'significant extent' to be at least 40% of the employee's time. So, if an employee spends at least 40% of his or her time at a particular place over a period of more than 24 months, there is no relief for the cost of the travel to and from that particular place as it then becomes part of ordinary commuting.

An employee may not have a normal place of work but may have a normal *area* in which they work. An example might be a district nurse who is required to cover a particular area but lives outside it. In this case the whole area would be considered to be the normal place of work and so costs of moving around in this area would not be deductible.

What if an employee doesn't have a permanent place or area of work? For example, 'site-based' employees have no fixed place of work, but are required to perform duties at several sites by their employer. These employees are allowed to set the full costs of travelling to and from sites against their employment income. They can also obtain relief for subsistence expenses when staying at a site.

As you can see, this area of allowable expenses can be difficult to apply in practice. Attempt the following activity to see if you have grasped the basics.

Activity

Consider the following situations, drawn from HMRC Guidance on employee travel expenses. Will relief for the cost of travel be available?

    (a) Dermot's employer sometimes requires him to attend his permanent workplace outside of normal hours, for example, on the weekend.

    (b) Doris has worked for 5 years at her employer's head office in Warrington. She is sent by her employer to perform duties at a branch office in Wigan for 18 months.

    (c) Ellery is employed as a financial adviser in Brighton. His employer sends him to an office in Bournemouth for one day a week over a 10 months period. He travels to Bournemouth directly from his home in Hastings.

Feedback

(a) No relief is available for Dermot because the journey is classified as 'ordinary commuting' i.e. between home and a permanent workplace, even though his employer requires him to be there after hours.

(b) Relief is available for the full cost of Doris' travel between home and the temporary workplace in Wigan (i.e. because her time there is less than 24 months).

(c) Ellery is entitled to relief for his travel to Bournemouth because he has gone there for a temporary purpose. He does not expect to spend more than 40% of his time there, nor does he expect to be going there for more than 24 months.

The amount of the relief

Having decided that a journey is eligible for tax relief by deducting the cost from the employee's employment income, the second task is to work out how much is deductible. As a general rule, the full cost of the travel will be deductible, regardless of the amount of allowance or reimbursement the employer pays. The cost of travel includes subsistence costs such as accommodation and meals that are attributable to the travel. It also includes car parking expenses, but not things like private phone calls, newspapers and laundry costs.

Activity

Consider the following situations, also drawn from HMRC Guidance on employee travel expenses. How much will each employee be entitled to deduct?

(a) Mary has to travel on business. Her employer pays a travel allowance to cover the cost of a plane fare. Mary travels by train instead, which is cheaper.

(b) Mathew receives payment from his employer to cover the cost of a hotel, but instead decides to sleep in his car.

(c) Mercy has to travel on business and receives a travel allowance from her employer to cover the cost of a standard rail ticket. She decides to travel first class.

Feedback

(d) Mary is taxable on the full payment from her employer, but can only claim relief for the cost of the train ticket.

(e) Mathew is taxable on the full amount received from his employer and cannot claim any relief because he hasn't incurred any expenses.

(f) Mercy is taxable on the full allowance from her employer, and relief is available for the cost of the first class ticket, even though this is more than the amount paid for by the employer. It is the actual cost of the travel that is allowed as a deduction.

Using your own car

We have explored the general rules for allowing travelling expenses as tax deductions, but what happens when the employee uses his or her own car? The question of whether the journey qualifies for relief is the same, but there are special rules for working out the cost of the journey, which could be quite complicated. To make the process simpler, the government has set out some rates of tax free allowance so that the employer can pay an amount to the employee to cover the cost of using his or her own car without creating a tax liability. The maximum rates payable before a taxable benefit will arise are given in the table below. These are called 'approved mileage allowance payments' or AMAPs. If they are exceeded both income tax and national insurance contribution liabilities (Class 1) will be created. The miles given are for *business miles* driven in a year (i.e. any private miles paid for by an employer will always be a taxable benefit).

If the rate of allowance paid by an employer does not exceed these amounts, then no tax is due on these payments and neither are any national insurance contributions required.

Type of vehicle	Rate
Car or van	40p per mile on first 10,000 business miles in the year
	25p per mile on excess over 10,000 miles
Motorcycle	24p per mile
Cycle	20p per mile

Employees using their own cars who do not receive any mileage allowance payments from their employers, or who receive less than the prescribed levels, will be able to claim tax relief on the difference as an allowable deduction against their employment income.

A rate of up to 5p per mile can also be paid (tax free) to the driver of the car if they carry a fellow employee as a passenger, provided they are also travelling on business. This rate will apply to passengers in both private cars, as discussed here, but also for company cars used for business travel. This allowance, however, cannot be reclaimed as a deduction if the employer does not pay the full amount – unlike the regular mileage rates.

Activity

Fred uses his own car when travelling for his employer. During the tax year he drove 8,600 business miles. How would Fred's tax computation be affected if his employer paid him the following rates for his business miles:
  a)   30p per mile
  b)   45p per mile.
  c)   4p per mile for the 2,000 miles he drove with a fellow employee in his car.

Feedback

a)   This payment is below the mileage allowance rate Fred is entitled to. He would receive £2,580 (30p × 8,600 miles) from his employer but could have been paid £3,440 (40p × 8,600 miles) before a taxable benefit arose. He is able to claim a deduction of the difference (£860) against his employment income.

b)   This payment is above the mileage allowance rate and so a benefit in kind is created. Fred will have to add £430 ((45p × 8600 miles) – £3,440) to his employment income and pay tax on this at his marginal rate of income tax.

c)   This rate is below the tax-free sum allowed and therefore no benefit would arise. He would receive £80 therefore tax-free. He is not able to claim the extra 1p per mile, however, as a deduction against his income.

Currently HMRC is engaged in a consultation on, amongst other things, how to make the process of approved mileage rates more environmentally sensitive.

We consider the situation where the employer provides a car for the employee to use later in the chapter under the heading of Benefits in Kind.

Other allowable expenses

There are a number of expenses other than travelling and the specific items listed earlier that may be deductible if they meet the *wholly, exclusively and necessarily* requirement. We will look at some of these in this section.

Phone calls

The cost of business phone calls made using a private phone are deductible, but usually no line rental for that phone can be claimed unless it can be proven to be solely dedicated to work related use.

Work clothing

An employee cannot claim the cost of work clothes, unless they are specialist or protective. In *Hillyer v Leeke*, the High Court denied the taxpayer a deduction for clothing that was 'ordinary civilian clothing...of the sort that is also worn off-duty'. In a 2010 case, the BBC television news presenter Sian Williams attempted to claim the cost of clothing, laundry and hairdressing as a deduction. The Tribunal held that she was not entitled to the claim, even though her work meant that she had to appear well dressed and groomed. The clothing was considered to be 'ordinary civilian clothing'.

Working from home

If you work from home by choice, for your own convenience, then the costs will not be deductible. If you are required to work from home by your employer, perhaps because you need access to facilities that are not available at your normal place of work, you will usually be able to claim a part of your additional domestic bills (e.g. heating, lighting etc.).

Education and Training

As a general rule, training is considered to be in addition to, rather than part of, the duties of employment and so not deductible. In HMRC v Banerjee [2009] EWHC 62 (Ch) however, the High Court found that the cost of training courses paid for by Dr Banerjee was deductible. This was because it was a condition of her contract of employment with the NHS that she had to undertake continuous training which meant that in this case it was a part of the duties of the job.

The area of allowable deductions from employment income is complex due to a lack of clear guidelines from legislation and case law. The 'necessary' rule, not present for sole-traders, causes many problems for employees seeking to claim tax deductions, often probably legitimately, for costs they incur in working for their employers but not fully reimbursed by them. Where many of these would be allowable for deductibility if the employee was instead self-employed, it seems a little unfair that they cannot claim these same costs just because of their employment status is different. This rule is unlikely to change in the near future however, because of the substantial cost it would imply to the Government to be more generous for employee claims for deductions.

Benefits in kind

In addition to receiving a wage or salary, many employees receive other benefits because of their employment. These so called *benefits in kind* may include things such as subsidised lunches, non-contributory pensions, private health care, sports facilities, child care, company cars etc. There is an endless list of such benefits in practice, however, tax treatments for them all must be determined to create an equitable tax system. Any benefit received as part of your employment must therefore be given a value that can be included in employment income calculations and be taxed accordingly. When computing a taxpayer's employment income all taxable benefits must be added to their wages or salaries in the tax computation. You have already briefly met the issue of national insurance contributions on benefits in kind in Chapter 4. In this section we will consider the income tax issues.

The tax treatment of some benefits in kind is dependent on the status (income level or office held) of the taxpayer while the tax treatment of other benefits in kind is independent of the status of the taxpayer. For most benefits, the general rule is that for status independent benefits, employees are assessed on the *cash equivalent* of the benefit. For status dependent benefits it is *actual cost of provision* that becomes the benefit. This however, becomes the marginal cost if the benefit is provided to non-employees as well.

The cash equivalent is taken to be the amount that the benefit could be sold for once the employee has received it. This rule tends to operate in favour of the employee because benefits in kind may have either no resale value, for example, a travel season ticket, or a low resale value, such as the second-hand value of a suit or uniform.

There are three levels of assessability to income tax for benefits in kind:

1. Benefits assessable on all employees;
2. Exempted benefits and
3. Benefits only assessable on higher paid employees and directors.

We will first consider those benefits which are assessable in the same way on all employees then go on to review the other two types.

1. Benefits assessable on all employees

This section reviews benefits in kind that all employees will be assessed on when they receive them irrespective of their status as an employee.

Vouchers

Any employee who receives cash vouchers, credit tokens or exchangeable vouchers as part of the reward for their employment will be assessable on the cost to the employer of providing the benefit. However, luncheon vouchers with a value of up to 15p per day are not subject to tax in the hands of the employee (this was a somewhat more valuable concession when it was first introduced!).

Accommodation

If an employee is provided with accommodation by an employer (that is not *job related* as defined below), the employee will be assessed for tax on the *annual value* of the property less any contributions made by the employee to the employer for the accommodation. The annual value is taken to be the rent that "might reasonably be expected to be obtained on a letting of the accommodation from year to year". This amount assumes the employee pays all the taxes, rates, bills etc associated with living in the property, but the employer pays to maintain the property. In practice, however, the annual value is typically taken to be the rateable value of the property, if this value is known, or a value estimated by HMRC if the property does not have a rateable value. The rateable value is the value used to compute the 1970s rating valuation for that property (i.e. the old valuation system is used from before Council tax was introduced).

If the property is not owned by the employer, but is simply rented by the employer for the employee, the employee will be assessed on the higher of the annual value and the actual rent paid by the employer.

If the accommodation either cost over £75,000 when acquired (or, if acquired more than six years before it was first provided to the employee, its market value on the date it was first provided to the employee was over £75,000), the accommodation is classified as "expensive" and a further benefit is charged to the employee. This is equal to the excess of the cost of providing the accommodation over £75,000 multiplied by the *official rate* of interest. The official rate is the interest rate given by the Treasury for various tax related charges – particularly loans (this rate varies periodically, but the latest rate can be found by looking at the 'Rates and Allowances' section on the HMRC website. For the purpose of this book, for simplicity, we will use 5%). The cost of providing the accommodation includes the costs of any improvements undertaken before the start of the tax year as well as the purchase price of the property. If the property is only available for part of the year, the benefit arising is reduced proportionately.

If the accommodation provided is *job related* then there is no assessable benefit in kind on the employee (although if the employee is a company director, then they may still incur a tax liability as the rules for directors can be more stringent). Accommodation is job related if either:

- the employee is required to live in the accommodation for the proper performance of their duties, for example a caretaker; or
- the employment is of the kind where it is customary to provide accommodation or the accommodation is provided to enable the better performance of the employee's duties, for example a clergyman, farm worker, pub manager or policeman; or
- the accommodation is provided for reasons of security.

If living accommodation is provided because of a person's employment, then alterations and additions to the accommodation which are of a structural nature, or repairs which would be required if the property were leased under the Landlord and Tenant Act 1985, are not assessable benefits.

Activity

George is provided with the use of a flat in Birmingham as part of his payment package for a new job. The flat cost George's employers £150,000 and is brand new. George is a management consultant and the flat allows him to live in the city close to his office. George pays all the bills associated with the flat's running and makes a £200 per month contribution to his employer for the use of the flat. The flat has an annual value of £6,000. What is the accommodation benefit in kind assessable on George, assuming an official interest rate of 5%?

Feedback

George's use of the flat would not be considered job-related, it is just a benefit he receives that makes his job easier to perform, but it is not necessary to enable him to do his job (he could live elsewhere and still do the job as well). He will therefore have the value of this benefit added to his employment earnings when his tax bill is calculated. The value to be added is:

	£
Annual value of the property	6,000
Additional value	
(£150,000 – £75,000) @ 5%	3,750
Less George's contribution	
£200 × 12	(2,400)
Benefit in kind	7,350

Additional accommodation related benefits in kind may also need to be paid if George earns over £8,500 per year as we will see below.

2. Exempted benefits in kind

Some benefits in kind are specifically excluded from assessment to tax in the hands of all employees. This section explores some of the most common of these.

Sports facilities

In-house sports facilities for employees do not have to be treated as a benefit in kind and are not therefore liable to tax.

Gifts

Employees are also not assessed on the benefit of any small gifts which are provided to them by third parties so long as the following conditions are met:

- the gift was not provided, or procured, by the employer or persons connected to the employer, (Note: a list of who are *connected persons* can be found in the Glossary); and
- the gift was not provided in recognition of services which have been, or are to be, performed.

If these conditions are met, the most an employee can receive tax-free by way of a gift from a third party is £250 p.a.

Parties, functions and meals

Tax free benefits can also be received by employees for annual parties or functions provided by the employer. There is a limit of £150 per head for the exemption to apply. The figure of £150 is not an allowance; if the expenditure exceeds this amount then the full amount will be assessable, not just the excess over £150.

Meals which are provided in the employer's canteen for the staff generally are not an assessable benefit. A special rule provides that meals provided to employees on designated 'cycle to work' days are also exempt.

Long service awards

Employees are not assessable on non-cash long service awards provided that they have worked for the organisation for at least 20 years, have not received a similar award within the past ten years and the cost to the employer of the award is no more than £50 per year of service. If a long service award is made in cash, it is taxable.

Suggestions

Rewards for suggestions are taxable, but there is an extra-statutory concession that exempts awards provided there is a formal suggestions scheme which is open to all employees and all of the following conditions are met:

- the suggestion relates to activities which are outside the scope of the employee's normal duties;
- if the award is more than £25 it is only made after a decision has been taken to implement the suggestion;

- awards over £25 either do not exceed 50% of the expected net financial gain during the first year after implementation or do not exceed 10% of the expected net financial gain during the first five years after implementation; and
- awards over £25 are shared equitably between any employees making the suggestion.

If the award exceeds £5,000 the excess is always taxable.

Relocation costs

If an employee has to move for work reasons the costs of relocation paid for by the employer up to a maximum of £8,000 are not taxed as a benefit in kind. If expenses of more than £8,000 are paid, the employee will be assessed on the excess over £8,000 as a benefit in kind. Note that it is not necessary for a taxpayer to sell a house in order to qualify for this relief.

Child care

A nursery place at a workplace nursery is not a taxable benefit. All other forms of childcare provision, including cash or vouchers, provided by the employer are generally taxable. From 6 April, 2006, however, employees can receive up to £55 per week (or £243 per month) free of tax and NICs for childcare so long as approved childcare providers are used.

Working at home

Employers are able to pay £2 per week, tax free, towards the additional costs employees incur when working at home – for part of the time or entirely. These costs do not need to be supported by evidence of actual costs incurred, as is usually required, to be paid as there is a concession from HMRC for up to these amounts to be paid tax-free. If amounts over £2 per week are paid, however, they can still be tax free if evidence of actual incremental expenditure resulting from working at home is provided.

Others

Free car parking space provided to employees is also a tax free benefit, provided it is at, or near, the employee's place of work.

Counselling or welfare services generally provided to employees is tax free.

No taxable benefit arises with benefits such as air miles or loyalty points that employees receive from employer's expenditure provided this is part of a publicly available scheme and not just given to them as an incentive, bonus etc.

Broadband internet access is a tax free benefit if provided by your employer for work purposes if there is no realistic way of determining any private usage of this benefit. (Note, however, the cost of a computer to use this access is a chargeable benefit – as we will discuss further below).

3. Benefits in kind assessable on higher paid employees and directors only

In addition to benefits in kind taxable on all employees and exempted benefits that no-one has to pay tax on, 'higher paid employees' and directors may be required to pay extra tax on some benefits in kind if they receive them. This section examines these.

The income tax legislation does not actually use the term 'higher paid employee', but we will use it for convenience. A higher paid employee is one whose employment earnings are £8,500 a year or more. Employment earnings for this purpose include not only direct cash payments in the form of salaries, commissions and fees etc. but also reimbursed expenses and benefits in kind, valued as if the taxpayer were a higher paid employee (other than the benefit of receiving a loan to purchase a home). This brings many lower paid employees into this category if they also get some benefits in kind.

This level of income might not sound to you like a 'higher paid' employee particularly. However, it is a level that was set some years ago (1979/80 to be precise when it rose from only £2,000) and has not been altered since, despite inflation and general rises in salaries and wages. Given the national minimum wage for those over 21 is £5.73 per hour (from October 2008), this means all full time employees should be paid more than this threshold – and therefore these rules now effectively apply to all full time employees and potentially, many part time employees also.

A director is any person who either acts as a director or on whose instructions the directors are accustomed to act, other than a professional advisor.

If a director owns 5% or less of the company's share capital and is either a full-time working director or the company is either non-profit-making or established for charitable purposes, he or she is not subject to these rules (unless he or she is also a higher paid employee).

All of the rules of this section apply to both higher paid employees and directors as we have just described, however, we will only refer to employees in our explanation to make the description simpler.

General rule – cash equivalents

The general rule for benefits in kind received by higher paid employees is that if because of their employment, an employee or members of the employee's family or household, receive any benefits, they are to be treated as part of the earnings and are chargeable to income tax under the employment income rules. The amount to be taxed as the benefit is the cash equivalent of the benefit (i.e. an amount equal to the *cost* of the benefit) less any contribution made by the employee to those providing the benefit.

The cost for this purpose is not defined in the tax legislation, but in *Pepper* v *Hart* (1992) the House of Lords found that cost should mean the marginal cost to the provider (i.e. rather than other possible costs such as the average cost) in circumstances where the benefit is also available to the non-employees. In this case the benefit received was school education provided to children of the taxpayer. The taxpayer successfully argued the value of the benefit was only the marginal cost of providing for an extra child and not the full cost of that place. This will usually have the effect of substantially lowering the value of the benefit to be taxed. Of course, if it is not possible to directly attribute any costs to the provision of the benefit to the taxpayer then there will be no assessable benefit.

Assets used by employees

If an asset is provided for the private use of a higher paid employee or a director then the assessable benefit is the annual value which is the greater of:

- 20% of the market value of the asset when first provided as a benefit to an employee, and
- the rent paid by the employer if the asset was rented.

If ownership of the asset is subsequently transferred to the employee the assessable benefit is the greater of:

- the excess of the current market value of the asset over the price paid by the employee; or
- the excess of the market value of the asset when it was first provided to the employee less the total of the annual benefits assessed on the employee so far for that asset over the price paid by the employee.

Activity

In the tax year ended 5 April 2007, Edward was provided with the use of a home entertainment system which cost his employer £3,000. During the year ended 5 April, 2011, Edward purchased this system from his employer for the agreed market value of £700. What is the amount of Edward's assessable benefit for 2010/11?

Feedback

The assessable benefit is the greater of:

1. The excess of the current market value of the asset over the price paid, in this case nil; or
2. The market value when first provided, less assessable benefits, less price paid i.e.:

	£
Market value when first provided	3,000
Less Assessable benefit (3 × 20% × £3,000)	(1,800)
Less price paid by Edward	(700)
Benefit in kind	500

Cars

One of the most important benefits in kind, in terms of the number of employees receiving it at least, is the company car. All higher paid employees and directors are assessed on a benefit if they are provided with a company car.

Company cars became widespread during the 1970s for a number of reasons. The most important was the wages legislation in force at the time which attempted to limit increases in wages. Providing cars to some employees was a way of increasing the rewards to employees despite this legislation. Providing company cars to employees was extremely tax efficient at the time. The employer could deduct the full cost of providing the car and the employee suffered relatively little tax on the benefit. At that time the provision of a company car also did not then lead to an increase in the national insurance contributions of either employees or employers.

During the 1980s and 1990s, successive Chancellors have turned their attention to the taxation of company cars and over a number of years the tax on this benefit has increased very substantially. While there may still be some limited tax advantages for some employees which encourage the use of company cars, the benefits are lower now than in the past. Employers are now required to pay national insurance contributions on company cars (under Class 1A – as we saw in Chapter 4) although employees are still not currently required to pay national insurance contributions on this benefit.

From 1994/95 all car benefits were assessed on their list price, rather than actual cost. This was to prevent abuse of the benefits in kind systems when car manufacturers quoted a higher retail price and then offered discounts. The actual benefit in kind was then calculated using a formula that was affected by the business miles driven in that tax year, the age of the car and any contributions made to the capital cost of the car by the employee.

A major rule change related to calculating the benefit of using a company car was introduced in April 2002. The new rules are based upon the CO_2 emissions of the car, rather than how it is used. The rates for 2010/11 are as follows:

CO_2 g/km	Taxable % Petrol	Diesel	CO_2 g/km	Taxable % Petrol	Diesel	CO_2 g/km	Taxable % Petrol	Diesel
120	10	13	160	21	24	200	29	32
125	15	18	165	22	25	205	30	33
130	15	28	170	23	26	210	31	34
135	16	19	175	24	27	215	32	35
140	17	20	180	25	28	220	33	35
145	18	21	185	26	29	225	34	35
150	19	22	190	27	30	230	35	35
155	20	23	195	28	31	235	35	35

In order to use this table of course you need to know the CO_2 emissions level of your company car is. For all cars registered after 1 January, 1998 these can be found either:

- on the cars registration document (V5)
- from the dealer
- in car magazines (for current models only usually)
- on the Society of Motor Manufacturers and Traders' website http://www.smmt.co.uk/co2/co2search.cfm

For cars registered before 1 January, 1998 the following rates apply:

Engine Capacity	Rate
up to 1400 cc	15%
1401 – 2000cc	22%
over 2000cc	32%

Once you have found the emission level of your car you simply look up the percentage rate in the above tables to determine the benefit in kind for the year. The CO_2 level is rounded *down* to find the correct percentage. This percentage is then multiplied by the list price of the car when it was new, to give you the annual benefit in kind that must be added to the car driver's employment income.

A new rate was introduced with effect from 6 April 2008 for cars referred to as QUALECs i.e. qualifying low emission cars. Where a car's CO_2 level is exactly 120g/km or lower, the rate to be used becomes 10% instead of the usual minimum rate of 15% (or 13% for diesels). For cars emitting between 1g/km and 75g/km of CO_2 this rate fell to 5% from 6 April 2010.

If the car is supplied with accessories that were not standard on the car when new then the cost of these must be added to list price of the car in this computation (unless the cost of the accessory is less than £100 in which case it can then be ignored).

In the above table the rates are given for petrol and diesel fuelled cars. If however, your car runs (or can run) on other fuels you may now get a reduction on these rates as part of the current Government's strategy to encourage the use of more environmentally friendly fuels. The chart below illustrates these reductions (full details can be found on the HMRC website). Reductions showed are based on the petrol fuel percentages in the above table.

Fuel Type	Reduction
Electric	6%
Hybrid Electric	3%
Gas only	2%
Bio-ethanol (e85)	2%
Bio-fuels (with separate CO_2 emissions rating)	2%
Bio-fuels – other	0%

The rates calculated by this system produce benefit in kind amounts for full tax years. If you do not have the company car for the full year these calculated rates are pro-rated proportionately for the part of the year the benefit is actually received. For example, if you only had a company car for 6 months of the tax year then only half of the annual benefit sum these tables gives you is taxable.

This system is designed to benefit people driving newer, lower emissions cars. It is designed to achieve the opposite of the old system which benefited older, higher business mileage cars.

If an employee must make a contribution to the employer towards the running costs of the car (not including insurance costs) this is deducted from the annual charge. However, if an employee makes a contribution towards the capital cost of the car, this is deducted from the list price for the purposes of this computation (i.e. affects each subsequent year's benefit computation then as long as the employee has use of that car). The maximum capital contribution that be used in this way however, is capped at £5,000 even if the actual contribution made by the employee was higher than this.

Fiscal Fact

According to a Revenue press release, the reform of company car tax has saved between 0.15 and .2 million tonnes of carbon, which is equivalent to around 0.5% of the CO_2 emissions from all road transport.

Fuel benefit

Where the employer provides a car for the employee to use then, in addition to the charge for the car itself, if the employee receives any fuel for private use, he or she is also taxed on the benefit of the fuel.

If the employee makes a contribution to the cost of the fuel which has been used, but does not reimburse the entire cost, the assessable benefit is not reduced. Hence, if the employee is going to make a partial contribution it is more tax efficient if he or she contributes to the cost of the car rather than to the cost of the fuel as such a payment would then reduce the overall benefit charge.

What cost should be repaid to ensure that the private fuel is fully reimbursed to avoid this fuel benefit charge? HMRC helpfully publish guidance figures to help an employer ensure they collect enough reimbursement. The current guidance (from 1 June 2010) proposes 12p (petrol), 11p (diesel) and 8p (LPG) per mile for cars of 1,400cc or less, 15p, 11p and 10p for cars between 1,400cc and 2,000cc, and 21p, 16p and 14p respectively for cars of more than 2,000cc. Lower rates may be acceptable however, so long as evidence of actual costs is then provided. (Note – these rates are reviewed twice a year currently so you should check them up on the HMRC website to confirm the current rates – search for 'advisory fuel rates').

For any reimbursement to count in preventing the fuel benefit falling due it must also be paid in the tax year (i.e. by the 5 April at the end of the tax year) or a short time after this date or the payment may not be counted as a recent case has illustrated (see *Impact Foiling Ltd v HMRC* 2006).

Fiscal Fact

Budget 2008 stated that the number of company car drivers getting free fuel for private use has dropped by approximately 600,000 since 1997 in part due to these various measures being introduced.

If the employee does not repay all the fuel costs related to private mileage, then to determine the fuel benefit, an emissions based charge, using the same table on the previous page, came into force on 6 April, 2003. Unlike car benefit itself (which multiplies the emissions level percentage by the car's new list price when it was new) the same relevant percentage is instead multiplied by a set monetary amount set for each tax year to go into the employee's tax computation. This amount is set at £18,000 for 2010/11 (£16,900 for 2009/10).

If an employee opts out of free fuel during the year, only the proportion (pro rata) of the annual charge will be assessable as a benefit. If the employee subsequently opts back in to receiving fuel paid for by the employer then they will have to pay the full annual charge – with no discount allowed for the opted out period.

Activity

Sarah, a higher paid employee, had the use of a 1600cc, petrol engined company car throughout the tax year. The car was first registered on 1 January, 2004, has an emissions rate of 196g/km of carbon dioxide and had a list price of £14,000 new (no accessories are attached to the car). Sarah contributed £50 per month towards the running costs of the car and £30 per month towards part of her private fuel. Sarah drove 18,000 miles in the year of which 70% is business mileage. Determine the benefit assessable to Sarah.

Feedback

Unlike the rules before April 2002, the number of business miles driven, age and engine capacity of the company car(s) used in the tax year no longer affect the car benefit in kind calculation.

The assessable benefit is therefore:

$(14{,}000 \times 28\%) - (£50 \times 12) = £3{,}320$

As Sarah only makes a partial contribution towards her private fuel a taxable benefit arises for this also. This will equate to £18,000 × 28% = £5,040. No reduction is given for her contribution towards her private fuel as it is not all paid back. Sarah's total benefit in kind cost related to her car is therefore £8,360 (£3,320 + £5,040). This should be added to her employment income for her tax computation.

It was very actually expensive for Sarah not to reimburse all her private fuel. If she had paid back the guidance price of 15p per private mile driven, she would have paid 15p × (30% × 18,000) = £810, or £67.50 per month. Not paying this extra £37.50 a month (£67.50–£30) therefore created a total of £4,230 (£5,040 – £810) as extra benefit which she could have avoided. She'd be better advised next year to make sure she pays back all her private fuel (unless she drives a lot more private miles).

Both of the charges for company cars given in the tables above are for full years. When the car is unavailable for part of the tax year then these rates fall pro rata to the time in the year the car was actually available to the taxpayer. Unavailable times obviously include before and after the car is available to the taxpayer, but also if the car is being repaired for at least 30 consecutive days during the year this period can also be deducted from the benefit computation. (Note that no reduction is made if you are unable to drive the car, only if the car can not be driven).

Activity

Jane, a higher paid employee, has an 1800cc, diesel engined company car which was first registered in 2004 when it had a list price of £24,000 and produces emissions of 162g/km of carbon dioxide. Fifty per cent of Jane's mileage was for business purposes and she makes no contributions towards the cost of the car or her private fuel. Her car has no accessories attached. Calculate Jane's car related benefits assessable in the tax year if:

a) Jane has the use of the car for the whole year and drives a total of 4,800 miles during the year.

b) Jane has the use of the car only from 5 October 2010 and she drives 4,800 miles between 5 October 2010 and 5 April 2011.

c) She has the car for the whole year but has a satellite navigation system fitted as an accessory to the car (not standard) costing £250.

Feedback

(a) As for Sarah above, Jane's business miles and the age of her car is not relevant to the computation.

The assessable car benefit is £24,000 × 24% = £5,760.

Her fuel benefit for the year will be £18,000 × 24% =£4,320

(b) As she only had the car for six months her car benefit rate is halved to £2,880. Note that this calculation should be done to the nearest day. Jane's fuel benefit will also be halved to £2,160.

(c) The cost of the accessory must be added to the list price of the car in the computation as it is more than the £100 minimum that can be ignored, therefore the car benefit calculation will change to add 20% of the cost of the accessory (20% x £250) to become a total of: £24,250 × 24% = £5,820.

Special rules for vans

For vans, as distinct from motor cars, special rules apply. These rules changed substantially on 6 April, 2007 to significantly increase the benefit rate for vans.

If an employee is provided with a van in which they are allowed to do private motoring, he or she will be taxed on a flat rate charge of £3,000 for the year. As for other vehicles, this benefit cost is pro-rated if the van is only available to the employee for part of the year. An additional charge of £550 (£500 for 2009/10) will apply if the employee is also provided with private fuel for the van.

These new rules bring the benefit associated with vans much closer to that of other cars. It is suggested this is necessary to reduce tax avoidance that was said to be occurring where employees are provided with vehicles that can be classed as vans just to reduce the tax benefit charge.

The only way for employees who are drivers of company provided vans to avoid these rules is if they prove they do no (or very few) private miles in the van. However, it is likely that these claims will be carefully examined with the introduction of these new rules to prevent abuse.

Accommodation for higher paid staff

Higher paid employees who are provided with living accommodation are assessed on the benefit of the accommodation as for all other employees (see earlier in the chapter). They are also, however, taxed on any other expenses which are paid by the employer which relate to the accommodation, for example, the cost of heating, lighting and repairs. They are also taxed on 20% a year of the cost of any furniture provided to them with the accommodation.

If the accommodation is job related, as we defined earlier in the chapter, a cap on these extras is applied. The maximum assessment of the ancillary services is then set at 10% of the employee's net employment earnings. Net employment earning is the employment income assessment after any allowable expenses and pension contributions but excluding the cost of any ancillary services. If the accommodation is not job related, the taxpayer will be assessed on the full cost to the employer of providing any ancillary services.

A director can only claim to be living in job-related accommodation if, as well as meeting the conditions given above, he or she has an interest in less than 5% of the company and he or she is either a full-time working director or the company is non- profit-making or is a charity, unless the accommodation is provided as part of special security arrangements.

Activity

Alexandra has a house in Yeovil and normally lives there but she has been transferred to London for two years to establish a new branch of the company she works for. Her gross salary for the tax year is £27,000. She has been provided with a flat in Mayfair which has an annual rateable value of £1,000. In this tax year the company paid £5,000 in ancillary services. Alexandra made a contribution of £1,000 to these services. Determine Alexandra's employment income for the tax year.

Feedback

Employment income assessment: Alexandra

	£	£
Salary		27,000
Accommodation benefits:		
Annual value (not job related)	1,000	
Ancillary services – cost:	5,000	
Less employee's contribution	(1,000)	5,000
Employment income		32,000

Note that, had this accommodation been job-related, the annual value charge (£1,000) would not have been applied and the ancillary services total would have been capped at 10% of Alexandra's net employment earnings i.e. £2,700. Her revised assessment would therefore have then totalled £28,700 (i.e. £27,000 + (£2,700 – £1,000)).

Loans to employees

If a higher paid employee or director, or a member of their family, receives a loan which was obtained because of their employment and either no interest was paid on the loan for the year or the amount of interest paid on the loan in the year is less than interest at the "official rate" published by HMRC, then the employee will be assessed on the cash equivalent of the benefit of the loan. The cash equivalent is equal to the difference between the interest the employee has paid on the loan to the employer (if any) and the interest calculated at the official rate. However, a minimum level of loan applies before this charge is commenced. If the total amount of all loans the employee has received from the employer does not exceed £5,000 then no tax liability will arise (i.e. the benefit is therefore ignored for tax purposes). Once the loan or loans exceed the £5,000 threshold however, it is all liable for a taxable benefit calculation, not just the excess over this amount.

The amount of the loan for this benefit computation is normally taken to be the average of the balance at the beginning of the year and the balance at the end of the year, if the loan had been in existence throughout the year. Otherwise the balance on the dates on which the loan was taken out and/or repaid is used instead. Only complete tax months in which the loan existed are taken into account (a tax month runs from the 6th of the month to the 5th of the following month). Under this circumstance the taxpayer can also make an election for interest at the official rate on the outstanding balance to be calculated on a daily basis if they want to, which is obviously more accurate, and therefore could lower their final tax bill.

If an employee receives a loan that comes under the 'qualifying loan' rules for tax deductibility (e.g. typically to buy necessary equipment to carry out their job as an employee) then no benefit will arise. Loans at full commercial rates to employees where the employer is in the business of providing loans, also give rise to no taxable benefit.

Activity

Harry, a higher paid employee, has loans from his employer that have been in existence all year:

(a) A loan of £50,000 at an interest rate of 3% pa which Harry used to finance the purchase of his main residence.
(b) A loan of £1,500 to buy an annual season ticket for rail travel at an interest rate of 2% pa.
(c) A personal loan of £2,000 at an interest rate of 5% which Harry used to refit the bathroom in his home.
(d) A loan of £1,800 at an interest-free rate to buy equipment he needs for his job.

Take the official rate of interest to be 5%. Determine the benefit assessable on Harry for the tax year.

Feedback

The loan d) is qualifying and therefore does not form part of any benefit calculations. The other loans can be totalled to calculate the total benefit arising.

		£
a)	50,000 × (5% – 3%)	1,000
b)	1,500 × (5% – 2%)	45
c)	no benefit as rate matches official rate	–
		1,045

Other benefits

It is not possible here to list and explain all the detailed rules relating to the full range of possible benefits in kind as so many exist; however, a number of other specific benefits in kind are worth mentioning more briefly because of their relative importance for large numbers of employees.

Mobile phones

Prior to the 1999 Budget the provision of a mobile phone to an employee was a taxable benefit in kind if any private use was allowed that was paid for by the employer. The final charge applicable to this benefit was £200 in 1998/99. This charge no longer exists and no benefit now arises from provision and use of a mobile phone even if private calls are allowed and paid for by the employer. The 2006 Budget however, restricted this benefit to a single phone per employee, for their use only, to prevent possible exploitation of this benefit by the giving of multiple phones for family members, as well as the employee, on a tax free basis. This restriction applies to all new phones issued to employees after 6 April 2006.

Computers

A second benefit worth extra comment is the loan of a computer to an employee for their home (i.e. part business, part private) use. Somewhat controversially and unexpectedly the rules for this benefit were changed in the 2006 Budget. The old rules continued to apply for all computers provided to employees up to 6 April 2006. The rule applied is; if you are a higher paid employee, then the first £500 per annum of the benefit that would arise is exempt. This is on the basis of computing the annual benefit of the loaned asset as normal, i.e. at

20% of cost when new plus any running costs (if these are also paid for by the employer). Therefore provided the total cost of providing the computer and running costs came to less than £2,500 (£2,500 × 20% = £500) it was tax free. Any excess over the £500 however, became a benefit in kind.

For all computers provided since 6 April 2006 however the tax free allowance element of £500 has been removed and the computer benefit is valued at the full 20% of the cost of provision, just like other loaned assets, to represent the private use element. This extra tax cost is only avoidable under these new rules if it can be proven that there is no private use of the computer of any kind.

For all other loaned asset benefits (other than cars) a rate of 20% of the cost when new applies each year as we saw at the start of this section.

Scholarships

A final special benefit you may come across is the provision of scholarships. We saw in Chapter 4 that scholarships paid to employees for their own education are exempt from tax. The situation is different, however, when the scholarship is for an employee's family members. For higher paid employees, if a scholarship of any kind is made available to the employee's family the employee is taxed on the actual cost of the scholarship, except when no more than 25% of the award is available because of the fact the recipient is a family member of an employee (i.e. at least 75% of the amount needs to be available to any applicant irrespective of any family ties to the giver of the scholarship).

You can see from this section that there are a number of benefits in kind that either have a low value, or are exempt from income tax. This gives rise to some tax planning opportunities for employers and employees. We will consider these opportunities in more detail, including salary sacrifice arrangements, in Chapter 11.

A summary of the benefits in kind treatment detailed in this section, together with some further examples, can be found as a handout in the student section of the website.

Pensions

Until 6 April 2006, an individual could derive a pension from at least three direct sources: the state pension schemes (basic pension and now state second pension or S2P), an occupational pension scheme and a personal pension scheme. A fourth type of pension available to everyone, working or not, had also been available since 6 April, 2001, called a *stakeholder pension*. A significant change however, occurred for pension provision in the UK on 6 April, 2006. While the state pension entitlement will continue, for now at least, the other methods of providing for your own pension have been rationalised into what is effectively now one scheme. The aim is to make pension provision easier understand, and therefore easier to invest in by more people.

The state pension schemes are funded from the Government's general tax fund, as discussed in Chapter 1. Entitlement to state pensions is determined by national insurance contributions made over your working life. Contributions to the state pension schemes have no income tax computation consequences, however, when state pensions are received on retiring, any receipts are potentially taxable as part of a taxpayer's employment income. State pensions receipts must therefore be added into the tax computations of anyone who receives them along with any other income they may receive when computing what, if any, income tax they must pay (this is listed a 'pension income' and is treated like employment income in the tax computation). The current rate of payment for state pensions can be found in the tables in Appendix A.

The new pension structure however, relates to other pension funds developed directly by taxpayers during their working lives. We will review the options now available to taxpayers for providing their own pension incomes below. In all cases however, for your tax computations the treatment is the same. If a taxpayer is in receipt of a pension it must be added to their employment or trading income computation as if it were an earned source of income. Non-cash benefits received as part of a pension are also taxable just like benefits received as part of employee incomes. The rules for taxing non-cash items are broadly the same as we reviewed in this chapter for benefits in kind.

Contributions to a pension made by taxpayers are allowed as deductions from their employment or trading incomes provided the contributions made are within the limits listed and detailed below. These deductions are in the form of a tax reduction included at step 2 of their tax computation. This means pension contributions continue to be a tax efficient way of saving for retirement as deducting the contributions from income makes them effectively tax deductible at the taxpayer's marginal tax rate.

A good source of information about pensions is the Government department responsible for this area of the economy – the Department of Work and Pensions (see their website at http://www.thepensionservice.gov.uk).

Current pension regime

A consultation proposing a new pension regime came to an end in April 2003 and details of the proposed changes were announced as part of Budget 2004. This new scheme commenced on 6 April 2006 (a date that was dubbed Pension 'A' day!).

Pension contributions have long been allowed as deductible expenditure from employment or trading income. This deduction has historically been allowed at the marginal rate of the taxpayer. This was introduced to encourage personal pension provision, rather than relying solely on state provision, by making contributions effectively tax free. Tax relief under the new pension regime is given to the taxpayer in one of three ways depending on the method by which the pension scheme operates.

Firstly, if they are an employee contributing to a pension directly through their salary then their deduction will be taken out before PAYE is computed to ensure that they receive the full tax deduction they are entitled to at the correct marginal rate. This is referred to as a 'net pay arrangement'.

Secondly, members may receive 'relief at source' by making their pension contributions net of the basic rate of income tax. A pension scheme member, for example, who wanted to pay £100 into the scheme, would actually pay only £80. The scheme administrator then claims the £20 from HMRC and credits the member with having paid £100. If the member is a higher rate taxpayer, they can get higher rate relief on their self assessment return by extending the basic rate band limit by the amount of the contribution (i.e. as is done for charitable donations - as illustrated in Chapter 4).

The third method is 'relief by way of claim'. This is where the member makes gross contributions to the pension fund, and no relief is given when the contribution is made. The taxpayer then claims relief by deducting the contribution from total income in his or her self assessment return, at step 2 of the income tax computation.

Fiscal Fact

The cost to the Treasury of income tax relief for contributions to approved pension schemes is estimated to be £19.7billion for 2009/10.

Under the current rules, in addition to keeping an annual earnings cap, a life-time maximum limit on the total size of the pension fund is also fixed. This is set at £1.8million for this tax year (£1.75million 2009/10). If your funds rise above this sum then a tax charge on the excess will need to be paid when the pension is taken (set initially at 55% if you take the benefits as a lump sum and 25% if you take them as income).

In addition to the cap on the overall size of the pension fund that can be accumulated, the annual maximum cap for the amount you can contribute to your pension funds each year and claim tax relief on the contributions is set at £255,000 for 2010/11 (£245,000 for 2009/10). If you wish to make contributions to your funds in excess of this sum you will be charged 40% tax on your contributions, rather than them being tax free.

These limits (£1.8million fund cap and £255,000 annual cap) were initially fixed for the next five years (until the end of 2015/16) by the first Finance Act 2010. However, with the Emergency Budget in June 2010 the Government announced a consultation to review the whole pension tax relief regime and so it is quite likely these rules will change for 2011/12 and beyond.

Once the taxpayer decides to start their pension they are allowed to take up to 25% of the accumulated fund as a tax free lump sum to do with as they wished. The remainder has to be invested in a product called an *annuity* – that provides a regular (usually monthly) payment to the taxpayer in return for the lump sum they invested. The larger the initial lump sum invested, and the better the current stock market conditions, the higher the annuity rate will be. This rate would normally be fixed for the remainder of the taxpayer's life so they have a fixed, known, level of income to rely on from then on.

The minimum age at which a taxpayer can take their pension is 55, but they can delay this until they are 77 (75 before 22 June 2010) if they wish to, to enable their fund to continue to grow so as to maximise their tax free lump sum and annuity levels. This flexibility is also important to allow the taxpayer to pick the market conditions that will give them the best long term rate for their annuity rather than forcing them to take a lower rate just because the market conditions were weak at the time they reached a particular age. The upper age (of 77) is likely to disappear as part of the new Government's pension review. This would then allow taxpayers to take their pension whenever they wanted after 55.

The Pension Credit

The 2002 Budget announced details of a new credit for pensioners that had been announced in the Pre-Budget report in November 2001. This new credit commenced in October 2003 and operates with similar aims to the Child Tax Credit and Working Tax Credit we discussed in Chapter 4. Its aim is to ensure no pensioner lives on less than £132.60 a week (£130 in 2009/10) or £200.40 a week as a couple (£198.45 in 2009/10). Direct credit payments are made to qualifying pensioners to ensure this is the case.

The Department of Work and Pensions reported that 2.7million pensioner households received this credit in their statistics reported in the Budget Report in April 2010.

For more details on this new tax credit see the following website: http://www.thepensionservice.gov.uk/pensioncredit

Summary

In this chapter we have focused on the taxation of income from employment. Since the majority of the UK workforce are employees it is an important area of the UK tax system. The general rule is that, unless specifically exempted, every benefit received from an employment is taxable, with just a very few deductions allowable. The tax treatment of individuals with gross emoluments of less than £8,500 a year is more generous than that of other employees. However, this limit has not increased for more than twenty years and so almost all employees are now subject to the more stringent tax regime. There are some tax planning opportunities for employers and employees. These particularly include the provision of some benefits in kind and planning for retirement.

You have encountered a number of different forms of tax relief in this chapter and the previous one, and may well be confused about how they all work. The following table should help clarify this for you.

Type of payment	how paid	how relief is given
Charges on income		
Patent royalties	net	Deduct gross amount paid (step 2) Add tax to tax liability
Copyright royalties	gross	Deduct gross amount paid (step 2)
Interest	gross	Deduct gross amount paid (step 2)
Gift aid donations		
Gift to charity	as if net	Don't deduct payment Extend basic rate band by grossed up amount
Pensions		
Relief at source	net	Don't deduct payment Extend basic rate band by grossed up amount (higher rate tax payers)
Net pay arrangement	gross	Paid before PAYE is calculated so relief is automatic, i.e. doesn't affect the tax computation.
Relief by claim	gross	Deduct gross amount paid (step 2)

Project areas

The taxation of income from employment provides a number of interesting areas to research. One such topic would be to undertake a comparison of the taxation of employment throughout the EU. Another interesting area of research is the question of the impacts and costs of altering benefits in kind, for example, extending the existing tax relief for workplace nurseries to all kinds of child-care costs.

A topical project would be an investigation into the provision of private versus company cars or of private fuel by employers. It would be interesting to find out how the role and use of company cars is changing in the UK as a result of the new rules introduced for fuel and for car benefit, or how many employers pay for their employees' private fuel and whether their decisions will change as a result of the Chancellor's measures.

Given the recent introduction of the radical changes to the pension regime, you could also look at how these differences have changed the nature of pension provision.

Discussion questions

1   Is it right to tax heavy users of vehicles more under the new emissions based rules when they need to use their cars for work?

2   Is it right to impose the extra 'necessary' rule, not present for sole-traders, on employees for deductibility of expenses from their taxable income?

3   Is it appropriate that some benefits in kind should not be taxable? (e.g. free coal to miners).

4   What are the implications for individual taxpayers, employers, the Government and society as a whole of our current pension provision options? Is the reduced focus on state pensions appropriate for those who can and can't fund their own pensions?

5   Sports people can receive payments related to their jobs tax-free provided those payments are gratuitous, for example testimonials or benefits (see *Moore v Griffiths* and *Reed v Seymour*). Is this fair to other workers?

Quick quiz

1   Iain receives luncheon vouchers of £3 per working day as part of his employment package. How much (if any) is chargeable as employment income?

2   Julia receives a mileage allowance of 30p per mile and drives her car 3,000 business miles during the year. How much (if any) is chargeable as employment income?

3   Keith is a high rate taxpayer whose employer supplies him with the use of a company house which cost £250,000 and has an annual value of £10,200. He makes no contribution towards the running costs which cost his employer £2,500 for the year. How much (if any) is chargeable as employment income, assuming an

official rate of 5%, and that the accommodation is not job related?

4   Lorna is provided with a diesel engined company car with a list price of £27,000 and an emission rating of 216 g/km. How much (if any) is chargeable as employment income?

Questions

Question 1   (based on ACCA Taxation December 1993).

Martin was appointed sales director of Multiple Mechanics Ltd on 1 July, 2010. His employment package was as follows:

1. Annual salary of £30,000 payable in equal instalments in arrears on the last day of each month.
2. A commission related to sales and payable annually shortly after the company's year end, 31 March. The commission to 31 March, 2010, £2,700, was paid on 30 April, 2011.
3. Company car, a Mercedes diesel 3000cc. The car was first registered on 1 August, 2006 has an emission level of 253g/km of carbon dioxide and had a list price of £30,000 when new. All running expenses, including private fuel, were to be paid for by the company but Martin was to pay the company £50 per month for private use of the car and £20 per month for private fuel, whatever the amount used. His total mileage from appointment to 5 April, 2011 was 16,000, of which 1,000 were private. These mileage figures were evenly spread over the period. The fuel consumption of the car averaged 5 miles per litre of fuel. Fuel cost an average 95 pence per litre.
4. A clothing allowance of £600 per annum payable monthly on the first day of each month.
5. A furnished flat, annual value £1,200, which was provided rent free until such time as Martin could find a suitable house in the locality, which was not until the summer of 2011. The flat had cost Martin's employer £120,000 in 2003 and the furniture had cost £10,000 at the same time.

Required: Show the amounts assessable as employment income on Martin for the tax year 2010/11. Assume the official rate of interest is 5%.

Question 2 (based on ACCA December 1990).

Maurice Thistlethwaite, aged 53, is a research chemist with Pulsating Paints Ltd. His wife Marjorie, aged 52, is a teacher with North Shires County Council. Details of their income and outgoings for the year ended 5 April, 2011 are as follows.

(a) Gross salaries

Maurice	£33,500 (PAYE paid of £5,986)
Marjorie	£19,000 (PAYE paid of £2,530)

Maurice paid 5% (gross) of his salary to an approved personal pension scheme under a relief at source arrangement and Marjorie paid 6% of her salary to the teachers' occupational pension scheme under a net pay arrangement.

(b) Pulsating Paints Ltd provided Maurice with a new 1500cc petrol engined car with a list price of £14,500 on 6 November, 2010. The car had no accessories added. This car's emission levels are km of carbon dioxide. His total mileage from that date 172g/to 5 April, 2011 was 8,000 miles of which 1,000 were on business. The company paid all running costs of the car, £1,200, including Maurice's private petrol.

(c) Maurice paid £100 to a relevant professional body of which he was a member and Marjorie paid £60 to her teaching union. Marjorie also purchased an academic gown during the year at the request of her employer. This cost £75.

(d) On 1 January, 2005 Maurice began performing as a magician at local charities and social clubs. It had been agreed with HMRC to treat the income as trading income and tax adjusted profits for the year are £3,000. Out of this income Maurice paid £900 (net) to his pension scheme in February 2010, under a relief at source arrangement.

(e) Maurice and Marjorie had joint accounts with the Barland Bank plc on which interest of £600 was paid and with the Barchester and Bognor Building Society on which interest of £4,000 was paid. No specific election on sharing this interest has been made.

(f) Investments in UK companies were held in joint names and dividends of £3,500 were received.

Required: Calculate the income tax payable for 2010/11 of Mr and Mrs Thistlethwaite.

Question 3 (Based on ACCA June 1999).

Rita, who is a fashion designer for Daring Designs Limited, was re-located from London to Manchester on 6 April, 2010. Her annual salary is £48,000. She was immediately provided with a house with an annual value of £4,000 for which her employer paid an annual rent of £3,500. Rita was reimbursed relevant re-location expenditure of £12,000. Daring Designs Limited provided ancillary services for the house in 2010/11 as follows:

	£
Electricity	700
Gas	1,200
Water	500
Council tax	1,300
Property repairs	3,500

The house had been furnished by Daring Designs Limited prior to Rita's occupation at a cost of £30,000. On 6 October, 2010 Rita bought all of the furniture from Daring Designs Limited for £20,000 when its market value was £25,000.

Daring Designs Limited had made a loan to Rita in 2008 of £10,000 at a rate of interest of 2%. The loan is not being used for a 'qualifying purpose'. No part of the loan has been repaid.

Rita was provided with an 1800 c.c. petrol engine company car from the start of the tax year with CO_2 emissions of 186 g/km. It had a list price of £18,500 when new in August 2007 and has had no accessories added. Daring Designs Limited paid for the petrol for all the mileage done by Rita until 5 December, 2010. On 5 December, 2010 the company discontinued the company car scheme and sold the car to Rita for £5,000, its market value at that date. Her mileage from 6 April 2010 to 5 December, 2010 was 20,000 of which 13,000 was on business. After that date Rita no longer used her car for business.

Required: Calculate the total income amount chargeable to income tax on Rita for the year 2010/11. Assume an official rate of interest of 5% per annum.

(Note: *answer available via lecturer's website*)

Further test questions for this chapter to test your knowledge can be found in the student section of the website at:

http://www.taxstudent.com/uk

Further reading and examples

Combs, A., Dixon, S. & Rowes, P. (2010), *Taxation: incorporating the 2010 Finance Acts*, Fiscal Publications: Birmingham.
– use this book for many other examples to further develop and test your knowledge of this chapter's contents. See
http://www.fiscalpublications.com/rowes/2010

6 Taxing trading and property income

Introduction

In this chapter and the next we will study the taxation of unincorporated businesses, which are businesses that are not run as limited liability companies, focussing on taxation of sole traders. In practice, unincorporated businesses are not treated as separate taxable entities for tax purposes. Rather, in the case of a sole trader, the trading income rules are used to determine the taxable income resulting from their business activities so that this can then be included in the taxpayer's tax computation alongside any other income categories they have to pay tax on for the tax year.

As property income is also calculated using similar rules to trading income, the final section of this chapter reviews this component of income.

At the end of this chapter you will be able to:

- state the badges of trade and use them to identify trading activities;
- identify income that is chargeable and expenses which are deductible under the trading income rules;
- convert accounting profits into trading profits for tax purposes; and
- compute property income and discuss the special property related tax schemes currently in operation.

Special rules for allocating profits to tax years (the basis period rules) are not covered in detail here but if you need to understand them for your course, detailed rules and worked examples relating to these provisions are available on the website.

Introduction to the trading income rules

In Chapter 4 we discussed how income which is taxed by direct assessment is assessed for tax purposes. Such income is taxed under one or other of the various tax categories. The basis of assessment that applies, and other rules to determine how much tax will be due on the income, depends on which category the income is assessed under. We saw in Chapter 5 how income from your job is taxed under the employment income rules. Income from a trade and income from a vocation or profession are taxed under the *trading income* rules. There are some small differences in the way that the tax due is calculated for trade and vocation/professional incomes (we'll meet one later by way of illustration), but for our purposes we can treat them as being the same for trading income computations.

Although we focus on sole traders, many of the rules also apply to partnerships as the other form of unincorporated business structure. We will not discuss the extra rules for partnership tax in more detail in this book however.* Many of the trading and property income rules also apply to companies, with some modifications that we will discuss further in Chapter 9.

There are approximately 3.5million people, or about 13% of the workforce, who are taxed under the trading income rules. They pay a total of approximately £14billion in taxes each year. While some trading taxpayers run large businesses many are running relatively small undertakings where they may be the only employee or where there are only a handful of other employees.

In general, sole traders and partners are assessed on the profits which arise in the business accounting period which ends during the tax year being assessed. However, before any taxable profit under the trading income rules can be calculated it is first necessary to demonstrate that trading is actually taking place. In this chapter we will review the principles referred to as the *badges of trade* which are used to determine this. Once the existence of trading has been established, you will then need to undertake at least two steps in order to determine the trading income for a tax year. These are:

1. determine which of the trader's accounts will form the basis period for the tax year; and
2. adjust the accounting profits in order to derive the tax adjusted trading profits.

---

* For more detailed information on Partnership taxation, we recommend you review Chapter 16 of our sister publication Combs, Dixon & Rowes' 'Taxation' – see the end of this chapter for further information on this book.

In order to fully determine the trading income assessment, you will need to establish the tax implications of any investment in fixed assets, so we will look at those rules in the next chapter.

Once you have been through each of these steps, the final trading income assessment will have been calculated for the sole trader. You can then add this amount to the tax computation as part of the aggregated income to determine the total income. The Thomas Lester example at the beginning of Chapter 4 showed you how to do this by adding trading income to the top part of the taxpayer's computation. Look back to this illustration if you need to be reminded which number we are now working towards determining.

Identification of trading activities

The first thing for us to do therefore is to consider when an activity is 'trading' and so is subject to trading income rules. The definition of 'trade' is quite wide and is defined to include 'any venture in the nature of a trade'.

For anyone who is not an employee, it is very important to determine whether money received in conjunction with carrying out an activity is trading income or not, as finding this out could significantly affect how much tax they have to pay on it.

Before 1965, if a receipt was held not to be trading income then it was likely to be a *capital gain* (i.e. selling something for more than its purchase price). At that time capital gains were not taxable and therefore obtaining receipts in this form was a tax free source of increased wealth. Since 1965 however, capital gains have been taxable in the UK. Until 1988 capital gains were taxed at the single rate of 30%. This rate was often lower than the taxpayer's marginal rate of tax and so even after 1965 there was an advantage to having a receipt of money classed as a capital gain.

Fiscal Fact

According to Gordon Brown's 2006 Budget Statement, since 1997 there were 575,000 new and additional businesses created in the UK and 105,000 additional self employed people giving a total of 4.3million businesses and 3.7 million self employed people at that time.

Until 2008, the distinction was less important because capital gains were taxed at the taxpayer's marginal rate of tax and so the amount of the tax saving that occurred due to the classification of the receipt as being outside of trading income largely disappeared. It has now re-appeared following Budget 2008 which created a new single rate of tax for capital gains tax for individuals at 18% – a rate which provides a lower marginal rate of tax than for income receipts for most taxpayers (we will discuss how to tax capital gains in more detail in Chapter 8).

Because of these different potential tax rates it is important to know whether or not trading is occurring, or some other type of activity (e.g. just a hobby or one-off activity), so that the correct method of taxing this activity is applied. For example, if you bought and sold a number of works of art or collectables (e.g. on Ebay), at what point would this go from being a hobby or occasional pastime (on which you may have to pay capital gains tax if you sell anything for more than you bought it for, but no income tax) to being a 'trade' you are engaged in (which is then subject to trading income tax rules)?

For most of us hobbies cost money rather than make money; HMRC will not give us tax relief on any losses related to hobbies, however, relief is often available for 'losses' incurred during the course of trading. Correct classification is therefore important for a variety of reasons.

The UK tax legislation does not define what constitutes trading. We must therefore look elsewhere, such as to case law or other sources of tax principles, for guidance in determining whether trading is taking place.

The Royal Commission on the Taxation of Profits and Income (1955: Cmd 9474) suggested an approach to resolving this issue that has become common practice. They proposed a series of tests to be applied to the activity which together would help indicate if it was a trade or not. These tests were called the 'badges of trade'. There were six 'badges' which can help to determine whether or not a particular transaction is, in fact, trading. None of the badges offer a conclusive test of trading by themselves, although some are stronger indicators than others. If trading is taking place it is likely that there will be evidence of this in more than one 'badge'. HMRC will use these tests in deciding whether they agree with a claim made by a taxpayer to be trading, or not. If they disagree with the taxpayer's self assessment, they may challenge the taxpayer and require them to pay tax on that activity differently.

Badges of trade

The six badges of trade are as follows:

1. The subject matter of the transaction.

If the property which forms the subject matter of the transaction does not provide either direct income or enjoyment to the owner, it is likely that the transaction will be considered to be trading. It seems unlikely that commodities or manufactured articles which are normally the subject of trading will be treated as anything other than a trade. For example, in *Rutledge v IRC* (1929) while in Berlin on business the taxpayer bought one million rolls of toilet paper from a bankrupt German firm for £1,000. The toilet rolls were sent to the UK and the taxpayer endeavoured to sell them. Eventually he found a buyer who bought the whole quantity for £12,000, earning him a considerable profit. The transaction was held to be 'in the nature of a trade' largely because of the quantity of the goods involved but also because of the nature of the goods (one million toilet rolls are unlikely to be used by the taxpayer personally!). This case demonstrates that even a single transaction can sometimes be trading.

In contrast, in *IRC v Reinhold* (1953) the taxpayer had bought four houses within a two year period intending to sell them on. The Court of Session stated that 'heritable property is not an uncommon subject of investment' and so the taxpayer was not considered to be trading on this occasion.

In the case of *Marson v Morton* (1986) the taxpayer bought land intending to develop it, but in fact sold it on for a profit. The taxpayer was held not to be trading, confirming that land can be held for investment purposes even if it does not yield an income.

2. The frequency of similar transactions.

Although a single transaction can be considered to be trading the repeated undertaking of transactions in the same subject matter is likely to be a stronger indicator that trading is being conducted.

In *Pickford v Quirke* (1927) the taxpayers formed a syndicate to buy and resell cotton mills. There were four such transactions over a period of time. The membership of the syndicate was not identical for each transaction. It was held that any one transaction would not have constituted trading but the four taken together did.

3. The circumstances responsible for the realisation.

There is a presumption that trading is not occurring if the property is disposed of to raise money for an unexpected event.

In the case of *The Hudson's Bay Company* v *Stevens* (1909) the taxpayer company had sold off a large quantity of land over a number of years which it had acquired in return for the surrender of its charter. The company was held not to be trading, the court offering the following explanation: 'The company are doing no more than an ordinary landowner does who is minded to sell from time to time as purchasers offer, portions suitable for building of an estate which has devolved upon him from his ancestors.'

4. Supplementary work on or in connection with the property realised.

Trading is more likely to be taking place if either work is done on the property to make it more marketable, or an organisation is set up to sell it. The courts have decided that if there is an organised effort to obtain profit there is a source of taxable income but in the absence of such effort the presumption will be that trading is not taking place.

In *Cape Brandy Syndicate* v *IRC* (1927) a group of accountants bought 3,000 casks of Cape Brandy, blended it with French Brandy, re-casked it and sold it in lots over a period of 18 months. They were held to be trading because they did not simply buy an article which they thought was cheap and then resold it; the syndicate bought the brandy intending to modify its character so that it could be sold in smaller quantities.

5. The motive for the transaction.

There is some evidence of trading taking place if the objective of undertaking the transaction is to make a profit. However, even in the absence of a motive to make a profit it may still be concluded that trading is taking place. The subject matter of the transaction may be crucial.

In *Wisdom* v *Chamberlain* (1968) the taxpayer, a well-known comedian, bought silver bullion as a hedge against an anticipated devaluation of the pound. It was held that the taxpayer had undertaken an 'adventure in the nature of a trade' when he realised a profit three months later, because the transaction was entered into on a short-term basis with the sole intention of making a profit from the purchase and sale of a commodity.

6. The length of ownership.

The presumption in this badge of trade is that the shorter the period of ownership the more likely it is that trading is taking place. This is a weaker badge than some of the others, however, because the short period of ownership can often be explained by the taxpayer if they need to, perhaps for example, by demonstrating a need for cash at the time of the sale. Hence there are many exceptions to this as a universal rule.

In addition to these six main badges of trade, other factors might be considered by HMRC when deciding whether trading is taking place. There could perhaps include:

- the source of finance for the transaction;
- the circumstances surrounding the acquisition of the asset; and
- whether the subject matter of transaction is in any way related to trades and other activities carried on by the taxpayer.

To summarise this section, and to illustrate the practical difficulties courts have in deciding over the trading question, attempt the following activity:

Activity

Stirling Hill is a vintage motor car enthusiast. On 1 January, 2009 he took out a loan of £40,000 at a fixed rate of interest of 10%, and spent £30,000 on having a workshop built. This was completed on 31 March, 2009, when a further £8,000 was spent on tools and equipment. On 6 April, 2009, Stirling bought a dilapidated vintage motor car for £3,000, and proceeded to restore it at a cost of £7,000 in spare parts. The restoration was completed on 30 June, 2009. Unfortunately, Stirling was made redundant on 15 September, 2009, and was forced to sell the motor car for £25,000. Not being able to find further employment, Stirling proceeded to buy three more dilapidated vintage motor cars on 15 October, 2009 for £4,000 each. The restoration of these was completed on 28 February, 2010 at a cost of £7,000 per motor car, and two of them were immediately sold for a total of £50,000. On 31 March, 2010 Stirling obtained employment elsewhere in the country, so he immediately sold the workshop for £25,000, and repaid the loan of £40,000. Stirling personally retained the tools and equipment, which were worth £4,500, and the unsold vintage motor car which was valued at £25,000.

You are required to:

(a) Briefly discuss the criteria which would be used by the courts in deciding whether or not Stirling will be treated as carrying on a 'trade' for his vintage motor car activities; and

(b) Explain whether or not you would consider Stirling to be carrying on an adventure in the nature of a trade.

Feedback

To answer this part of the question you need to discuss the six badges of trade set out above.

The acquisition and disposal of the first car, taken in isolation, is unlikely to be deemed to be trading because:

- Vintage cars are often owned and restored by individuals in order to derive enjoyment and/or as investments.
- The length of ownership after the restoration work is completed does not suggest trading is taking place.
- The circumstances surrounding the sale of the car suggests that the disposal was a forced sale rather than trading.

However, the loan taken out to build and equip the workshop and help to finance the acquisition of the car might be taken to be a sign that trading is taking place. The acquisition and disposal of the next three cars is likely to be treated as an adventure in the nature of a trade because:

- Stirling devoted the whole of his time to the activity.
- There were three acquisitions and disposals.
- Two of the cars were sold as soon as their restoration was completed.

If, as seems likely, Stirling Hill is deemed to be trading it is now necessary to determine whether the first transaction will be deemed to be trading as a result of the subsequent transactions. To decide this we need to refer to case law again. In the case mentioned above of *Pickford* v *Quirke* (1927) the taxpayer bought a mill and sold all the assets. This would normally be treated as a capital transaction but the taxpayer carried on to asset strip a total of four mills. The courts decided that the taxpayer was trading and that the three later transactions could be taken into account when deciding whether the first transaction was trading.

In the case of *Leach* v *Pogson* (1962) the taxpayer set up 30 driving schools which were then sold. Again the courts decided that the 29 later transactions could be taken into account when deciding whether the first transaction was trading and hence the taxpayers were considered to be trading.

Finally, in the case of *Taylor* v *Good* (1974) the taxpayer bought a country estate, intending to live in the house. His wife refused to live in the house and so he instead obtained planning permission to build 90 houses on the land. He then sold the property to a property developer having owned the property for about four years. The courts decided that the transactions undertaken to enable the taxpayer to sell the property at a profit were not enough for the first transaction, the acquisition of the property, to be considered trading.

On balance it seems likely that Stirling Hill will be taken to be trading on all his transactions. Do you agree? You might like to think about what arguments Stirling Hill could offer against this decision if he challenged it in court.

Adjustment of profits

Now that you are able to identify trading activities you need to be able to calculate the taxable profits that arise from any trading transactions.

Taxable profits are made up of the difference between trading receipts and allowable expenses during a period of assessment, although we actually start with the net profit for accounting purposes to work this out, as we will see later. In order to calculate the taxable profits you will need to:

- determine which accounting period will form the basis of assessment for the tax year
- identify taxable income and allowable expenditure which relates to the basis period.

In this section we will first discuss the recognition of income and expenditure for tax purposes in general terms. Then we will explore specific trading receipts that form part of the trading income. Finally we will consider allowable expenses under the trading income rules.

Recognition of income and expenditure

Clearly it is important for each year's tax computation to determine in which period income and expenditure will be recognised as having been received or incurred. Under the trading income rules, taxpayers are assessed on profits arising, calculated using accounting profits as a starting point, and determined using Generally Accepted Accounting Practices (GAAP). Profits are calculated as 'revenue receipts less revenue deductions' and any deductions should follow normal accounting principles in the first instance.

It used to be possible to adopt a cash receipts basis for a business, but since the introduction of self assessment, only new barristers in their first seven years of practice can now use a cash basis. For other businesses therefore the accruals basis for recognising income and expenses (as done for accounting purposes) will be used for determining trading profits for tax computations.

We will now look more closely at the calculation of trading income to illustrate how these general rules are applied in practice.

Trading receipts

A receipt is a trading receipt if it is a payment for services or goods supplied by the taxpayer. But how do we determine when a trading receipt has been received in practice, and how much should be recorded in our tax computation? There are a number of rules and principles we must apply in practice to answer this question to ensure we don't either under or over-estimate the amount we need to record (so we don't under or overpay tax). These include, for example:

1. The receipt must be income and not capital;
2. Voluntary payments received are not trading receipts; and
3. Goods taken from the business for private purposes must be valued at market price and not cost.

We will now examine each of these principles in more detail:

1. Income versus capital receipts

As a general rule, to be taxable as trading income, a receipt must be income not capital. Capital receipts are instead generally taxed under the capital gains tax rules (see Chapter 8). A receipt falling under the capital gains tax rules will usually attract less tax than if it is taxed under the trading income rules and so the correct classification of items as income or capital is very important. The distinction has proved difficult to draw in practice, however, and a number of tests have been developed over a long period of time. The most straightforward is to determine if the receipt relates to an asset that is part of the fixed capital (therefore likely to be a capital receipt) or is part of working capital of the business (therefore likely to be an income receipt). A difficulty with applying what seems a fairly straight forward rule, however, is that whether an asset stock in trade or a capital asset depends on the type of business being carried on. You will have looked at this distinction if you have studied accountancy and will have seen how difficult this can be to determine.

The courts have devised a broad test, called the 'trees and fruit' test, which can be applied to help resolve this issue in practice. Here the analogy is that the tree is the enduring part (considered to be the capital), producing the fruit, which is the recurring product (considered to be the income).

One characteristic of income receipts is that they are often recurring, i.e. they occur again and again, compared to capital receipts which are often (but not always) one-off items. So how often a taxpayer receives a particular kind of payment may be a clue as to whether it is income or capital.

In order to decide whether a receipt is income or capital, we also need to think about what it is paid for and how it relates to the taxpayer's particular activities. Case law gives us a number of examples and general principles that can be used to help make this decision.

For example, what if a payment is received in return for a taxpayer restricting his or her activities in some way (e.g. agree not to trade in a particular area)? If the payment is to compensate the taxpayer for not being able to use a business asset at all, sometimes referred to as 'sterilisation' of the asset, then it will probably be a capital receipt. However, if it is to substitute for a receipt that would have been a trading receipt, then it is more likely to be income.

In *Higgs v Olivier* (1952), Sir Lawrence Olivier received £15,000 from the makers of the film Henry V, in which he starred, in return for an agreement not to act in another film for 18 months. This payment was separate from the fee he was paid for starring in the film. The Court of Appeal held that the payment was for a substantial restriction of his income earning activities, and so was not a trading receipt. If a restriction is not substantial, or only short term, it may be classified as an income receipt.

In *Glenboig Union Fireclay Co Ltd v IR Commrs* (1922) the company leased some fireclay fields and the seam ran underneath a railway track. The railway company paid a large sum of money to stop the company from working the fireclay seam, and the House of Lords held that this was a capital receipt. It was considered to be a payment for the sterilisation of an asset of the business.

In *Burmah Steamships Co Ltd v IRC* (1930), the company bought a ship that needed extensive repairs before it was seaworthy. The repairer took longer than agreed to finish the repairs and so paid compensation to the company, calculated by reference to the profits lost during the delay. This was held to be income because the compensation filled a 'hole' in the taxpayer's profit.

Some other areas where the distinction between capital and income arise are:

- Compensation for cancellations of commercial contracts or connections. Where the compensation relates to contracts which are relatively small compared to the overall size of the business activities, they will usually be income in nature and form part of the trading profits. Receipts which are compensation for contracts which are large compared to the size of the business, on the other hand, are generally considered to be capital.

- Appropriations of unclaimed deposits and advances.
- Receipts from the sale of information. This receipt is covered by statute, unlike the two above which have been decided by means of case law. Provided that the vendor continues to trade after the sale, the receipt will be treated as a trading receipt.
- A trade debt which has been deducted as a trading expense and is subsequently cancelled is treated as a trade receipt.

Sometimes a particular payment can be divided into both capital and income parts for tax purposes. This is what happened, for example, in the case of *London and Thames Haven Oil Wharves v Attwooll* (1967) where £100,000 compensation was paid after a tanker crashed into a jetty, causing serious damage. The sum was split into a capital sum, which was intended to be used to rebuild the jetty, and an income receipt, which was compensation to the jetty owners for loss of income due to the accident. The income part alone of this sum would qualify as a trading receipt.

2. Voluntary payments

Payments made on a voluntary basis for some personal quality of the taxpayer are not generally trading receipts. In *Murray v Goodhews* (1976), the brewing company, Watneys, made *ex gratia* (voluntary) lump sum payments to landlords of public houses when they terminated tied tenancies, partly as an acknowledgement of the good relationship they had with their tenant and partly to preserve their good name. These sums were held not to be trading receipts in the hands of the landlords since the amounts of the payments had no connection with the profits earned nor was it linked with future trading relations between Watneys and the taxpayer.

However, in *McGowan v Brown and Cousins* (1977), the taxpayer, an estate agent, received a lower than usual fee for acquiring property for a company in the expectation that he would be retained to deal with letting the property. The company owning the property later paid the taxpayer £2,500 as compensation when they retained another agent instead to deal with the lettings. The payment was held to be a trading receipt this time despite the lack of a legal obligation to pay it.

3. Goods taken for private purposes

For tax computation purposes, goods disposed of, other than in the ordinary course of business, must be accounted for at market value as a trading receipt. In *Sharkey* v *Wernher* (1956) the taxpayer who ran a stud farm as a business also raced horses as a hobby. She transferred five horses from her stud farm to her racing stables and recorded the cost of breeding the horses as a receipt of the stud farm. The Inland Revenue (as it was then) argued that the market value of the horses should be entered in the accounts rather than cost, and the courts agreed. The rule derived from this case applies to all goods taken by owners for their own use, as well as goods they give to others for non-business purposes. Finance Act 2008 has now enshrined this rule in statute. Beware, as this is usually different to the way such adjustments are made in accounting (where cost is used not market value). We will illustrate this principle for you later with an example when we discuss common adjustments needed to convert accounting profits to tax profits.

This rule can also apply if goods are sold at less than their market value. However, provided that the disposal can be shown to have been made for genuine commercial reasons (e.g. as the result of a sale or special offer) the rule in *Sharkey* v *Wernher* does not apply. Additionally, the rule applies to traders only. It does not apply to professional persons (i.e. it does not apply in relation to intangible goods or services). In *Mason* v *Innes* (1967) the novelist Hammond Innes gave the manuscript of *The Doomed Oasis* to his father. The writer had deducted allowable travelling expenses from his income which had been incurred while researching the book. The Inland Revenue (as it was at the time) wanted to assess the writer on the market value of the script. Lord Denning said:

> "Suppose an artist paints a picture of his mother and gives it to her. He does not receive a penny for it. Is he to pay tax on the value of it? It is unthinkable. Suppose he paints a picture which he does not like when he has finished it and destroys it. Is he liable to pay tax on the value of it? Clearly not. These instances therefore show that that *Sharkey* v *Wernher* does not apply to professional men."

This latter example is one of the main differences between business income and professional income categories. Other examples are beyond the scope of an introductory tax course.

Deductible expenses

Having looked at the income element in determining a trader's taxable income we should now consider the allowable expenses that can be deducted from this income. For expenditure to be an allowable deduction for tax purposes it must satisfy three criteria:

1. it must be incurred *wholly and exclusively* for the purposes of the trade;
2. it must be a *revenue* item, not a *capital* expense (unless specifically allowed for in the legislation); and
3. it must not be specifically disallowed by statute.

We will now examine each of these concepts in more detail:

1. Wholly and exclusively

Only expenditure that is wholly and exclusively for the purposes of the trade or business will be deductible to determine taxable profits. This concept is similar to the one we met in Chapter 5 in the context of employment income, except the requirement there was for expenses to be wholly, exclusively and *necessarily* for the purposes of employment. For a self employed taxpayer there is no need, however, to prove an expense they incur is necessary to perform their income earning activities, as long as the wholly and exclusively aspects are met then an expense can be allowable. This means more expenses may be allowable for self-employed taxpayers than for employees.

There are two situations where a business is likely to fall foul of the wholly and exclusively requirement. The first is when the payment is too remote from the business activities, which is tested for using what is called the *remoteness test*. The second is where the expenses have a dual purpose, using the *duality test*.

The remoteness test

This test considers whether the expense is related to the day to day running of the business, or whether it really relates to an activity outside of the business. For example, consider the decision whether subscriptions and donations are deductible or not. Subscriptions to trade associations will generally be deductible as it is generally easy to see the benefits that arise to the business from membership of a trade association, and it is closely related to the running of the business. Subscriptions and donations to political parties on the other hand are likely to be disallowable, as they are usually remote from the business activities of most businesses. It is therefore difficult to create a case to demonstrate how they can relate to business operations directly. In one case, however, a donation to a political party was held to be allowable where this link to business operations was held to have been made (i.e. payment was not considered to be remote). This was the case of *Morgan v Tate and Lyle Ltd* (1954) where a donation to the Conservative Party was allowed because it was made in order to resist the nationalisation of the sugar industry proposed by the Labour Party which would have led to the cessation of the business.

Donations to charity will generally not be deductible as they are remote from the business activities. However, by extra statutory concession, where the donations are only small and are to local charities, they are often allowable as a deduction in practice.

In applying the remoteness test you also need to consider in what capacity the proprietor has incurred the expense. In a 1906 case, *Strong & Co of Romsey Ltd v Woodifield*, a guest at a hotel was injured when a chimney fell, and the company paid an amount of damages to the guest as compensation. These were considered to be paid by the company in its capacity as an owner of property, and not in the context of the business operations and so were not allowed as a deduction.

Similarly, a misappropriation, or theft, of profits by the owner or a director of the business will be considered to be outside of the business activities and not deductible (e.g. see *Curtis v J & G Oldfield* (1933)). On the other hand, if the theft is by a member of the staff, the loss will usually be an allowable deduction.

The duality test

If an expense has a dual purpose, for example, the sole trader gets some private, as well as business related, benefit from the expense, then the duality test will operate to deny deductibility of the expense. In *Caillebotte v Quinn* (1975) the taxpayer, a self employed carpenter, claimed the difference between the cost of eating at home (at 10p a meal) and the cost of eating in a café (at 40p) for those days when he was working away from home. It was held that the expenditure was disallowable because he ate to live as well as to work and so the expenditure was 'tainted' by the private purpose.

There have been a number of other cases dealing with this rule, such as *Mackinlay v Arthur Young McClelland Moores & Co* (1990) where the House of Lords ruled that removal costs paid to two partners to move house were disallowable. It was accepted that the partnership benefited from the move because the partners were able to work at different offices, but there was a duality of purpose where the business and private benefits were too closely intertwined to separate them from each other. In another case, *Mallalieu v Drummond* (1983), a lady barrister tried to deduct the cost of the clothes she wore in court. The House of Lords said that in addition to a business purpose, there were other purposes, namely to provide 'warmth and decency' which meant that the expense had a dual purpose and was not deductible.

Sometimes it is not possible to split an expense into a business and a personal element directly. However, when this occurs, it may be possible to split the payment up using an acceptable allocation formula and allow the business portion as a deductible expense. A widespread example of this situation that occurs for a large number of self-employed taxpayers is the treatment of expenses relating to a car which is used for both business and pleasure. The proportion of business miles compared to total miles can be used to determine the proportion of expenses such as servicing, insurance and petrol which are allowable deductions.

Other examples of this occur for taxpayers who undertake all or part of their business from their home. Part of the cost of running their house is deductible from their trading profits as long as they can justify how these shared costs are allocated to the business correctly.

2. Revenue not capital expenditure

The second question we need to consider in determining if an expense is deductible is whether it is a revenue or capital expense. As we discussed above, there is a need to distinguish between revenue and capital receipts as generally only revenue income is part of trading income for tax computations. Equally revenue expenses are normally deductible from trading profits whereas capital expenses have to be dealt with differently - using the capital allowances rules (we'll discuss these rules in Chapter 7). These principles will sound familiar to those of you who have studied accounting where what goes directly into the Profit and Loss account, or what needs to go into the Balance Sheet, is considered on a very similar basis.

The distinction between *revenue* and *capital* expenditure for tax deductibility has developed over the years, largely from case law, which tries to be consistent in its treatment of revenue income and expenditure. The tests that are used to determine whether a receipt is capital or revenue, as we discussed above, are generally also used to test whether expenses are of a capital or revenue nature. These rules largely follow normal accounting principles, however, there is not always a clear cut distinction and some cases appear to be at odds with these tests. For example, in the case of *Lawson v Johnson Matthey plc* (1992) a payment of £50 million was made as part of a deal with the Bank of England in order to save the banking subsidiary from a threat of insolvency. Despite the size and one off nature of the payment it was allowed as revenue expenditure.

The question of how often a payment is made can play a part in deciding whether it is capital or revenue in nature. As we saw with receipts, capital payments are often one-off, single payments, whereas revenue payments are often recurring. One of the tests the courts have established is the *enduring benefit test*, where we ask 'does the expense bring into existence something that has enduring benefit for the trade?' If so, it is probably capital and therefore not deductible.

In *Tucker v Granada Motorway Services Ltd* (1979), the rent payable by the taxpayer company under a lease agreement was calculated based on the previous year's takings, which included an amount of tobacco duty. By paying a lump sum to the lessor, the company was able to have the formula changed to take out the tobacco duty and so in the future the rent paid under the lease would be lower. The House of Lords held that this was a capital payment, because it created an enduring benefit, i.e. future reduced rent payments.

To help explain these rules in more detail, and to show you how these rules work in practice, let us review some commonly encountered items for which the revenue/capital distinction is important:

Self education expenses

Expenditure on a training course for the proprietor of a business which is intended to provide new expertise, knowledge or skills brings into existence an intangible asset which has enduring benefit for the business and is therefore really of a capital nature. On the other hand, if the training course is to update expertise, knowledge or skills already possessed by the proprietor it will normally be regarded as revenue expenditure.

Repairs and improvements

Amounts spent on repairs to an asset will generally be allowable for tax purposes but amounts spent on improvements will be disallowed.

As a general rule, repair means restoring an asset to its original condition, whereas an improvement means making the asset bigger or better in some way, therefore changing its character. Given the frequency of these kinds of payments occurring in business, this distinction is very important to understand. Normal accounting principles are used as guidance when differentiating between repair and improvement expenditure and case law has been used to decide marginal cases.

Two types of expenditure cause particular difficulties. The first is expenditure which is incurred to renovate assets soon after they were acquired. When a taxpayer buys an asset, the purchase price is, of course, a capital expense. What if the asset needs to be repaired soon after purchase? There is an argument that if the asset was purchased for a low price because it needed to be repaired, then the cost of those repairs is a capital expense, because it is an additional purchase cost. In *Law Shipping Co Ltd v IRC* (1924) a ship, which was built in 1906, was bought in December 1919 for £97,000. The ship was ready to sail with freight that was booked for transport at the time of the purchase. The required periodic survey of the ship (for sea-worthiness etc.) was then considerably overdue and an exemption from the survey had to be obtained. The ship was granted a Lloyd's Certificate for a single voyage to enable it to be taken into dock to undergo its survey. The purchaser had to spend £51,558 on repairs.

It was agreed that the expense of keeping a ship, which is employed in trade, in proper repair is normally an expense 'necessary for the purpose of trade' (i.e. a revenue expense), even if that expense is deferred. In fact, had the previous owners undertaken the repairs, they would have been able to set the costs against their income for tax purposes. However, the accumulation of repairs required extended partly over a period during which the ship was used, not in the purchaser's trade, but the seller's. A ship which is dilapidated is worth less than a ship which has been well maintained and is in good condition. The condition of the ship at the time of the sale was reflected in the price paid. The value of the ship was presumably increased by the repairs undertaken and hence some of the cost of the repairs should be treated as capital expenditure since they increased the value of a capital asset.

It was held that most of the expenditure was incurred because of the poor state of repair of the vessel when it was bought and this amount was disallowed as a capital expense, but £12,000 of the total expenditure was allowed for post-acquisition repairs.

In a contrasting case of *Odeon Associated Theatres Ltd* v *Jones* (1972) a cinema had been bought which was in a fairly dilapidated condition after the Second World War. The cinema was used for a number of years by its new owners before it was refurbished. In this case all of the refurbishment expenditure was allowed despite the poor condition of the cinema when it was bought.

There are two essential differences between the two cases which led to the differing conclusions. First, when the cinema was bought, the purchase price was not reduced to reflect the condition of the property which was both usable and used immediately after purchase. In the *Law Shipping* case, however, the purchase price did reflect the condition of the ship which was not seaworthy immediately after purchase. Second, the Court of Appeal decided that the costs of refurbishment for the cinema were deductible expenses in accordance with accounting principles (i.e. would go directly to the Profit and Loss account, not to the Balance Sheet) and therefore tax principles should not deviate from the normal accounting rules unless there was strong reason to – which they argued was not so in this case.

The second area which has depended on case law for clarification concerns the question of *repair or replacement*. That is, has an asset been repaired or effectively replaced following the expenditure? The cost of replacing part of an asset will generally be deductible as a revenue expense, but if it is the whole of the asset that has been replaced, it will generally be considered capital expenditure and therefore not be deductible.

To illustrate these situations, we can use the example of the case of *Samuel Jones & Co (Devondale) Ltd* v *CIR* (1951) where expenditure on a new chimney to replace the existing one was allowable because the chimney was held to be a subsidiary part of the factory. In a second case, *Brown v Burnley Football and Athletic Co Ltd* (1980), the football club replaced a wooden spectators' stand with a concrete structure which also provided additional accommodation. The expenditure was disallowed because the entire stand was replaced, which was held not to be part of a larger asset, but a distinct and separate part of the club.

Professional fees and charges

In some cases you will need to look behind the expenses to see what they relate to in order to classify them as revenue or capital. This is the case with professional fees and charges. Where they relate to capital assets or non-trading items, then they will not be deductible. Use the following activity to see how these rules can be applied.

Activity

For each of the following legal and professional charges decide whether they are allowable deductions for the purposes of computing trading income:
1.   Charges incurred in issuing shares.
2.   Charges incurred when obtaining a long (more than 50 years) lease.
3.   Charges for trade debt collection.
4.   Charges incurred with respect to an action for breach of contract.

Feedback

The first two charges would be disallowed because they relate to non-revenue items. The third charges would be allowable and the fourth charges would be allowable provided that the contract itself has the quality of revenue and not capital.

However, while this rule works most of the time, it is not always possible to classify all legal and professional charges using this rule alone and some further exploration of the actual purpose of the expenditure must be entered into to determine if it can, or cannot, be deductible. For example, the normal fees for preparing accounts and agreeing tax liabilities are allowable while legal fees incurred during tax appeals are not deductible, regardless of the outcome of the appeal. However, accountancy expenses incurred due to a HMRC investigation will be allowable provided that taxable profits for earlier years are not increased and that an increase, if any, made to the taxable profits of the year under review does not lead to interest charges or penalties.

Costs of obtaining finance

In relation to loans, interest on qualifying loans for partners or employees is treated as a tax relief, and dealt with in the personal tax computation (as we saw in Chapter 4). However, for the self-employed, interest on other types of business loans such as overdrafts, credit cards and hire purchase agreements will be allowable as revenue expenses (i.e. fully deductible in the year it is accrued) so long as they meet the 'wholly and exclusively' rule. If there is any private use of the assets purchased with the loan then this part of the interest paid is not tax deductible. Note, however, that interest paid on overdue tax is not an allowable expense (for what should be obvious reasons!).

The incidental costs of obtaining finance for the business could be considered to be capital expenses on the basis that they are one-off expenses. A special rule, however, provides that if the interest paid on the loan is tax deductible, then the incidental costs of obtaining the loan will also be deductible. This includes fees, commission, advertising and printing but does not include any stamp duty costs.

Registration of Patents

A patent is an item of intellectual property that is an asset of the business. It would be reasonable therefore to classify the cost of registering a patent as a capital expense, however the legislation specifically allows for this cost to be deductible.

Staff secondments

Where staff of the business are seconded to work for another organisation, but the business continues to pay their wages, it is arguable that the wages are no longer paid wholly and exclusively for business purposes. By special provision, where the secondment is to a charity or to an educational institution, the business can continue to claim the salary of the seconded employee as a tax deduction.

Lease premiums

If a taxpayer leases premises he or she may be required to pay a premium when the lease is granted as well as periodical rent. Because it is a one-off payment related to the acquisition of a right to use whatever is being leased, a lease premium is really capital in nature. However, a special provision allows for the premium to be claimed as a deduction. The lessee can claim the amount on which the landlord is assessable under property income; spread over the term of the lease agreement.

Activity

The lessee of business premises pays a premium of £36,000 on the grant of a 25 year lease. How much, if any, can be claimed as a deduction under the trading income rules?

Feedback

For the landlord, under the property income rules (see later in this Chapter) the assessment will be the amount of the premium reduced by 2% for each year of the lease except the first. Therefore 48% (24 × 2) of the premium is not taxable and the remaining 52% is taxable. The property income assessment is therefore 52% of £36,000 or £18,720.

The tenant can claim a deduction for that amount spread over the lifetime of the lease, i.e. £18,720 ÷ 25 or £748.80 each year.

3. Specifically disallowed items

The final of our three criteria for deductibility of expenses in trading income tax computations is whether the expenses are specifically disallowed by legislation.

There are a number of items which would appear to be deductible for trading income purposes using the first two rules we outlined at the start of this section (namely incurred wholly and exclusively for the purpose of trade and not of a capital nature) but are specifically excluded from being deductible by legislation. The following are some of the more commonly encountered cases in this category.

Fines and penalties

Any payments made which are held to be contrary to public policy, such as fines or penalties, are disallowable. However, in practice, deductions for parking fines incurred by employees parking the employer's cars during the course of their employer's business are usually allowed, although such fines incurred by directors and proprietors are never allowed.

With effect from 1 April, 2002, deductions also cannot be claimed for any payments, such as bribes, made overseas that would be a criminal payment if made in the UK.

Entertainment

Most expenditure on hospitality and entertainment is disallowed. This includes entertaining customers and clients whether they are UK based or overseas. The main exception is the entertainment of genuine employees of the business. This expense, as with most expenses relating to employees, is fully deductible. You will recall from Chapter 5, however, that where an employee is entitled to attend an annual Christmas party or similar, the value of which is more than £150 a person, a benefit in kind will arise to the employee. The full cost of the function will still be deductible to the employer however much they spend per employee.

Gifts

Gifts to charities are given special treatment in the personal income tax computation outside of the trading income calculation. Businesses may, however make gifts to other categories of people, including customers and employees. As a general rule, gifts to customers are disallowed unless they cost less than £50, contain a conspicuous advertisement for the business and are not food, drink or tobacco. Gifts to employees are allowable deductions for the business, but may be a taxable benefit in kind in the hands of the employee as we saw in Chapter 5.

Expensive car leases or hire charges

The cost of hiring or leasing plant and equipment for business purposes is generally deductible. The ongoing lease rental payments are of a revenue nature, not a capital expense which the outright purchase of these items would be.

For lease agreements entered into before 6 April 2009, there was an exception to this general rule in the case of expensive motor vehicles. Where a car cost more than £12,000, the amount of car hire, or lease expense, was restricted using the following formula:

$$\text{Lease or hire expenses} \times \frac{£12,000 + \frac{1}{2}\,(\text{cost of car} - £12,000)}{\text{cost of car}}$$

This tells you how much of the lease expense is deductible for tax purposes, the rest is disallowed.

For car lease agreements entered into on or after 6 April 2009 the expensive car restriction has been removed. A new restriction refers to the CO_2 emissions of the vehicle instead. For leased cars with CO_2 emissions of more than 160g/km a flat 15% disallowance applies, i.e., only 85% of the lease payments are deductible.

Do note however, that since 17 April, 2002, where the car is a low-emission vehicle, this special rule will not apply and the full amount of the lease expense will be deductible irrespective of the cost.

Redundancy payments

Where payments are made to staff who are made redundant, they will be deductible so long as it can be shown that they are wholly and exclusively for the purposes of the trade. If the payments are made by a business that is ceasing to trade, however, there is a restriction on the amount that can be claimed as a tax deduction. The limit is the statutory amount plus three times this statutory amount for each employee (i.e. a total of four times whatever that employee's statutory redundancy pay entitlement is).

Pre-trading expenses

Expenditure can only be a deductible expense from trading income if it is incurred on or after the date on which the business commences to trade. However, expenses incurred in the seven years prior to this date will be treated as a loss which arises on the date of commencement provided they relate directly to the new business. The reason for treating it this way relates to the way in which the basis period rules work for commencing businesses.

If your course of study requires you to understand the basis period rules (e.g. allocating accounting profit to tax periods during the opening and closing periods of a business' life), you can find further explanations and worked examples on the website.

Appropriations of profit and provisions

Where a sole trader makes drawings from the business profits, this is an appropriation and is not deductible. As such, any drawings must be included in the taxable profit calculation.

Another item which is not deductible is a provision for accounting purposes. For tax purposes, to be deductible an expense must be reasonably certain to arise. Where for accounting purposes an adjustment is made to profit in the interests of prudence, for example a provision for doubtful debts, this will not be deductible. In the case of adjustments to debtors, for tax purposes, only debts written off or which are reasonably estimated to be bad will be deductible.

A further example of an unacceptable provision is *depreciation* for accounting purposes. Where depreciation is included in the accounts, it cannot be claimed as a tax deduction. As depreciation is related to apportioning the costs of capital assets over time and may be subject to abuse (at least in theory) to affect reported tax profits, the tax system has its own regime for calculating allowable costs related to the purchase of certain capital assets (called capital allowances) which we will examine more closely in the next chapter.

A question of timing

The timing of expenses deductions usually follows the accounting rules, i.e. expenses are deducted for tax purposes in the year in which they accrue (not when they are paid). There are two main exceptions to this general rule. One is for payments to employees. A special rule says that if a business deducts payments to employees on an accrued basis, but then the actual payment is not made until more than 9 months after the end of the accounting period, then the deduction is disallowed and deferred to the following year.

Another variation is for pension contributions made by a business for its employees. Where contributions are made to registered pension schemes, they are deductible in the period in which they are paid, which is different to the accounting treatment. In addition, a special rule applies where there is an increase of more than 210% in the level of employer contribution from one period to the next. In such cases, if the excess contribution is more than £500,000, the deduction is spread over two or more years, depending on the level of the payment.

Calculating tax adjusted trading profits

You can now identify taxable revenues and allowable deductions for trading income purposes. As mentioned earlier, rather than start a whole new calculation of net profit for tax purposes, instead we start with the net accounting profit. This is then adjusted to take into account those cases where the tax treatment of items is different to the accounting treatment. Because the final figure we are calculating is the trading income, adjustments also need to be made to remove items that are dealt with under different categories, for example, savings or property income. In undertaking this computation for exam questions, or in practice, you may find it helpful to use this pro forma to undertake the adjustment of profits to the trading income (Note: figures are for illustration only):

Computation of the trading income assessment:

	£	£
Net profit per accounts		20,000
Add:		
Expenditure in the accounts which is not deductible for tax purposes	3,000	
Income which is taxable but not directly credited to the P & L account	1,000	4,000
		24,000
Less:		
Income in the accounts which is not taxable	2,000	
Expenditure not in the accounts which is deductible for tax purposes	3,000	(5,000)
Tax Adjusted Trading income		19,000

To see how this is useful in practice, see the following activity.

Activity

Monica has been in business for a number of years. Her profit and loss account for the year to 31 August, 2010 is as follows:

	Note	£	£
Sales			100,000
Less: Cost of sales			(40,000)
Gross profit			60,000
Add:			
Bank interest		500	
Profit from sale of plant		300	
Rental income		1,000	1,800
			61,800
Less:			
Rent and rates		3,000	
Insurance		1,000	
Heating, lighting and power		1,500	
Repairs and renewals	(a)	1,500	
Telephone	(b)	400	
Motor expenses	(c)	500	
Bad debts	(d)	200	
Wages and salaries	(e)	20,000	
Legal fees	(f)	300	
Sundry expenses		1,000	
Interest on a credit card		100	
Depreciation		3,000	(32,500)
Net Profit			29,300

Notes:

(a) This figure includes £1,000 spent on furnishing a new showroom and £200 redecorating the reception area.
(b) 30% of the telephone cost relate to private use.
(c) 20% of the motor expenses relate to private use.
(d) Bad debts is made up of £120 trade debt written off and £80 increase in the general provision for bad debts.
(e) This figure includes drawings of £8,000.
(f) The legal fees related to the purchase of plant and machinery.

Required: Determine the tax adjusted trading profit for the year ended 31 August, 2010.

Feedback

	£	£
Net profit per the accounts		29,300
Add: Disallowed expenditure		
Drawings	8,000	
Capital expenditure	1,000	
Telephone 400 × 30%	120	
Motor expenses 500 × 20%	100	
General provision for bad debts	80	
Legal fees	300	
Depreciation	3,000	12,600
		41,900
Less: Non-trading income		
Rental income	1,000	
Bank interest	500	
Profit from sales of plant	300	(1,800)
Tax adjusted profit		40,100

Notes:

- Drawings are not allowable as they represent an appropriation of profit by the proprietor.
- The £1,000 spent on furnishing the new showroom is capital expenditure. This may qualify for capital allowances which we will discuss in the next chapter. Note that the cost of redecoration, which has to be done periodically, is of a revenue nature, so no adjustment is necessary for that expense.
- Private expenditure must be excluded under the wholly and exclusively rule (e.g. for telephone and car expenses).
- General provisions are not allowable for tax purposes.
- To decide whether legal fees are deductible, you must consider what they relate to. Here it is for purchase of plant and machinery, a capital transaction, and so the legal fees are also considered to be capital and disallowable.
- Accounting depreciation is not deductible for tax purposes (capital allowances related to these assets will potentially be claimable instead as we will see in the next chapter).
- Rental income is taxed as property income and so must be excluded from the trading income computation. It will appear in a separate part of Monica's overall tax computation.
- Bank interest is taxed as savings income and so must also be excluded here. Again, it is instead listed separately in Monica's overall tax computation.
- Profit on sale of plant is a capital receipt and must be excluded.

There may be capital gains tax liability on this item, see Chapter 8 for details of how this could be calculated and taxed.

To draw together all the points made in this chapter, we will use another activity. You are advised to work through this long example carefully so that you can be sure you understand how the principles we have discussed are translated into a trading profit adjustment and how these are placed into a simple tax computation.

Activity

Roger Riviere is a self-employed wholesale clothing distributor who commenced trading on 1 July, 1997. His summarised accounts for the year ended 30 June, 2010 are:

		£	£
Sales	(1)		400,000
Opening stock	(2)	40,000	
Purchases		224,000	
		264,000	
Closing stock	(2)	(32,000)	232,000
Gross profit			168,000
Wages and national insurance	(3)	52,605	
Rent and business rates		31,140	
Repairs and renewals	(4)	3,490	
Miscellaneous expenses	(5)	665	
Taxation (Roger's income tax)		15,590	
Bad debts	(6)	820	
Legal expenses	(7)	1,060	
Depreciation		570	
Loss on sale of office furniture		60	
Transport costs		4,250	
Interest	(8)	990	
Motor car running expenses (Roger's car)	(9)	2,000	
Lighting and heating		1,250	
Sundry expenses (all allowable)		710	
Relocation expenditure	(10)	2,400	117,600
Net profit			50,400

Notes to accounts:
1. Sales include £500 reimbursed by Roger's family for clothing taken from stock. This reimbursement represented cost price.

2. Stock: The basis of both opening and closing stock valuations was 'lower of cost or market value' less a contingency reserve of 50%.

4. Wages: Included in wages are Roger's drawing of £50 per week, his national insurance contributions of £320 for the year and wages and national insurance contributions in respect of his wife totalling £11,750. His wife worked full-time in the business as a secretary.

5. Repairs and renewals: The charge includes £3,000 for fitting protective covers over the factory windows and doors to prevent burglary.

6. Miscellaneous expenses:

	£	£
Theft of money by employee	65	
Political donation to Green Party	100	
Gifts of 100 'Riviere' calendars	500	665

7. Bad debts:

	£	£
Trade debt written off		720
Loan to former employee written off		250
Provision for bad debts (2% of debtors)	450	
Less: Opening provision	(600)	(150)
		820

8. Legal expenses:

	£
Defending action in respect of alleged faulty goods	330
Costs in connection with lease of new larger premises	250
Successful appeal against previous year's income tax assessment	200
Defending Roger in connection with speeding offence	190
Debt collection	90
	(1,060)

9. Interest:

	£	£
Bank overdraft interest (business account)	860	
Interest on overdue tax	130	990

10. Motor car running expenses. One-third of Roger's mileage is private. Included in the charge is £65 for a speeding fine incurred by Roger whilst delivering goods to a customer.

11. Relocation expenditure. The expenditure was incurred in transferring the business to new and larger premises.

The following information is also provided:

1. Capital allowances for the year to 30 June, 2010 are £480 (in Chapter 7 we will show you how to undertake the computation to produce these numbers).

2. Roger was born on 8 April, 1969 and, due to his rapid aging, decided to make a pension contribution this year to his pension fund of £13,500 under a 'relief at source' arrangement.

3. Roger has no other sources of income.

You are required:
a)   To prepare a profit adjustment in respect of the accounting period to 30 June, 2010 showing the tax adjusted profit.
b)   To calculate the Class 4 national insurance contributions payable for 2010/11 (using the data provided)
c)   To prepare an estimate for Roger of the income tax payable for 2010/11 and to advise him when the tax will become due for payment.

Feedback

(a)   Profit adjustment statement year ended 30 June, 2010

	£	£
Net profit per accounts		50,400
Add:		
(1) Sales: Goods for own use (see working 1 below)	333	
(3) Wages: Roger's drawings (appropriation)	2,600	
Roger's NIC (private)	320	
(4) Capital cost of fitting covers	3,000	
(5) Miscellaneous:		
Political donation (not wholly and exclusively)	100	
Taxation (private)	15,590	
(6) Loan to former employee (not business)	250	
(7) Legal expenses:		
Lease of new and larger premises (capital)	250	
Cost in connection tax appeal (private)	200	
Defending re: speeding offence (private)	190	
Depreciation	570	
Loss on sale of office furniture (capital)	60	
(8) Interest: on overdue tax (private)	130	
(9) Motor car running expenses:		
Fine (not deductible)	65	
1/3 of remaining expenses (private)	645	
(10) Re-location expenditure (capital)	2,400	26,703
Less:		
Capital allowances	480	
(Chapter 7 will discuss this item further)		
(2) Stock adjustment for contingency (working 2)	8,000	
(6) Reduction in general bad debt provision	150	(8,630)
Tax adjusted trading profit		68,473

(b) Class 4 National insurance contributions

8% × (£43,875 – £5,715) + 1% (68,473 – 43,875) = £3,298.78

(c) Computation of income tax liability 2010/11

	Non-savings £	Total £
Income:		
Trading income		
(adjusted profits)	68,473	68,473
Total Income	68,473	68,473
Less Personal Allowances	(6,475)	(6,475)
Total Taxable Income	61,998	61,998

Roger has made pension contributions of £13,500. This is the gross amount of the payment. As we saw in Chapter 5, basic tax relief for the pension payment is obtained by Roger making the payment net of income tax at the basic rate. That is, he will pay only £10,800 (£13,500 × 80%). Higher rate relief is given by extending his basic rate band by the gross amount of the premium, £13,500. Roger's basic rate band is therefore increased to £50,900 (£37,400 + £13,500).

Tax Due:

		£
Non savings income	50,900 @ 20%	10,180.00
	11,098 @ 40%	4,439.20
Tax Liability		14,619.20

Workings
1. Goods taken for Roger's own use must be included at market value. They have been reimbursed at cost, so we need to increase Roger's profit by the tax profit associated with goods costing £500:

	£
Sales £500 × 400/240	833
Less cost of sales	(500)
Profit	333

The sales price of the goods for Roger's own use is arrived at by multiplying the cost of those goods (£500) by Roger's gross sales figure (£400,000) divided by the restated cost of sales (£240,000) – see working 2 below.

2. The valuation of stock for tax purposes is on the basis of 'lower of cost or market value'. Therefore the cost of goods sold by Roger for tax purposes is:

Opening stock	80,000
Plus purchases	224,000
	304,000
Less closing stock	(64,000)
Cost of goods sold	240,000

Roger has only deducted cost of goods sold of £232,000 in his profit and loss account – a further deduction of £8,000 is required.

Basis of assessment

Tax is raised for individuals for tax years (6 April to following 5 April). These are called 'Assessment Years'. For employed people it is easy to assign their income to these periods to calculate their income tax liability as most employees are paid on a weekly, or monthly, basis – so we can just add up their payslips for the twelve month period (or use their P60 issued annually by their employer if they have this). For self-employed people paying tax on trading income however, this is not quite so straightforward because their income is based on their accounts, as we have just seen in the previous section. Accounts are produced in periods usually, but not always, of twelve months in length. These accounting periods may start and finish at different point during the year to the tax year, as suits the business. To perform tax computations for self-employed people we therefore need rules for how to allocate their trading income to tax years.

In this section we will discuss how these rules operate in the UK at present. These rules were introduced in 1998/99 for all unincorporated businesses as part of the self-assessment regime currently in operation in the UK for individual taxpayers.

As described in Chapter 4, the normal basis of assessment for unincorporated businesses is the *current year* basis. Under the current year regime the general rule is that the profits arising in the tax year will be assessed in the tax year. This is sometimes termed the *actual* basis because the actual profits arising in the tax year form the basis of assessment for the tax year. In particular, the profits in the tax year in which the business commenced will be taxed on the actual basis. However, if a sole trader or partnership uses an annual accounting date which is not 5 April the basis of assessment of a tax year will be the 12 months to the accounting date which falls in the tax year.

Since not every business will use 5 April as an accounting date, the accounting period ended in the tax year will normally form the basis period for the tax year.

To ensure you understand these rules, try the following activity.

Activity

For each of the following annual accounting dates state the tax year for which they will form the basis period.
- a) 30 June, 2009
- b) 31 August, 2008
- c) 30 November, 2009
- d) 31 January, 2009
- e) 31 March, 2011
- f) 30 April, 2010.

Feedback

The tax years for which these accounts form the basis period are:
- (a) 2009/10
- (b) 2008/09
- (c) 2009/10
- (d) 2008/09
- (e) 2010/11
- (f) 2010/11

There are some circumstances in which the normal basis of assessment cannot be applied. These usually fall in the opening and closing years of a business trading or when the business decides to change its accounting date. Further explanations and worked examples for these extra rules can be found on the website.

Loss relief

What happens then, if the expenses of a trading business exceed the revenue for tax purposes? In such a case, there are a number of possible ways of relieving the tax loss. The loss can be offset against other categories of income that the taxpayer has during the year (sideways relief). Alternatively, the loss can be carried forward to the following year to offset trading income for that year. Finally, the loss can be carried back to previous years to be offset against the general income of that year. We will look more closely at these rules in the following chapter.

Property income

Having examined how trading income is computed, the final income component we will examine is property income. Most income from land and property located in the UK is taxed under the property income rules. This includes rents, lease premiums (if the lease is for not more than 50 years), income from rights of way or sporting rights over land or income from letting of fixed caravans or permanently moored house boats. The exceptions to this rule are hotels and guest houses as these are treated as trading income (use the rules therefore contained in the earlier parts of this chapter).

Taxable income from UK property is pooled (i.e. added together) to create one net profit or loss from all property belonging to a taxpayer. This profit or loss is calculated in the same way as trading profits are computed (i.e. as discussed in the previous section). Receiving money from UK property is referred to as running a 'property business'.

Income from most property (apart from furnished holiday lettings) is treated as 'unearned' income in a taxpayer's income tax computation, not 'earned' income. A key implication of this is that it cannot be used as a source of income to count towards deductible pension contributions, nor can this type of property usually gain from business asset rates for rollover relief when calculating capital gains tax on property sales. The rules for furnished holiday lettings are different – these can count for pension contributions and for business asset rates of rollover relief etc. We will examine these specific differences later in this section.

The basis of assessment for property income is the income for the tax year, computed using the accruals basis as we did for trading income. However, for very small, simple businesses, for example where income is only received from one property, it is likely that the cash received basis will be acceptable if you wish to argue this case with the Revenue.

The property income accounts will include the total income from land and property in the UK, regardless of the source, less total allowable expenses – i.e. to follow the same principles as we outlined above for trading income. Examples of allowable expenses include:

- expenses incurred wholly and exclusively for the purpose of the business such as repairs, insurance, advertising, legal costs, etc.;

- capital allowances for plant and machinery which enable taxpayers to carry on their business (unless the property is a dwelling where no capital allowances are available – see Chapter 7 for more on this);

- capital allowances for landlords of residential property on loft and cavity wall insulation up to a value of £1,500; and

- rent paid by the property business to another landlord (e.g. when rental income results from sub-letting).

If the rental comes from a furnished dwelling (of any kind other than holiday lettings), an allowance is given as a deduction from the profits earned in the property business for the usage of fixed assets in the business either on *'wear and tear' basis* or by using an alternative *renewals basis*. The 'wear and tear' rules allow for usage of fixed assets to be claimed at 10% of the relevant receipts from furnished lettings as relief for the wear and tear of furniture and equipment provided as part of the letting. Relevant receipts are gross receipts less any sums for services which would normally be borne by the tenant (payment of the council tax by the landlord would be an example of this).

Alternatively, the taxpayer may elect to use the renewals basis to spread the cost of the use of fixed assets in the business. The renewals basis entitles the taxpayer to deduct the cost of replacing furniture. Note, however, that the initial costs of acquiring furniture are not allowable expenses if the renewals basis is chosen, only the replacement costs when this occurs.

Unlike normal trading businesses (see Chapter 7), these are the only capital expenditure deductions allowed for property businesses.

The following activity illustrates how property income can be assessed in practice.

Activity

Andrew has a furnished house which is let for £4,800 per annum payable monthly in advance. Andrew incurred the following expenditure in the tax year.

		£
June 2010	Replacement of doors and windows with double glazed units.	1,500
July 2010	Annual insurance premium runs from 1 August to 31 July (last year's premium was £600)	900
November 2010	Redecoration	500
June 2011	Repairs to boiler – the work was undertaken and completed in January 2010	200

Andrew claims the 10% wear and tear allowance. Andrew's tenant left in May 2010 without paying the rent due for May. Andrew was unable to recover the debt but he let the house to new tenants from 1 July, 2010. Determine Andrew's property income assessment for 2010/11.

Feedback

	£	£
Rent accrued 400 × 11		4,400
Less allowable expenses:		
Doors and windows replacement	1,500	
Insurance (4/12 × 600 + 8/12 × 900)	800	
Redecoration	500	
Repairs to boiler	200	
Bad debt – May 2010 rent	400	
Wear and tear 10% × (4,400 – 400)	400	(3,800)
Property income assessment		600

Loss relief

In general, losses arising under property income rules are carried forward and set against the first available property income profits in the future. If a loss arises across all a taxpayer's property business, the assessment for that year will be nil. If a loss arises for one part of the business only it will be netted against any gains in other parts first however, as part of the pooling of property income. As with trading losses, where it is to be used as a relief against general income, it is included in the tax computation at step 2.

An illustration of the property income loss rules can be found on the website. This demonstrates how they work in practice.

Furnished holiday lettings

A special tax position exists for furnished holiday lettings (including both houses and caravans). Income from this kind of property is assessed under property income rules, however, the regulations which apply to trading income are used to determine the taxable income as this income is normally treated as "earned income" unlike other property income (which you will recall we said at the start of this section is treated as unearned income). This means normal capital allowances can be claimed (i.e. instead of wear and tear allowance or renewals basis as for other dwellings), capital gains tax relief for the disposal of business assets (i.e. entrepreneurs' relief and rollover relief, which are explained in Chapter 8) is available and loss relief can be claimed under the regulations which apply to losses incurred by traders (see Chapter 7).

Because these profits are treated as earned income the taxpayer can also provide for retirement by making contributions to a pension fund that include this income in their computation (see the later section in this chapter for more detail on pensions). However, no Class 4 national insurance contributions are due on this income source as Class 4 only applies to income assessed under trading income.

Note that the basis period rules for property income rather than trading income still apply to income from furnished holiday lettings despite this special treatment.

To be eligible for this advantageous treatment the accommodation must be let commercially with the aim of making a profit. Also, the following three rules must apply:

1. The property must be available for letting to the public for at least 140 days in the tax year, and
2. must have actually been let for at least 70 of those days.
3. For at least 155 days (including the 70 days from rule 2) the property must not normally be occupied by the same tenant for more than 31 days.

In addition, if the taxpayer owns more than one property each of which satisfies the 140 day rule, they will all be deemed to satisfy the 70 day rule providing their average number of days let is at least 70.

Activity

Leonard owned four furnished houses in a village in the Yorkshire Dales which are let as holiday homes. None of the houses is normally let to the same tenant for more than 31 consecutive days. The numbers of days for which each house was available for letting and actually let in 2009/10 were:

House	Days available	Days let
1	160	85
2	175	50
3	130	115
4	160	65

Determine Leonard's potential averaging claims.

Feedback

House 3 does not satisfy the 140 day availability rule and so cannot be included in an averaging claim. If no averaging claim is made, only house 1 qualifies as furnished holiday accommodation.

Possible averaging claim	Average days let
House 1 and 2	67.5
House 1 and 4	75.0
House 2 and 4	57.5
House 1, 2 and 4	66.7

Averaging house 1 and 4 is beneficial because the average number of days is 75. No other averaging claim would succeed.

The furnished holiday lettings rules only applied to UK property, until 6 April 2009 when they were extended to property in the European Economic Area. It was proposed that the special rules for furnished holiday lettings would be abolished in 2010/11, however the Emergency Budget in June 2010 confirmed these rules would continue for 2010/11 but be subject to revised plans from April 2011.

The 'rent a room' scheme

If an individual lets one or more furnished rooms in his or her main residence then rents received up to a limit of £4,250 in 2009/10 (unchanged in the last few years) are exempt from tax under property income. If another individual is also receiving rent from letting accommodation in the same property (for example, as joint owner) the limit of £4,250 will be halved. If the total receipts are in excess of £4,250 (£2,125 if halved) then the taxpayer has a choice as to how they are taxed. Either the excess receipts over £4,250 (£2,215) is taxed in full (i.e. no deductions are allowed) or they can choose to be taxed on a normal trading computation principle (i.e. the gross rents received minus any allowable deductions, such as heating costs is taxed instead - although note that for capital expenditure deductions, such as for the furniture for the room, normal capital allowances are not available as this is in a dwelling house, instead the 10% 'wear and tear' allowance would be applied for these expense). The taxpayer has the choice of which of these two calculations should determine their taxable income in this case.

Any income arising from the 'rent-a-room' scheme is normally likely to be treated as part of property income in the taxpayers' tax computation. If a trade is being carried out however, (e.g. if meals are cleaning/laundry services are also provided in addition to just the charge for the use of a room itself) then this income can probably be added to trading income totals.

Fiscal Fact

The estimated cost to the UK Government of allowing the rent-a-room scheme for 2009/10 is £120 million.

Premiums on leases

When a lease is granted the lessee may have to pay a premium to the lessor. A premium is a lump sum payment at the commencement of the lease and is different to the regular lease or rental payments made throughout the course of the lease. In fact, some leases are structured so that the lessor receives very little rent for the duration of the lease but has to depend on the lease premium for income from the property. This situation is most typically found in commercial (e.g. office space) leases.

If the lease term is more than 50 years (termed a *long lease*) then the premium is taxable as a capital gain rather than an income. If the lease is for 50 years or less (a *short lease*) income tax is paid on the value of the premium less 2% of the premium for each complete year of the lease after the first year. Written as a formula the assessable amount of the lease premium therefore equals:

$$P - (P \times (L - 1) \times 2\%)$$

where P is the premium on the lease and L is the length of the lease.

Activity

Amanda granted a 21-year lease on a property on 1 January, 2011 for an initial premium of £30,000 and an annual rent of £6,000 payable monthly in advance. Determine Amanda's property income assessment for 2010/11 and 2011/12.

Feedback

In 2010/11 the assessment on the premium of the lease is £18,000 (£30,000 − (£30,000 × (21 − 1) × 2%)). The rent due in 2010/11 is £1,500 (£6,000 × 3/12). Hence the total property income assessment for 2010/11 is £19,500 (£18,000 + £1,500). In 2011/12 the property income assessment will be £6,000.

We saw earlier that if the property is used for business purposes, the lessee on a short lease can claim a tax deduction against their trading profits of the annual equivalent of the amount of premium they paid and on which the landlord is liable to pay tax in each year of the lease. In the activity above, Amanda's tenant would therefore be able to claim a deduction of £18,000÷21 = £857 in each year of the life of the lease.

Note that the above rules on premiums only apply on the granting of the lease (i.e. from landlord to lessee) not if it is subsequently assigned (i.e. from one lessee to another lessee).

In some cases a premium may actually be paid by the landlord to the lessee (rather than the lessee to the landlord) perhaps as an inducement to the lessee to take on the lease. This occurs most commonly in commercial leasing. This type of premium is usually called a *reverse premium*. When a reverse premium is paid the landlord can usually either treat the payment made as an enhancement expenditure against their capital gains tax bill when they sell the property (see Chapter 8 for details of how this works in practice), or as an allowable business expense if they are a property developer or dealer. Of course, the lessee must declare the receipt of the premium as income on which they will have to pay tax (under trading income if the property rented is used for this business, or under property income if it is not for commercial use).

Summary

This chapter looks trading and property income components. It outlines how to distinguish between a trading activity and an activity which is carried out as a non-trading activity, maybe as a hobby. It outlines how the 'Badges of Trade' are used in practice for this assessment given we have no legal definition for trading. As accounting profit for the business is the foundation for trading income assessments, it then focuses on how to adjust the accounting figures to arrive at amounts that will be acceptable for the tax computation. This involves manipulation of both receipts and expenses from the accounts. A detailed worked example is then provided to illustrate these principles in practice.

The question of what happens when a trading activity results in a loss will be considered in Chapter 7.

Property income is discussed illustrating the specific rules used for computing this component of income, particular focusing on how income from furnished holiday letting property can be taxed differently to income from other dwellings. The special rules for the 'rent-a-room' scheme and for lease premiums were also outlined.

Project areas

This chapter provides a rich source of material for projects including the:

- impact of taxation on reported profit.
- differences between trading and non-trading activities in practice
- classification of expenses into revenue and capital items
- use of different recognition bases for reporting profits
- advantages of income from furnished holiday lettings being considered to be trading income. Does it just give special tax breaks to rich people with second homes distorting local housing in some areas of the UK?

Quick quiz

(Assume all the following relate to activities that are trading)

1. Matthew charges £800 to his profit and loss account for bad and doubtful debts. This figure consists of £300 trade debts written off, £150 staff loan written off, £100 increase in specific provision and £250 increase in general provision. What amount (if any) is to be added back in the course of adjusting profits for tax purpose?

2. Nola leases a car for use in her business, which costs £25,000 when new, for £4,200 per annum. How much of this annual cost is deductible given that the lease was entered into prior to 6 April 2009? What difference would it make if the lease was entered into on or after 6 April 2009?

3. Orlando spends £500 on 100 T-shirts, printed with his business logo, to give to his customers, and spends £200 per head on a Christmas party for his 5 staff. How much (if any) of this expenditure is deductible?

4. Pauline takes goods costing £90 from her business stock for her own personal use. She normally sells such items for £115. What adjustment is required to her net profit for tax purposes if she pays nothing for the goods?

5. Quentin pays a lease premium of £10,000 for the 15 year lease of his business premises. How much of this (if any) can he deduct?

6. Rachel incurs legal fees for her business of £500 being £30 for debt collection, £270 for the acquisition of new business premises and £200 for registration of a patent. How much (if any) can she deduct?

7. Gerald rents a house to a tenant for a rental payable monthly in advance. The annual rent of £8,400 was increased to £8,600 on 6 October, 2010. How much is assessable as Gerald's property income?

8. In 2010/11, Heather receives a lease premium of £48,000 in respect of a 40 year lease. How much (if any) is chargeable as property income?

Questions

Question 1 (based on CIMA May 1992 - updated).

The following events occurred and were reflected in the profit and loss account of Mr Jones' self employed business for the year ended 31 March, 2011.

Debits

(a) Expenditure of £8,500 was incurred on the reconstruction of a roof on a second-hand warehouse which was recently purchased. This had been damaged in a fire some months before Jones acquired it.

(b) During the year a director was convicted of embezzlement and the amount of the loss, as established in court, was £18,000.

(c) Due to a contraction of the trade, a works manager was made redundant. His statutory redundancy entitlement was £12,000 and the total gratuitous lump sum paid to him (including the £12,000) was £38,000.

(d) For the whole of the year, one of the senior managers was seconded to work full-time for a national charity. Her annual salary, included in the salaries charged in the profit and loss account, was £24,000.

(e) Costs of £24,000 were incurred in constructing a crèche to be used for employees' children. Administration costs include £8,000 in respect of the running costs of the crèche incurred during the year.

Credits

(f) £24,000 was received from an insurance company in respect of damage caused to a processing plant as a result of a fork-lift truck colliding with it. The cost of repairing the plant was £18,000 and this was credited against the repairs account. The additional £6,000 was an agreed sum paid for loss of profits while the plant was unusable and this was credited to the profit and loss account.

(g) A gain of £30,000 arose on the sale of selected investments. No details of the original cost or disposal price are given at this stage.

(h) Mr Jones has included in his sales figure for the year, sales amounting to £50,000 to X Ltd, a company in which he has an interest. These sales have been heavily discounted and, if they had been made at the normal retail price, would have been sold for £80,000.

Required: Indicate, giving full reasons and quoting case law where appropriate, how each of the above items would be dealt with in arriving at the tax adjusted trading profit figure for the year.

You must state in your answer whether each item would be added to or subtracted from the profit shown by the profit and loss account (which is not given) or left unadjusted.

Question 2 (based on ACCA Paper 7 December 1999 - updated)

The following items have been charged against profit in the accounts of William Oakley, a shoe manufacturer, for the year ended 31 March, 2011:

1. In Repairs and Renewals an amount of £2,000 was included for the fitting of security bars over the factory windows as a precaution against theft.
2. A loan of £100 to a former employee was written off.
3. Gifts of 'Oakley' calendars in December 2010 costing £12 each.
4. Incidental costs incurred in obtaining a bank loan, £350.
5. A donation of 5 pairs of running shoes, costing a total of £200, when sponsoring a local charity raising money by organising a marathon.
6. A lease rental of £4,000 per annum on a car provided for a senior employee. The car cost £14,000 and the lease commenced in 2008.
7. Registering a patent for a new shoe design, £1,275.
8. A parking fine of £100 incurred by an employee (not William) on a business trip to Manchester.
9. Payment of £6,000 re-location expenses to a new employee.
10. In Repairs and Renewals an amount of £2,000 to re-condition a second-hand stitching machine bought for £10,000. The repairs were necessary before the machine could be used in the business.
11. Cost of a course in computer skills, costing £350, for William himself who had no previous computer experience.

Required: You are required to state how you would deal with each of the items when preparing the tax adjusted profit computation for the year ended 31 March, 2011. You should give a brief explanation for your treatment of each item.

(Note: answer available via lecturer's website)

Question 3

Vincent's profit and loss account for the year to 31 August, 2010 was as follows:

	£		£
General expenses(1)	114,000	Gross trading profit	295,000
Repairs and renewals(2)	20,000	Bad debts recovered	
Legal and accounting charges(3)	1,200	(previously written off)	400
Subscriptions and donations(4)	3,000	Commissions received(5)	800
Manager's remuneration	40,000	Bank interest (net)	1,000
Salaries and wages to staff	38,000		
Depreciation	20,000		
Rent and rates	1,500		
Net profit	59,500		
	297,200		297.200

Notes

(1) General expenses include the following:

	£
Travelling expenses of staff	1,000
Entertaining suppliers	600

(2) Repairs and renewals include the following:

Redecorating existing premises	300
Renovations to new premises to remedy wear and tear of previous owner (the premises were usable before these renovations)	500

(3) Legal and accounting charges are made up as follows:

Debt collection service	200
Staff service agreements	50
Tax consultant's fees for special advice	730
Audit and accountancy	220
	1,200

(4) Subscriptions and donations include the following

Donation to a political party	700
Staff Canteen facilities – running costs	500

(5) The commissions received were not incidental to trade

(6) Capital allowances for tax purposes for the year — 4,000

(7) No payment to Vincent is included in the Manager's remuneration or Salaries and Wages to staff

247

Required: Compute Vincent's tax adjusted profits and, assuming he has no other income or deductions, calculate the income tax and national insurance contributions payable.

(Note: answer available via lecturer's website)

Question 4 (Based on ACCA December 1999).

In 2010/11 Theresa received various income from property she owned. Details of the income and corresponding expenses were:

(i)   Rent from letting out a room in her house for £3,000.

(ii)   Rent from a furnished flat. The flat had been let on a lease which expired on 23 June 2010 at an annual rent of £5,000. The property was re-let from 24 June 2010 on a seven-year lease at an annual rent of £8,000. In addition the incoming tenant was required to pay a premium of £3,000.

Expenditures in the year ended 5 April 2011 were:
a) An annual insurance premium of £450 was paid for the flat on 1 May 2010. (£400 was paid on 1 May 2009).
b) Water rates and council tax £1,200.
c) Sundry repairs £350.

The rent on both leases was paid in advance on the usual quarter days, 25 March, 24 June, 29 September and 25 December.

(iii)   Rent from a holiday cottage, which fulfils the requirements to be treated as furnished holiday accommodation. The rent received was £4,200 and the following expenditure was incurred:

	£
Insurance	500
Water rates and council tax	900
Sundry repairs and decorating	400
Cleaning	240
Accountancy	100
Advertising	400
Capital allowances on furniture and fittings, adjusted for private use	500
	3,040

Theresa stayed in the cottage for the whole of August but it was available for letting the remainder of the year.

Required:

(a)   Calculate Theresa's property income for the year 2010/11 assuming any necessary election is made. Calculations may be made to the nearest month.

(b)   State the tax advantages of income from property being treated as income from furnished holiday accommodation.

(Note: answer available via lecturer's website)

Further test questions for this chapter to test your knowledge can be found in the student section of the website at:

http://www.taxstudent.com/uk

Further reading and examples

Combs, A., Dixon, S. & Rowes, P. (2010), *Taxation: incorporating the 2010 Finance Acts*, Fiscal Publications: Birmingham.
– use this book for many other examples to further develop and test your knowledge of this chapter's contents. See http://www.fiscalpublications.com/rowes/2010

7 Capital allowances and trading losses

Introduction

This chapter continues the subject discussed in Chapter 6 – the taxation of unincorporated businesses. Here we consider the tax treatment of capital assets under the capital allowances rules. Although we focus in this chapter on examples related to unincorporated businesses, you need to be aware that in fact these rules also apply for employees and companies that are eligible for capital allowances. We also consider the special tax rules that apply when an unincorporated business makes a loss.

At the end of this chapter you will be able to:

- identify plant and machinery that qualify for capital allowances;
- undertake capital allowance computations for plant and machinery;
- calculate capital allowances for Industrial Buildings;
- state the capital allowance rules for patents; and
- state the special tax rules that deal with the offset of trading losses for unincorporated businesses.

Overview of capital allowances

You will remember from the previous chapter that neither depreciation nor actual capital expenditure itself (as a general rule) is an allowable deduction for income tax computations. Tax relief for capital expenditure is instead given by means of capital allowances. This ensures consistent treatment of capital assets for tax purposes, rather than allowing the multiple possible treatments that would occur if accounting depreciation policies were used in tax computations. It also allows for special tax treatment of particular assets, asset groups or types of company as Government policy may require. We will see how the current special treatments are applied later in this chapter.

The current legislation relating to capital allowances is contained in the Capital Allowances Act 2001 (CAA 2001).

Capital allowances are available to businesses on certain, but not necessarily all capital assets.

The capital allowances allowed as a deduction each year are a fixed percentage of the value of the capital asset, or pool of assets, in question. They are usually given on a *reducing balance* basis and are called *writing down allowances* (WDA).

For expenditure on capital assets to be eligible for capital allowances they must fall into one of these categories:

- plant and machinery;
- integral features;
- industrial buildings;
- patents; and
- agricultural buildings and works.

The first three categories are the most common and so we will concentrate on these in this chapter. The rules for patents will be commented upon briefly at the end of this chapter.

Plant, machinery and integral features

To calculate capital allowances for plant and machinery and integral features, we need to go through a number of steps to decide:

1. whether the capital asset qualifies for capital allowances in the first place;
2. if so, which pool the asset belongs to and the rate of capital allowance;
3. whether the Annual Investment Allowance or First Year allowance applies;
4. whether the asset requires some special treatment; and
5. whether any disposals need to be dealt with.

Only after considering each of these steps, will you be ready to do a full capital allowance computation for the year.

Capital allowances pro forma

This is what a capital allowance computation will look like for a straightforward case. It is important to make sure you deal with things in a logical order. If you know the way to lay out a capital allowances computation you will be able to calculate the capital allowances for a business with relative ease. Therefore, this is the way we have laid out the answers to activities in this section and we advise you to use it wherever you do a capital allowance calculation.

Capital allowances on the main pool for plant and machinery (numbers given are just for illustration).

	£	Main Pool £	Allowances £
Balance brought forward		130,000	
Additions qualifying for AIA:			
Plant	60,000		
AIA	(60,000)		60,000
Writing down allowance:			
Disposals		(40,000)	
		90,000	
Writing down allowance (90,000 × 20%)		(18,000)	18,000
Sub-total		72,000	
Written down value c/f		72,000	
Allowances for the accounting period			78,000

The 'allowances' column at the end is the one in which we record the amounts that will be allowed as a deduction in the computation of the tax adjusted trading income for the business (or other qualifying activity).

Fiscal Fact

The estimated cost to the government of providing capital allowances under income tax and corporation tax is £20,600 million for 2009/10.

Take careful note of the order in which adjustments are made to the value of the capital allowance pool in the above proforma. This order is important to ensure you calculate the correct writing down allowances each year. We will now consider each of the steps in turn so that you can see how the capital allowance computation is constructed.

Step 1: Does the asset qualify?

The first step is to decide whether the capital asset purchased by a business qualifies for any capital allowances or not. Like previous legislation on capital allowances, the CAA 2001 does not define what exactly constitutes plant and machinery and so it is necessary to look to case law for guidance. There has been a considerable amount of case law on this subject. One of the most important is *Yarmouth v France* (1887) in which the status of a horse was questioned. Lindley LJ concluded:

> "There is no definition of plant in the Act but in its original sense, it includes whatever apparatus is used by a businessman for carrying on his business, not his stock-in-trade which he buys or makes for sale; but all goods and chattels, fixed or moveable, live or dead, which he keeps for permanent employment in his business."

The *Yarmouth v France* decision therefore excludes trading stock from the meaning of 'plant' and implies that business premises are also excluded.

A number of subsequent cases have refined this definition somewhat. In *Wimpey International Ltd v Warland* (1988) three types of asset were excluded from the definition of plant and machinery:

- assets which are not used for carrying on the business;
- assets with a useful life of less than two years; and
- assets which form part of the setting in which the business was carried on, as opposed to assets actively used in the business.

As this judgment is actually the cumulative result of a number of earlier cases, it would be useful for us to review some of the more interesting ones. Understanding these rules is important as not having capital expenditure allowed as a tax deduction has significant cost implications for businesses.

The last requirement is referred to as the 'function v setting' test and has been the subject of a considerable number of cases, as it can be a difficult test to apply in practice. In *CIR v Barclay Curle & Co* (1969) the costs of building a dry dock was held to be expenditure on plant and machinery because the dock played an active part in the operation of the company's trade. In *Cooke v Beach Station Caravans Ltd* (1974) the costs of excavating and installing a swimming pool were held to be expenditure on plant and machinery because the swimming pool performed a function, that of 'giving buoyancy and enjoyment to the swimmers'.

In *Benson* v *Yard Arm Club* (1978) a ship which was being used as a floating restaurant was held to be ineligible for capital allowances because it failed the functional test. However, in *CIR* v *Scottish and Newcastle Breweries Ltd* (1982) it was held that light fittings, decor and murals performed the function of creating an atmosphere and so were plant. In contrast, in *Wimpey International Ltd* v *Warland* (1988) a raised floor was held not to be plant as it was considered setting, despite the argument made on the grounds that it was just there to make the restaurant attractive to customers.

In another case, *Carr* v *Sayer* (1992), quarantine kennels were held not to be plant, despite being purpose built.

In the case of *Brown* v *Burnley Football and Athletic Co Ltd* (1980) expenditure on a new football stand was held not to be plant because it did not perform a direct function in the business, just provided the setting. You will remember from the last chapter that *Burnley Football and Athletic Co Ltd* had also failed to claim the expenditure as a repair because the entire stand was replaced. Today, however, such expenditure would in fact be allowed under the special provisions currently in force, as below.

The following expenditure is automatically deemed to be plant and machinery by statute:

- expenditure on equipment in order to comply with fire regulations for a building occupied by the trader;
- expenditure on thermal insulation in an industrial building;
- expenditure in order to comply with statutory safety requirements for sports grounds;
- expenditure on computer software;
- expenditure on alterations to buildings connected to the installation of plant and machinery; and
- expenditure on personal security equipment.

In order to claim capital allowances, a person carrying on a trade must incur capital expenditure on machinery or plant wholly or partly for the purposes of the trade, and the machinery or plant must belong to him or her. The extent to which assets can be described as plant and machinery is highlighted in *Munby* v *Furlong* (1977) when a barrister successfully argued that his law library was plant because it was the apparatus used for carrying out his profession.

Integral features

One of the problem areas for deciding what qualifies as plant and machinery is items that are attached to buildings. In 2008/09 the government introduced a new category of items that qualify for capital allowances, called integral features. It consists of the following items which are integral to a building:

- An electrical system (including a lighting system);
- A cold water system;
- A space or water heating system, a powered system of ventilation, air cooling or air purification, and any floor or ceiling that is part of such a system;
- A lift, escalator or moving walkway; or
- External solar shading.

This measure was first announced in Budget 2007, and there was a considerable amount of consultation with business about the design and technical approach of this new measure. Some items that were previously treated as part of a building and therefore didn't qualify as plant and machinery for capital allowance purposes now qualify under this category. The category does not just include newly acquired items; it also extends to replacements where the whole or the majority (more than 50%) is replaced within a 12 month period.

Once we have decided whether a new capital asset qualifies for capital allowances by being either plant and machinery or integral features, the next step is to decide how much the capital allowance will be.

Step 2: Pooling and rates

If businesses were required to calculate capital allowances for each and every asset separately, the compliance costs would be very high. In order to reduce these costs, and keep the system relatively simple, the Government allows taxpayers to 'pool' certain categories of assets and perform a single calculation based on the aggregate value of the pool. There are two pools, a 'main pool' and a 'special rate pool'. There are some special rules for items that are not put into either of these pools, which we will come back to later.

For both the main and special rate pools, capital allowances are calculated on a reducing balance basis. This means that the starting point in any year's computation is the balance brought forward from the previous year. Before calculating the annual writing down allowance, however, we first must add to the balance brought forward the value of any new items, and subtract the value of any disposals. This again is in the interest of simplicity, and means that new items qualify for writing down allowances for the full year, and items disposed of don't qualify for any writing down allowance in the year of disposal writing down allowance is not apportioned for the part of the period that the asset has been owned, it is either allowed for the whole period or not at all. This is an important difference from the way depreciation may be computed for accounting profit calculations where part year ownership may be taken into account.

Main pool

The main pool consists of plant and machinery other than long life assets (see below) or items that have to be treated separately (which we consider later). For expenditure incurred before 6 April 2008 (1 April 2008 for companies) the rate at which the writing down allowance was calculated on the main pool was 25%. After these dates the rate changed to 20%. Where a business has an accounting period that spans the introduction of this new rate, a hybrid rate may have to be calculated, based on the number of days in each period.

Special rate pool

The Finance Act 2008 introduced a new capital allowance pool, referred to as the 'special rate pool', which attracts a rate of 10% writing down allowance. As with the main pool, a hybrid rate may be needed if the accounting period spans the changeover date.

Initially, there were three categories of asset that qualify for the special rate, long life assets, integral features, and thermal insulation. FA 2009 included a fourth: high CO_2 emission cars.

Long-life assets are those items of plant and machinery purchased since 26 November 1996 that have a useful life of 25 years or more when new.

Prior to 6 April 2008 (1 April 2008 for companies) the rate of writing down allowance for long-life assets was 6% and they were put into a separate pool but from these dates they form part of the special rate pool.

Note, however, that the long-life asset rules only apply to businesses spending more than £100,000 per annum on such long-life assets. Also, some assets are never treated as long life assets including:

- machinery or plant in a building used wholly or mainly as (or for purposes ancillary to) a dwelling-house, retail shop, showroom, hotel or office
- cars (including hire cars) and taxis
- sea-going ships and railway assets bought before the end of 2010.

As most small businesses (and often many medium sized ones too) will not spend more than £100,000 a year on long-life capital assets, these assets are instead dealt with as part of the main pool, and not put into the special rate pool.

Basis periods

The rates of writing down allowance, 20% for the main pool and 10% for the special rate pool, assume that we are dealing with a normal 12 month accounting period. What happens, however, if the taxpayer's business has an accounting period that is not 12 months in length? In this case the relevant rate needs to be reduced, or expanded, pro-rata to the length of the accounting period (e.g. an 18 month accounting period will result in 20% × 1.5 worth of allowances for the main pool).

Step 3: AIA and FYA

In this step, we need to consider whether the new capital asset qualifies for either the annual investment allowance (AIA) or first year allowance (FYA). These two forms of incentive have recently been introduced in order to stimulate investment in new capital assets. Let us consider each of these in turn.

Annual investment allowance

With effect from 6 April 2008 (1 April 2008 for companies) a new system of encouraging investment was introduced, called the annual investment allowance (AIA). The AIA allows businesses (of any size) to claim an allowance of 100% of the first £100,000 of expenditure on plant and machinery and integral features. Prior to 6 April 2010 (1 April for companies), the AIA limit was £50,000. If a business has a chargeable period that spans this date, a transitional amount has to be calculated based on the number of months falling before and after the date of the change.

Activity

What would be the maximum AIA that a company with a calendar year chargeable period from 1 January 2010 to 31 December 2010 could claim?

Feedback

They would be able to claim:
(a) the proportion of their year to which a limit of £50,000 applied i.e. from 1 January 2010 to 31 March =
3/12 x £50,000 = £12,500

(b) the proportion of their year to which a limit of £100,000 applied i.e. from 1 April 2010 to 31 December 2010 = 9/12 x £100,000 = £75,000

i.e. their maximum AIA claim could be £87,500 (£12,500 + £75,000)

The allowance is available to individuals carrying on a qualifying activity, which includes trades, professions, vocations, ordinary property business (and also includes being an employee) as well as companies.

If the business spends more than £100,000 in the year the excess is then added to the relevant pool and receives a normal year's WDA for that pool (i.e. 10% or 20%).

The AIA can only be given for the chargeable period in which the expenditure is incurred, so any unused allowance (i.e. if a business spends less than the £100,000 in any year) can't be carried forward. It also can't be transferred to another business. The allowance can't be claimed in the period when the qualifying activity ceases, and is not available for cars. Apart from these restrictions, businesses have a choice about how to apply the allowance to best effect, so as to maximise their capital allowance claim.

First-year allowances

From time to time over the recent history of the capital allowance regime, the Government has offered an incentive by way of a 'first year allowance'. This is a special rate of allowance that is allowed in the period in which new capital assets are acquired. Like the annual investment allowance, first year allowances provide an incentive for businesses to purchase plant and machinery by bringing forward the tax deductibility of the capital expenditure.

The old FYA rules

Prior to 6 April 2008 (1 April 2008 for companies) when the new AIA regime started, first year allowances were restricted to certain sizes of business. The rate of first year allowance was at least 40% from July 1997 until 5 April 2008 (31 March 2008 for companies), with some periods where it was 50% for those businesses that were classified as 'small'. For the 2007/8 year, the relevant rate was 40% for medium businesses and 50% for small businesses.

These first year allowances for small and medium sized enterprises were not available for expenditure on plant and machinery for leasing, cars, ships and railway assets but could be claimed for all other allowable plant and machinery purchased by the business.

A normal writing down allowance was not available in the same year as the first-year allowance. However, unlike writing down allowances, first year allowances were not scaled to the length of the accounting period when it is not the usual 12 months. The full, standard, first year allowance rate was claimed irrespective of the actual length of the accounting period in which a purchase qualifying for first year allowances is made.

Fiscal Fact

The cost of provision of FYAs for SMEs was estimated to be £640million when last available in 2007/08. The new 40% FYAs for 2009/10 were expected to cost the Treasury £1.64billion.

The 2009/10 FYA

When the government introduced the new AIA in 2008/09, it abolished the first year allowance that had previously applied to SMEs. It was estimated that 95% of businesses spend less than £50,000 annually on new plant and machinery etc. As one of the measures introduced in Budget 2009 to help businesses weather the financial crisis, the Government has reintroduced the first year allowance system at the rate of 40% for 2009/10 only. This time, however, it is not restricted to SMEs and applies to all businesses small, medium and large. So the 5% of businesses that have expenditure in excess of £50,000 per annum could apply a 40% rate to new acquisitions over and above the AIA that would otherwise go to the main pool. The remaining 60% of expenditure was then transferred to the main pool balance carried forward so that it will be included in the writing down allowance computation for the following year. Note, however, that the 2009/10 FYA was restricted in that it did not apply to special rate expenditure (i.e. long life assets or integral features), cars or assets for leasing. The 2009/10 FYA ceased on 5 April 2010 (31 March 2010 for companies), and the AIA was increased to £100,000 instead.

Activity

Mulder, a small sole trader, prepares accounts to 5 April annually. His main pool of unrelieved expenditure on plant and machinery brought forward on 6 April, 2010 was £20,000. During the year ended 5 April 2011, the following transactions took place:

			£	
31 August 2010	Bought	Plant	20,000	
31 October 2010	Sold	Plant	5,000	(originally cost £10,000)
31 March 2011	Bought	Plant	38,000	

Calculate the capital allowances for the year ended 5 April 2011.

Feedback

To perform this calculation there is a series of questions we need to ask:

1. Do the new additions belong in the main pool? Yes, they are neither long life assets nor special rate assets.
2. Do the new additions qualify for AIA? Let's assume they do.
3. For disposals, which is lower, the net disposal proceeds or the original cost? It is the lower of the two that we must use.

	£	Main Pool £	Allowances £
Written down value b/f		20,000	
Additions qualifying for AIA:			
Plant (£20,000 + £38,000)	58,000		
AIA	(58,000)		58,000
Balance to main pool		nil	
Sale/proceeds		(5,000)	
		15,000	
WDA 20%		(3,000)	3,000
Written down value c/f		12,000	
Total allowances for year			61,000

In this example, had the new plant and machinery purchased in the tax year exceeded £100,000, the excess would simply have been added to the main pool (or other pools as necessary) and increased the sums available for the 20% (or other rate as applicable) WDV for that period.

Step 4: Special treatment

Having looked at the rules that apply to main pool and special rate pool items, we now consider some categories of capital asset that require special treatment. First we consider the special case of cars. We then consider items that qualify for enhanced capital allowances, which gives immediate write off (100% allowance) in the year of acquisition. We finally consider some categories of capital asset that need to be treated separately, i.e. they are not included in either the main or special rate pools.

Cars

The capital allowance system has always treated cars differently from other plant and equipment and the rules for cars were changed with effect from 6 April 2009 (1 April 2009 for companies). Before that, cars that cost more than £12,000, termed *expensive cars*, were not pooled but had their own separate computations for each car. The reason for this was that the writing down allowance for 'expensive' cars was limited to a maximum of £3,000 or, if the chargeable period is less than twelve months, a pro-rata proportion of £3,000. If the person carrying on the trade incurred only a part of the expenditure actually incurred on the provision of the motor car, (such as there being some private usage) only a proportionate part of £3,000 could be claimed.

In the 2002 Budget a relaxation on the maximum writing down allowance for expensive cars was given. If the expensive car is a low emission car (emitting less than 110g/km of carbon dioxide) then for all new purchases after 17 April, 2002 the maximum allowance did not apply and the full 20% of the value of the car could be claimed.

When the car is disposed of the balancing allowance or charge was calculated in the normal way and was also reduced if there was a private use element as described above.

The following activity illustrates how expensive car capital allowance cap applies in practice (for cars purchased before the change of rules on 1 or 6 April 2009).

Activity

Roger has traded for many years making up accounts to 5 April each year. On 31 August, 2008 he bought a car for £20,000 which used 75% of the time for business purposes. Determine the capital allowances which can be claimed on the car for 2008/9 and for 2009/10 and 2010/11.

Feedback

The capital allowances computation is:

	Expensive car £	Allowances £
Year ended 5 April 2009		
Acquisition	20,000	
WDA (capped)	(3,000) × 75%	2,250
WDV c/f	17,000	
Year ended 5 April 2010		
WDA (capped)	(3,000) × 75%	2,250
WDV c/f	14,000	
Year ended 5 April 2011		
WDA (WDV c/f @20%)	(2,800) × 75%	2,100

This is an expensive car purchased before the new rules came into effect for expensive cars, therefore it must be separately pooled, with suitable capping in writing down allowances allowed. The maximum writing down allowance is £3,000 and this is the amount by which the tax written down value is reduced for each year where (20% × WDV) exceeds this limit. However, because the car is only used 75% for business purposes, Roger can only claim 75% of the applicable allowances for each year.

Note the running balance of the car's written down value is reduced by the full writing down allowance, even though only the business part can actually be claimed.

In the 2010/11 tax year however, the WDA (20% × WDV to date) now is less than £3,000 so this total is used instead (although of course the 75% business cap still applies to the allowable capital allowances). While this car does not then move into the main pool, the normal 20% per annum WDA's will be given for each subsequent year of ownership until the car is sold.

It is important to remember that cars do not qualify for either the AIA, or the FYA.

For cars purchased after 6 April 2009 (1 April 2009 for companies), there are be three possible treatments depending on the level of CO_2 emissions. Cars with emissions below 110 g/km qualify for a 100% allowance. Cars with medium range emissions, i.e. between 110 and 160 g/km go into the main pool with writing down allowance of 20%. Finally, those with high emissions of 160g/km or more, go into the special rate pool and receive a writing down allowance of 10%.

Note however, the value of the car no longer gives it a different 'expensive' or otherwise status and therefore a different tax treatment. The value of the car is now irrelevant for determining the applicable capital allowance rate. It is just the CO_2 emissions rating that will determine what annual capital allowances rate it will get. However, where private usage of the car occurs, it will continue to have to be separately pooled so only the business proportion of the relevant allowances each year will be applied.

Enhanced (100%) capital allowances

Since the 2000 Budget the government has introduced a number of enhanced capital allowances for certain 'green' capital items where the rate of allowance is 100%. The enhanced 100% capital allowance is available to all businesses, small, medium and large and also applies to assets for leasing, letting or hire purchase from 17 April 2002. In summary, the 100% ECAs are as follows:

Date of effect	Qualifying items	Eligibility
1/4/01	Energy saving plant and machinery [1]	Any business
1/4/01	Flat conversions [2]	Any business
17/4/02 to 31/3/13	Low emission cars [3]	Any business
1/4/03	Water conservation equipment [4]	Any business
to 31/3/13	Refuelling equipment [5]	Any business
to 1 or 6/4/15	Zero-emission goods vehicles [6]	Any business

Notes:

(1) A list of qualifying items can be found at http://www.eca.gov.uk, the Department of Environment, Transport and Regions website. Initially included were boilers, motors, refrigeration equipment, thermal screens, lighting and pipe insulation. Added in 2002 Budget were heat pumps, radiant and warm air heaters, and solar heaters.

(2) To quality for this allowance, the conditions that must be met are:

– that the property must have been built before the start of 1980;

– the money is spent on renovating or converting space that is underused or vacant (for at least a year) above shops or other commercial premises;

– the property must not be more than five floors high and not part of an extension to the property.

– the flats once converted can only be for short term letting, must have separate access, be no bigger than four rooms, not be a high value flat and must not be let to connected persons.

(3) These cars are registered after 12 April, 2002 which are electric cars or emit not more than 110 g/km of carbon dioxide (120 g/km prior to 6 April 2008). The allowance also applies to plant and machinery purchased to refuel natural gas or hydrogen fuelled vehicles and apply whether the assets are purchased, leased or hired.

(4) This includes flow meters, leakage detection equipment and efficient taps and toilets. From April 2008 there are additions to this category including waste water recovery and reuse systems.

(5) For natural gas, bio-fuel and hydrogen refuelling equipment.

(6) This measure commenced 1 April 2010 for companies and 6 April for other businesses. It applies to vehicles that cannot, under any circumstances, provide CO_2 emissions when driven, are design primarily to convey goods or 'burdens' and on which expenditure occurs by these applicable dates.

Fiscal Fact

The estimated cost to the government of providing enhanced capital allowances for energy saving technology is £100 million for 2009/10.

Capital allowances are a deduction in the tax computation. This means that they are only really useful as an investment incentive if you are a taxpayer. With effect from 1 April 2008, this situation has been partly addressed as companies in loss situations that are entitled to enhanced capital allowances will be able to convert them to cash refunds of up to 19% of the expenditure up to a maximum of £250,000 (or the total of their annual PAYE and NIC liabilities – whichever is the greater). According to the Government, this will deliver a cash flow benefit to loss making companies that invest in environmentally friendly products and technologies. Note that this special cash refund only applies to companies and not to sole traders, which some commentators feel is unfair and may lead to some businesses switching to being companies just for tax purposes.

The following activity illustrates the use of AIA and enhanced capital allowances (ECAs):

Activity

Philip, who runs a small printing business, buys a computer and software costing £2,500 on 1 May, 2010. He also purchased a delivery van for £5,500 on 19 June, 2009 and a qualifying boiler on 25 June, 2010 for £3,600. His normal accounting year runs to 30 June each year and the brought forward written down value of his capital assets at 1 July, 2009 was £15,000. No other purchases or sales of assets occurred in the year. Calculate the capital allowances available to Philip for the year ended 30 June, 2010.

Feedback

	£	Main Pool £	Allowances £
Additions qualifying for ECA:			
Boiler	3,600		
ECA (100%)	(3,600)	–	3,600
Additions qualifying for AIA:			
Plant (£2,500 + £5,500)	8,000		
AIA	(8,000)		8,000
Balance to main pool		nil	
Writing down allowance:			
Written down value b/f		15,000	
WDA 20%		(3,000)	3,000
Written down value c/f		12,000	
Allowances for tax year			14,600

Philip gets all of his expenditure on the computer and delivery van as a deduction under the AIA rules. He can also receive 100% ECA on the boiler and so in this way he can get all the eligible tax allowances for this purchase immediately. Note that it is important to list enhanced FYAs separately to AIAs available assets as these are entitled to a 100% allowance rate even if the taxpayer uses up all their AIA in any given year.

Recap

At this point, we can now create an order of priority for the different allowances we have considered so far as follows:

1. ECA is top priority so your first question must be 'does the new asset qualify for 100% ECA as a 'green' asset?
2. We can then consider the AIA – do the other new assets qualify for AIA? If so, up to £100,000 becomes fully deductible.

3. Finally, what is left, i.e. the assets that don't qualify for ECA or AIA; or AIA expenditure in excess of £100,000, will be placed in either the main pool or the special rate pool and receive a 20% or 10% writing down allowance respectively.

> If you are required to know the rules for 2009/10, when the temporary FYA operated, you will find a diagram on the website to show the decision making process for new assets acquired in 2009/10.

Separately pooled assets

To determine the correct capital allowances, some plant and machinery needs to be treated either separately, rather than being placed into either the main or special rate pools. In this section we will review these situations. These include assets with some private use, leased assets, and short life assets.

Private use of assets

If plant and machinery is only partly used for the purpose of trade (e.g. the owner also gets some private benefit from their ownership) the capital allowances and charges described above are reduced by the fraction A÷B, where A is the proportion of the time during which the asset was used for the purpose of trade while B is the total period of ownership. Because of the need to apply this fraction for each asset with any element of private usage, a separate capital allowances computation must be carried out for *each asset*. This means you should create a separate column in your proforma for assets with any private usage. Only the business use part of the total capital allowances can be claimed. See the example (Roger) below which illustrates how this works in practice.

Leased assets

Assets which are owned by the business and leased to other people are not pooled. Instead, they are aggregated in a separate pool (i.e. they also get their own column in the computation but not separate columns for each leased asset). The calculation of the writing down allowances is exactly as for the main pool however (i.e. normal 20% reducing balance rules apply etc.). Remember, however, that AIA can be claimed on new purchases of assets leased out, but they did not qualify for the FYA.

Short-life assets

The taxpayer may elect for certain machinery and plant to be treated as a short-life asset and de-pooled (i.e. given separate treatment on an asset by asset basis like expensive cars above) in order for the balancing allowance to be computed when the asset is disposed of. This is a useful concession as it means the full allowances for the asset can be claimed sooner rather than the taxpayer only receiving 20% of it, on a reducing balance, each year as part of the main pool of plant and machinery for the remainder of the life of the business (Note, however, this option is not available for special rate pool items).

The election to treat a purchased capital asset as a short life asset must be made not more than two years after the end of the chargeable period, or its basis period, in which the capital expenditure was incurred and once made is irrevocable. However, if the asset is not disposed of in a chargeable period ending on or before the fourth anniversary of the end of the chargeable period in which the cost of the asset was first recorded, then the tax written down value of the asset is transferred into the general pool at the beginning of the next chargeable period. From then on it will receive the normal treatment for other capital assets and the advantage of gaining a balancing allowance (if applicable) early is lost.

The legislation identifies a number of assets which cannot be treated as short-life assets, these are:

- ships;
- cars; and
- machinery or plant provided for leasing.

An example can be found on the website to illustrate the operation of the short life asset rules.

Step 5: Disposals

When assets are disposed of, we need to calculate a balancing adjustment. This will happen in the year in which a trade ceases, or when an item that has been kept out of the pools is sold and the process is similar to profit or loss on disposal computations we perform for accounting purposes, and is to ensure the correct changes have been made to the records over the life of the asset.

Note that any disposals are dealt with before calculating this year's writing down allowance. This means that no writing down allowance is allowed in the year of disposal

When performing this balancing adjustment computation we compare the disposal proceeds (or original cost if lower) with the written down value. If the written down value exceeds the disposal value, then a balancing allowance equal to the whole of the excess can be claimed. This balancing allowance is effectively an additional capital allowance claim. If the disposal value exceeds the written down value, a balancing charge equal to the excess will be levied on the taxpayer. This can be thought of as a 'negative capital allowance' and is effectively added to the trading profit for that year.

It is important to note also that the disposal value deducted from the pool total when an asset is disposed of is equal to the lower of the net proceeds of disposal, including any insurance money received, and the capital expenditure incurred on the acquisition of the machinery or plant, that is, the lower of the original cost or its disposal value.

In the case of pooled assets, a balancing charge will arise if the disposal value is more than the balance in the pool. A balancing allowance, however, will not be allowed until such time as the qualifying activity itself ends (for example when the trade ceases to operate). This is the reason for using the 'short life asset' option that we discussed earlier. If a taxpayer thinks that he or she will sell an asset within four years and make a loss (balancing allowance), by de-pooling the asset, the balancing allowance can be claimed in the year of disposal.

Activity

Catherine retired on 31 December, 2010 after trading for many years. On 6 April, 2010 the tax written down value of her capital allowances pool was £10,000 and of an expensive car, which was acquired in 2006 and used solely for the purposes of the business, was £4,500. The plant and machinery in the general pool had originally cost £12,000. Catherine sold the plant and machinery for £16,000 and the car for £3,000 when she retired. Calculate the capital allowances and charges for 2010/11.

Feedback

Remember, expensive cars acquired before 6 April 2009 were always treated as items that are not pooled and have their own column, therefore, the capital allowances computation is:

	Main Pool £	Expensive Car £	Allowances £
WDV b/f	10,000	4,500	
Disposal proceeds/cost	(12,000)	(3,000)	
	(2,000)	1,500	
Balancing allowance		(1,500)	1,500
Balancing charge	2,000		(2,000)
Net capital allowances			(500)

Although the plant in the main pool was sold for £16,000, it had originally only cost £12,000 so this is the figure we use as the disposal value to work out the balancing adjustment.

Small pools

As part of the process of simplifying the capital allowances regime, particularly for small businesses, and in response to suggestions from business, the Government has decided to allow for small pools to be written off. With effect from 6 April 2008 (1 April 2008 for companies), it is possible to write off small pools of unrelieved expenditure, which are those where the balance brought forward is less than £1,000. This applies to both the main pool and special rate pool, but not to single asset pools such as expensive cars and short life assets. It is not compulsory to write off all of any small pools, and the taxpayer can choose how much, if any, to be written off each year.

Waiving rights to capital allowances

All or part of the capital allowance entitlement for any given year can be waived by the taxpayer. This means a taxpayer can make a choice each year whether or not to claim any of their capital allowance deduction. Any amount waived simply has the effect of increasing the balance of qualifying expenditure which is eligible for capital allowances in future years.

Clearly it is usually in the interest of the business to claim tax relief as quickly as possible, but this may not always be the case, such as if the business makes a loss that year. Rather than adding to this loss, the business may decide instead to carry forward their capital allowances by not including the deductions they could claim in this year's computation. Instead, the value of the pool will remain the same and so their claim is effectively deferred to offset against profit in later years.

A business might also waive the capital allowance on the following occasions:

- if taxable profits would be reduced to such an extent that it would not be possible for the taxpayer to use all of his or her personal allowances
- if the taxpayer believed that his or her marginal rate of tax would increase significantly in future years and so the deduction will be more valuable to them in the future.

Industrial buildings

Having examined the general rules for capital allowances on plant and machinery, we will now look in more detail at the second capital allowance category; industrial buildings.

An industrial building is a building or structure in use for the purposes of:

- a trade carried on in a mill, factory or other similar premises; or
- a transport, dock, inland navigation, water, sewerage, electricity or hydraulic power undertaking; or
- a tunnel, bridge or toll road undertaking; or
- a trade which involves the manufacture or storage of goods or materials; or
- a trade involving working of any mine, oil well or other source of mineral deposits, or ploughing or cultivating land (other than land occupied by the person carrying on the trade) and other agricultural operations on such land, or threshing the crops of another person, or catching or taking fish or shellfish.

A building provided by a person carrying on any of these trades (or 'undertaking for the welfare of workers employed by that person') is deemed to be an industrial building.

The legislation specifically excludes from the definition of an industrial building any building or structure in use as, or as part of, a domestic dwelling, retail shop, showroom, most hotels or offices. However, if the non-qualifying part of the building is less than 25%

of the cost of the whole building, then all the building remains eligible for industrial buildings allowance. If the non-qualifying part is more than 25% of the cost of the whole building then only the relevant percentage relating to the qualifying part of the building can receive capital allowances.

A normal writing down allowance of 1% (2% for 2009/10) on a *straight line* basis (be careful - not the reducing balance basis as is used for plant and machinery) is available from the point when the building is brought into use. In order to be eligible for a writing down allowance a person must *have an interest in* (e.g. own) the qualifying building, at the end of the period. However, when a building is the subject of a long lease the lessee is often deemed to be the person having an interest in the building provided that both the lessor and the lessee make an election to that affect. This means the lessee can then receive the capital allowances on the building instead of the actual owner.

Expenditure incurred on preparing, cutting, tunnelling or levelling land in order to prepare it as a site for the installation of machinery or plant is treated as expenditure on an industrial building for capital allowance purposes.

As for plant and machinery, the writing down allowance is reduced for short basis periods for both income tax and corporation tax purposes.

The Government is of the view that the IBA is now an outdated and poorly focussed subsidy. For this reason, and also the desire to simplify the tax system, Budget 2007 announced that IBAs were to be phased out by the start of the tax year 2011/12. This is achieved by allowing a proportion of the IBA. For the 2008/9 year, 75% of the full IBA rate for that year (4%) was allowed (i.e. this translates into an IBA rate of 3%), 2009/10 it was 50% (i.e. an IBA rate of 2%), 2010/11 it is 25% (i.e. an IBA rate of 1%) and then will be nil for 2011/12.

Industrial buildings and structures, including qualifying hotels and commercial buildings, located in enterprise zones are eligible for an initial allowance of 100% of the cost, including VAT, provided the site was included in the zone not more than ten years before the expenditure. There is no requirement that buildings in an enterprise zone be in use in order to claim the allowance, but only the last buyer before the building is brought into use may claim the allowance. This allowance is not being restricted year on year by the phase out of IBA

– instead the full 100% rate will continue to apply until 2011 when it will also stop.

Activity

Bob has traded for many years and makes up accounts to 5 April each year. On 1 January, 2008 he bought a new factory for £100,000 which was brought into use on 1 April, 2008. Determine the industrial buildings allowance available for the years ended 5 April, 2008 to 5 April, 2011 inclusive.

Feedback

	Building £	Allowances £
Year ended 5 April 2008		
Cost	100,000	
WDA 4% × Cost	(4,000)	4,000
WDV c/f	96,000	
Year ended 5 April, 2009		
WDA 3% × Cost	(3,000)	3,000
WDV c/f	93,000	
Year ended 5 April, 2010		
WDA 2% × Cost	(2,000)	2,000
WDV c/f	91,000	
Year ended 5 April, 2011		
WDA 1% × Cost	(910)	910
WDV c/f	90,090	

If the building was not in use as an industrial building on the last day of the period, and was not used for any other purpose, the writing down allowance is still available, provided that the period of disuse is temporary. In practice so long as the building is used as an industrial building at some time in the future the period of disuse will be considered to be temporary. However, if the building is used for a non-industrial purpose at any time, a notional writing down allowance continues to be deducted as before, but *no* capital allowance may be claimed by the taxpayer for that period (i.e. as for private use of plant and machinery).

Prior to March 2007, a balancing adjustment was calculated on the sale of an eligible property disposed of within 25 years of the date first used for eligible purposes. The purchaser could then claim the IBA over the remaining life. With effect from 31 March 2007, purchasers will now stand in the shoes of the seller and just take over any remaining claim without the need to calculate a balancing adjustment.

Fiscal Fact

The Government estimated that the removal of IBA will generate an extra £300million in tax revenue in the years 2007/08 to 2009/10.

Patents

If patent rights are purchased (i.e. rather than developed in-house) and used for trading purposes, a separate capital allowances pool is formed for all rights held on which writing down allowance of 25% per annum on a *reducing balance* basis is available for tax purposes, if the owner wishes to use them. These rules however, only apply to un-incorporated business. For companies with expenditure on patent rights after 1 April, 2002, the write downs used in producing the accounts are now used rather than the 20% tax capital allowance (see the intangible assets description in Chapter 9 for further details).

The rules for balancing allowances and charges are as for the general pool for plant and machinery. If sale proceeds exceed the original cost the deduction from the pool is limited to the original cost, as for plant and machinery, however, the excess of proceeds over the original cost is taxed as miscellaneous income, and not as trading income as plant and machinery are.

Trading losses

In this section we will look at the special tax rules that apply for dealing with losses on trading activities.

Calculating a loss is simple. If, after adjusting the profits for tax purposes, the end result is a negative amount, i.e. the expenditure exceeds the income, then you have a trading loss for tax purposes. Such a loss can be used to influence past, present or even future tax bills as they can be used to relieve profits earned in other periods or from other categories. However, a loss can only be relieved once and the taxpayer may have to make a choice about how best to use the loss.

A taxpayer who incurs a trading loss has a number of alternative ways of obtaining relief. Each has advantages and drawbacks. There are special rules for losses incurred in the early years of business, or at the end of the life of a business, but in this chapter, we will only consider the position of an established, on-going business. In this case, the loss can be relieved by:

- Deducting it from general income, for the current year, the year before, or both years; and
- Carrying it forward to be offset against subsequent trade profits.

Deduction from general income

Where a taxpayer carries on a trade in the tax year and makes a loss in that year, he or she can claim a deduction for that loss against general income for that year as a tax relief (step 2). If there is still some loss left over after applying it against general income of the year, the remaining part can then be used to offset general income tax paid in the previous tax year. This is done in practice by creating a credit equivalent to the loss available to be carried back. This credit can then be used to claim a repayment of tax previously paid or can be used to offset later year taxes (see below) – the taxpayer has the choice.

Alternatively, the taxpayer can choose to first use the loss in the previous tax year and then, if there is still some left over, use it in the current year. This means that the taxpayer has to think about how much tax saving can be made from each course of action.

There are some conditions that have to be met for this relief to apply. The main condition is that relief against general income is not available unless the trade is "commercial". This means that it is carried on during the year on a commercial basis and with a view to making a profit. There are also special rules for 'hobby' farms and market gardens.

Losses have to be used up to the full extent of the net income of the year to which they are applied. This can mean the loss of personal allowances for that year (as losses are deducted at step 2 of the tax computation – before personal allowances are dealt with at step 3).

A concession was announced in November 2008 as a result of the financial crisis, and enacted in Finance Act 2009. Trade losses incurred by un-incorporated businesses in the 2008/09 or 2009/10 tax years (for companies this period was restricted to accounting periods ending between 24 November 2008 and 23 November 2009) are allowed to be carried back for three years instead of just one. While there is a no restriction on the amount of loss that can be carried back to the previous year, there is a limit of £50,000 on the loss that can be carried back to the earlier two.

Fiscal Fact

According to Budget 2009, an estimated 140,000 loss making businesses (both unincorporated and incorporated) will benefit from the extension of loss carry-back to the preceding three years.

Carry forward

As an alternative to deduction from general income, a trading loss can be carried forward to be relieved against subsequent trade profits. The most important restriction here is that the loss can only be offset against the profits of the same trade in later years, not against general income or profits from a different trade. Any loss that is not used up in the following tax year can then be carried forward to the next year and so on indefinitely until it is all eventually used up.

There are some drawbacks to this form of relief. Once a taxpayer has decided to use this form of relief, there is no flexibility, and the first available profits have to be used to relieve the loss. If the taxpayer has little income from other sources, this could mean a loss of personal allowances. There is also a delay in receiving the relief, until the year of assessment for the year in which profits are next made. As well as having potentially serious cash flow implications, the relief may be worth less because the tax rate applied to the relief is the one in force when the relief is received, not when it was incurred.

In addition, the law is strict about what exactly constitutes the 'same trade'. In *Gordon and Blair Ltd v IRC* (1962), losses incurred from the trade of brewing could not be carried forward and relieved against profits earned from bottling. Whether the same trade is being carried on is a question of degree and so the facts of each case must be considered carefully. Hence there is an element of risk in choosing to receive relief in this way.

If your course requires you to also know the other special cases of loss relief, additional material and examples can be found in the student section of the website at:

http://www.taxstudent.com/uk

The rules for dealing with trading losses for companies are slightly different to these, which apply to sole traders. We will briefly examine the rules for corporation tax in Chapter 9.

Summary

This chapter continues our examination of the tax rules related to unincorporated businesses. It looks at the capital allowance rules for capital assets. We examined what kind of plant and machinery qualifies for capital allowances and how they are calculated. We also examined the rules for Industrial Building calculations and discussed the special cases of allowances for expenditure on patents. Finally, we briefly reviewed the basics of how trade losses can be handled.

Project areas

This chapter provides some scope for projects including the:

- effectiveness of capital allowances as tools for accurately reflecting the real cost of using assets in businesses
- question of whether increasing capital allowances leads to increased investment in plant and machinery (i.e do incentives like the new AIA, or enhanced 100% FYAs, work to encourage investment).
- implications of having different accounting and tax treatments for capital assets
- reasons why cars are singled out for special capital allowance treatment

Quick quiz

1. Samuel bought a motor car for use in his business on 1 September, 2010. The car cost £15,000 and has CO_2 emissions of 165 g/km. He draws up his accounts to 31 December each year. How much capital allowance can he claim this year if the car is used solely for business purposes?

2. Theresa bought a motor car for use in her business on 1 September, 2010. The car cost £15,000 and is not electric, but has CO_2 emissions of 110 g/km. How much capital allowance can she claim?

3. Umut has a year end of 31 October for his business, which he has operated for several years. What AIA will he be entitled to for the 2010/11 year?

4. Vivian buys a state of the art computer for her small business on 30 June, 2010 at a cost of £2,500. What capital allowance can she claim for her year ended 30 September, 2010? Should she treat it as a short life asset?

5. Walter sold an expensive car for £3,000 which had a tax written down value of £8,000 at the start of the year. He used the car 75% for business purposes and had purchased it in October 2007. What adjustment is required to his capital allowance claim for the year?

6. Xenia builds an industrial building for use in his trade which costs £100,000 for the land, £62,000 for site preparation, £20,000 for architects fees and £392,000 in building costs. Which cost or costs qualify for industrial buildings allowances?

Questions

Question 1   Luke Skyrunner has a medium sized business manufacturing high quality toys. The opening balance in his main pool of assets was £10,000. All vehicles are used 100% for business purposes. During the year ended 30 June, 2010, the following transactions occurred in relation to his fixed assets:

29 July, 2009	New van purchased for £14,000
25 October, 2009	New car (CO$_2$ emissions 190g/km) purchased for £16,000
15 February, 2010	Plant (bought on 1 August, 2001 for £8,000) was sold for £7,000
1 May, 2010	New plant purchased for £86,000
15 May, 2010	New car (CO$_2$ emissions 180g/km) purchased for £20,000
30 May, 2010	New lift installed in the warehouse for £58,000

Required: Calculate Luke's maximum entitlement to capital allowances for the year ended 30 June, 2010.

Question 2   Jack Hammer owns a large manufacturing operation with branches all over the UK. The following information is provided for the year ended 31 March, 2010 in relation to industrial buildings:

(a) In November 2008, Jack purchased a new factory (not in an enterprise zone) and immediately brought it into use for qualifying purposes. The cost of the factory consisted of:

	£
Land	50,000
Site preparation costs	10,000
Construction cost of the factory	175,000
Additional cost of general office space within the factory	33,000

(b) Jack had purchased an office block in an enterprise zone during the year ended 31 March, 2009. In that year, he only claimed an initial allowance of 50% of the original cost of £200,000.

Required: What are the maximum industrial building allowances that Jack can claim for the year ended 31 March, 2011?

Question 3   (based on ACCA Paper 7 December 1994).

Joseph Kent commenced in business on 1 January, 2004 as a self employed joiner making conservatories. His business qualifies as a medium business for tax purposes. His tax-adjusted profits before capital allowances were as follows:

	£
Year ended 31 March, 2009	35,000
Year ended 31 March, 2010	24,000
Year ended 31 March, 2011	42,000

Capital additions and disposals were as follows:

Additions	£
1 October, 2008 car 1 (at valuation)	12,200
1 October, 2008 trailer	2,000
1 October, 2008 plant and machinery (not energy-saving)	8,000
1 October, 2008 car 2	13,000

Disposals	
1 January, 2010 plant and machinery (at less than cost)	3,000
1 March, 2010 car 1	7,000

The balance in the main pool at 1 April 2008 was £1,000.

Private use of cars 1 and 2 is 20%. No claim is made to treat any of the assets as short-life assets.

Joseph manufactured the conservatories in rented premises until 1 January, 2011 when he purchased a new factory unit for £20,000 on an industrial estate (not an enterprise zone).

All assets were brought into use immediately on acquisition.

Required: Calculate the trading income for Joseph for the period ending 31 March, 2009 and the years ending 31 March, 2010 and 31 March, 2011.

(Note: answer available on lecturers' website)

Question 4 (based on ACCA Paper 2.3 December 2004).

Richard Desk has been a self-employed manufacturer of office furniture since 1993. His income for the previous three years is as follows:

	2008/9	2009/10	2010/11
Trading profit/(loss)	8,800	(26,300)	8,600
Property income	nil	3,000	2,800
Bank interest	600	400	500

Required: Calculate Richard's taxable income for each year on the basis that he relieves the trading loss against general income in the previous year.

(Note: answer available on lecturers' website)

Further test questions for this chapter to test your knowledge can be found in the student section of the website at:

http://www.taxstudent.com/uk

Further reading and examples

Combs, A., Dixon, S. & Rowes, P. (2010), *Taxation: incorporating the 2010 Finance Acts*, Fiscal Publications: Birmingham.
 – use this book for many other examples to further develop and test your knowledge of this chapter's contents. See
 http://www.fiscalpublications.com/rowes/2010

8 Capital taxes

Introduction

Until capital gains tax was introduced in 1965, capital receipts were largely free of tax. This meant that increases in wealth through growth in capital value, as opposed to receiving income, resulted in substantially less tax being paid on them. Some of the incentive to classify a receipt as capital rather than income has now been removed by the introduction and development of capital gains tax, although there are still differences between the operation of the income tax and capital gains tax systems, as you will see in this chapter. During its life capital gains tax has undergone many changes as successive Chancellors have attempted to improve the tax. In recent years, capital gains tax has become increasingly different for individuals and for companies. For this reason, in this chapter we consider the basic principles and their application for individual taxpayers. We will examine how capital gains tax works for companies in Chapter 9.

There are other forms of taxes on capital transactions in operation in the UK at present and in this chapter we will also briefly describe the operation of stamp duty and inheritance tax.

After reading this chapter you will be able to:

- describe the introduction and development of capital gains tax;
- calculate the capital gains tax liability which arises as a result of a range of transactions;
- describe the capital gains tax reliefs available to taxpayers;
- briefly describe the application of stamp duty; and
- briefly describe the operation of inheritance tax.

Capital gains tax

We saw in Chapter 6 that one of the key concerns of the income tax system is to distinguish income receipts from capital receipts given, as a general rule, capital receipts are not subject to income tax. One consequence of not taxing capital receipts is that it creates a distortion in the tax system, i.e. an incentive for taxpayers to manipulate transactions so that they fall to escape tax as capital receipts rather than attract tax as income receipts. Many tax systems do tax capital receipts to reduce these distortions, however, not always at the same rates, or using the same rules, as for income.

The first modern attempt to tax capital gains in the UK was a short term capital gains tax introduced in 1962. The tax was replaced in 1965 by James Callaghan, as Labour Chancellor, by a full capital gains tax which was intended to tax profits which were not subject to income tax. You will remember from Chapter 2 that taxes are sometimes introduced into a tax system because they are seen to be needed to make it fairer. Capital gains tax is certainly an example of this.

Today capital gains tax accounts for only 2–3% of the revenue raised by direct taxation but, as James Callaghan said at the time he introduced it, the tax was not primarily introduced to raise revenue for the Government but to 'provide a background of equity and fair play'. So it has an importance beyond the sums it raises in tax revenue.

There is no intention in the UK tax system to subject a receipt to both income tax and capital gains tax. If a receipt is subject to income tax then no capital gains tax liability will arise.

Fiscal Fact

It is estimated that 130,000 individual taxpayers paid capital gains tax in 2008/09. They are expected to pay around £7.8billion in CGT in that year however, for 2009/10 this sum is estimated to drop dramatically to £2.5billion – a sign of the economic situation in the UK in that period.

Look again at some of the legal cases in Chapter 6 which are used to determine whether trading has occurred. Some of these pre-1965 cases may not be brought today because if the receipt is not seen to be a trading receipt it will now be considered under capital gains tax. Of course, there are differences between the treatment of capital gains and income, despite this mutual relationship, that mean they are not completely inter-changeable as far as taxpayers are concerned. For example, capital gains cannot be included in the calculation of net relevant income for pension contribution purposes, so increasing wealth via capital gains won't help you build your tax-free pension funds.

The tax was not intended to be retrospective so only gains which arose after 6 April, 1965 are liable to capital gains tax. There were two ways of achieving this aim. Firstly, the 'Budget day value' at 6 April, 1965 could be substituted for the original cost of assets acquired before that date. This would enable the tax to be levied only on gains which arose after 6 April, 1965. The second solution was to 'time-apportion' the gain. That is the total gain which arose throughout the period of ownership was calculated and then apportioned to the periods of ownership prior to and subsequent to 6 April, 1965. Only the gain which was attributable to the later period of ownership was subject to capital gains tax. You are unlikely to encounter assets owned before April 1965 in an introductory tax course.

The effects of inflation

The question of what to do with gains resulting from inflationary increases in prices is one that affects all countries that try to tax capital gains. Inflation results in changes to the real value of capital assets and creates a key question of whether to tax the inflation component of any change in value. The problem became particularly acute in the 1970s and 1980s when inflation was relatively high.

When capital gains tax was first introduced no relief was given for the effects of inflation. Broadly speaking tax was paid on the difference between the allowable costs of acquiring the asset and the disposal proceeds. In 1985 the law was amended to give full relief for inflation. The retail price index (RPI) was chosen as the inflation measure to be used for capital gains tax computations. The changes in the RPI between the date the asset was purchased and sold produced an *indexation allowance* that was used to reduce the total gain and remove the effects of inflation on the asset's value.

For disposals on or after 30 November, 1993 the indexation allowance cannot be used to create a loss (i.e. the minimum it can reduce the taxable gain to is zero) or increase a loss if one exists before the indexation allowance calculation.

After a period of consultation the then Chancellor, Gordon Brown, announced a major reform of capital gains tax for individuals in his 1998 Budget. In the interests of simplicity, the system of indexation allowances was replaced (for individuals) by a fixed reduction based on the time of ownership of the asset, called *taper relief*. The new rules meant that for individual taxpayers the taxable amount of any chargeable gain diminished the longer they owned the asset.

The rules were intended to encourage individuals to undertake long-term investment by holding assets for relatively long periods. Taper relief was significantly more generous for business assets (i.e. assets used for business purposes) than non-business assets to encourage investment by entrepreneurs.

So, for individuals, an indexation allowance was not given for periods of ownership after April 1998. Instead, taper relief applied, ranging from 5% for non-business assets held for 3 years to a rate of 75% for business assets held for at least 2 years.

With effect from 6 April 2008, taper relief has now been abolished for individuals initially replaced with a flat rate of tax at 18% for everyone. For any gains arising on or after 23 June 2010, the rate rises to 28% for higher and additional rate income tax payers. These rates are, however, lower than comparable income tax rates, perhaps providing some acknowledgement of the impact of inflation on this source of increased wealth. The justification for this new flat rate system (ironically perhaps) was to further simplify the system that the introduction of taper relief had already been supposed to have simplified.

In 1992 there was a Consolidation Act and legislation relating to capital gains tax is now contained in the Taxation of Chargeable Gains Act 1992 (TCGA 1992). We will examine how these rules work for individual taxpayers, in practice, with examples as we go through this chapter.

Rebasing to 1982 values

In 1988 the tax was rebased so that gains before March 1982 were no longer liable to capital gains taxation.

Prior to 6 April 2008, taxpayers could make an irrevocable election for the market value on 31 March, 1982 to be used instead of the actual costs for all of their assets, except quoted securities, which were held on 31 March 1982. From 6 April 2008 onwards, the market value on 31 March 1982 automatically applies.

The charge to capital gains tax

A liability to capital gains tax arises when a *chargeable person* makes a *chargeable disposal* of *chargeable assets*. You need to be able to define each of these terms and list exemptions to capital gains tax to understand the effect of capital gains tax.

Chargeable person

A chargeable person may be:

- An *individual who is either resident or ordinarily resident in the UK during the tax year in which the chargeable disposal occurs*. If the individual is resident *and* domiciled in the UK, disposals anywhere in the world may give rise to a capital gains tax liability.
- A *partner in a business*. A partnership does not have a separate legal identity. When a partnership makes a chargeable disposal of partnership assets the partners are individually liable to tax in proportion to their share of the capital gain.

The legislation contains a list of exempt persons who are not therefore liable to capital gains tax on asset disposals (but also therefore cannot claim any losses). These are:

- charities using gains for charitable purposes;
- approved superannuation funds;
- local authorities;
- registered friendly societies;
- approved scientific research associations; and
- authorised unit and investment trusts.

Whilst companies are also chargeable persons for capital gains tax purposes, they don't pay a separate capital gains tax like individuals do. Instead, corporation tax is charged on their total profits including their chargeable (capital) gains. We will discuss the taxation of companies more fully in Chapter 9.

Chargeable disposal

The term *chargeable disposal* includes the sale or gift of all or any part of an asset. It also includes the loss or destruction of an asset, the appropriation of assets as trading stock and the receipt of a capital sum in return for the surrender of rights to assets. An example of this latter case is the sale of rights which attach to shares when a company makes a rights issue. The chargeable disposal is deemed to take place when the title to the asset passes to its new owner.

A number of disposals are *exempt disposals* and do not give rise to a capital gains tax liability. These are:

- transfers of assets on death – the assets are instead deemed to be acquired by their new owners at their value at the date of death;
- transfers of assets to provide security for a loan or mortgage; and
- gifts of assets to charities and national heritage bodies.

Where an asset is damaged, and the taxpayer receives a capital sum as compensation (e.g. from an insurance payout), a special rule may apply. So long as the compensation is used to restore the asset (or most of it) the taxpayer can elect to have the compensation reduce the allowable cost of the asset instead of creating a chargeable disposal. This election can also be made if the capital sum is small (less than 5% of the value of the asset). Making such an election has the effect of delaying the capital gains tax payment until the restored asset is eventually disposed of.

Chargeable assets

All assets are *chargeable assets* unless they are specifically exempted from capital gains tax by law, or other regulation. Here is a list of some of the more common exempt assets:

- motor vehicles (whatever their age);
- national savings certificates, premium bonds and SAYE deposits;
- foreign currency, provided it was for private use;
- decorations for valour (e.g. brave conduct medals) unless the chargeable person purchased them rather than being awarded them personally;
- damages for personal or professional injury;
- life assurance policies when disposed of by the original owner;
- works of art or scientific collections given for national purposes are treated as being disposed of on a no gain/no loss basis;
- gilt-edged securities, for example Treasury loans, Treasury stocks, Exchequer loans and War loans;
- qualifying corporate bonds (debentures);
- the disposal of debts, other than debts on a security, by the original creditor;
- pension and annuity rights;
- betting and gambling winnings; and
- investments held in individual savings accounts (ISAs).

In addition, in certain circumstances tangible moveable property, also called *chattels*, is exempt from capital gains tax, as is an individual's only or main residence. We will consider both of these categories later as they are not always fully exempt.

If a taxpayer disposes of exempt assets no chargeable gain, or allowable loss, arises.

The basic computation

In this section we will study firstly the computation of the chargeable gain, or allowable loss. We will then illustrate how the calculation is applied in practice using a number of transactions.

The pro forma for calculating the chargeable gain or allowable loss is (numbers are for illustration only):

	£
Gross proceeds on disposal (or market value)	20,000
Less incidental costs of disposal	(1,000)
Net proceeds	19,000
Less allowable costs	(4,000)
Chargeable gain/(loss)	15,000

As you will see later, this calculation is done for each disposal of a non-exempt capital asset, the results are then aggregated and an annual exemption applied (for individuals) to the combined total so that a certain amount of the total gain each year is tax free. For 2010/11 the annual exemption amount (AEA) is £10,100 (unchanged from 2009/10). The following activity provides an overview of the CGT computation. We will then explore each stage of this computation in further detail.

Activity

Ernie sold a chargeable asset on 1 July 2010. He had no other chargeable gains or losses in the tax year. If the chargeable gain on disposal of the asset was £15,000 (as computed above) what would be his capital gains liability if his taxable income for income tax purposes is:
  (a) £10,000
  (b) £45,000?

Feedback

(a) If Ernie had any other gains or losses, these should be aggregated first using the computation approach above. As he doesn't, the next thing to take into account is his AEA – of £10,100 this year. This should be deducted from the gain leaving a chargeable sum of £4,900. The CGT liability is then computed using Ernie's income tax bands. In this case Ernie has a taxable income of £10,000 (making him a basic rate income tax payer) the chargeable gain of £4,900 is added to this sum and, as this would not take him beyond the basic rate band limit (£37,400), it would all be taxed at 18% i.e:

$$£4,900 \times 18\% = £882$$

(b) If Ernie has taxable income of £45,000 he is a higher rate taxpayer and pays tax on his chargeable gain at 28% i.e.:

$$£4,900 \times 28\% = £1,372$$

We will now consider each of the elements of the capital gains tax computation in more detail.

Gross proceeds on disposal

In general, the proceeds received from an *arm's length* transaction are used when performing a capital gains tax computation. An arm's length transaction occurs when vendor and purchaser are not *connected* in any way that could affect the price agreed between them i.e. the price is one which two strangers might mutually agree. If the disposal is not 'a bargain at arm's length' the consideration used for the computation will be the market value of the asset at the point of the sale, regardless of the value of any consideration actually given.

Disposals to connected persons and gifts are always taken to be not at arm's length. The market value is also used if the consideration for the disposal cannot be directly valued for any reason.

Connected persons are generally:

- For an individual – his or her spouse, siblings, direct ancestors, lineal descendants and their spouses. He or she is not, however, connected for tax purposes to lateral relatives like uncles, aunts, nephews and nieces.
- Companies are connected to each other if they are under common control. A company is connected to a person if, either alone or with individuals connected to him or her, that person controls it.

Sometimes a taxpayer may try to reduce tax liability by disposing of assets piecemeal to connected persons. Where this kind of disposal is made, the disposal proceeds for each transaction will need to become an equivalent proportion of the value of the total of the assets transferred. Transactions in parts of an asset are likely to be considered to be linked if they occur within six years of each other.

For example, a majority shareholder of a company may pass their shares on to the next generation in a series of small gifts. If it were not for the above anti-avoidance legislation this would perhaps give a lower market value than if the shares were transferred in one single transaction.

There are strict rules for calculating the market value of some assets. When calculating the market value no reduction is made if several assets are sold at the same time. So if a large number of shares are disposed of to a connected person, then no account is taken of any reduction in the share price due to the size of the disposal. For example, the market value of quoted securities is taken to be the lower of the:

- 'quarter-up': the lower of the two prices quoted in the Daily Official List plus a quarter of the difference between the two prices, and
- 'mid price': half way between the highest and lowest prices at which bargains were recorded on the date of disposal excluding bargains at special prices.

Incidental costs of disposal

The incidental costs of disposal include fees, commission or remuneration paid for the professional services of a surveyor, valuer, auctioneer, accountant, legal adviser or agent as well as the cost of transfer or conveyance such as stamp duty. It also includes advertising to find a buyer, but does not include any payment of interest or any cost that is allowed as part of a trading profit computation.

Allowable costs

Allowable costs include the following:

- The base cost of acquiring the asset – this will usually be the purchase price. However, there are a number of situations in which some other value will be used. For example, if the asset is inherited rather than bought, the market value at the date of death will be an allowable cost. There are other examples which we will consider later on.
- Any incidental costs of acquisition such as legal fees.
- Any capital expenditure incurred in enhancing the asset or establishing, preserving or defending title to, or a right over, the asset. For enhancement expenditure to be allowed the benefits of the expenditure must be reflected in the state or nature of the asset at the time of disposal. There are a number of specific exclusions from this category of allowable expenses. These are

the costs of repairs, maintenance and insurance and any expenditure which is either an allowable deduction for income tax purposes or was met by public grants, such as home improvement loans.

Capital losses

If a taxpayer incurs a capital loss in a year, the loss is first usually set against any gains for that year. If the taxpayer then still has an overall net loss for the tax year, that is losses for the year as a whole exceed the total gains, the net loss is carried forward to future fiscal years.

Losses carried forward are set against the first available gains in future years. In that year any losses for that year are deducted first before any prior year losses brought forward are then deducted. However, the brought forward losses are used to enable the taxpayer to gain the full benefit of the annual exemption limit. Any remaining amounts still not used are then carried forward to the subsequent year.

Losses brought forward can only be deducted from the net gain in the year to the extent that the gain is greater than the current year's annual exemption.

We can illustrate these rules with the following example:

Activity

Ewan had the following capital gains and losses:

Year	Gain £	Loss £	Annual exemption for year £
2008/09	4,000	9,000	9,600
2009/10	7,500	3,000	10,100
2010/11	12,000	nil	10,100

Calculate Ewan's net chargeable gain for each year.

Feedback

2008/09	£
Gain	4,000
Loss	9,000
Net loss	(5,000)

Ewan's annual exemption is wasted for this year and the loss of £5,000 gets carried forward to the next year.

2009/10	£
Gain	7,500
Loss	(3,000)
Net current year gain	4,500
Annual exemption	10,100
Net chargeable gain	nil

Ewan's annual exemption covers his net current year gain and he pays no capital gains tax in this year. The £5,000 loss from year 1 does not reduce his gain to zero; rather it is carried forward to 2009/10.

2010/11	£
Gain	12,000
Loss	nil
Net current year gain	12,000
Loss brought forward	(1,900)
Annual exemption	10,100
net chargeable gain	nil

In 2010/11, Ewan has a net chargeable gain of £12,000. The annual exemption is £10,100. This means that Ewan only has to use £1,900 of his loss brought forward to make the chargeable gain equal to the annual exemption. He is then left with £3,100 of the loss to be carried forward to 2011/12.

Calculation of the capital gains tax liability

Basis of assessment

For individuals, capital gains tax is charged on the chargeable gains accruing during the year of assessment after the deduction of:

- allowable losses occurring during the year, and
- any allowable losses accruing from a previous year of assessment which have not already been allowed as a deduction from chargeable gains.

Allowable losses cannot be carried back except on the occasion of the taxpayer's death – they can only be carried forward as we discussed in the previous section.

A year of assessment for individual's capital gains tax runs from 6 April to the following 5 April, i.e. just like the income tax year. Capital gains tax is charged on a current year basis (i.e. what arises in the year of assessment). The tax is payable on the later of the 31 January following the year of assessment and 30 days after the issue of a notice of assessment from the HMRC. Hence, for disposals made in the fiscal year 2010/11 the tax will be payable on 31 January, 2012.

Therefore, in order to maximise the gap between making the disposal and paying the tax (i.e. to reduce the effective impact of the tax by using the effects of inflation on the fixed costs), disposals should be made as early as possible during the fiscal year (other constraints allowing).

Rate of tax

An individual can realise capital gains up to the annual exempt amount (AEA) each year before any liability to this tax arises. The annual exemption amount therefore operates for capital gains tax in a similar way as personal allowances do for income tax i.e. it is a tax free threshold. The allowance is usually increased in line with the increase in the RPI and rounded up to the next multiple of £100 each year, although it has not been increased for 2010/11.

Fiscal Fact

It is estimated that an increase in the annual capital gains tax exemption of £500 for individuals and £250 for trustees would cost the government £30million in 2010/11 if it were introduced with effect from April 2010. In Budget 2009 the actual increase was £500 for individuals.

Capital gains tax is a separate tax to income tax, and for gains between 6 April 2008 and 22 June 2010 that meant no link to income tax levels was needed when computing CGT liabilities. Instead a separate fixed rate (flat rate of 18%) was applied to any gains arising in that period making the computation fairly straightforward to do.

However, new rules were introduced in the Emergency Budget in 2010 that are similar to the pre-6 April 2008 CGT computation approach, where there is an explicit link between these two taxes. After 22 June 2010, the rate of tax to be applied to net chargeable gains in excess of the annual exemption amount depends on the income tax band(s) the gain falls into. It is considered to be, in effect, the very top part of income for purposes of determining the applicable rate to pay on the gains.

If the capital gain falls into any band below the basic rate band limit (£37,400 for 2010/11) it is taxed at 18%. If it falls into the higher rate or additional rate bands it is taxed at 28%.

These new rules have therefore created a small anomaly for CGT computations in 2010/11 for disposals of assets between 6 April 2010 and 22 June 2010. The previous rules that applied a flat 18% rate to all gains apply to any gains arising in that period of the tax year. Gains arising after the 22 June may be subject to the 28% rate if the recipient is a higher or additional rate taxpayer. The 18% rate will continue to apply otherwise. The date the gain arose is therefore critical to the tax charge that applies this year as it will make 10% difference in the tax paid for some taxpayers.

Also, if an individual has more than one gain during the year, and they arise either side of the new rule introduction date, the taxpayer can choose how to apply their AEA. This will usually be applied to whichever one produces the lowest final combined CGT liability of course.

The following activity illustrates how the current rules for CGT apply (source – based on Budget Note 20, Budget June 2010).

Activity

In 2010/11 Emily's taxable income, after all allowable deductions and the personal allowance, is £27,400. She sells an asset in May 2010 and realises a chargeable gain of £17,000. In November she sells another asset, realising a chargeable gain of £25,100. Emily has no allowable losses to set against these gains. Neither gain qualifies for any relief. What is her CGT liability for 2010/11?

Feedback

Emily's taxable income is £10,000 less than the upper limit of the basic rate band (£37,400 – £27,400). As she has two chargeable gains to use her AEA between she will need to make a choice how to apply her AEA this year. She is best to set her AEA against the later gain (because part of that gain is liable to tax at the higher CGT rate) leaving £15,000 (£25,100 – £10,100) of that gain still taxable. The first £10,000 of the £15,000 is taxed at 18% and the remaining £5,000 is taxed at 28%. The £17,000 chargeable gain Emily realised in May 2010, before the change in rates on 23 June 2010, is taxable at the old 18% rate.

Emily's total CGT liability for 2010/11 therefore is:

May 2010 gain:

£17,000 x 18% = £3,060

November 2010 gain:

Taxable gain = £25,100 – AEA of £10,100 = £15,000

Basic rate band remaining un-used:
£37,400 – £27,400 income = £10,000

£10,000 of the £15,000 will be taxed at 18% = £1,800
Remaining £5,000 at 28% = £1,400

Total CGT liability for 2010/11:
£3,060 + £1,800 + £1,400 = £6,260

To confirm this is the best use of the AEA try re-computing the CGT liability if the AEA is applied to the May 2010 gain instead.

Husband, wife and civil partners

Capital gains tax gets a little more complicated when it comes to its treatment of spouses and civil partners. For most purposes spouses and civil partners are treated as separate people. They each have the full annual exemption limit and each pays tax on their capital gains at either 18% or 28% depending on their marginal rate of income tax. As they are treated separately it is not possible for losses to be transferred from one spouse, or civil partner, to the other.

However, if an asset is jointly owned any chargeable gain, or allowable loss, on disposal to a third party must be split up between the husband and wife, or civil partners. This is normally done by apportioning the gain between them using the beneficial interest of each in the asset.

Disposals between a husband and wife, or civil partners, living together, however, are treated on a 'no gain or loss' basis. This is done by taking the net proceeds to be the amount that makes the chargeable gain nil, regardless of any consideration actually given.

These rules obviously often give good scope for tax planning. Assets can be transferred between spouses or civil partners before their final disposal to make the best use of annual exemption allowances or may enable gains to be taxed at 18% instead of 28% if transferred from an higher rated income tax partner to a basic or non-taxable partner. The legislation also offers opportunities to maximise the benefit to be obtained from capital losses. We will review tax planning in more detail in Chapter 11, however, to illustrate these ideas, work through the following example.

Activity

Richard and Judy are a married couple. In May 2001, Judy bought a chargeable asset for £10,000 (net of incidental costs of acquisition and on which no further capital expenditure was incurred), which she gave to Richard in November 2010. Richard sold the asset for £20,000 in March 2011. Calculate the chargeable gain that arises when Richard sold the asset.

Feedback

The transfer from Judy to Richard will be on a no gain/no loss basis. This means Richard is treated as having acquired the asset at the same value as Judy did in May 2001 – i.e. £10,000.

Assuming Richard is a basic rate tax payer with taxable income of £15,000, when Richard sold the asset:

	£
Proceeds	20,000
Less Deemed cost	(10,000)
Chargeable gain	10,000
CGT liability £10,000 x 18%	1,800

Note: the 18% rate would apply as the chargeable gain, together with his taxable income, does not exceed the income tax basic rate band. Also, as Richard has an annual allowance this year of £10,100, this may mean this sale attracts no CGT, as the £10,000 chargeable gain does not exceed the £10,100 AEA he is entitled to if he does not have other gains to use his allowance against.

This transfer may have made particular sense if Judy had perhaps disposed of other assets using up her allowance this year and would therefore have had to pay 18% CGT on this disposal if she hadn't transferred it to Richard first. Even if Richard has used up his allowance, the transfer would still make sense if Judy was a higher rate income tax payer and would have otherwise paid CGT at 28%.

Special capital gains tax rules

Now that you are able to calculate the basic capital gains tax charge on a disposal there are some special situations which you need to be able to deal with. Broadly speaking there are two potential difficulties when calculating a capital gain that you should know how to handle. Firstly, it may not be possible to use the actual disposal proceeds in the calculation and secondly, allocating allowable costs may not be straightforward.

For example, suppose an individual buys a large plot of land and then sells a small part of it. It is likely that the large plot is worth more per acre than the part sold. If the taxpayer is allowed to apportion costs by reference to the areas sold, a lower chargeable gain will arise than if the cost is apportioned according to the market value of the part disposed of and the part retained. Perhaps understandably, the legislation requires that the allowable costs are allocated according to market values when part disposals are made.

We will look at how gains on part disposals are calculated later in this section, but first we examine the sale of chattels, another example of an anomaly in calculating capital gains tax. We will conclude this section with a discussion of negligible value claims.

Chattels

Chattels are tangible, movable, property. Assets such as cars, paintings and horses are chattels. Securities and land are not chattels. *Wasting chattels* are chattels with an estimated remaining useful life of 50 years or less. Hence a horse, as an example, is a wasting chattel but a painting will probably not be.

Wasting chattels are usually exempt from capital gains tax which at first sounds like a generous concession as it could then perhaps exclude lots of assets. However, there are two special exceptions we must consider to this general rule. First, you will remember that cars are entirely exempt from capital gains tax anyway. Second, assets which are used during the course of a trade, profession or vocation and are eligible for capital allowances are subject to capital gains tax even if they are wasting chattels. The capital gains tax computation for such assets depends on whether a loss arises or not. If a loss arises, the allowable cost is reduced by the lower of the loss and the capital allowances, including any balancing allowance or charge given for the asset. If a gain is made the rules set out next, relating to the relief available for chattels, apply as normal.

A relief is available for all chattels subject to capital gains tax which have a relatively low value. If the proceeds of sale are £6,000 or less, no capital gains tax liability will arise. This is true even if the asset was eligible for capital allowances. If the sale proceeds exceed £6,000 the chargeable gain is equal to the lower of:

- $5/3 \times$ (gross proceeds − £6,000); and
- the indexed gain.

It is not possible to give a benchmark of when it is no longer worth checking both calculations, and so for relatively low value chattels both calculations will have to be done to be sure which applies.

The following activities illustrate the chattel rules we have just explained.

Activity

Jack sold a valuable book in June 2010 for £6,600. He had bought the book for £100 in November 1984 in an antique shop. Calculate the chargeable gain.

Feedback

A book is a chattel, but as the proceeds are more than £6,000 it is not exempt, although the maximum gain calculation can be used to cap any gain.

	£
Proceeds	6,600
Less cost	(100)
Chargeable gain	6,500

$5/3 \times (£6,600 - £6,000)$ £1,000

The chargeable gain is the lower of £6,500 and £1,000. Hence the chargeable gain will be £1,000.

If a chattel is sold for less than £6,000 any allowable loss is calculated as if the chattel had been sold for £6,000. This will have the effect of reducing or extinguishing the loss, but cannot create a gain.

Wasting assets other than chattels

Not all wasting assets are chattels. Examples include registered designs and copyrights with less than 50 years to run. In such cases the allowable cost is the full original cost of the asset written down over its useful life on a straight line basis. Note that this rule does not apply to leases, which generally don't lose value evenly over their life. Special rules apply for leases to work out how much of their cost is deductible.

Activity

Stephen sold a registered design, a business asset with a 30 year life and a remaining life of 14 years, for £12,000 in March 2011, which had cost £10,000 in March 1995. Calculate the chargeable gain.

Feedback

	£
Proceeds	12,000
Allowable cost	
10,000 × 16/30	(5,333)
Chargeable gain	6,667

Chattels for which capital allowances are available and which are used throughout their period of ownership in a trade, profession or vocation do not have their allowable cost written off.

Part disposals

A taxpayer may dispose of all or part of an asset. For example, he or she may dispose of one chair from a set of four. Alternatively he or she may dispose of a part share in an asset, for example selling a third interest in a race horse. A part disposal may still be a chargeable disposal even if the rest of the asset is still owned by the seller. Under these circumstances special rules apply to determine how much gain may be taxable. Only part of the allowable cost is included in the capital gains tax computation. To calculate this sum, multiply the allowable cost which relates to the entire asset by:

$$\frac{A}{A+B}$$

where A is the value of the part disposed of and B is the market value of the remainder.

To some extent this legislation acts as an anti-avoidance measure. If we take the example of the chairs, a set of four valuable chairs will be worth more than the aggregate values of a single chair and a set of three and equally a set of three chairs will be worth less than three-quarters of the value of the four chairs. This leads to a lower allowable cost and so a higher chargeable gain.

Activity

Susan gave a third interest in a painting of her great-grandfather, which had been commissioned at a cost of £30,000 in April 1982, to her daughter for her 21st birthday in June 2010. The market value of the third disposed of was estimated to be £20,000. The market value of the remaining two-thirds of the painting was estimated to be £55,000. Calculate Susan's chargeable gain.

Feedback

The allowable cost using market value in June 2010 is:

$$\frac{£20,000}{£20,000 + £55,000} \times £30,000 = 8,000$$

	£
Proceeds (deemed to be market value)	20,000
Less allowable cost	(8,000)
Chargeable gain	12,000

The legislation which deals with the part disposal of small areas of land is a little different. Where there is a part disposal of land, it will not be treated as a disposal if the taxpayer elects, so long as two conditions apply:

- the total consideration for all disposals of land for the year is not more than £20,000; and
- the consideration for the transfer of this land is not more than one-fifth of the value of the total just before the transfer.

In this situation the consideration for disposal is deducted from any allowable expenditure when computing the gain on disposal of the rest of the land.

This special rule can also be used where part of a holding of land is compulsorily acquired, for example by a local government authority, so long as the consideration is small in relation to the market value just before the transfer (in practice, less than 5%).

Negligible value claims

If an asset becomes effectively worthless the taxpayer can make a negligible value claim, which means the asset is deemed to be sold at its then market value and immediately re-acquired at the same value. This enables the taxpayer to create a capital loss which can be relieved in the normal way. Of course, the allowable cost on any subsequent disposal becomes the market value at the date of the negligible value claim which could lead to a future capital gains tax bill if the value of the asset goes up again later.

We have now considered most of the special situations which you need to be aware of. However, there are two more important ones that you need to know something about. The first is the treatment of quoted securities and the second is the treatment of houses which either have some element of private use as well as being used for other purposes or are not considered the taxpayer's principle private residence throughout the period of ownership.

Securities

Special rules are needed for calculating the capital gains on the sale of securities because a taxpayer may undertake many transactions in the same securities and in these cases a *matching problem* may arise. For example, suppose a taxpayer acquires a number of ordinary shares in a company on several different dates. When they make a disposal it will be necessary to calculate the allowable cost of the shares. As the shares are effectively identical, but will probably have been purchased at different prices, rules are needed to determine which shares are actually being sold. This is much the same problem as arises in the valuation of stock for accounting purposes and many of the same techniques offer possible solutions, for example, First-in, First-out (FIFO), Last-in, First-out (LIFO) and average cost. In addition, there are circumstances when it may be difficult to identify the appropriate allowable costs, for example when rights and bonus issues are made. Since 1985, indexed weighted average cost has been the method used to address these problems.

The rules for matching acquisitions to disposals of quoted securities are quite complex. If you need to be able to do this for your course of study, there are detailed worked examples and further explanations on the website.

Capital distributions

A capital distribution is a repayment of share capital rather than a dividend which is paid from income.

A capital distribution is treated as a part disposal for capital gains tax purposes. Provided it has a value of more than 5% of the value of the shares, then the normal part disposal rules we examined earlier in the chapter will apply.

However, if the capital distribution is 5% or less than the value of shares the distribution can be deducted from the allowable cost of the shares. This has the effect of deferring any gain until a future disposal occurs. HMRC are able to exercise their discretion when applying this rule if, for example, they suspect tax avoidance is being deliberately entered into, although the taxpayer may appeal if the deduction is disallowed.

Reorganisations

During a reorganisation new shares, and possibly debentures, are exchanged for the original shareholding. If the exchange is for only one class of securities, for example ordinary shares, there is no difficulty. The allowable cost of the original holding becomes the allowable cost of the new holding.

If, however, shares are exchanged for more than one class of securities, such as ordinary shares and debentures, it is necessary to apportion the allowable cost of the original securities to the new holdings. If any of the new securities are quoted the allowable cost is split in proportion to their market values on the first day on which they are quoted after the reorganisation.

Takeovers and mergers

The way in which share exchanges which occur during a takeover or merger are valued is exactly as you might expect from reading the sections on reorganisations and capital distributions.

New shares and securities received in exchange for existing holdings do not lead to a capital gains tax liability. Their allowable cost is derived from the allowable cost of the original holding as described in the section on reorganisations above. If new capital is introduced it becomes an allowable cost. If part of the consideration is in the form of cash a capital distribution is deemed to have taken place and the procedure described in the section on capital distributions is followed.

Private residences and capital gains tax

An individual's only, or main, residence (termed their *principal private residence* or 'PPR'), including grounds of up to 5,000 square metres, is exempted from capital gains tax provided that he or she has occupied the whole of the residence throughout the period of ownership.

This exemption has helped to contribute to an attitude of homeowners to any increase in the value of their property that differs from the way they think about other capital assets. Homeowners are in a unique position to become highly geared, with loans of up to 100% (or even more in some cases) of the value of their house. This means that even a small increase in the value of houses could generate a nice tax-free increase in the value of the owner's equity. This has led to a sense of economic well-being when the price of houses goes up among the more than 65% of households who own their own homes. Few people however, see increases in house prices in the same light as increases in other commodities. Imagine the impact of applying capital gains tax to principal private residences. Increases in value would no longer be seen as beneficial to the same extent because of the large amount of tax which may be payable each time an individual moves.

There is some pressure on the Government to levy tax on the gains made by homeowners (as we discussed in Chapter 3) but it is hard to imagine a government accepting the level of unpopularity which would surely be the result of enacting such a policy and therefore we can probably expect no major change in this area in the near future.

There are, however, some restrictions to this generous rule that you should be aware of. For example, a husband and wife can claim only one principal private residence between them unless they are legally separated. If you own more than one property, and live in them both at any time, you must elect (i.e. tell HMRC in writing) which of them is your principal private residence. The sale of the other will be subject to capital gains tax under the rules explained below. This implies you can only have a single principal private residence at any one time. You must tell HMRC which is your principal private residence within two years of residing in the second or subsequent property.

Where the taxpayer has not occupied the residence throughout their period of ownership a capital gains tax liability may arise. To calculate the proportion of the gain which is exempt from capital gains tax multiply the total gain, calculated in the normal way, by:

$$\frac{\text{Period of deemed occupation since 31 March, 1982}}{\text{Total period of ownership since 31 March, 1982}}$$

(Remember that capital gains which arose prior to 31 March, 1982 are no longer taxable.)

Provided that the residence was the taxpayer's principal private residence at any time during their period of ownership, the last 36 months of ownership are deemed to be a period of occupation, even if the taxpayer nominates another property to be their principal private residence during this period. This measure is designed to help taxpayers who have moved house and are trying to sell their old house and may otherwise be caught by the capital gains tax rules.

Fiscal Fact

The cost of exempting gains on PPRs is estimated to be a huge £3,800 million for 2009/10

There are a number of other occasions when a period of absence can be treated as a period of deemed occupation provided that the property both before and after the period of absence (although not necessarily immediately before or immediately after) was occupied as the taxpayer's principal private residence. The periods of deemed occupation are not affected if the property is actually let to tenants during them or not.

The periods of deemed occupation are:

- any periods of absence totalling up to three years;
- any periods during which the taxpayer was required to live abroad in order to fulfil employment duties; and
- any periods totalling up to four years during which the taxpayer was required to work elsewhere in the UK in order to fulfil employment duties.

Strictly, therefore, each period of absence should be followed by a period of occupation. However, as an extra-statutory concession, if a taxpayer's employment requires him or her to work in the UK immediately followed by a period of working abroad or vice versa the periods will still be allowed as periods of deemed occupation.

To try and make these complicated rules somewhat clearer we will illustrate them with the following example.

Activity

John bought a house on 1 April, 1986 for £45,000. He lived in the house until 30 June, 1988 when he obtained work in another part of the country. The house was let until he returned on 1 April, 1992. On 1 May, 1997 he went to work abroad until 1 May, 2002 when he returned to the UK and moved in with his friend. The house was sold on 1 January, 2011 for £220,000. John incurred fees and costs of £5,000 relating to the sale.

Feedback

It is first necessary to calculate the proportions of exempt and chargeable months to the period of ownership since 1 April, 1986. The total period of ownership is 297 months (24 years 9 months from 1 April 1986 to 1 January 2011).

Period	Exempt months	Chargeable months
1/4/86–30/6/88 (occupied)	27	0
1/7/88–31/3/92		
(working away (in UK) <4 years)	45	0
1/4/92–30/4/97 (occupied)	61	0
1/5/97–31/12/07 (see below)	0	128
1/1/08–1/1/11 (last 36 months)	36	0
	169	128

The period from 1 May, 1997 to 31 December, 2007 is not exempt because the absence was not followed by a period of owner occupation. Had John re-occupied the house after this period instead of moving in with his friend, even if only for a short time, the period from 1 May, 1997 to when he moved out would also have been exempted under the working away rules, and the normal principal private residence exemption.

Now the chargeable gain can be calculated:

	£
Gross proceeds	220,000
Incidental costs of disposal	(5,000)
Net proceeds	215,000
Less allowable cost	(45,000)
Gain	170,000

Private residence exemption:

$169/297 \times 170{,}000$	(96,734)
Chargeable gain	73,266

Taxpayers living in job-related accommodation will be able to claim any residence which they own as a principal private residence provided that they intend to occupy it as their main residence in due course. (Look back to the benefits in kind section of Chapter 5 for a definition of job-related accommodation).

Lettings

If a lodger lives with a family, sharing living accommodation and eating with them, there is no liability to capital gains tax. However, if part or all of a property is let for residential purposes, the principal private residence exemption may extend to gains which relate to the period of letting. This relief is available if:

- the owner is absent and lets the property during a period which is not considered a deemed period of occupation; and
- only part of the property is let.

The relief available is the lowest of:
- the gain accruing during the letting period;
- £40,000; and
- the total gain which is exempt under the principal private residence provisions. However, this relief cannot turn a gain into an allowable loss for capital gains tax purposes.

Business use

If part of the residence is used wholly for business purposes, then any gain which is attributable to that part is taxable. This is an important point to bear in mind when deciding whether to claim that part of a residence is used for business purposes, perhaps an office or a workshop. In the short term it may be possible to set some expenses against income for income tax purposes but it may give rise to a substantial liability for capital gains tax purposes in the future if that use is claimed to be exclusively for business purposes.

Reliefs from capital gains tax

As you have already seen, capital gains tax is largely intended to create a fair and equitable system of tax and to reduce the incentives to artificially create a capital receipt rather than an income receipt to decrease the amount of tax payable on the transaction. However, there are a number of situations when relief is available to mitigate the impact of capital gains tax.

Businesses often sell an asset intending to replace it with another. For example, a business may move to new premises and thus sell the existing land and buildings they own in order to purchase the new property. Rollover relief (which defers capital gains tax due) may be available if the proceeds from a sale of assets are invested in new assets. You may consider this to be entirely reasonable since, although a liability to capital gains tax has arisen because of the sale, the business is clearly no better off than they were just before they sold the property, and probably needs the money it has raised from the sale to buy the new asset. In reality the taxpayer has simply exchanged one asset for another.

Such a favourable tax treatment will also encourage a business to reinvest their money into other businesses assets rather than to take it out of the economy. This is arguably good for an entrepreneurial society.

If the new asset is a depreciating asset then the taxpayer may claim *holdover relief* rather than rollover relief. This relief works in a similar way to rollover relief, as we will see below.

If a taxpayer makes a chargeable disposal for less than the market value of the asset (e.g. as a gift) then, providing both the donor and the beneficiary make an election, some or all of the chargeable gain can be deferred and transferred to the beneficiary by means of gift relief. This enables assets to be passed from one generation to the next without a capital gains tax liability arising and hence the name gift relief.

Finally, a new form of relief, introduced in Budget 2008, is the Entrepreneurs' relief, which is designed to reduce the capital gains tax liability for a business proprietor who sells all or part of his or her business as a going concern.

We will now consider each of these reliefs in more detail, in turn.

Rollover relief

If the consideration received for the disposal of capital assets is used, by the taxpayer, to acquire other capital assets, then rollover relief may be available. This will allow the disposal of the old asset to occur as if it gave rise to neither a gain nor a loss but the allowable cost of the new asset is then reduced by the amount of the gain on the old asset. This way the new asset absorbs the gain from the old asset and holds it until such time as it is disposed of. Both the old and the new assets must be used solely for the purpose of trade and also must fall into one of the following classes (Note: it does not matter if they fall into different categories.):

Class 1: any land or building or part of a building used only for the purpose of trade – fixed plant or machinery which does not form part of a building

Class 2: ships, aircraft and hovercraft

Class 3: satellites, space stations and spacecraft

Class 4: goodwill

Class 5: milk quotas and potato quotas

Class 6: ewe and suckler cow premium quotas.

Class 7: fish quota

Class 8: Lloyds syndicate rights

In order to claim the relief the new asset must be acquired between 12 months before and three years after the disposal of the old asset (although sometimes HMRC can be persuaded to extend this period). It is not necessary for the old and new asset to be used in the same business, just that they belong to the same taxpayer.

If the total proceeds from the sale of the old asset are reinvested in the new asset, then full relief will be given. However, if some of the proceeds are not reinvested then a chargeable gain equal to the lower of the chargeable gain before rollover relief and the amount which has not been reinvested will be subject to capital gains tax immediately.

Activity

Mike bought a ship in March 1999 for £500,000 and sold it for £1,000,000 in September 2010. He bought a factory in November 2010 for £850,000. Both assets are or were used in his trade. Determine any chargeable gain that arises on the sale of the ship assuming that rollover relief is claimed and compute the chargeable gain arising when Mike sells the factory in June 2011 for £1.5 million (assuming current rules apply in 2011).

Feedback

Disposal of ship	£
Proceeds	1,000,000
Less allowable cost	(500,000)
Chargeable gain	500,000
Less amount not reinvested	
£1,000,000 – £850,000	(150,000)
Gain eligible to be rolled over	350,000

The chargeable gain is £150,000 as this is the amount not re-invested and is lower than the gain calculated (£500,000).

Base cost of the factory:	£
Cost	850,000
Less rolled over gain	(350,000)
Base cost of the factory	500,000

Disposal of factory	£
Proceeds	1,500,000
Less allowable cost	(500,000)
Chargeable gain	1,000,000

Holdover relief

Rollover relief cannot be claimed, however, if the replacement asset is depreciable i.e. if it is, or within the next 10 years will become, a wasting asset. Instead, we use holdover relief. Remember that a wasting asset has a life of 50 years or less and so holdover relief is going to apply to any replacement asset with a life of 60 years or less. Plant and machinery is always treated as a depreciating asset while freehold land and buildings are never treated as depreciating assets for this purpose.

Holdover relief is given by reducing the amount of the chargeable gain according to the amount reinvested as we did with rollover relief, but instead of using the gain to reduce the cost of the new asset until it is finally sold, the gain is instead 'held over' until it crystallises, at which time it becomes chargeable.

The held-over gain becomes a chargeable gain on the earlier of:

- the date on which the taxpayer disposes of the replacement asset;

- the date on which the replacement asset ceases to be used for the purposes of a trade carried on by the taxpayer; or
- ten years after the date of the acquisition of the replacement asset.

If, before the held-over gain crystallised, the replacement asset is itself replaced by an asset which is not a depreciating asset then some or all of the held-over gain can be transferred to the new asset.

Activity

May bought a workshop in February 2001 for £25,000 and ran a business making and selling soft furnishings. In July 2005 she sold the workshop for £40,000 and in August 2005 she bought fixed plant for £50,000 to use in the new premises she was renting. In January 2008 May bought a new workshop for £35,000 and in October 2010 she sold the fixed plant for £80,000. Determine May's chargeable gains on each of the transactions, assuming that holdover/rollover relief is claimed where appropriate.

Feedback

July 2005 disposal:	£
Proceeds	40,000
Less allowable costs	(25,000)
Chargeable gain	15,000

The entire proceeds of £40,000 can be considered to have been reinvested in plant within the time period allowed for relief to apply, and so the £15,000 gain can be held over and no chargeable gain arises from the first transaction.

January 2008 purchase:

When the new workshop (not a depreciating asset) was bought part of the held-over gain from the first workshop could be rolled over to the new workshop. Rolled-over gains can be held indefinitely as long as the new asset is owned and as such is a better place to have the gain attached to than the plant. May is probably better off moving as much of the held-over gain (£15,000) onto the new workshop therefore that she can. The base cost of the new workshop would be £25,000.

	£
Total gain held over	15,000
Less proceeds not reinvested	
40,000 – 35,000	(5,000)
Gain eligible to be rolled over	10,000

The £5,000 not eligible to be rolled over continues to be held over until the charge crystallises.

October 2010 disposal of plant:

	£
Proceeds	80,000
Less cost	(50,000)
Chargeable gain	30,000

August 2015:

The remaining held-over gain of £5,000 crystallises as a result of the 10 year rule, and will be chargeable to capital gains tax in 2015/16.

Incorporation relief

At present rollover relief is also available where a business and all its assets (other than cash) are transferred to a company in exchange for shares in that new company. This relief is referred to as incorporation relief. It is automatically applied normally, however incorporations can be done without application of this relief if the taxpayer so elects. This may be in their favour if they wish to use up allowances where they may otherwise be lost. If a taxpayer wishes to do this they must normally inform HMRC of their decision no later than the second anniversary of the 31 January following the tax year in which the transfer occurs.

The relief works by deducting any chargeable gains from the disposal of business assets from the value of the shares received and the company is treated as receiving the assets at their market value. The relief only applies if the business is transferred to the company as a going concern.

Activity

Zigmund decides to incorporate the business he has operated for a number of years as a sole trader. He transfers the business to the company as a going concern, and there is a chargeable gain of £75,000 for the business assets transferred. The market value of the shares in the new company is £200,000. What is the effect of incorporation relief on this transaction?

Feedback

The gain on the business asset is rolled over by reducing the value of the shares, so that the cost of the shares becomes £125,000 (200,000 – 75,000). This means that when Zigmund later sells the shares, the gain will crystallise at that time.

If only part of the consideration given by the company for the business is in the form of shares, for example part of the price is paid in cash, then only a proportion of the chargeable gain can be rolled over in this way and deducted from the value of the shares, based on the market value of the shares compared to the total consideration for the transfer of the business.

Gift relief

Gift relief is available if an individual makes a disposal, otherwise than as a bargain at 'arm's length' (i.e. 'gives' it away, or sells it at less than its true value), of a qualifying asset and both the transferor and the transferee elect for the transferor's gain to be reduced to nil. For the purposes of gift relief an asset is a qualifying asset if:

- it is, or is an interest in, an asset used for the purposes of a trade, profession or vocation carried on by:
  - the transferor, or
  - his or her personal company, or
  - a member of a trading group of which the holding company is his or her personal company or
- it is shares or securities of a trading company, or of the holding company of a trading group, and either:
  - the shares are not listed on a recognised stock exchange, or
  - the trading company or holding company is the transferor's personal company.

If the election is made the transferee is deemed to acquire the asset at its market value less the gain which would otherwise have arisen.

Activity

Joe runs an IT firm. In October 2010, his daughter Lorna joins the business. Joe decides to gift to her the goodwill in the business. This was acquired for £150,000 in April 2000 when Joe first acquired the business and its market value in October 2010 was £450,000. Both parties elect to treat the gift under the gift relief rules. What would be the heldover gain and Lorna's allowable cost?

Feedback

The chargeable gain needs to be computed for Joe. This will be £300,000 (£450,000 – £150,000). This then reduces the allowable cost of the asset in Lorna's hands to £150,000 (£450,000 –£300,000). Joe has no capital gains tax liability to deal with and the gain is transferred to Lorna to pay tax on instead when she disposes of the goodwill in the future.

If the transferee provides some consideration the transferor's deferred gain is instead equal to the gain less any excess of the consideration over the allowable costs, excluding any indexation allowance. This deferred gain is termed the held-over gain.

Activity

Alan sold the goodwill of a small paper recycling business to his daughter Sarah on 30 May 2010. The goodwill had a market value of £300,000 but Alan sold it to Sarah for £100,000 and both claimed gift relief. Alan had bought the goodwill in May 2000 for £50,000. Sarah intends to sell the business in April 2012 and believes that she will be able to obtain a price of £400,000 by then. Determine Alan's chargeable gain and advise Sarah on the amount of any chargeable gain if she sells the business as planned.

Feedback

	£
Alan	
Deemed proceeds	300,000
Less allowable cost	(50,000)
	250,000
Less gain held over	
£250,000 – (£100,000 – £50,000)	(200,000)
Chargeable gain	50,000
Sarah – if sold in April 2012	
Proceeds	400,000
Less allowable cost (£300,000 – £200,000)	(100,000)
Chargeable gain	300,000

Alan's chargeable gain is £50,000, while Sarah's chargeable gain will be £300,000 if she sells the business as planned.

If the taxpayer makes a disposal by way of a gift to a charity or for national purposes, or for a consideration which would give rise to an allowable loss, then the disposal and acquisition is treated as being made for a consideration that results in neither a gain nor a loss on the disposal. The recipient of the asset is deemed to have acquired the asset at the same time and for the same consideration as the donor of the gift.

A gift is for national purposes if it is made to the National Gallery, British Museum or National Trust or to a university, among others.

It should be noted that no gift relief is available for any transfers of shares or securities to a company by individuals or trustees after 9 November, 1999.

If an individual gifts shares in a company to another person, however, an apportionment calculation must be done as only gains related to chargeable business assets are eligible for gift relief. Any sum represented by non-eligible assets (for gift relief), like investments held by the company whose shares are being gifted, become chargeable instead on the transferor.

Entrepreneurs' relief

A new form of relief was introduced with effect from 6 April 2008 to complement the capital gains tax reforms introduced in 2008 (i.e. the abolition of indexation and taper relief for individuals replaced by a single flat 18% tax rate). Entrepreneurs' relief was introduced following public concern that the changes to the rate of capital gains tax would be detrimental to people selling all or part of a business as a going concern, or on cessation of the business, particularly as many small business owners treat the increase in goodwill which they will realise on sale of their business as a form of retirement provision.

Where individuals involved in running a business dispose of all or part of that business and make a gain on the disposal, the first £5million for any disposals after 22 June 2010 (£1million until 5 April 2010, £2million for disposals 6 April 2010 to 22 June 2010) of gains that qualify for the relief will be charged to capital gains tax at a simple, fixed rate of 10%, instead of the normal 18% or new 28% CGT rates. Before the 22 June 2010, this relief was achieved by reducing the gain liable to capital gains tax by 4/9ths. This resulted in an *effective* rate of 10% (5/9ths x 18%), but was a more complicated way of achieving this same outcome.

The £5million limit is a lifetime limit, so a taxpayer may be able to make several claims until this total is reached.

The relief also applies to gains which arise on the disposal of shares in a trading company, providing that the individual making the disposal has been an officer or employee of the company and owns at least 5% of the ordinary share capital of the company.

Prior to 22 June 2010 entrepreneurs' relief was not granted automatically, it had to be claimed by the taxpayer or the full 18% would be applied. The claim had to be made within one year of 31 January following the tax year in which the disposal occurred. For gains arising after 22 June 2010, no claim is now needed and the 10% rate automatically applies until the £5million limit is reached.

The following activity illustrates how this relief can be applied (source: based on Budget June 2010, Budget Note 20):

Activity

Bethan has previously used £1million of her lifetime entrepreneurs' relief limit. In 2010/11 her taxable income, after all allowable deductions and the personal allowance, is £17,400. In May 2010 Bethan realises a chargeable gain of £3million on the disposal of a business. In December 2010 she sells another business, realising further chargeable gains of £7million. Both disposals qualify for entrepreneurs' relief (subject to the lifetime limits). Bethan has no allowable losses to set against these gains. What would her CGT liability be for 2010/11 assuming she has no other gains in the year?

Feedback

The £3million gain realised in May 2010 is subject to the £2million lifetime limit for entrepreneurs' relief (for qualifying disposals from 6 April 2010 to 22 June 2010) of which Bethan has previously used £1million. The gain is reduced by 4/9 of £1million and the remainder is charged to CGT at the single rate of 18%:

£2million – £1million relief already claimed = £1million

Chargeable gain=£1million–(4/9 x £1million) x 18% = £100,000

The increase in the lifetime limit from 23 June 2010 means that £3million of the £7million gain from December is chargeable at the 10% rate of CGT (i.e. £300,000). This is because £4million (£1million previously + £3million in May 2010) has already used up part of this (albeit now enlarged) lifetime limit.

Bethan's taxable income is £20,000 below the basic rate band (£37,400 – £17,400) but clearly the £3million of the gain charged at 10% must then take priority over any other gains in determining whether total income and gains exceed the basic rate band so the remaining £4million gains, less the AEA, are charged at the higher rate of 28%.

(£4million – £10,100) x 28% = £1,117,172

Bethan's total CGT liability for 2010/11 would therefore be:

£100,000 + £300,000 + £1,117,172 = £1,517,172

Stamp duty

Stamp duty was introduced into the UK in 1694, and is therefore one of the oldest taxes still in existence in this country. Its origins can be traced all the way back to Roman times however. Stamp duty is a tax on transactions, imposed when certain types of property changes hands. As such it can therefore be thought of as a capital tax in the same category of taxes as capital gains tax.

Like income tax, when stamp duty was first introduced it was only supposed to be temporary and was introduced to provide revenue for the King and Queen (William and Mary) to 'carry on the war against France'.

Stamp duty was charged on certain documents when first introduced. These included insurance policies, documents in court proceedings, grants of honour, grants of probate (wills) and letters of administration.

Stamp duty is now administered in the UK by HMRC via various Stamp Duty offices that can be found spread around the UK.

Payment of stamp duty used to be denoted by affixing a stamp to the transfer document or receipt which is the subject of the duty. With the introduction of Stamp Duty Land Tax (SDLT) in December 2003, provision is now made for electronic conveyancing, i.e. without documentation. Stamp duty is calculated at either a flat rate or *ad valorem* i.e. varying according to the value of the transaction to which it relates.

Property transactions

The most common form of stamp duty now is on transfers of property, (land and buildings) both residential and non-residential commercial and on share transactions. It is always payable by the purchaser in a transaction to which it applies.

A major reform of stamp duty on land and buildings was announced in Budget 2002 in order to close a number of loopholes in the new tax rules and reduce some distortions recognised as existing in the old system. This process of modernisation was continued in Budget 2003, with further changes taking effect from December 2003. Under the previous stamp duty regime, transactions were sometimes structured so as to avoid or reduce payment of stamp duty and the government was concerned that this was interfering with commercial decision making. The new regime includes increased powers of enforcement for HMRC to reduce this problem.

Fiscal Fact

According to the 2006 Budget statement there were 160,000 new houses built in 2005 and 200,000 were either built, or at least started, in 2007/08 according to the Communities and Local Government Department in May 2009. With the current housing and credit 'crisis' however, this number is currently much lower.

From 1 December, 2003, SDLT applies to all land transactions. This includes the purchase of freehold land as well as the acquisition of an existing lease. The only exemptions to this are the sales of school owned land and of zero carbon homes (on the first £500,000 of purchase price only in the latter case) from 1 October 2007.

The act of entering into a contract to purchase land is not enough to be considered a land transaction (i.e. what is called an 'exchange' in house purchase terms) rather it is generally 'completion' or the point at which possession occurs that is important. As the date of completion normally occurs before possession is allowed, this will normally be the date of the transaction for SDLT.

The rates of tax on transfers of property vary from 0% to 4%. The table below shows you how the property related stamp duty rates apply in the UK. These rates are not in cumulative bands like income tax however. As soon as the value of the property transferred crosses a boundary, all of the transaction is taxed at the higher rate, not just the excess over the lower band.

Various special provisions apply for SDLT. For property located in disadvantaged areas, a lower rate range applies, in keeping with the current Governments' aim to encourage urban regeneration. Further, stamp duty on shared ownership homes is not required until buyers own 80% of the equity in their homes. Also, as part of the growing range of apparently environmentally motivated tax concessions, relief from stamp duty now applies to all zero-carbon flats on their first sale with effect from 1 October 2007 (currently until 30 September 2012). This only applies however, for flats up to a sale value of £500,000 (although more expensive zero-carbon flats still get a £15,000 deduction on the normal SDLT).

Value of property (£)	Stamp duty rate %	
Residential property	*Non 1st time buyers*	*1st time buyers*
0 – 125,000*	0	0
125,001 – 250,000	1	0
250,001 – 500,000	3	3
over 500,000	4	4

Non-residential property	
0 – 150,000	0
150,001 – 250,000	1
250,001 – 500,000	3
over 500,000	4

Prior to 23 March 2006, the lower limit for residential property was £120,000. As part of the Government's attempt to correct the problems arising as a result of the recession, a stamp duty 'holiday' was granted for properties valued at less than £175,000 from 2 September 2008. This holiday was expected to expire on 3 December 2009, but Budget 2009 announced continuation of this holiday until 31 December 2009, at which time the 0% rate threshold reverted to £125,000. In the case of residential property in disadvantaged areas, the threshold is £150,000 instead of £125,000. The first Finance Act 2010, however, changed the rules again, this time just for first home buyers. For first home buyers, the 0% rate will apply up to £250,000.

Fiscal Fact

The minimum 0% theshold for residential property SDLT was raised by £5,000 to £125,000 in the 2006 Budget. This measure brought an additional 40,000 homebuyers into the 0% band according to the Treasury's estimates reported in the Budget.

Activity

(a) Rhona enters into a contract to buy a residential house, not in a disadvantaged area and not her first home, for £243,000. How much SDLT will she have to pay on completion?
(b) What if this sale falls through and instead Rhona buys a house for £252,000. How much SDLT will now be due on completion?

Feedback

(a) The house is in the 1% band and so she will have to pay £243,000 × 1% = £2,430 in SDLT.
(b) The house is in the 3% band so all the value is subject to 3% SDLT i.e. £252,000 × 3% = £7,560.

Note that an increase of only £9,000 in the value of the property has resulted in an extra £5,130 in taxes (i.e. an effective marginal tax rate of 57%).

Leases

SDLT also applies to the grant of a new lease. Any premium payable on the grant of the lease is subject to SDLT using the tables above, except if the rental for a year is more than £600, then the zero rate band does not apply.

There is also SDLT due on the lease, based on the net present value of the rent payable. For residential property, the rate is 0% up to £125,000 and 1% on the excess over £125,000. For non-residential property the rate is 0% up to £150,000 and 1% on the excess.

Note that this is not calculated on the same basis as for sales of property, rather the progressive rate scale (see below) means that only the excess over the threshold is chargeable.

Activity

Lewis is granted a 15 year lease over a warehouse building which is not in a disadvantaged area. He pays a premium of £50,000 and the net present value of the rent is £190,000. How much SDLT will he have to pay?

Feedback

	£
On the premium £50,000 × 1%	500
On the rental 1% × (190,000 – 150,000)	400
Total	900

Share transactions

The other main area to which UK Stamp Duty is applied is transactions in shares. The table below shows the current rates of duty that are applied when shares are purchased using a stock transfer form.

Purchase price (£)	Duty (£)
1,001 – 2,000	10
2,001 – 3,000	15
3,001 – 4,000	20
4,001 – 5,000	25
5,001 – 6,000	30
6,001 – 7,000	35
7,001 – 8,000	40

8,001 – 9,000	45
9,001 – 10,000	50
over 10,000	0.5% of transaction rounded up to next multiple of £5.

Transactions with a purchase price of less than £1,000 are exempt from stamp duty, with effect from April 2008.

When you buy shares through a stockbroker, it will usually be a paperless (electronic) transaction. In this situation, Stamp Duty Reserve Tax is paid at a flat rate of 0.5% of the amount paid for the shares.

Administration

Payment of stamp duty on share transactions is made by taking, or sending, the documents to be stamped to a Stamp Duty office. These offices can be found in various UK cities. Documents that need stamping should be presented to one of these offices within 30 days of the transaction occurring. If you are late making this presentation for payment you have to pay charges and interest as a penalty. The maximum penalty is an amount equivalent to the duty, or £300, whichever is less. This becomes a minimum of £300 if your presentation for payment is more than a year late. Interest is charged on overdue payments at normal official rates in addition to this penalty.

For property transactions, a self assessment system is now in operation that requires the purchaser to send HMRC a return notifying them of the completion of a taxable transaction within 30 days of the effective date of the transaction. The tax due should accompany this notification. Failure to submit a return and/or pay the tax due results in similar interest and penalty charges or legal proceedings that are linked with the self assessment procedures for other taxes, such as income tax.

Inheritance tax

Inheritance tax in its current form was introduced in 1986. A tax on the transfer of property on death has, however, been part of the UK tax landscape in some form or another since the eighteenth century. Like capital gains tax and stamp duty it is a further example of a capital tax in operation in the UK at present as it related to capital transfers (i.e. to inheritances in this case).

An inheritance tax liability will arise when a chargeable person makes a transfer of value of chargeable property. Let's consider each of these terms further.

- *Chargeable person.* Inheritance tax only applies to individuals and not to companies. All individuals are potentially liable for inheritance tax, for UK domiciled persons on all chargeable property wherever it is located, and for non-UK domiciled persons on UK situated property only. (You can check Chapter 12 to find an explanation of the concept of domicile for tax purposes).
- *Chargeable property.* All property is potentially chargeable to inheritance tax, although there are some exemptions or exclusions which we will consider briefly below - see the website chapter for full details.
- *Transfer of value.* The key trigger for inheritance tax to arise is a transfer of *value* between its current 'owner' and the person or entity to whom it is being given. This does not always just arise on an individual's death however. A transfer of value is essentially a gift of an asset by a chargeable person which results in a decrease in the value of that person's estate (total net worth). Usually the decrease in value we consider for inheritance tax purposes will be the open market value of the property at the time of its transfer. Some transfers, or dispositions, are not caught by the inheritance tax net however, including genuine commercial activities and those that are allowable expenses for income tax or corporation tax purposes. Also excluded are dispositions for the maintenance of the transferor's family.

Lifetime transfers

There are three types of transfer made during the lifetime of an individual:

- *Exempt transfers:* These include certain gifts, for example, between spouses or to charities, small gifts and those within the annual exemption, currently £3,000 per annum. No inheritance tax is payable on these either during the transferor's lifetime or on death.
- *Potentially exempt transfers* (PETs): These are gifts to another individual or certain types of trust. No inheritance tax is payable during the lifetime of the transferor, however some tax will be payable if he or she dies within seven years of the transfer.

- *Chargeable Lifetime Transfers* (CLTs): These are mainly gifts to discretionary trusts. Here lifetime inheritance tax is payable at a rate of 20%, and if the transferor dies within seven years of the transfer, another 20% becomes payable to bring the rate up to the full inheritance tax rate of 40%.

Payment of inheritance tax on lifetime transfers depends on when the transfer is made. For transfers made after 5 April and before 1 October in any year, payment is required by 30 April of the following year. Where the transfer is made after 30 September and before 6 April in any year, payment is required within six months of the end of the month in which the transfer is made.

Inheritance tax payable on death

When an individual dies, inheritance tax is calculated at the rate then applicable, currently 40%, subject to a nil rate band of £325,000 for the current tax year (unchanged from 2009/10 and frozen at this level until 2014/15). The nil rate band is applied first against lifetime transfers, i.e. CLTs and PETs which were made in the preceding seven years. Any remaining nil rate band after lifetime transfers have been considered then reduces the value of the total estate left at the point of death. The remainder of the estate after all the nil-rate band has been used up is taxed at 40%.

Inheritance tax payable on death transfers is due six months after the end of the month in which the death occurs.

From 9 October 2007, the inheritance tax rules have been relaxed somewhat for married couples and civil partners. They are now allowed to share their nil-rate bands so that any unused sums from these bands on the first partner's death can be added to the surviving partner's nil-rate band increasing it for when they subsequently die.

Fiscal Fact

Despite the fact the published rate of inheritance tax is 40%, HMRC estimates that only 6% of value bequeathed in the UK is taxable due to the use of tax planning and the effect of the threshold; 94% of all estate value therefore is not subject to IHT. The estimated number of taxpaying estates in 2008/09 is 21,000.

Business property relief

Special relief applies to business property so that businesses do not have to be sold in order to pay any inheritance tax due on transfer of an on-going business. Property which qualifies for this relief includes unincorporated businesses and shares in unquoted companies, so long as they have been owned for at least two years prior to the transfer.

Tax planning

Capital gains tax is a tax which is amenable to tax planning because the timing of events is often within the control of the taxpayer. Tax planning is also an important issue because it is possible to incur a significant capital gains tax liability if good advice is not taken.

Consider the disposal of a company on retirement – the taxpayer can sell either the shares of the company or the business's assets and wind the company up.

If the assets are sold a capital gains tax liability will accrue to the company. When the company is then liquidated the taxpayer will incur a second capital gains tax liability on the gain received on the shares. If instead the shares are sold directly, then only the gain on the shares will be taxable.

However, for a number of reasons the purchaser may rather buy the assets than the shares. If the company is sold the purchaser also acquires the liabilities and obligations of the company whereas acquiring the assets is more straightforward.

These factors, often together with many more, will become part of the negotiations which are entered into before the business is sold.

In general, capital disposals should be made as early as possible in the fiscal year in order to delay the payment of tax as much as possible to allow inflation to reduce the impact of the tax charge. An individual or married couple should try to fully utilise their annual exemption limit(s) each year since, if it is not used in the year, it cannot be carried forward.

If at all possible losses should not be wasted by being set against current gains which would otherwise have benefited from the annual exemption limit.

It is important to obtain good tax advice before making a large disposal so that any exemptions and reliefs available can be claimed.

Summary

Capital taxes, including capital gains tax, stamp duty and inheritance tax, are generally levied for reasons of equity and to reduce tax avoidance.

Capital gains tax was introduced in 1965. In the early years there were many changes in the legislation which were needed to correct fundamental flaws in the original legislation. One of the most important developments was the introduction of the indexation allowance. Of course, this also significantly reduced the amount of tax which was collected by the Government but it might be argued that it made the tax 'fairer'- which seems to be one of the most important motivating characteristics of capital gains tax. Now that the indexation allowance and taper relief have gone, the question of whether the tax is still fair must be raised again.

Taxpayers, both individuals and companies, pay tax on their chargeable gains. However, there is considerable scope for tax planning as the taxpayer can often choose the date on which to make the disposal. There are a number of reliefs which are available to taxpayers including relief on a principal private residence, rollover relief, holdover relief, incorporation relief and gift relief. Remember also that gains on assets held in pension funds and personal equity plans are not subject to income tax or capital gains tax. These reliefs, together with the annual exemption limit, enable most individuals to avoid any liability to capital gains tax.

The 2010/11 year is particularly complicated for capital gains tax because unusually the Government chose to make key changes effective part way through the year. In particular, these are the introduction of the new 28% rate for higher and additional rate taxpayers, the increase in the entrepreneurs' relief lifetime limit to £5 million, and the change to way in which the entrepreneurs' relief is calculated. We saw how these changes affect computations in various activities in this chapter.

Stamp duty is imposed on documents which evidence certain transfers of property. Finally inheritance tax, which only applies to individuals, taxes the value of estates on the death of individuals, and sometimes also transfers of property during a taxpayer's lifetime.

Project areas

Because of the introduction and subsequent abolition of the taper relief regime for individuals, there is great increased scope for dissertations on the subject of capital gains tax. A survey of holders of chargeable assets, especially chargeable business assets, to determine if it affects their decision to hold or sell might be interesting. A comparison of the taxation of capital gains in more than one country is likely to be interesting. The question of whether capital gains tax is a fair tax is worth asking.

In the area of stamp duty you might like to consider what the impact of this tax is on the housing and share markets. What would now happen to these markets if it was revised for example?

For IHT, how has the significant increase in personal wealth of homeowners over the last 20 years or so affected the role of IHT as part of the tax system? Is this taxation of PPRs by the back door?

Discussion topics

1. It is sometimes possible for individuals to arrange their affairs in order to have receipts taxed as income rather than a capital gain and vice versa. For example, directors planning to sell a family company could either pay themselves high salaries taxable under ITEPA 2003 or take relatively low salaries thus increasing the funds retained in the business, leading to a higher value for their shares when the company is sold. List the taxation consequences of making this decision and discuss the circumstances in which income may be preferable to capital gains.

2. What impact do stamp duties have on capital transactions, if any?

3. Is inheritance tax an unfair tax in that it taxes people on the results of their life-time's hard work when they die?

Quick quiz

1. Andrew bought a fixed asset (not exempt from capital gains tax) for use in his business in June 1989 for £1,700 and sold it in May 2010 for £5,000. Compute the chargeable gain.

2. In August 1999, Barbara bought a second hand hearse at an auction for £4,000 which she then sold to the Atherstone Vintage Car Museum for £7,000 in April 2010. What are the capital gains tax consequences?

3. Charlie bought a valuable modern impressionist painting for £3,400 in May 1998. He sold it in February 2011 for £5,500. What are the capital gains tax consequences?

4. In August 2010 Davina sold part of her trading business and realises a gain of £450,000 before entrepreneurs' relief. She has not previously made any claims for entrepreneurs' relief and has no other capital gains or losses for the year. If she claims entrepreneurs' relief, how much capital gains tax will be payable?

5. Eddie was given a chargeable asset (not a chattel) in August 2000 with a market value of £7,000. In June 2010 he was successful in claiming that the asset had a negligible value of only £50. What allowable loss (if any) will Eddie be entitled to?

6. Felicity sold one quarter of a parcel of land in May 2010 for £200,000. She had originally bought the land in May 2002 for £500,000 and the remainder was valued at £860,000 immediately after the part disposal. What is her chargeable gain?

Questions

Question 1 (based on ACCA June 1990).

James purchased a house in Oxford, 'Millhouse', on 1 July 1992 and took up immediate residence. The house cost £50,000. On 1 January 1993 he went to work and live in the United States where he stayed until 30 June 1995. On 1 July 1995 James returned to the UK to work for his United States employers in Scotland where it was necessary for him to occupy rented accommodation. On 1 July 1996 his mother became seriously ill and James resigned from his job to go and live with her. His mother died on 30 September 1997 leaving her house to James. James decided to continue to live in his mother's house and finally sold 'Millhouse' on 30 June 2010 for £200,000.

Required: Calculate, before the annual exemption, the capital gain assessable on James for this sale in 2010/11.

Question 2 (based on ACCA December 1988).

(a) Arthur bought 300 hectares of land to be used in his business for £120,000 on 1 February 1988. On 1 July 2010 he sold 50 hectares of the land for £40,000. On 1 July 2010 the value of the remaining 250 hectares was £187,500.

Required: Calculate Arthur's capital gain in 2010/11 (before annual exemption).

(b) Margaret sold her holiday home, which had never been her main residence, on 6 April 2010 for £65,000. She had purchased the home on 6 April 1982 for £25,000. The following amounts of enhancement expenditure were incurred:

6 October, 1985	Central heating system	£1,000
6 May, 1995	Extension to rear	£4,000

Required: Calculate Margaret's capital gain in 2010/11 (before annual exemption).

(c) On 3 August 2010, her 55th birthday, Anne retired from running her nursing home and gave the business to her daughter, Jocelyn. Both Anne and Jocelyn are resident and ordinarily resident in the UK. Anne had owned the business for the previous 15 years. The chargeable gain was £200,000, before any reliefs.

Required: State the reliefs (other than annual exemption) which can be claimed and outline the effect of claiming them.

Question 3 During the year ended 5 April 2011 Eric (a higher rate tax payer) disposed of the following property:

(a) A small cottage in Devon which he had inherited in August 1984 when its value was £20,000 and he subsequently used as a holiday cottage for his own use. In September 1985 he had added a conservatory to the property at a cost of £3,500. Eric did not use the cottage as his main residence, and he sold it for £225,000 in July 2010. Eric incurred legal and estate agent's fees of £1,500 on the disposal of the property.

(b) A vacant 8 hectare plot of land for £52,800 in February 2011. The plot was part of a 12 hectare plot originally bought by Eric for £31,700 in October 1985 and not used by him as a business asset. Incidental costs of disposal were £1,300. The remaining 4 hectare plot was valued at £22,000 in February 2011.

Required:

(a) Calculate Eric's capital gain for the year of assessment 2010/11 after the annual exemption.
(b) Calculate the amount of capital gains tax payable by Eric for 2010/11, stating when the tax must be paid.

Question 4   (based on ACCA June 2004).

Alice Lim disposed of the following assets during 2010/11:

(a)   On 24 June 2010, Alice sold a freehold office building for £152,000. The office building had been purchased on 2 March 2002 for £134,000. Prior to this on 15 April 2002 Alice had sold a freehold warehouse for £149,000. The warehouse had been purchased on 20 November 1999 for £93,000. Alice made a claim to roll over the gain arising on the disposal of the warehouse against the cost of the office building. Both the office building and the warehouse were used entirely for business purposes in a manufacturing business run by Alice as a sole trader.

(b)   On 9 January 2011 Alice sold 50,000 £1 ordinary shares in Alilim Ltd, an unlisted trading company, for £275,000. Alilim Ltd had been formed on 17 October 2002 in order to incorporate a retail business that Alice had run as a sole trader since 18 May 1998. The market value of the retail business on 17 October 2002 was £300,000. All of the business assets were transferred to Alilim Ltd. The consideration consisted of £200,000 £1 ordinary shares valued at £200,000, and £100,000 in cash. The transfer of the business assets resulted in total chargeable gains of £120,000. This figure is before taking account of any rollover relief that was available on incorporation.

(c)   On 27 February 2011 Alice sold 40,000 £1 ordinary shares (a 40% shareholding) in Family Ltd, an unlisted trading company for £230,000. Alice had acquired the shares on 21 March 2003 when she purchased them from her mother for £120,000. Alice's mother had originally purchased the shares on 19 December 1998 for £128,000. Alice and her mother elected to hold over the gain arising on 21 March 2003 as a gift of a business asset. The market value of the shares on that date was £168,000.

Required: Calculate the capital gains arising from Alice's disposals during 2010/11. You should ignore the annual exemption.

(*Note: answer available on the lecturer's website*)

Further test questions for this chapter to test your knowledge can be found in the student section of the website at:

http://www.taxstudent.com/uk

Further reading and examples

Combs, A., Dixon, S. & Rowes, P. (2010), *Taxation: incorporating the 2010 Finance Acts*, Fiscal Publications: Birmingham.
– use this book for many other examples to further develop and test your knowledge of this chapter's contents. See http://www.fiscalpublications.com/rowes/2010

9 Corporation tax

Introduction

Corporation tax is charged on the profits of companies. Until 1965 companies were taxed under the income tax legislation. In 1965 a reform of the tax system led to the introduction of corporation tax as a separate tax. As you will learn in this chapter, there are still many similarities between the ways in which companies' profits are taxed under corporation tax rules and the taxation of sole traders and partnership profits, which are subject to income tax rules. However, there are some important differences between corporation tax and income tax that you need to be aware of.

At the end of this chapter you will be able to:

- describe the imputation system of taxation;
- state the basis of assessment of tax for companies;
- determine the profits chargeable to corporation tax;
- calculate a company's corporation tax liability; and
- determine the date on which the corporation tax is due

Details of other, more complicated, aspects of corporation tax can be found on the website, specifically tax implications of corporate losses and company groups.

The liability to corporation tax

For corporation tax purposes a company is defined in the Companies Act (1985) as being either a corporate body or an unincorporated association. The definition of a company extends to organisations such as clubs and political associations which are therefore subject to corporation tax. The definition excludes partnerships, which are subject to income tax like sole traders.

UK resident companies are liable to corporation tax on their total world-wide profits arising in an accounting period regardless of whether the profits are remitted to the UK or not. However, dividends received by a UK resident company from other UK resident companies are not liable to further corporation tax in the hands of the recipient. The exact details of how to determine the residence of a company for tax purposes is further considered in Chapter 12.

The capital gains of a company are not subject to capital gains tax. Instead, its capital gains are subject to corporation tax along with their other income and profits.

The imputation system of taxation

In Chapter 2 we considered whether companies should be liable to tax, given they are just collections of other taxpayers operating in business using a particular legal structure. We also reviewed the principal methods of taxing companies that are used in practice despite this possible issue. When corporation tax was first introduced in 1965 the *classical system* was used. Under the classical system the relationship between a company and its shareholders is ignored for tax computations. A company pays tax on its profits without reference to its dividend policy and its shareholders pay tax on their dividends received without any relief for the tax already paid by the company on those profits. This is a simple system but does lead to distributed profits effectively being taxed twice, once in the hands of the company and then again in the hands of the shareholders. This is how company profits are taxed in some parts of the world.

Fiscal Fact

In 1973-74 it is estimated that 175,000 companies paid corporation tax, by 2007/08 the number had reached 940,000.

In 1973 the problem of double taxation of distributed profits led the Government to switch to an *imputation system* under which shareholders were given a tax credit for some of the corporation tax which had been paid by the company. The tax credit was used to offset at least some of the shareholder's liability to income tax resulting from their dividend receipts from the company. This is the system still in operation in the UK. (If you need to, look again at the way in which dividends are included in a tax computation in Chapter 4 to see how these credits are applied in personal tax computations). The primary advantage of the imputation system of company taxation over the classical system is that the impact of double taxation on distributed profits is reduced.

For the current tax year the tax credit is set at a rate of 10%. Taxpayers receive a tax credit equal to 1/10th of any gross dividend from a UK company. Gross dividends, that is the dividend actually received together with the related tax credit, received by basic rate taxpayers, are subject to income tax at a rate of 10%. This means that non-higher rate taxpayers are able to use their tax credit to fully satisfy their tax liability on their dividends received. Higher rate taxpayers are taxed at a rate of 32.5%, and from 6 April 2010 additional rate taxpayers pay 42.5%, on their gross dividends received, although of course they are able to use the 10% tax credit to reduce this tax liability.

Individual non-taxpayers are not able to reclaim the tax credit under the current tax system and therefore suffer tax on dividend income from UK companies even though they would not pay tax on income of other types. This may seem a little unfair, but it is the way the UK tax system works at present.

Calculation of the corporation tax payable

You will recall that for income tax, the ITTOI Act 2005 removed the remaining schedules and cases for income tax and re-classified them by categories of income (employment income, trading income, etc.). This didn't change the rules for how income tax is computed, just how it is classified. For companies, the Corporation Tax Act 2009 has had the same result. Companies are taxed on the full amount of the profits or gains or income arising in the accounting period for a company (whether or not received in or transmitted to the UK), after any deductions authorised by the Corporation Tax Acts. Despite coming from a common Act originally, there are a number of key differences between how the rules are applied to sole traders to calculate income tax on their profits and to companies to calculate corporation tax on their profits and capital gains In this section we will examine the key similarities and differences that exist in the legislation at present.

In order to calculate corporation tax payable you will need to undertake a number of steps. These are:

1. Determine the accounting period(s) which are to be assessed.
2. Adjust accounting profits for tax purposes and allocate income and allowable expenditure to the correct period.
3. Calculate the profits chargeable to corporation tax.
4. Ascertain the rate at which corporation tax will be charged.

In the first section of this chapter we will review each of these stages in order.

1. Determining the accounting period

Look for the similarities and differences between the basis of assessment for companies and unincorporated traders when reading this section. Many of the calculations are the same but there are some important differences.

Corporation tax is assessed and charged for any accounting period of a company on the full amount of the profits arising in the period, whether or not received in or transmitted to the UK, minus allowable deductions.

An accounting period of a company starts, for corporation tax purposes, whenever:

- the company comes within the charge to corporation tax; usually on commencing to trade as a company; or
- an earlier accounting period of the company ends without the company then ceasing to be within the charge to tax (i.e. each period flows immediately after the previous one for companies still in operation).

An accounting period of a company ends, for the purposes of corporation tax, on the earliest of the following:

- 12 months after the beginning of the accounting period;
- an accounting date of the company or, if there is a period for which the company does not make up accounts, the end of that period;
- the commencement of a winding up;
- the date on which the company ceases to be UK resident; or
- the date on which it ceases to be liable to corporation tax.

Be careful that you do not confuse accounting periods for tax purposes (called 'accounting periods') with the company's reporting period for financial accounting purposes (called 'periods of account'). Whilst these two are often the same (usually 12 months long and ending on the same day) this is not always the case. The key rule to remember is a company's accounting period for tax purposes cannot be more than 12 months long. If the period of account (for reporting purposes) is longer than 12 months (e.g. perhaps in a year when a company moves its year-end date) then the period of account must be split up into more than one accounting period for the tax calculations. If the accounting period is less than 12 months then it becomes its own chargeable period. This is one of the important differences between sole traders and companies. Sole traders can have tax periods longer than 12 months as we discussed in Chapter 6.

Activity

Apply the above rules to determine the accounting periods for tax when a company changes its year end from 31 December to 31 March by having a 15-month period of accounts starting on 1 January, 2010.

Feedback

For this company, 1 January, 2010 is the start of an accounting period because it is immediately after the end of the previous accounting period (i.e. 31 December 2009). Since it must end at the latest 12 months after it starts, the first accounting period must run from 1 January, 2010 to 31 December, 2010. The second accounting period must commence as soon as the first one finishes and so it begins on 1 January, 2011. It ends at the end of the period of account i.e. 31 March, 2011. This company will therefore have two accounting periods covering the 15 month period of account; one for the first 12 months and the other for the final 3 months.

Try the next activity to be sure that you understand the difference between accounting periods and periods of account.

Activity

State the accounting periods for each of the following periods of account:
- Green Ltd. has a period of account for the 6 months to 31 December, 2010.
- Yellow Ltd. has a period of account for the 15 months to 31 January, 2011.
- Pink Ltd. has a period of account for the 26 months to 31 March, 2011.

Feedback

Green Ltd.
The accounting period is the same as the period of account, i.e. the 6 months to 31 December, 2010.

Yellow Ltd.
The first 12 months of the period of account forms an accounting period. The remaining 3 months of the period of account creates a

second accounting period. Hence the 12 months to 31 October, 2010 and the 3 months to 31 January, 2011 are the accounting periods.

Pink Ltd.
The accounting periods are made up of two 12-month periods and a 2-month period, namely the 12 months to 31 January, 2010, the 12 months to 31 January, 2011, the 2 months to 31 March, 2011.

2. Allocating profits to accounting periods

Income and expenses incurred by a company are normally simply allocated to the accounting period in which they occur to form part of the tax computations however, the fact that companies can't have an accounting period of more than 12 months may cause problems for this simple allocation process. This is not something that causes problems for sole traders who can have tax accounting periods of more than 12 months. For example, in the activity above you saw that a 15-month period of account was split into two accounting periods for tax purposes, the first one 12 months long and the second one three months long. If this happens we must then split the income and expenses of the company between the two periods in the following ways:

- Trade profits and miscellaneous income before capital allowances is *apportioned* on a time basis. In our example 12/15ths would be included in the first accounting period while the remaining 3/15ths would be included in the second accounting period. This apportioning approximates reality but won't necessarily reflect exactly when any particular income is earned.
- Capital allowances, including balancing allowances and charges, are calculated for each accounting period by computing figures based on actual expenditure or disposals. Do not forget that writing down allowance percentages need to be reduced for short accounting periods as they are normally cited on a per annum basis e.g. 20% per annum for main pool plant and machinery (25% prior to 1 April 2008). Also note that for companies, although a short period of account will result in an adjustment to the capital allowances available, there are never any reductions in capital allowances for private usage of assets owned by the company, because a company is an artificial legal

entity and can't have "private" expenses. Instead private use may be charged on the user as a benefit in kind under employment income rules, as the user will probably be an employee or director.

- Property income used to be allocated to the period in which it was due, however, since FA 1998, it is treated like trading income and time apportioned.
- Bank Interest (and other non-trading loan relationships e.g. Building Societies) are allocated on an accrued basis.
- Other income is usually allocated on an actual basis to the period to which it relates.
- Charges on income are allocated to the period in which they are paid.
- Chargeable gains are allocated to the period in which they are realised.

Activity

Cherry Ltd. makes up accounts for the 18 months to 31 March, 2011. The company's results for the period of account are:

	£
Trading income before capital allowances	300,000
Bank interest (gross) received:	
31/03/10	1,200
30/9/10	1,000
31/3/11	1,100
Chargeable gains on disposal of assets:	
31/12/09	5,000
6/6/10	3,000
31/12/10	7,000
Charges on income paid:	
31/12/09	15,000
31/12/10	20,000

Calculate the chargeable profits for each of the accounting periods within the period of account.

Feedback

The period of account will be split into two accounting periods, the 12 months to 30 September, 2010 and the 6 months to 31 March, 2011. The chargeable profits are:

	12 months to 30/9/10	6 months to 31/3/11
Trade profits		
12/18 × 300,000	200,000	
6/18 × 300,000		100,000
Bank interest received	2,200	1,100
Chargeable gains	8,000	7,000
	210,200	108,100
Less charges on income	(15,000)	(20,000)
	195,200	88,100

Note – Interest received by companies is taxed on an accrued, not received, basis, you should assume the payments received on 30 September 2010 and 31 March 2011 represent all interest outstanding on those dates.

Now you need to be able to adjust the company's trading profits for tax purposes. As for income tax, the easiest way of calculating the trade profits is to follow the proforma given here. (Note – the numbers are used in the proforma to make it easier to follow – they do not relate to the previous example.)

Adjustment of trade profits for the accounting period ended 31 December 2010.

	£000	£000
Net profits per accounts		3,270
Add expenditure disallowed		530
		3,800
Less: Income not assessable	120	
Expenditure not included in the accounts which is an allowable deduction	180	
Capital allowances	500	
		(800)
Tax Adjusted trade profits		3,000

In the next section we will consider some areas where companies are treated differently to sole traders. There are three of these; loan relationships, research and development, and intangibles.

Loan relationships

Sole traders account for gains and losses on loans, such as government stock and company debentures, using a combination of the income tax rules (for interest accrued and payable) and the capital gains tax rules (for any capital gain or loss when the loan is disposed of). Different rules apply to companies for loan relationships.

If the company receives a loan related to its trading activity, the interest payable (or other debt costs) are allowed as a trading expense and can therefore be deducted in working out their trade profits.

If they lend money as part of their trade, any interest receivable is treated as a trading receipt and is also included in the trade profits calculation.

Where a company borrows or lends money for the purposes of its trading activities, it is referred to as a *trading loan relationship*. Examples of trading loan relationships are bank overdrafts, loans to buy business premises or plant and machinery, and debentures. (Note: You will not usually see a company *receive* income under a trading loan relationship unless they are in the business of making loans but it is still useful to know how this should be handled).

Income and gains from *non-trading loan relationships*, i.e. those which are not related to the company's trading activities, are dealt with under the non-trading loan relationship rules for companies as we will see later.

For all loan relationships, trade and non-trade, profits and losses (referred to as credits and debits respectively) are treated as income for companies, i.e. the capital/revenue distinction, which we discussed in Chapter 6, does not apply. This is a further important difference between sole traders and companies for tax purposes.

Research and development

Companies are entitled to a special tax credit on research and development (R&D) expenditure. These rules were introduced in April 2000 for small and medium sized companies and then extended in April 2002 to large companies. The credits are only available to companies and not to sole traders and partnerships so the rules are another example of how the UK tax system treats companies differently from other forms of business.

To qualify for the credits, companies must spend more than £10,000 (£25,000 before 1 April 2003) on research and development in a 12 month period. This is defined by reference to Department of Trade and Industry guidelines which, at its most basic, implies the project seeking the credits must be aiming to extend overall knowledge or capability in a field of science or technology, for example, creating a new process or product.

Valid expenses include non-capital expenditure which directly relates to R&D activity, such as staff costs and consumables. The allowable expenses were extended in the 2004 Budget to include expenditure on software development and any power, fuel or water expenditure directly related to the research and development activity.

The system works by allowing small and medium sized companies to deduct 175% of valid expenditure in their tax computation (this was 150% prior to 1 April 2008). For larger companies the credit is 130% (previously 125%). What happens then, when a company is in a loss situation and can't get the benefit of the extra tax deduction? In that case, the company may be eligible for a special payment from the government of £24 for every £100 of actual R&D expenses. This only applies to SMEs, however, and if they claim a cash payment in this way, they then lose the special 175% deduction.

In addition to R&D tax credits related to non-capital expenditure items, there is a separate 100% capital allowance for R&D capital expenditure such as the purchase of new buildings or machinery.

Fiscal Fact

The cost to the Government of providing research and development credits is estimated to be £710million for 2009/10.

Intangibles

New rules were introduced with effect from 1 April, 2002 for companies' income and expenses relating to intangible assets. This includes the treatment of intellectual property such as patents, trademarks and copyright, as well as goodwill. Goodwill that only appears in the consolidated accounts and not in the individual company's accounts does not come under these rules, however.

Companies can now claim tax relief for any amortisation claimed in the accounts for such assets (or impairment losses under International Financial Reporting Standards (IFRS)), or at a fixed rate of 4% per annum if the accounting treatment is not considered appropriate to use (e.g. as the asset is not amortised in the accounts or is amortised over a very long period). The company must justify why this will be the case to HMRC. Capital allowances are no longer available to companies for patent rights or know-how bought on or after 1 April, 2002.

If a company sells an intangible asset which was created or acquired after 1 April, 2002, any loss will be deductible from the total trading income and any profit will be taxable. In this way, the new rules remove the capital/income divide for these types of assets in a similar way to the loan relationship rules. If a profit arises but the proceeds are reinvested in a new intangible asset, the difference between the original cost and the disposal proceeds can be rolled over into the cost of the new intangible. This rollover rule applies to all intangibles, not just those acquired after 1 April, 2002, and for companies it supersedes the rollover capital gains tax rules we saw in Chapter 8.

3. Profits chargeable to corporation tax

Now that the trade profit has been computed and allocated to the correct accounting period for the tax computation we can calculate the rest of the profits chargeable to corporation tax (often referred to as PCTCT). This computation is the equivalent for companies of calculating taxable income for sole traders i.e. it is the aggregation of all their income sources minus any charges.

Once again we will use a proforma (with example numbers in it) to illustrate how to do this:

PCTCT for the accounting period ended 30 September, 2010

	£000
Property income	500
Trade profit	3,000
Non-trading loan relationship	1,500
Miscellaneous income	300
Chargeable gains	700
Total profits	6,000
Less charges on income (gross)	(1,000)
Profits chargeable to corporation tax (PCTCT)	5,000

It is important to note that dividends received by a UK company from other UK companies are excluded from the tax computation because they are not subject to further corporation tax in the hands of the receiving company.

We have already explored how to determine trade profit earlier in the chapter but you need to know a little more about some of the other items in the proforma before you are ready to calculate the profits chargeable to corporation tax for specific companies. We will consider the relevant points in the order in which they appear in the pro forma above.

Property income

Income from land and buildings owned by companies is taxed regardless of whether the property is located in the UK or not. Property income includes rents due, income from holiday lettings and furnished lettings, premiums on short leases, ground rents and payments for sporting rights.

Property income will be determined using all the same trade profit rules that you are familiar with. This means that the accruals basis will be used for income and expenses, including management expenses for the property, i.e. they will be treated as trading expenses are. Because this is in line with normal accounting principles, no tax adjustment will generally be necessary.

Interest payable by a company on a loan related to rental property is dealt with under the loan relationship rules, as such it is not an allowable property expense. Capital allowances will also be deducted to determine the property income.

If a property loss occurs, provided the business is conducted on a commercial basis, the loss can be set against total company profits for the same period, or carried forward to set against future total profits.

Non-trade loan relationships

Income and other amounts receivable in this category by companies usually relates to interest from bank and building society accounts and other interest receivable that is not to do with trading activity. This income is assessed on an *accrued basis*. Trading loan relationships are dealt with under trade profits, as we discussed above.

Note that, unlike individuals, companies always receive interest *gross* from banks and building societies (therefore, no grossing up is needed and no 'tax deducted at source' deductions are required).

Any amounts receivable or payable under non-trading loan relationships must be pooled. If the net figure is positive (debits are less than credits) then the total becomes the loan relationship income for the company. If a net deficit exists then it can either be set against other income for the same accounting period, surrendered as group relief if the company is part of a group (see the Company Groups chapter on the website for more details on this option), carried back against any surpluses on non-trading loan relationships in the last twelve months or carried forward to set against future non-trading profits (i.e. future PCTCT less trade profit). This process applies not just to interest, but also to other gains and losses for loan relationships, for example when a loan is written off. As we noted earlier, the capital/revenue distinction is not applicable to loan relationships for companies.

Charges on income

Charges on income have traditionally been payments made net of basic rate tax. They are deducted from the aggregate of income and profit from all sources to arrive at PCTCT, in much the same way as reliefs are allowed for individuals under income tax.

Patent royalties used to be treated as charges on income for companies. Since 1 April 2001, however, patent royalties are paid gross by companies if they are paid to another UK company (or any other company that pays UK corporation tax). If patent royalties are paid to a person other than a company, income tax must be deducted at the basic rate (20%). From 1 April 2002 corporate patent royalty payments are no longer classed as a charge on income (as we discussed earlier) but instead will be a trade profit deduction (if the patent is held for trade purposes).

The special treatment of charitable gifts for individual taxpayers i.e. the extension of the basic rate band, does not apply to companies. They are treated as 'charges on income' for companies (strictly now called 'charitable donations relief' as part of the Corporation Tax Act 2010 changes to terminology) and they are paid gross by the company (so no grossing up will be required).

Donations to local charities which small in amount and are made wholly and exclusively for the purpose of the trade are allowable deductions from the trade profits. An example of such a donation might be a gift to an employees' welfare organisation. Of course, no payment can be both an allowable deduction from the trade profits and a charge, it must be used as one or the other and treated correctly in the tax computation.

The charges that are added back in the adjustment of trading profits computation are equal to the amount which is included in the profit and loss account. This figure will usually be determined using the accruals basis rather than the cash paid basis. The amount allowed as a charge in the calculation of profits chargeable to corporation tax is the cash actually paid. Hence the two figures may not be the same and may need to be adjusted.

In summary therefore, from 1 April 2002 the only item you will see treated as a charge on income for companies is charitable donations under the Gift Aid Scheme.

Companies and income tax

Where a payment is paid net of tax, for example a patent royalty to an individual, the company must account to HMRC for the tax they have withheld. This is a separate calculation to the corporation tax computation. The income tax withheld is netted against any income tax that is withheld from the company as recipient and the difference is paid/reclaimed. Companies are required to submit quarterly returns to HMRC to reconcile any income tax on items received and paid. This process used to include all patent royalty (at 20%) and interest payments (at 20%), but since 1 April 2001, these payments can be made between UK companies without deduction of tax. Income tax will only need to be deducted from patent royalties and interest where either the payer or recipient is not a UK company, for example a partnership.

The following activity illustrates the key points from above for you.

Activity

Bournemouth Ltd had the following results for the year ended 31 March, 2011

	£000	£000
Gross profit on trading		1,200
Investment income (a)	300	
Profit on sale of land (b)	200	500
		1,700
Less: Depreciation	100	
Directors' emoluments	150	
Gift aid	30	
Audit and accountancy fees	45	
Legal costs (c)	20	
Salaries	100	
Premium on lease written off (d)	25	
Miscellaneous expenses	30	(500)
Net profit for year		1,200

Notes:

(a) Investment income:

	£000
Dividends from UK companies (gross)	200
Loan interest from UK company (gross- non-trading loans)	100

(b) Profit on sale of land:

The profit on the sale of land relates to a plot of vacant land no longer required by the company. The chargeable gain is	150

(c) Legal costs:

Costs re debt collection	5
Costs re issue of shares	12
Costs re renegotiations of directors' service agreements	3

(d) Lease premium
The lease premium written off relates to a lease taken out
at the beginning of the accounting period for a warehouse
for a period of 17 years. The premium paid was   25
(e) Capital allowances have been calculated as   50

Required: calculate the profits chargeable to corporation tax.

Feedback

First you needed to calculate the trade profit:

Trade profit	£000	£000
Net profit per accounts		1,200
Add: Depreciation	100	
Gift (treat as a charge on income)	30	
Legal costs (not allowable as capital)	12	
Lease premium written off (W1)	25	167
		1,367
Less: Investment income (loan relationship)	300	
Profit on sale of investments	200	
Capital allowances	50	
Lease premium (Working 1)	1	(551)
Adjusted trade profit		816

Working 1
The amount of the lease premium assessable on the landlord under
the property income rules is:
£25,000 – [£25,000 × (17 – 1) × 2%] = £17,000.

The amount which is allowable for the lessee in the accounting
period ended 31 March, 2011 is therefore £17,000 ÷ 17 = £1,000.

Now you can calculate the profits chargeable to corporation tax.

	£
Trade profit	816,000
Non-trading Loan relationship	100,000
Chargeable gains	150,000
	1,066,000
Less charges paid (gift)	(30,000)
Profits chargeable to corporation tax	1,036,000

You will notice the treatment of the lease premium is the same as for
individuals as we saw in Chapter 5.

Note that we do not cover the situation where a company makes losses in detail in this book, but you can find a section of the website dealing with this if you need it for your course.

4. The rate of corporation tax payable

Having now learnt the basics of the first three stages of calculating corporation tax, we now need to work through the actual computation of the tax liability.

The rate of corporation tax is set for *financial years*, rather than the *tax years* of the income tax legislation. A financial year (FY) runs from 1 April to the following 31 March i.e. the financial year 2010 (or FY 2010) runs from 1 April, 2010 to 31 March, 2011. The rate of corporation tax for a financial year is set after the year has started, in the annual Finance Act. Hence the rate for the financial year 2010 is set in the Finance Act 2010.

Calculation of corporation tax

The calculation of corporation tax is different from that for income tax in that once you have decided which tax rate band the company falls into, that rate then applies to all of the profits chargeable to corporation tax. There are no cumulative calculations to perform as with individuals to allocate the total income across tax rate bands. The tax rate bands for corporation tax for the current financial year (FY07) are as follows:

Profits £	CT rate	
0– 300,000	21%	Small profits rate
300,001 – 1,500,000	21 – 28%	On a sliding scale
over 1,500,000	28%	Full rate

The small profits rate was scheduled to increase to 22% for FY09; however, this was delayed last year as a result of the financial crisis. Therefore, a single company with profits of £100,000 will pay £21,000 in corporation tax (i.e. tax rate of 21% applies) and a company with profits of £2,000,000 will pay £560,000 in corporation tax (i.e. tax rate of 28% applies).

In the Emergency Budget in June 2010 it was announced the small profits rate will fall, instead the proposed rise, to 20% from 1 April

2011 as part of the new Government's reforms of corporation tax. The full rate of corporation tax is also set to fall to 24% by 1 April 2014).

Use of the sliding scale

Let us now consider how the sliding scale works for profits between £300,000 (called the *lower relevant maximum amount* or *LRMA*) and £1,500,000 (called the *upper relevant maximum amount* or *URMA*).

Profits falling within this band are subject to a sliding scale of rates and so a formula is used to calculate the tax due. The corporation tax due is calculated using the next highest rate (i.e. 28% currently), and then a deduction is computed, (referred to as *marginal relief*), to reduce the actual corporation tax that will be payable.

There are complications when a company receives dividends from other UK companies which we will consider later, but for a company that does not receive dividends from other UK companies, the marginal relief formula is:

$$\text{Fraction} \times (M - P)$$

where M is the upper limit of the tax rate band you are considering and P is the company's profits for tax calculation purposes. The relevant fraction is currently 7/400.

Activity

Holborn Ltd has profits chargeable to corporation tax of £400,000 for the year ended 31 March, 2011. Calculate Holborn Ltd's corporation tax liability for the year.

Feedback

	£
Corporation tax at the next highest rate: 28%	112,000.00
Less marginal relief:	
$\dfrac{7}{400} \times (1,500,000 - 400,000)$	(19,250.00)
Corporation tax liability	92,750.00

You will remember from Chapter 1 that to calculate the average tax rate, you can divide the tax liability by the taxable income. If you do this you will see that the average tax rate for Holborn Ltd is 23.19%, which falls between 21% and 28% as we expected.

The use of this marginal relief formula ensures that there is a smooth progression from one rate band to the next in the intervals where the sliding scale applies.

There is another way of looking at this calculation where marginal relief calculations need to be performed. You know that if the company's profits had been £300,000, tax of £63,000 would be payable, so it is possible to say that the additional £100,000 which encroaches into the marginal rate band has attracted therefore £29,750 in tax, which means the marginal tax rate is 29.75% (i.e. £27,750 ÷ £100,000). A 29.75% marginal tax rate will in fact occur, if there is no franked investment income (see below), for any profits within the small companies' marginal rate band. You could try the calculation with another profit figure between £300,000 and £1,500,000 to satisfy yourself that this is the case throughout the sliding scale band.

The role of franked investment income

Franked investment income (FII) is the name given to the sum of the dividends a company receives from other UK companies, plus the related tax credit on those dividends, (currently at the rate of 10%). You have already seen that such dividends are not subject to corporation tax as profits in the hands of the recipient company and are not therefore included in the PCTCT calculation itself. FII is important, however, as when a company receives FII it needs to be used along with the PCTCT when determining the rate of corporation tax a company must pay. This system is sometimes referred to as "exemption with progression", because while the UK dividends are exempt from corporation tax, they may be used to force the company to progress into a higher tax bracket.

A new 'profits' figure is used to determine this rate, which is PCTCT + FII. To prevent confusion with other profits figures, this amount is always referred to as 'profits' (i.e. in quotes).

So, to calculate corporation tax for a company that receives UK dividends, you should use the 'profits' figure to decide which rate band the company falls into, and then apply that rate, as before, to the PCTCT. A company with PCTCT of £1,300,000 and FII of £300,000 will therefore pay tax at the rate of 28% on the £1,300,000, i.e. £364,000, as the PCTCT + FII is £1,600,000, which falls into the 28% bracket of corporation tax.

The inclusion of FII also means we have to modify the marginal relief formula that we saw earlier. The full formula is:

$$\text{Fraction} \times (M - P) \times I \div P$$

where M is the upper limit of the rate band, P is the 'profits' figure and I is now the PCTCT. (Note that P here is now not just PCTCT, as it was for the company without FII, but PCTCT + FII).

Activity

Assume Holborn Ltd from the previous activity received dividends from other UK companies of £90,000 for the year. Calculate Holborn's revised tax liability.

Feedback

	£
PCTCT	400,000
FII 90,000 × 100 ÷ 90	100,000
'Profits'	500,000
Corporation tax on PCTCT of £400,000 @28%	112,000
Less marginal relief:	
$\dfrac{7}{400}$ × (1,500,000 – 500,000) × $\dfrac{400,000}{500,000}$	(14,000)
Corporation tax liability	98,000

This gives an effective or average corporation tax rate of 24.5%. This also illustrates that even where a company has the same PCTCT as another, the tax liability they both face may be different depending on the level of dividends they each receive from other UK companies.

Associated companies and short accounting periods

The rate bands we have been using are for a single company computation. Where a company has associated companies, however, the bands are divided between the total number of associated companies, including the one you are calculating tax for.

Companies are associated with each other if either one controls the other or if both are controlled by the same person or persons, who may be individuals, partnerships or other companies. Associated companies do not have to be UK resident. Control for these purposes is defined as holding over 50% of the share capital or 50% of the voting power or being entitled to over 50% of the distributable income or of the net assets in a winding up (see the Company Groups chapter on the website for further details).

The bands are also pro-rated if the accounting period for which you are calculating tax is less than 12 months. Remember that it can never be more than 12 months for a company.

The following two examples demonstrate these variations:

Activity

Ealing plc has profits chargeable to corporation tax of £290,000 and franked investment income of £40,000 for the year ended 31 March, 2011. Calculate Ealing's corporation tax liability. It has two associated companies.

Feedback

	£
PCTCT	290,000
FII	40,000
'Profits'	330,000

First we must apportion the rate band thresholds to reflect the existence of the associated companies. There are three associated companies in total, and so the rate band thresholds become £100,000 and £500,000 (instead of £300,000 and £1,500,000).

The 'profits' lie between £100,000 and £500,000 so marginal relief applies. (Note that you do not need to gross up here because the question has given you the FII figure, not the dividend received figure – watch out for this)

	£
Corporation tax on PCTCT £290,000 @ 28%	81,200
Less marginal relief	
$\frac{7}{400} \times (500,000 - 330,000) \times \frac{290,000}{330,000}$	(2,614)
Corporation tax liability	78,586

(i.e. an effective corporate tax rate of $78,586 \div 290,000 = 27.1\%$)

Note how 'M' in the formula has become the revised threshold figure.

Activity

Felixstow plc prepared accounts for 9 months to 31 March, 2011. Felixstow has profits chargeable to corporation tax of £160,000 and franked investment income of £40,000. Felixstow has one associated company. Determine the corporation tax payable.

Feedback

	£
PCTCT	160,000
FII	40,000
'Profits'	200,000

The limits for marginal relief are reduced by a quarter because the accounting period was only 9 months long. The limits are then divided by the total number of associated companies, in this case there are two associated companies. Hence the lower limit is £300,000 × 9 ÷ 12× ½ = £112,500 and the upper limit is £1,500,000 × 9 ÷ 12× ½= £562,500.

	£
Corporation tax payable on PCTCT 160,000 @ 28%	44,800
Less marginal relief	
$\dfrac{7}{400}$ × (562,500 − 200,000) × $\dfrac{160,000}{200,000}$	(5,075)
Corporation tax liability	39,725

Year ends straddling 31 March

As the rates of corporation tax are set on an annual basis, what happens to companies with year ends other than 31 March which straddle two financial years?

If the appropriate rate for the two years is the same there is no difficulty. The profits chargeable to corporation tax are taxed at the rate prevailing for the two years and only one tax computation needs to be done.

If the rate of tax changes between the two years, however, the profits chargeable to corporation tax are apportioned to the two financial years on a time basis. This has happened a number of times in the last ten years – and in particular recently for FY07 when the small companies' rate (as the small profits rate was then called) rose from 19% to 20%. For FY08, we saw both the small companies' rate and the full rate change. FY09 and FY10 have not seen a change in rates for any corporations so accounting periods straddling 31 March 09 and 31 March 10 do not need to be split.

The following example illustrates how to handle this situation:

Activity

Lilac Ltd has 30 June as a permanent accounting date. In the year to 30 June, 2007, Lilac Ltd generated profits chargeable to corporation tax of £9,000. In 2007/8, the small companies' rate of corporation tax was 20% while in 2008/9 the rate was 21%. Calculate Lilac Ltd's tax liability for the year to 30 June, 2008.

Feedback

Profits	Tax rate		Tax liability
£	%		£
9,000 × 9/12	20		1,350.00
9,000 × 3/12	21		472.50
		Tax payable	1,822.50

The first nine months of the accounting period fall in the 2007/08 year (FY 07) and so the profits attributable to this period are taxed at 20%. The remaining three months of the accounting period fall in the 2008/09 year (FY 08) and so the profits attributable to this period should be taxed at 21%.

Where there is a rate change there are also implications for associated companies we need to be careful of. Where the year must be split to charge different corporation tax rates, the limits for associated companies will also have to be apportioned across the end of the tax year (although no such restriction is required if the business are only associated in one of the periods and not both).

Chargeable gains for companies

Companies are not liable to capital gains tax as a separate tax, but their chargeable gains and allowable losses are subject to corporation tax. This mean they will not pay tax on chargeable gains at the fixed rates of 18% and 28% like individuals do. They will instead pay tax on chargeable gains at their marginal rate of corporation tax.

Many of the same rules apply to companies that we examined in Chapter 8 for individuals. There are a few exceptions you should be aware of, however. For example, unlike individuals, companies do not have an annual exemption allowance to set against their chargeable gains, and they are also compensated for changes due to inflation using an indexation allowance rather than lowered rates of tax.

The pro forma for calculating the chargeable gain or allowable loss is (numbers included only for illustration purposes):

	£
Gross proceeds on disposal (or market value)	12,000
Less incidental cost of disposal	(2,000)
Net proceeds	10,000
Less allowable costs	(2,500)
Unindexed gain/(loss)	7,500
Less indexation allowance	(1,000)
Indexed gain/(unindexed loss)	6,500

For disposals of chargeable assets by companies you need to know how to calculate the change in the retail price index as disposals by companies use this percentage change as the means to adjust for inflation and get what is called an 'indexation allowance' from the date of purchase to the date of sale.

The indexation allowance is applied to all items of allowable costs (except incidental costs of disposal as these are taken to already be in current money value). The allowance is designed to compensate for the inflation part of the increases in the value of the asset so that companies only pay tax on the real gains they make – not those solely due to inflation. It does this by using the percentage increase in the retail price index from the later of March 1982 and the month in which the asset was acquired until the month in which the disposal took place. March 1982 was the date before which gains are no longer deemed chargeable to CGT for individuals. The same rule applies for companies' chargeable gains calculations.

Hence the indexation factor for companies is:

$$\frac{\text{RPI for month of disposal} - \text{RPI for the later of the month of acquisition and March 1982}}{\text{RPI for the later of the month of acquisition and March 1982}}$$

The retail price index figure for the appropriate months can be found in the RPI table in the rates and allowances section in Appendix A.

The indexation factor should be stated as a decimal correct to *three decimal places*. It is important you round to three decimal place or your answers will be wrong – it is not more accurate to use more decimal places in this case.

Be careful in use of indexation allowance as it cannot create or increase a loss for the chargeable gains computation. At best it will reduce the gain to zero.

The following activities will illustrate how to compute indexation allowances for chargeable gains computations for companies:

Activity

Calculate the relevant indexation allowance for an asset purchased in January 1989 and sold in April 2010.

Feedback

a) Using the RPI tables in the Appendix A, the indexation allowance will be:

$$\frac{222.8 - 111.0}{111.0} = 1.007$$

(Don't forget to round the indexation factor to three decimal places)

The indexation allowance is equal to the indexation factor multiplied by the allowable cost. Each element of the allowable cost has a separate indexation calculation as the expense may have been incurred at different times. For example, if there is enhancement expenditure this also is indexed but from the date of the expenditure on the enhancement, not from the date of the original acquisition of the asset of course.

Activity

Cream Ltd sold land and buildings for £200,000 in April 2010. The property cost £50,000 when bought in December 1991. Cream Ltd spent £30,000 extending the building in June 1996. Calculate the chargeable gain on the property.

Feedback

	£	£
Proceeds		200,000
Less allowable costs		
Cost	50,000	
Enhancement expenditure	30,000	(80,000)
Unindexed gain		120,000

	£	£
Indexation allowance		
$\dfrac{222.8 - 135.7}{135.7}$		
$0.642 \times 50,000$	32,100	
$\dfrac{222.8 - 153.0}{153.0}$		
$0.456 \times 30,000$	13,680	(45,780)
Indexed gain		74,220

Other aspects of taxation of chargeable gains for companies

The treatment of the disposal of chattels, part disposals and negligible value claims is the same for companies as it is for individuals, subject only to the differences set out above.

The principal private residence relief, gift relief and entrepreneurs' relief, are not available to companies.

Rollover relief and holdover relief are normally available to companies, however, an amendment was made in the 2002 Budget for companies for some assets. These rules apply to expenditure and receipts by companies related to intangible assets after 1 April, 2002 (e.g. goodwill and the various quotas we listed in the rollover relief section earlier). A form of rollover relief, but not the same as normal rollover relief, is available on realising intangible assets where the proceeds are reinvested in new intangibles. This means these assets are removed from normal rollover relief rules if they are purchased after 1 April, 2002 (although the company has the right to choose which set of rules it wishes to apply if the assets were owned on 1 April, 2002).

Companies also need special rules for determining the cost of quoted securities, in much the same way as we saw for individuals. The rules for companies are slightly different however, and you will need to see the website for an explanation and worked examples.

Payment of corporation tax

In the UK, companies are required to use a system of *self-assessment* for their corporation tax computation. Self assessment for companies commenced for accounting periods ending after July 1999, whereas individuals have been self-assessed for their income since the 1996/97 tax year.

The primary difference between the previous payment system for companies (called 'pay and file') and the self-assessment system is that no assessments are now raised by HMRC. Instead, a company is required to perform its own tax computation and pay over the tax due according to this computation on the correct dates. If HMRC wishes to query the calculations, they now have up to one year from the date the return is due to be filed (or at least a year after the return is filed if filed late) to say so. If they do not query the computation within this time then the year is completed.

In conjunction with the changes to the assessment rules, companies are also now required to maintain full records of all the information they use to do their tax computation for 6 years beyond the end of the period of assessment. Companies failing to be able to produce records if asked to by HMRC in this period could be prosecuted.

The advantage of the self-assessment scheme to HMRC is that they can operate a 'process now – check later' approach for dealing with corporate tax returns. This enables them to spread their work load throughout the year in more flexible ways than was previously the case. A disadvantage of the scheme for the company is that they now need to employ more expert help in completing their returns, which increases their compliance costs.

Budget 2009 introduced a somewhat controversial change that requires large companies to nominate a 'senior accounting officer' who will be required to certify each year that the tax accounting arrangements for the company are appropriate. If he or she fails to comply with this new rule, a personal fine of up to £5,000 could be imposed. It seems this new measure is in response to the G20 summit which took place in London in April 2009, and focussed heavily on regulation and transparency.

Payment dates

Companies that pay tax at the small profits rate mostly pay their corporation tax liability 9 months after their accounting period end. However, for large companies there is a requirement for quarterly instalments of their corporation tax liability to spread their payments throughout the tax year.

Companies that pay full corporation tax, with no marginal relief, are required to pay a percentage of the total tax liability in four equal payments. The actual quarterly dates on which payments should be made are calculated using the rule – the first payment is due on the 14th day of the 7th month of the accounting period, then in three further equal payments at quarterly intervals.

Activity

Calculate the corporate tax payment dates for a large company with a 12 month accounting period ending 31 December, 2010.

Feedback

The due dates will be:

1st instalment	14 July, 2010
2nd instalment	14 October, 2010
3rd instalment	14 January, 2011
Final instalment	14 April, 2011

You should note that the final instalment is not due until 3 months and 14 days after the accounting period ends. This enables the company to ensure all their records have been completed for the accounting period so that a full determination of the tax due is possible.

Where accounting periods exist of less than 12 months, then fewer than four payments will be made. The final instalment will always be due 3 months and 14 days after the end of the accounting period. Earlier instalments are only due if the due dates of the usual gaps (six months and 13 days then 3 monthly intervals) fall before the due date for the final instalment.

This means:

Accounting period length	Instalments due
less than 3 months	final
3–6 months	first + final
6–9 months	first, second + final
9–12 months	all four instalments

Activity

Calculate the instalment dates due for a company with an accounting period of 1 January, 2008 to 31 July, 2010.

Feedback

Final instalment	14 November, 2010
First instalment	14 July, 2010 (14th day of 7th month) Second
instalment	14 October, 2010 (3 months after 14 July)
Third instalment	not due (would be due 3 months after 14 October, 2010 which would fall after final instalment)

Where a company has an accounting period of less than 12 months the amounts of tax due at each instalment should be calculated using the formula:

$$\frac{3 \times \text{CTL}}{n}$$

where:

- CTL is the amount of the company's total tax liability for the accounting period due for payment by instalments
- n is the number of months in the accounting period.

Where a company has reasonable grounds for believing that its total tax liability at the end of the year will be less than the total amounts that will be paid based on amounts currently being paid in instalments, then the company can adjust subsequent payments to reflect the correct liability (or make a claim for a repayment if they have already paid too much).

Corporation tax reform

For some years now the Government has been consulting widely on possible reform to the corporation tax system in the UK. One of the issues being discussed is the possibility of making tax profits and accounting profits the same so that companies only have to create one set of computations for both financial reporting and for tax computation purposes.

In some countries tax profit and accounting profit are already much more closely aligned, but in the UK the computation of tax profits has always been separate, even though it uses the accounting profit as the starting point, as we have illustrated.

One of the unique features for the tax profit calculation is the need to separate different types of income into different categories. One reason for separating different income sources is to give special treatment to losses (i.e. where the income from that source is less than the associated expenses). Whether or not this should continue is also under debate.

Several new measures introduced in recent years have deliberately adopted accounting rules for tax purposes. For example, the new rules which allow companies to deduct goodwill written off the in accounts for tax purposes allow the accounting value to be used to work out the tax deductible amount. Some have suggested that now all listed companies use International Financial Reporting Standards, and perhaps other companies will eventually also do likewise, not only will it be possible to use accounting profits for tax purposes, but also that company tax systems will be able to be harmonised between countries.

As accounting standards develop, and more judges look at the way accounting profits are calculated when tax profits are in dispute, the prospects for closer alignment of accounting and tax profits increases.

One argument against using accounting profits for tax purposes is that it won't allow the Government to use the tax system to provide special incentives. There are also public policy implications, for example, the Government in the UK has decided that fines and penalties should not be allowed as deductions for tax purposes even though they will appear in the accounts.

The Treasury released a discussion document in conjunction with the Pre Budget Report in November 2009, in which it is proposed to allow small companies to use accounting profits for tax purposes, or be taxed by reference to cash flows rather than profit. The Institute for Chartered Accountants in Scotland has spoken out against these proposals, suggesting they are not helpful to small business and simplification to the current system would be preferable to such radical changes – despite the possible compliance cost benefits this might bring for small businesses. These questions are unlikely to be resolved in the immediate future and the ways in which corporation tax should be reformed will be an ongoing debate.

Further reforms to the system of paying and filing self assessment tax returns for companies was also recently proposed in a major review of the way the HMRC operate their electronic services. This report, called the Carter Review and published at the same time as the 2006 Budget (and revised during 2007), suggested that, for example, companies should file their tax returns sooner than they are at present. On-line filing of corporation tax returns will be required for accounting periods ending after 31 March 2010. HMRC have also mandated the use of XBRL for corporation tax return filing from April 2011.

In addition to the reduction in rates for corporation tax over the next few years, the new Government announced in its June 2010 Emergency Budget that a business forum is to be established to consult on wider changes to the international tax system, so we can expect further reforms in the corporation tax area in the near future.

Basic tax planning of UK resident companies

Companies which are family owned and managed may have some flexibility when remunerating their owner/managers. Paying dividends or providing benefits in kind rather than high salaries may reduce the total national insurance contributions which must be paid. For example, when employees make contributions to a pension scheme the contributions are allowable deductions for tax purposes but not for national insurance contributions. However, if the contributions are made by the employer, then they are fully deductible for tax purposes and do not give rise to a liability to either employee or employer national insurance contributions. Hence it may be tax efficient for small companies to operate non-contributory pension schemes.

Companies may have marginal rates of tax of 21%, 28% or 29.75% depending on their profits chargeable to corporation tax. Ideally companies should plan their affairs so as to avoid paying tax at a marginal rate of 29.75% being the highest marginal rate they might face. A little thought may help a company to save tax at the highest possible rate. For example, a company may reduce its profits chargeable to corporation tax by increasing its contribution to the company pension scheme in years in which profits fall within the marginal rate band. Similarly it may be possible to defer a chargeable gain to a period with a lower marginal tax rate.

Summary

This chapter has provided you with the skills needed to calculate the corporation tax liability of companies which are resident in the UK.

In order to calculate a company's tax liability it is necessary to undertake a number of steps:

- identify each source of income for a company;
- determine the category of income which is used to calculate the taxable income for each source of income;
- using the current year basis (which applies to the income and expenditure of companies) to calculate the income that is assessable and determine any deductions from that income which are allowable for tax purposes; and
- determine details of any charges on income which are paid by the company.

This will enable you to calculate the profits chargeable to corporation tax using the small companies limit, and the marginal relief equation if necessary to determine the main corporation tax liability.

The imputation system was also briefly explained in this chapter.

You have been able to compare and contrast the taxation of companies with the taxation of individuals. You might like to list the similarities and differences and decide if the differences between the two are sufficient for one business medium to be preferred to the other. However, it is important to remember that tax is just one aspect of the environment in which businesses operate. Other considerations are at least as important, for example the benefit of limited liability and the ability to raise extra finance. We will look at this more in Chapter 11.

Discussion topics

1. What are the key differences between the application of trading profit rules for sole traders and for companies? Do these differences need to exist?

2. In what way is the classical system a better company tax system than the imputation system – and vice versa? Why is the imputation system generally favoured around the world?

3. Why are tax years and financial years different?

4. Is the Government right in no longer repaying the tax paid by companies on profits that belong to non-taxpayer shareholders?

5. Why are special rules needed for describing how loan relationships, research and development costs and intangibles costs should be allocated to accounting periods for tax computations?

6. Could the sliding scale way of dealing with marginal relief be organised another way to achieve the same ends?

7. Is it fair to have stepped progression in corporate tax rates in some profit bands but not them all? Should the tax bands for companies not be cumulative as they are for individuals?

8. Should large companies have to pay their corporate tax bills so much earlier than smaller companies have to?

9. What might the implications be for corporation tax if all companies start using International Financial Reporting Standards for their financial reporting?

Quick quiz

1. Grotius Ltd prepares accounts for the sixteen months to 31 December, 2010. What are its accounting periods for corporation tax purposes?

2. Helvetius Ltd receives dividends from a UK company of £132,000. How will they be treated for corporation tax purposes?

3. Isocrates Ltd acquires a patent during the year ended 30 June, 2010 and charges amortisation in its accounts at the rate of 3%. How will it be treated for corporation tax purposes?

4. Justinian Ltd licences a partnership to use its patent and accrues patent royalties of £3,900 (net) for the year. How will this be treated for corporation tax purposes?

5. Knox Ltd, a company with no associated companies, has PCTCT of £1,000,000 and FII of £50,000. Compute its corporation tax liability for the year ended 31 March, 2011.

6. Lycophron Ltd has a corporation tax liability of £500,000 and has an accounting period of 5 months to 31 May, 2010. When will its instalments of corporation tax be due?

Questions

Question 1   Ultimate Upholsterers Ltd is a UK resident trading company which manufactures leather upholstered chairs. It has been trading for many years. The company's results for the year ended 30 September, 2010 are summarised as follows.

	£
Trading profits*	375,000
Net dividend from UK company (received 29 May 2010)	18,000
Gross (non-trading) loan interest accrued	12,000
Gross (non-trading) debenture interest payable	10,000
Profit on sale of land	37,000
Writing down allowances on plant and machinery	49,000

* As adjusted for taxation, but before capital allowances and adjustment for the lease premium on the factory (see below).

The company operates from a factory, which meets the definition of 'industrial building' in the Capital Allowances Act. The factory was first occupied by Ultimate Upholsterers Ltd on 1 October, 1984, under the terms of a 25-year lease which had been acquired for £50,000.

The land had been purchased in March, 1983 for £10,000 and sold in February 2010 for £47,410.

Required: Calculate the corporation tax payable for the year ended 30 September, 2010. The indexation factor for March 1983 to February 2010 is 1. 637.

Question 2   ABC Ltd (a company with no associates) has a corporate tax liability of £1.8 million for FY10.

Required: Calculate the due dates for instalments of corporation tax ABC Ltd will have to pay and the amounts due on each of these dates if:

(a) The company has a 12 month accounting period to 31 October, 2010;

(b) The company produces accounts for 8 months to 30 June, 2010 instead (assume the amount of the tax liability is not affected for the purpose of this question).

Question 3   Unsurpassable Umbrellas Ltd is a UK resident trading company with no associated companies, which began to trade in 1964. Accounts have always been prepared to 31 December and the summarised results for the year ended 31 December, 2010 are as follows:

	£
Adjusted trade profit	330,000
Income from property, after expenses	4,000
Bank interest receivable	1,900
Chargeable gain (17/3/10)	8,200
Gross debenture interest accrued	28,200
Dividend from UK company (17/2/10)	14,000
Dividend from UK company (17/7/10)	18,000

Notes: Dates in brackets are dates upon which the transactions occurred.

Required: Calculate the corporation tax payable for the year ended 31 December, 2010.

(Note: answer available on lecturer's website)

Question 4   Pendulum Ltd is a medium sized UK company that owns a gymnasium and leisure facility in Stafford. The company has been trading for several years. During the year ended 31 March, 2011, the company's accounts revealed the following:

	£	£		£
Depreciation		43,150	Trading profit	262,772
Directors' fees		37,840	Building society interest accrued	759
Patent royalty payable (1)		3,500	Debenture interest accrued (gross)	1,200
Gift aid donation		5,000		
Entertaining customers		730		
Salary and wages		16,500		
Non trading loan interest payable		700		
Rent of business premises		3,000		
Audit fee		1,320		
Trade expenses (3)		25,328		
Net profit before taxation		127,663		
		264,731		264,731

(1) The patent royalty is payable to a UK company and is accrued at 31 March, 2011.

(2) £100 of the £700 non-trading loan interest payable was accrued as at 31 March, 2011.

(3) The trade expenses include the following items:

	£
Legal expenses in respect of the following:	
The non trading loan	500
Staff service agreements	90
Gifts to customers:	
6 bottles of malt whisky	280
1,000 diaries bearing the company's name	1,250
Redecoration of café area	3,200

(4) The written down value of plant and machinery on 1 April, 2009 was £263,504. On 1 August, 2010 the company sold some plant for £9,400 which had originally cost £11,000. On 31 January, 2011 plant costing £10,500 was acquired. On the same day, a low emission car costing £13,000 was purchased for the use of the marketing director of the company, who used the vehicle 50% for private purposes.

Required: Compute Pendulum Ltd's trade profits, PCTCT, and corporation tax payable for the accounting period 31 March, 2011. State when the tax will be payable.

(Note: answer available via lecturer's website)

Question 5 Burgundy Ltd bought an office block to use in its business in August 1982 for £100,000. In April 2010 the company sold the building for £300,000 and at the same time bought another office block to use in its business.

Assuming that Burgundy claims rollover relief calculate the chargeable gain arising on the disposal of the office block if the replacement office block has a cost of:
(a)   £380,000
(b)   £280,000
(c)   £180,000.

(Note: answer available via lecturer's website)

Question 6 Navy Ltd sold a warehouse used exclusively for business purposes for £200,000 in November 2002 realising a chargeable gain of £50,000. The company also bought fixed plant for £240,000 in November 2002. The company elects to hold-over the gain on the warehouse against the fixed plant. How will the held-over gain be treated (assuming current tax rules still apply) if:

(a) Navy Ltd sells the fixed plant in January 2010
(b) Navy Ltd sells the fixed plant in April 2014
(c) Navy Ltd bought another warehouse for business use in December 2003 and elected to transfer the held-over gain on the fixed plant to the new warehouse which cost £220,000
(d) The new warehouse in part (c) cost £185,000.

(*Note: answer available via lecturer's website*)

Further test questions for this chapter to test your knowledge can be found in the student section of the website at:

http://www.taxstudent.com/uk

Further reading and examples

Combs. A., Dixon, S. & Rowes, P. (2010), *Taxation: incorporating the 2010 Finance Act*, Fiscal Publications: Birmingham.
– use this book for many other examples to further develop and test your knowledge of this chapter's contents. See http://www.fiscalpublications.com/rowes/2010

James, S. & Nobes, C. (2010) *Economics of Taxation: 10th edition*, Fiscal Publications: Birmingham.
–useful additional perspective on the role and design of corporation taxation in the UK.

For more information about how different systems of corporation tax work to reduce the double taxation of dividends, see Oats, L (2002) "Taxing Companies and Their Shareholders" in *The International Tax System*, Lymer & Hasseldine eds, Springer.

Value Added Tax

Introduction

VAT (Value Added Tax) has become an increasingly important source of income for the government since it was introduced in 1973. The Treasury expects to raise £60.7billion from VAT in the fiscal year 2010/11, which is easily the third highest tax revenue source for the UK Government after income tax and national insurance contributions.

At the end of this chapter you will be able to:

- state the broad principles of the UK's VAT system;
- state the criteria for compulsory registration and deregistration for VAT and explain the advantages and disadvantages of registration;
- identify taxable supplies and calculate a trader's VAT payable/repayable;
- list which goods are standard rated, zero rated and exempt from VAT and explain the differences in their treatment;
- describe the main characteristics of the administration of VAT including various special schemes that currently exist in the UK;
- state the VAT consequences of importing and exporting goods and services; and
- describe the system for administering VAT which operates within the EU.

Background

VAT was introduced in April 1973 partly as a consequence of the UK joining the European Union. It replaced a tax called purchase tax, and introduced three classifications into which all goods and services are allocated – zero rated, exempt and standard rated. Sales and purchases of goods and services (from UK based or overseas traders) are taxed according to their classification into one of these three categories.

When VAT was first introduced it was seen to be a relatively simple tax however, it has increased in complexity and can now be a difficult tax to apply in practice. It has become a specialist area of tax compliance and planning.

The legal basis for VAT is contained in the Value Added Tax Act (VATA 1994) and subsequent Finance Acts. VAT was, until 2005, administered by HM Customs and Excise. However, like other taxes, VAT is now managed by HMRC.

Principles of VAT

VAT is an *indirect tax* and is the UK's primary *expenditure tax*. VAT is borne by the final consumer, although it is charged whenever a *taxable person* makes a *taxable supply* of goods or services in the course of business at each stage in a supply chain for any taxable supply. It is a tax on turnover, not on income or profit like the majority of other taxes we have seen in this book.

Before giving more detail of how VAT operates in practice, let's review what we mean by the terms taxable persons and taxable supplies.

A taxable person

A person is a taxable person for the purposes of VAT while he or she is registered under the Value Added Tax Act 1994. As we see below, a trader is required by law to register for VAT once their annual turnover of a taxable supply reaches a registration threshold that is set each year as part of the budget. For this tax year this is set at £70,000. However, any trader making a taxable supply can register for VAT even if their turnover for the year is less than the threshold that year.

A taxable person can be an individual or partnership, company, club, association or charity.

A taxable supply

A taxable supply includes all forms of business supply made in return for consideration (i.e. for money or payment in kind) unless it is explicitly exempted from VAT by law or regulation. For example, in addition to the normal sales activities a business may engage in, the following transfers are all taxable supplies:

- Any transfer of a whole asset is a supply of goods. The transfer of any share of an asset is a supply of services.
- The supply of any form of power, heat, refrigeration or ventilation.

- The grant, assignment or surrender of a major interest in land.
- The transfer of fixed assets or current assets, including transfers to the registered trader whether or not for a consideration.
- Business gifts are taxable supplies unless the transfer is either a gift of goods made in the course or furtherance of the business (which cost the donor not more than £50) or a gift to an actual or potential customer of the business of an industrial sample which is not ordinarily available for sale to the public.
- Goods which were owned by the business and are put to any private use or are used, or made available to any person, including the registered trader, to use for a private purpose are taxable at cost.
- Goods lent to someone outside the business or hired to someone are a taxable supply of services.

A taxable supply is considered to have occurred once the ownership of the asset being supplied transfers from one person to another. This means the actual physical transfer of the asset, if it is a good, may happen after the supply has actually been made and supplies of services will have occurred for VAT purposes once the service has been carried out.

The value of a taxable supply

If the supply is for a consideration in money, then VAT should be added to the price charged for the good or service. If the supply is for a consideration which is not wholly in money (e.g. involving payment in kind) then, the money value of the consideration is taken to be the VAT inclusive price.

The market value of a supply of goods or services is taken to be the amount which would be payable by a person in an *arms' length* transaction. This means that if a business makes a taxable supply to a *connected person* the VAT will be due on the price that would have been charged on the supply had this transaction been with an unconnected recipient. This rule ensures the correct amount of VAT is charged on all supplies.

The standard rate of VAT until 3 January 2011 is 17.5%, and so this amount should be added to the value of the sale of a good or service to determine the total amount to be collected from the customer. The VAT proportion of the total consideration is $17.5 \div (100 + 17.5) = 7/47$. This proportion is called the *VAT fraction* and can be used to find how much VAT will have been paid on any standard rated supply if you are only given the VAT inclusive amount of the supply.

For the period from 1 December 2008 until 31 December 2009, a different standard rate applied (15%) introduced to try and stimulate spending and reduce the severity of the recession. This means that the VAT fraction for this period is 3/23. Budget 2010 announced an increase in the VAT rate to 20% to take effect on 4 January 2011. The VAT fraction from that date will be 1/6 (20/120).

Input and output tax

The VAT system operates by registered traders collecting VAT from customers they supply to on behalf of the Government – VAT is therefore an example of an indirect tax. Registered traders can also, however, reclaim VAT they suffer on their purchases. These two parts of the VAT system from the trader's perspective are referred to as *input tax* and *output tax*.

Input tax is the VAT a taxable person has to pay:

- on the supply to him or her of any goods or services;
- on the acquisition by him or her of any goods from another EU member state; or
- paid or payable by him or her on the importation of any goods from a place outside the EU provided that the goods or services are, or will be, used for the purposes of a business carried on by the taxable person.

A taxable person's output tax is the VAT charged on supplies made. The difference between input and output tax is the amount they pay over to the Government on a regular basis. We will see how this works in practice on the next page.

The tax point

VAT is accounted for on a periodic basis, usually quarterly, and so we need to know the date on which transactions occur in order to determine which time period it belongs to. The deemed date of supply of taxable goods or services is termed the *tax point*. The basic tax point is the date on which a supply of goods or services is treated as taking place.

A supply of goods will be treated as taking place when:

- the supplier sends the goods to the customer;
- the customer collects the goods from the supplier; or
- the goods are made available for the customer to use. This might occur, for example, when the supplier assembles something at the premises of the customer.

A supply of services is any taxable supply which is not a supply of goods. As no physical transfers may take place when services are supplied, the supply of services will be treated as taking place at the time when the services are carried out and all the work is finished.

A trader can choose to use these basic tax points, however, if a tax invoice is issued within 14 days of the date on which the supply is considered to have taken place according to the basic rules, the supply can be treated as taking place at the time the invoice is issued instead. This makes the practical process of accounting for VAT more straight forward as it is then linked with the accounting part of the transaction not the physical movement of goods or supply of the service. HMRC can, at the taxpayer's request, substitute a period longer than the 14 days. For example, many companies generate all invoices at the end of the month and so some invoices may be generated more than 14 days after the basic tax point. If this is the case then it is likely that this end of month date will be treated as the date of supply.

The impact of VAT on registered traders and final consumers

The easiest way to illustrate the operation of VAT we have outlined so far in this chapter, and its actual impact on registered traders and their consumers, is to use an example. The following activity illustrates the cascade effect of VAT where traders account for VAT on their value added at each stage on a production process.

Activity

Susan runs a small farm as a business on which she keeps rare breed sheep. She sells fleeces for £200 to a local manufacturer, Country Crafts Ltd, which employs spinners and knitters to produce garments which are sold for a total of £600 to a shop, Country Clothes Ltd, which sells the clothes to members of the public for £1,000. All three businesses are registered for VAT purposes.

None of the above amounts include VAT, which you can assume is levied at the standard rate of 17.5% on each of the transactions. Calculate the impact of VAT on the transactions described above.

Feedback

Taxable person	Cost (£)	Input tax (£)	Net sales price (£)	Output tax (£)	VAT payable to HMRC (£)
Susan	0	0	200	35	35
Country Crafts	200	35	600	105	70
Country Clothes	600	105	1,000	175	70
					175

Note that the VAT suffered by the final consumer is £175 which is exactly the amount payable to HMRC over the three transactions (£35 + £70 + £70).

Each person has to pay input tax on taxable supplies received and charges output tax on taxable supplies made.

The difference between the output tax charged and input tax paid must be paid to HMRC. This simple example does not illustrate it, but if there is an excess of input tax over output tax the excess can be reclaimed from HMRC.

You can perhaps notice therefore that as registered businesses collect VAT from their customers, but can deduct (reclaim) VAT they pay on their inputs, these businesses are not affected by the direct cost of VAT. The only impacts they suffer are the cost they must bear to administer the tax and any impact on cash flow between when they pay input tax and receive output tax.

Registration and deregistration

A registered trader is a sole trader, partnership or company who is registered for VAT. Failure to register carries severe penalties as well as a liability to pay the VAT which should have been accounted for.

Initial registration

A person who makes taxable supplies, but is not already registered for VAT, becomes liable to be registered:

- at the end of any month, if the value of taxable supplies for the preceding twelve months has exceeded £70,000 (2010/11 or FY09 – £68,000), or
- at any time, if there are reasonable grounds for believing that the value of taxable supplies in the period of the next 30 days will exceed £70,000.

In determining the value of a trader's supplies for this purpose supplies of goods or services that are capital assets of the business are ignored.

The trader will be registered from the end of the month following the 12-month period in which they exceeded the limit. If HMRC and the trader agree to an earlier date, this will be used instead.

If a trader's taxable supplies will not exceed £70,000, then they are not required to register for but they may choose to do so, as we will see later.

Where a business is split so as to keep each part below the registration threshold, HMRC can treat it as a single business in determining if registration is required.

As soon as it becomes known that a trader is required to register they should keep VAT records and begin to charge VAT on any taxable outputs they supply (although they cannot issue VAT invoices until a VAT registration number is received). During this period the trader should notify customers that the price charged is VAT inclusive and a full tax invoice should be sent within 30 days of receiving the registration number.

Traders who should register, but fail to do so, will still be liable for VAT on taxable supplies made from the date on which they should have registered. If it is not possible to collect the VAT due from customers retrospectively, then they will be liable themselves for the tax they should have collected. This could prove very expensive of course as it could equate to up to 17.5% (or 20%) of the value of all the supplies made since they should have registered.

Fiscal Fact

The cost to the government of allowing small traders not to register for VAT where their turnover doesn't exceed the registration threshold was estimated to be £1.6 billion for 2008/09.

Voluntary registration

It is possible to register for VAT even if the business' turnover is below the registration limit. There are a number of benefits of voluntary registration:

- input tax suffered can now be reclaimed; and
- the trader may appear to be a larger business than they actually are which may increase their status with customers.

The key disadvantages of voluntary registration are:

- customers who are not VAT registered cannot reclaim the output tax now charged on the supply and so the trader may lose their competitive edge with non-registered customers; and
- the administrative burden of registration (e.g. completing quarterly VAT returns and handling queries from HMRC) should not be overlooked.

The tax status of a trader's customers is an important factor when deciding whether voluntary registration is likely to be beneficial. Let's consider this in a little more detail with an example.

Activity

Elaine makes patchwork quilts. She can make a maximum of 40 quilts in a year which she can sell on the open market for £500 each (before VAT). She does not think that customers would be willing to pay any more. Alternatively she has been made an offer to sell her total production for the year to an exclusive retail outlet, again for £500 a quilt excluding VAT. The materials to make a quilt cost £100 before VAT.

Under what circumstances should Elaine apply for voluntary registration of VAT?

Feedback

Sales to public	If registered £	If not registered £
Value of supply		
40 × (£500 × 117.5%)	23,500	
40 × £500		20,000
Less output VAT		
40 × (£500 × 17.5%)	(3,500)	
Net sales	20,000	20,000
Less costs 40 × £117.50	(4,700)	(4,700)
Reclaimed VAT	700	
Profit	16,000	15,300

The difference in the two positions is therefore a result of the extra cost to Elaine of her input tax – if she is a registered trader, this is not a cost she will have to bear. However, if she registers she will need to start charging her customers £587.50 (£500 + 17.5%) for her quilts, rather than £500 if she does not register. She must be certain that her sales will not be offset by this extra price as she only needs to lose 2 sales of her 40 to then have a lower overall profit.

If Elaine took the option of selling to the retailer instead, the numbers would be the same (i.e. a profit of £16,000 if she registered and £15,300 if she did not) but now as long as the retail outlet was also a registered trader, then the extra cost associated with the output VAT charge would not directly affect this transaction. It would just become part of the retail outlet's input VAT which they can then reclaim. It would be up to the retailer how much of this extra cost to pass on to their own customers.

Deregistration

Deregistration may also be compulsory or voluntary. Compulsory deregistration will occur if the trader ceases to make taxable supplies.

A trader may ask to be voluntarily deregistered if they can satisfy HMRC their taxable supplies, net of VAT, for the following 12 months will not exceed £68,000, the deregistration limit for this year (2009/10 or FY09: £66,000). Traders can not claim to be voluntarily deregistered if they intend to cease to trade (it will be compulsory when they do cease to trade) or if there will be a suspension of taxable supplies for a continuous period of 30 days or more in the next 12 months (their registration cannot be suspended therefore by trading inactivity alone).

The date of a voluntary deregistration is the later of the date on which the request is made or an agreed date between the trader and HMRC.

Fiscal Fact

The number of registered VAT traders was 1,942,000 in 2009/10.

Taxable supplies and exempt supplies

The example above (Elaine) illustrated the use of the standard rate (17.5% currently) for calculating the VAT due. There are actually three possible rates of VAT. The standard rate (17.5% or 20% for the period from 4 January 2011), a lower rate (5%) and zero. It might appear strange to have a rate of zero for some items, but it is an important part of the VAT system as we will see later. The general rule is that any supply that is not exempt, lower rated or zero rated will be taxable at the standard rate. In this section we consider what types of supply fall in these categories and how this classification affects the VAT system.

Exempt supplies

The exemptions to VAT are contained in Schedule 9 of the VATA 1994. The Schedule contains a number of groups, which are listed here, together with some important examples of exempt goods and services.

Group 1   Land, including:
- granting of any interest in or right over land
- holiday accommodation
- mooring fees including anchoring and berthing.

Group 2   Insurance.

Group 3   Postal services provided by the post office.

Group 4   Betting, gaming and lotteries.

Group 5   Financial services. Including:
- provision of credit
- issue, transfer or receipt of, or any dealing with, any security or secondary security.

Group 6   Education, including:
- provision of education or research by a school, eligible institution or university or independent private tutor
- supply of any goods or services incidental to the provision of any education, training or re-training.

Group 7   Health and welfare, including:
- supply of services by registered medical practitioners, ophthalmic opticians and dentists
- provision of spiritual welfare by a religious institution as part of a course of instruction or a retreat.

Group 8   Burial and cremation.

Group 9   Supplies to trade unions and professional bodies if in consideration for membership.

Group 10   Entry fees for sports competitions (if non profit making).

Group 11   Works of art when disposed of to public bodies.

Group 12   Fund-raising events by charities and other qualifying bodies (this was extended in the 2000 Budget to include participative events and events on the internet).

Group 13   Provision of cultural services (e.g. admission charges for museums, zoos, galleries, exhibitions, etc).

Group 14   Supplies of goods with unrecoverable input tax.

Group 15   Gold purchased as an investment.

A business of making any of these exempt supplies cannot charge VAT on the supply to a customer. If the trader only makes exempt supplies, they cannot register for VAT and therefore cannot reclaim any input tax they pay. Effectively, they become the final consumer in any supply chain and therefore must bear the full VAT costs as part of the costs of their business.

Fiscal Fact

For 2009/10, exempting education from VAT is estimated to cost the Government £1,050 million; health services exemption £1,150 million, postal services £200 million; finance and insurance £6,050 million and betting/gaming/lottery dues £1,400 million.

Zero rated supplies

Zero rated goods and services are defined in Schedule 8 of the VATA 1983. The Schedule has a number of groups, listed below, together with some important examples of zero rated goods and services.

Group 1   Food, including:
- food of a kind used for human consumption
- animal feeding stuffs.

Exceptions include (these are standard rated instead):
- supply in the course of catering, including all food which is consumed on the premises and all hot food
- ice cream, confectionery and chocolate biscuits
- spirits, beer and wine
- pet food.

Group 2   Sewerage services and water for non-industrial use

Group 3   Books, including:
- books, booklets, brochures, pamphlets and leaflets (but not stationery).
- newspapers, journals and periodicals.

Group 4   Talking books for the blind and handicapped and wireless sets for the blind when supplied to a charity.

Group 5   Construction or conversion of buildings, for residential or charitable purposes.

Group 6   Sale by builders of restored 'protected buildings' (i.e. listed) if used for residential or charitable purposes.

Group 7   International services.

Group 8   Transport (apart from those with less than 10 seats which are standard rated, such as a taxi or hire car).

Group 9   Caravans and houseboats.

Group 10   Gold supplied between capital banks (through a new scheme of investment gold was introduced at the start of 2000).

Group 11   Bank notes.

Group 12   Drugs, medicines, as prescribed by a medical practitioner and aids for the handicapped.

Group 13   Certain exports, etc. (see further explanation on export handling later)

Group 14   Tax-free shops.

Group 15   Sales by charities of donated goods and some supplies to charities e.g. some advertising (not for paid staff), etc.

Group 16   Children's clothing and footwear and some protective clothing e.g. crash helmets and bike helmets (children's and adults – latter being added in the Finance Act 2001).

The VAT system is complex and full of anomalies, for example, individual knitting patterns are taxable supplies but booklets containing more than one pattern are zero rated. The classification or exclusion of supplies into or from these groups gives rise to lots of disputes and litigation between taxpayers and HMRC.

Fiscal Fact

Currently the UK and Ireland are the only EU countries to zero rate food, water, books or children's clothes. It is estimated the cost of zero rating these items will be £14,250 million in lost tax revenues for 2009/10.

A zero rated supply is still a taxable supply; the VAT is calculated at 0% – but it still is in effect charged, it is therefore not the same as being exempt. Businesses making zero rated supplies can still register and reclaim input tax as a taxable person. As such, businesses will often prefer to be classed as making a zero rated supply rather than exempt supplies. Traders making only zero rated supplies can request exemption from registration. Traders with this exemption are responsible for notifying HMRC if there is any change in the nature of their supplies.

Lower rated supplies

A handful of items that would normally fall into the standard rated category are, by special exception instead, taxed at a lower rate of 5%. These are termed lower-rate supplies. This category includes:

- Domestic fuel or power (or for charity use);

- Installation of energy-saving materials in the home or a charity property (e.g. loft insulation);
- Government grant-funded installation, maintenance and repair of central heating systems or water heating system in homes;
- Ground source heat pumps (new from 1 June, 2004);
- Qualifying security goods installed in the homes of qualifying pensioners (when installed as part of a Government grant funded scheme);
- Renovations and alterations of homes that have been left unoccupied for at least two years;
- Women's sanitary products;
- Children's car seats, seat bases and booster seats/cushions;
- Certain conversions, alterations or renovations of non-residential property into residential property;
- Contraceptives (from 1 July 2006 – although note that prescription contraceptives are a zero rated supply);
- Nicotine patches and gum (and related 'over the counter', non-prescription, smoking cessation products). Initially this is for one year only (1 July, 2007 to 30 June, 2008) but was extended in Budget 08; and
- Housing alterations to provide mobility aids for the elderly, for example, grab rails and stair lifts (from 1 July, 2007).

Fiscal Fact

The cost to the Treasury of lower rated supplies of domestic fuel and power is estimated to be £3,600 million for 2009/10.

The VAT fraction (for determining VAT exclusive costs from a VAT inclusive price) on lower rated items is 1/21 (i.e. 5/(100 + 5)).

Accounting for VAT

You next need to understand the principles of accounting for VAT in a business and you need to know the basic legislation and practices which deal with the accounting for VAT.

VAT returns

Registered traders will pay and collect VAT over a *tax period*. They must submit a *VAT return*, together with any VAT payable, within one month of the end of a tax period.

A tax period is the length of time covered by their VAT return. It is normally three months long and ends on the last day of a month. HMRC have classified trades and businesses into various groups and allocate a tax period to a registering business, by reference to the type of trade that is being carried on, when the business first registers for VAT. This enables HMRC to spread their work evenly throughout the year so they receive roughly equal numbers of VAT returns each month. However, variations on this general rule are allowed. For example, a trader who operates four-week periods can apply to use this basis for VAT periods rather than using month ends. Some businesses also prefer to have one of the tax periods ending on the same date as the accounting year end to aid their accounting process and this is likely to be acceptable to HMRC.

It is even possible to shorten the length of the tax periods to one month. This would be attractive to traders who regularly receive a repayment of VAT (i.e. their input tax regularly exceeds their output tax for reasons we will explore later), and so could decrease the impact of VAT on their cash flow. However, this option carries the penalty of having to complete twelve VAT returns a year and so may not be a favourable option for many smaller businesses.

At the other extreme, small businesses can elect to complete only one tax return a year, although they must still pay VAT throughout the year (as we will see below).

A transaction must be accounted for in the tax period in which the tax point occurs. The transaction is subject to the relevant rate of VAT which prevails on the date of the tax point.

A VAT return, called a VAT 100, is completed at the end of each tax period and sent to HMRC (in paper form or also now via electronic submissions if the registered person wants to do it this way – although from April 2008 returns have had to be electronically filed for businesses with turnover exceeding £5.6million. From 1 April 2010, newly registered businesses and those with turnover greater than or equal to £100,000 will have to file their VAT returns on-line. The VAT return includes the following information:

- output tax collected in the period
- input tax paid in the period
- net amount payable or repayable

- value of supplies to other EU countries
- value of acquisitions from other EU countries
- input VAT due on acquisitions from other EU countries.

If an excess of input over output tax exists for the period this is repayable to the business. If the output tax exceeds the input tax (as would be normal for most businesses that are profitable over time) this difference will be paid over to HMRC from the sums collected by the registered person during the period.

Fiscal Fact

From 4 January 2011 the Government is raising the VAT rate to 20% from its current level of 17.5%. They estimate that this will create additional tax revenue of £2.8billion in 2010/11 and between £12-13billion in each of the next 4 years.

Tax invoices

Once a person is registered for VAT they must provide a tax invoice to other registered people whenever they make a taxable supply to them. The trader must also retain a copy of the tax invoice (in paper or electronic form) to illustrate what output tax has been charged on the supplies they have made.

A tax invoice must include at least:

- supplier's name, address and registration number
- tax point
- invoice number
- name and address of the customer
- description of the goods or services including, for each type of goods or services supplied:
  - quantity purchased
  - unit price where supply can be measured in units
  - rate of tax
  - tax exclusive amount
  - type of supply, for example sale or hire
  - rate of any cash discount available and separate totals of the cash discounts which applies to zero rated and exempt supplies.

Retailers may issue less detailed invoices when the VAT inclusive total value of the supply is less than £250. They need only disclose:

- supplier's name, address and registration number
- date of the supply
- a description of the goods or services supplied
- rate of tax
- the total amount chargeable including VAT.

From January 2004 a European Commission directive (2001/115/EC) on invoicing came into force in the UK. These rules make the general items of information mandatory as listed above but also add additional items if necessary. They allow invoicing of small businesses and for small valued items to be simplified further than in the past and allow for electronic transfers of VAT invoices in some circumstances. They also introduced rules for outsourcing the burden associated with accounting for VAT – even allowing customers to self bill (i.e. generate invoices for themselves) under some circumstances.

Cash operated machines, for example in car parks, do not need to provide a tax invoice if the total value of the invoice is less than £25. Purchasers can still reclaim the input tax on these costs even though they do not have a tax invoice, as a practical concession from HMRC.

Mixed supplies

Sometimes goods and services are sold as a unit but are, in fact, made up of a mixture of standard rated, lower rated, zero rated or exempt supplies. For example, if a book and cassette tape is sold together, perhaps as a foreign language course, the book is zero rated and the tape is standard rated. This is called making a mixed supply.

In this case the supplier must apportion the value of the supply between the different components using an equitable basis. VAT is then levied on each part at the appropriate rate. The legislation does not offer one method to be used to apportion the value, but acceptable methods are likely to include apportionment using the cost to the supplier of the components and apportionment using the open market value of each component.

Sometimes it may not be possible to apportion the value in this way. It is then necessary to consider the sale as a composite supply and one rate will be applied to the whole of the supply.

Cash discounts

With the exception of imports from non-EU-member states, if a cash discount is offered for early settlement of the invoice, then the VAT is levied on the value of the supply net of the cash discount. This rule applies whether the discount is actually taken up, or not. For imports from outside the EU the discount offered is ignored for the purposes of VAT unless it is actually taken up.

Input tax: more detail

So far we have simply suggested that registered traders can reclaim input tax they pay against output tax they charge provided that they have a VAT invoices to prove these amounts. In principle this is correct, but there are a number of special situations that you need to know about where these basic principles of VAT are varied.

We will start by considering capital expenditure, then VAT and cars, and finally list the occasions on which input tax cannot be reclaimed or restrictions on reclaiming may be imposed.

Capital expenditure

Capital expenditure is not usually differentiated from revenue expenditure for VAT purposes. All input tax is therefore fully recoverable as it is incurred. When a capital asset is disposed of, then VAT is charged on the disposal price just as for any other taxable supply.

VAT and cars

The exception to the VAT on capital expenditure rules is the treatment of cars. Generally, input tax on cars cannot be reclaimed. Equally, registered traders do not account for output tax when the car is subsequently sold, unless it is sold at a profit, when output tax must be levied on the profit element. However, there are a number of exceptions to these rules. VAT can be reclaimed on cars:

- acquired new and intended to be sold (i.e. if you are a car dealer);
- intended to be leased to or used in a taxi business, a self-drive hire business or a driving school.

Where input VAT on a car is recoverable, output VAT must be accounted for in the usual way when the car is eventually disposed of.

Accessories bought at the same time as the car suffer the same treatment as the car itself, but if they are acquired and fitted after the car was acquired, the input VAT can be reclaimed, provided that the expenditure is for business use.

Travelling and car maintenance costs

While VAT on the acquisition of a new car is generally not recoverable, what happens to the VAT on petrol and maintenance costs?

By concession, provided that a car is owned by a business and used for some business purposes, the VAT on the full cost of any repair and maintenance costs is reclaimable, even if the car is also partly used for private purposes.

VAT on fuel used for business purposes is reclaimable even if the fuel is paid for by an employee who is then reimbursed, either through a mileage allowance or by repayment of the cost of the fuel.

If a business provides its employees with petrol for private use, and the employee does not fully reimburse the company for the cost of the fuel, the business is considered to have made a taxable supply of that fuel to the employee. VAT car fuel scale charge tables can be accessed from HMRC website to show how this output tax should be charged. However, if the business chooses not to try to reclaim the input tax on the fuel they do not have to account for this special output tax.

If an employee reimburses an employer for the cost of either the use of the car or any private fuel used, then the payment is treated as if it were VAT inclusive provided that the payment is equal to or exceeds the cost of the private fuel.

Bad debts

What happens when a supply is made to a customer, VAT is charged, but the customer doesn't pay, i.e. the debt goes bad? In this situation, the trader can obtain a refund of the amount of tax chargeable on that debt. Where the trader has supplied goods or services and has accounted for and paid tax on the supply, if either the whole or any part of the debt has subsequently been written off in the accounts, and a period of six months from the date on which payment was due has elapsed, the trader is entitled to a refund of the output tax previously paid.

On the opposite side, registered traders must repay any input VAT which they have reclaimed on supplies for which they have not actually paid and on which bad debt relief is then claimed by the supplier, as we have just discussed. This ensures repayments made to suppliers for their bad debts are collected from the buyers whose debt was not paid and so the Government does not end up 'out of pocket'.

Those who use the annual accounting scheme for VAT (explained later in this chapter), and hence only complete one VAT return a year, will be able to account for output tax and claim bad debt relief on the same return.

Input tax specifically disallowed

In addition to non-recoverable input tax on the acquisition of cars discussed above registered traders also cannot reclaim input tax on expenditure on:

- Business entertaining, unless the expense is allowable for income tax or corporation tax purposes (see Chapter 6 for more on this).
- Living accommodation being paid for by the business on behalf of its directors.
- Non-business items which have been recorded in the business accounts.

If the taxable supply is partly for business use and partly for private use, the registered trader may either reclaim all of the input tax, and then account for output tax on the value of the supply taken for private use, or reclaim only the business element of the input tax. If the taxable supply is a service, then only the second method can be used.

Note that non-reclaimable input tax is deductible as an expense for income tax, corporation tax and capital gains tax purposes, just like other expenses, if the related expenditure is deductible for trading income or capital gains tax purposes.

Self-supply

A self-supply occurs when a trader produces a marketable output and then instead of selling it, uses it during the course of their business instead. For example, a business may own a printing operation which produces stationery which is used by the business.

If a trader makes a supply to themselves, output tax must be charged as if it were a supply to a third party. Input tax charged on the supply is only reclaimable up to the level of output tax they charged themselves on the supply. (i.e. input tax reclaimed cannot exceed output tax on the supply).

Partial exemption

Input tax is only recoverable if it has been paid on acquiring goods and services which are directly attributable to taxable supplies made by the trader. Remember that taxable supplies includes standard rated, lower rated and zero rated supplies.

If a trader's outputs consist of both taxable and exempt supplies, then the rule is that only input tax which relates to taxable outputs is recoverable. The trader cannot reclaim input tax on the goods or services they purchased that went into making their exempt output supplies. This type of trader is referred to as 'partially exempt' to recognise this fact.

This necessary matching of inputs and taxable outputs is achieved by firstly determining how much input tax can be related directly to taxable outputs and exempt outputs. The input tax which relates directly to taxable outputs is fully reclaimable and that which relates to exempt supplies is not deductible. The remaining input tax is apportioned between taxable supplies and exempt supplies by using the percentage:

$$\frac{\text{Taxable turnover excluding VAT}}{\text{Total turnover excluding VAT}} \times 100$$

This is then rounded up to the next whole percentage point. The following items are omitted from this calculation:

- goods acquired and sold without any work being done to them.
- self-supplies.
- capital goods acquired for use within the business.

HMRC may be willing to allow an alternative basis to be used to allocate input tax between taxable and exempt supplies but this will not happen automatically and the trader will need to seek approval directly for the use of any alternative method.

As a concession to this allocation rule, if the amount of input tax which is deemed to relate to exempt supplies is less than an average of £625 a month (£7,500 pa) the above apportionment is ignored and all of the input tax is reclaimable anyway. This concession helps to reduce some of the compliance costs that would arise for managing a very small amount of exempt input tax.

The treatment of partial exemption is a complex area of the VAT rules and many cases exist in this area.

From 1 April 2009, it is now possible for a registered trader to use last year's annual percentage rather than perform separate calculations for each quarter. A potential problem with using last year's annual percentage is that actual proportions of total to taxable supplies might vary during the year, but it has the advantage of smoothing out seasonal fluctuations and may help the cash flow of the business. An annual adjustment will still be required, but whereas under the old rules this took place in the first VAT return of the following year, for tax years ending on or after 30 April 2009, the calculation can be done in the final VAT return for the year.

Special schemes

You need to be aware of some of the special VAT schemes which are available to registered traders that affect how VAT is accounted for between the trader and HMRC. There are many VAT schemes in operation (and new ones are introduced from time to time). We illustrate only the most commonly used ones here. The payments on account scheme (see later) is compulsory for large organisations but other schemes are offered to taxpayers on a voluntary basis. The schemes don't normally alter the amount of VAT which must be paid (the exception being the new flat rate scheme which is deliberately designed to do this); they merely affect either the date of payments to HMRC or the administration of VAT.

In practice the take-up of these voluntary schemes is very low despite the apparent attractiveness of some of them. This may be partly due to the stringent conditions for joining the schemes, some of which have been relaxed in recent budgets to encourage wider take-up as we will see.

The payments on account scheme

Companies which have to pay £2 million a year or more to HMRC complete their VAT returns in the normal way once each quarter but are required to make two payments on account in each quarter in addition to the usual end of quarter payment. The first payment is made a month before the end of the quarter and the second payment is made at the end of the tax period. The final payment, which is sufficient to cover the remaining VAT liability for the tax period, is made at the usual time, i.e. one month after the end of the tax period. This means, in practice, that the trader will make a payment to HMRC at the end of each month of the year.

HMRC will use the previous twelve months' information in order to determine the monthly payments of the scheme members usually on the basis of 1/24th of the trader's total VAT liability for the previous year. Traders can opt to pay their actual VAT liability instead, however, if they so wish. This may be cheaper for them to do if their activity is less than in the previous year.

The cash accounting scheme

The cash accounting scheme allows members to bend the normal tax point rules we examined earlier in the chapter. Instead members of this scheme can use the following tax points:

- for output tax; the day on which payment or other consideration is received, or the date of any cheque, if later.
- for input tax; the date on which payment is made or other consideration is given, or the date of any cheque, if later.

This means members of the scheme only pay VAT on actual cash transactions. This can provide a considerable cash flow advantage to many businesses as it also avoids them having to deduct output tax on a VAT return when they have not yet received the payment from their customer.

Taxable persons are eligible for admission to the scheme if:

- the value of their taxable supplies for the next year after application is not likely to exceed £1,350,000 (up from £660,000 with effect from 1 April 2007);
- they have made all the returns which they are required to make and all their VAT payments are up to date
- they have not, in the last twelve months up to date of application, been convicted of any VAT offence.

The scheme does not apply to hire purchase agreements, conditional sale agreements or credit sale agreements.

Members of the scheme may remain in the scheme unless at the end of any quarter or relevant accounting period the value of taxable supplies made in the 12 months up to that point has exceeded £1,600,000 (increased from £825,000 with effect from 1 April, 2007) and in the year then beginning is expected to exceed £1,600,000. If this is the case, they must notify HMRC and stop operating the scheme on the anniversary of joining it.

Current members can withdraw themselves from the scheme if:

- they want to at any point; or
- they are unable to comply with the requirements of the scheme for any reason (e.g. their accounting systems do not comply).

HMRC can terminate membership of the scheme in certain circumstances.

A person whose membership has been terminated has to account for, and then pay in the current period, all the tax they owe to return to the normal VAT rules.

Fiscal Fact

Budget 2007 estimated that the increase in the cash accounting threshold to £1.35 million will allow an extra 56,000 businesses to benefit from the scheme.

The annual accounting scheme

Under this scheme, members:

- pay 90% of tax liability as estimated by HMRC for that current accounting year. This payment is normally made by direct debit from their bank account in nine equal monthly instalments commencing on the last day of the fourth month of their current accounting year. An option to pay in three larger instalments in the year was also introduced with effect from 25 April, 2002. Payments are then equal to 25% of the previous year's VAT liability.
- supply a return for the year by the last day of the second month following the end of that accounting year, together with any outstanding payment due to HMRC for their liability for tax declared on the return.

Taxable persons are eligible to apply for membership of the scheme if:

- the value of taxable supplies in the year from the date of application to join will not exceed £1,350,000;
- they have made all the VAT returns which they are required to make;
- total credits for input tax did not exceed total output tax in the year prior to application for authorisation; and
- they have not had membership terminated in the three years preceding the date of application for authorisation.

Members can remain in the scheme once they have been allowed to join unless:

- at the end of any current accounting year the value of the taxable supplies made by them in that year has exceeded £1,600,000, in which case their authorisation will be terminated immediately;
- at any time the value of taxable supplies made so far in the current accounting year will exceed £1,600,000 in which case they have 30 days in which to notify HMRC who may then terminate their membership

They are expelled from the scheme for non-compliance with its rules. As with the cash accounting scheme, HMRC can terminate membership in certain circumstances.

Why may a business choose to use the annual accounting scheme?

Feedback

The annual accounting scheme is useful in managing business cash flows as payments are predictable throughout the year and only one VAT return needs to be completed, helping to reduce compliance costs. However, it does require monitoring of the various membership limits to ensure the turnover maximum is not exceeded as well as some planning to ensure monies are available for payments when they fall due, irrespective of the cash flow position of the business. If you are down-scaling your business, or just having a less profitable year, larger payments may need to be paid than would otherwise be the case as payments due will be based on the previous years figures. This is of course reversed if you have a better year again the following year.

Retail schemes

There are a number of special schemes which are used by retailers. The normal VAT legislation requires registered traders to maintain detailed records of every transaction. Retailers who make a mixture of standard rated, zero rated and exempt supplies face particular problems with accounting correctly for VAT. Retailers are allowed therefore to keep less detailed records by using one of the schemes and calculate output tax in a way which better suits their circumstances. Some of the schemes require totals for different sorts of supply rather than details of individual transactions while others allow the VAT liability to be estimated using purchases and mark-up percentages. The retail schemes are only available to retailers who cannot reasonably be expected to account for VAT in the normal way.

Retail schemes are not just for small traders. Individually agreed schemes for businesses with taxable retail turnover in excess of £100 million per annum have recently been introduced. From 1 April 2009, retailers with a turnover of more than £130million are required to enter into bespoke schemes and are no longer able to use the published schemes.

The second-hand goods scheme

The second-hand goods scheme is available to traders who buy second-hand goods from individuals who are not registered traders. HMRC can allow a reduction on the taxable supply amounts of such second-hand goods as such traders will typically have to charge output tax but not have any input tax to offset against it.

The maximum reduction available is equal to the amount of tax which would have been due had the purchase of the goods been a normal taxable supply. This means that VAT is due only on the trader's profit margin rather than on the total sales price of the goods. Hence the trader has to only account for output tax of $7/47^{ths}$ ($1/6^{th}$ after 3 January 2011) of the difference between their purchase price and their selling price.

Under this scheme the member selling the second-hand goods does not have to create a tax invoice when they make a sale. A registered trader who buys goods from a trader who is using the second-hand goods scheme will not therefore be able to reclaim the input tax because he or she will not have received a tax invoice.

This scheme can apply to sales of all second-hand goods, works of art, antiques and collectors' items. The scheme cannot, however, be applied to precious metals and gemstones.

Flat rate scheme

The 2002 Budget introduced a new scheme for VAT payment aimed at offering smaller businesses a significant compliance cost saving in handling VAT issues. The new scheme, available since 25 April, 2002, is for businesses with:

- VAT-exclusive taxable turnover of up to £150,000 per annum and;
- VAT-exclusive total turnover (i.e. including exempt or other non-taxable (income) up to £187,000 per annum.

However, from 1 April 2009, the second of these criteria no longer applies and only taxable turnover will be used to decide if the trader is eligible for the scheme.

The scheme allows businesses to account for VAT using a flat rate percentage applied to their tax-inclusive turnover (including exempt or zero rated income). The rate that applies depends on the nature of the business as different flat rates will apply to different businesses. To illustrate the range in these rates; the lowest flat rates can be enjoyed by suppliers of food and of children's clothing (flat rate of 2% applies) whereas the highest rate applies to builders who charge for labour only (flat rate of 13.5% applies).

With effect from 1 January, 2004, these rates have been reduced in some cases, for example, the rate applicable to taxi operators has been reduced from 10% to 9%. In addition, newly registered businesses are entitled to an extra 1% discount in their first year of operation.

In conjunction with the rise in the standard rate form 4 January 2011, the fixed rate tariffs will also rise. The full range of rates for both levels of VAT can be found on the HMRC website.

Businesses using this scheme still issue VAT invoices to and collect VAT from their customers but don't have to track input or output VAT specifically to calculate their VAT charge or repayment. The only exception to this is for capital purchases in excess of £2,000 (VAT inclusive). For such purchases traders who normally use the flat rate systems can recover the input tax on these purchases directly in the normal way (i.e. as for non-flat rate users). Of course, if these assets are subsequently sold, full VAT must be charged on the sale price and accounted for as output tax in the usual way (i.e. capital assets over £2,000 continue to be accounted for as normal even for traders registered to use the flat rate scheme).

The use of the flat rate scheme could save businesses significant compliance effort by reducing much of the separate accounting that otherwise needs to occur for recording the input and output VAT appropriately. This scheme needs careful monitoring, however, as it may not produce a lower tax bill for all business depending on the make-up of supplies and inputs.

Imports and exports

Since the creation of a Europe without trade barriers (the 'Single Market') on 1 January, 1993 it has become necessary to differentiate between transactions with traders resident in other countries in the European Union and those resident in countries outside the European Union when a trader completes a VAT return. The way we account for VAT on transaction with these two groups of purchasers and suppliers is different. We will outline differences in this section.

Imports

Imports into the UK may come from other EU member states or from countries which are not members of the EU. The VAT treatment of imports depends on the source country of the goods.

We will discuss the detail of the arrangements which are currently in force within the EU member states later in this section. First, we will consider imports from countries from outside the EU.

Goods

Tax on the importation of goods from places outside the member states will be charged and payable as if it were a customs duty. VAT due and any associated customs duty on imports is often in fact paid at the same time by traders. The rate of the duty is the same as the rate which would apply if the same goods were supplied in the home market by a registered trader. The registered trader is then able to reclaim the duty paid on the goods as input tax in the normal way.

A registered trader can apply for approval to make deferred payments until a fixed payment day once a month. Payment day is the 15th day of the next month following the one in which the amount of duty deferred fell due to be paid. Each period under this scheme commences on the 16th day of a month and ends on the 15th day of the next month. On each payment day an approved person has to pay to the Commissioners the total amount of customs duty deferred.

Services

If services are supplied to a registered trader who is UK resident by a person resident overseas, either within the EU or from outside the EU, the *reverse charge system* will be used.

Relevant services include:

- transfers and assignments of copyright, patents, licences, trademarks and similar rights;
- advertising services;
- services of consultants, engineers, consultancy bureaux, lawyers, accountants and other similar services; data processing and provision of information;
- banking, financial and insurance services including re-insurance; any other service supplied to a registered trader provided that it is not exempt.

The reverse charge system requires the recipient trader to treat the supply received as if they were also the supplier. This means they account for a notional output tax, which then becomes the actual input tax on the supply.

Overseas (non-EU) companies can register for VAT in the UK if they wish to. If they do so they then follow the usual rules for charging VAT on their supplies we have examined in this chapter.

Under this circumstance no reverse charging is then necessary by the recipient of the supply, even though the supplier comes from outside the EU.

Non-EU based suppliers of broadcast electronic services (e.g. via the Internet) to UK based non-registered recipients have also been required to charge VAT from July 2003 at the rate applicable for that sale in the customers' country. This, in effect, requires some non-EU based suppliers to become registered traders in at least one EU member country and to comply with their VAT regulations in making suppliers of services in the rest of the EU. That member state country will then reimburse any taxes due to countries to whom that supplier has made supplies.

Imports of works of art, antiques and collectors' pieces from outside the EU are subject to VAT at a reduced rate of 2.5%.

Exports

A supply of goods is zero rated if HMRC are satisfied that the person supplying the goods has:

- exported them to a place outside the EU member states (evidence must be produced); or
- shipped them for use as stores on a voyage or flight to an eventual destination outside the UK, or as merchandise for sale by retail to persons carried on such a voyage or flight in a ship or aircraft.

VAT within the EU

The principles of the EU requires that, in effect, no borders should exist when goods and services are sold or purchased between suppliers and customers in more than one member state. This means that VAT should be applied as if both parties were in fact in the same state.

In reality this situation has not yet come about fully. In the meantime, the current position can be outlined as follows:

If a registered person in one member state supplies goods or services to a registered person in another member state they should make the supply at a zero-rate in the country of origin (i.e. no output tax is accounted for, but input tax associated with the supply can be reclaimed). The customer will then account for output VAT on the purchase in their accounts at whatever VAT rate is applicable in their home country. The VAT suffered can also then be treated as their input tax in their country and accounted for as normal. This is the same reverse charging process as we described above for services purchased from non-EU suppliers by EU registered persons. This has a net effect of zero so that the trader is in the same position as if they have acquired the goods from a trader in their own country. For this system to be applied evidence of the transfer or supply of the goods or services must be available and both traders must be able to provide details of the registration numbers of the other.

If the supply from a registered trader is to a non-registered customer (or one who has not proved their registered status by providing their registration number) then the supply should be made including VAT at the origin country's rate, as if it had been supplied within the supplier's own country.

Summary

In this chapter you have read about the operation of VAT, one of our most important taxes in the UK.

VAT has to be paid whenever a taxable person makes a taxable supply of goods or services in the course of business. Unless a supply of goods or services is specifically exempt in the legislation it is a taxable supply. With the exception of domestic fuel and a handful of other supplies, which are taxable at 5%, taxable supplies are either standard rated or zero rated. The standard-rate of VAT for the UK has been 17.5% for a number of years, but reduced to 15% for the period 1/12/08 to 31/12/09 and increased to 20% from 4/1/11.

A trader must register if turnover exceeds certain limits, for this tax year the limit is £70,000 a year. A trader whose turnover is lower than the registration limit may choose to register voluntarily.

A registered trader is able to reclaim allowable input tax but must account for output tax on taxable supplies.

VAT is normally paid quarterly to HMRC on the basis of invoices received and issued in the quarter. However, there are a considerable number of special schemes, some of which are compulsory for some businesses, which require VAT to be accounted for on a different basis.

There is debate about the acceptability of further increases in the amount of revenue which is raised using indirect taxation. This debate was considered in the first three chapters.

Project areas

Not all countries around the world use a VAT style tax on expenditure. Review how other countries tax expenditure and discuss the relevant merits/disadvantages of each approach.

The harmonisation of VAT within the EU provides considerable scope for dissertation titles. There are also opportunities for comparative studies, for example the special schemes on offer to small businesses in EU member states.

Since 1979 there has been a significant shift in taxation in the UK from direct taxation to indirect taxation. A number of titles suggest themselves, for example, is it possible for there to be further shifts from direct taxes to indirect taxes? Alternatively would a shift back towards direct taxation be possible or desirable?

From 1 July, 2003 a new VAT regime has been imposed on non-EU companies selling electronic services (e.g. via the web) to European customers. This resulted in VAT having to be charged to consumers of these services where previously they were VAT free. This was welcomed by EU companies, who always had to charge this, but not of course by non-EU based companies. What are the implications of this for the growing market of electronic business related services in the UK?

Lower and zero rating particular items costs the UK Government lots of lost revenue. Should they instead impose a fixed rate on all purchases to collect as much tax as possible – and to improve fiscal neutrality? What would be the implications of so doing?

Quick quiz

1. Kieran makes taxable supplies of £72,000 p.a. Is he required to register for VAT?

2. Louise offers her customers a 5% discount for prompt payment. She sells a standard rated item for £500 in December 2010 to a customer who does not take up the discount. How much VAT should she charge?

3. Maurice owns a business which makes wholly zero rated supplies totalling £50,000 p.a. Should he register for VAT?

4. Nigella is registered for VAT and is partially exempt. During the year she incurred the following input tax:
   – attributable to taxable supplies   £50,000
   – attributable to exempt supplies   £5,000
   – unattributable   £4,000
   The total value of supplies for the year was £500,000 of which £100,000 was exempt. How much of Nigella's input tax is recoverable?

5. Omnibus Ltd is a company that makes office furniture. It received an order on 30 July, delivered the goods to the customer on 20 August and issued an invoice on 30 August. Payment was received on 13 September. What is the tax point for VAT purposes?

6. Portia uses the cash accounting scheme and in the quarter ended 31 September 2010 invoices sales of £6,000 plus VAT; purchases raw materials for cash of £4,000 plus VAT and receives cash from debtors of £5,525. How much VAT is due?

Questions

Question 1   (based on past CIMA exam question May 1988).

A trader started in business, selling mainly foodstuffs which are zero rated for VAT purposes, on 1 January, 2010 and the following information was extracted from his records for the year ended 31 December, 2010.

The purchases (but not the sales) are inclusive of VAT.

	£
Fixed assets purchased (all standard rated)	9,000
Other standard rated purchases and expenses	4,000
Sales of zero rated foodstuffs	65,000
Sales of standard rated items	8,000

He approaches you shortly after the end of the year and informs you that he does not intend to register for VAT since 'the sales liable to VAT were well below the threshold'.

Required: Advise him on the position regarding VAT registration, and show the final value added tax position which would have applied for the above year if the trader had registered voluntarily at the start of the year.

Question 2   Victor commenced trading as a garden centre business on 1 May, 2002, and became registered for VAT on the same day. Supplies made (exclusive of VAT) for the 31 October, 2010 quarter are:

	£
Standard rated supplies	88,400
Exempt supplies	11,600
Total supplies	100,000

Input tax for the quarter is £24,000, of which £18,000 directly relates to taxable supplies and £1,500 to exempt supplies.

Required: Compute the deductible input tax for the quarter ended 31 October, 2010.

Question 3 (based on ACCA June 2004).

Sandy Brick has been a self employed builder since 2000. He registered for VAT on 1 January 2011 and is in the process of completing his VAT return for the quarter ended 31 March 2011. The following information is relevant to the completion of this VAT return:

(1) Sales invoices totalling £44,000 were issued to VAT registered customers in respect of standard rated sales. Sandy offers his VAT registered customers a 5% discount for prompt payment.

(2) Sales invoices totalling £16,920 were issued to customers that were not registered for VAT. Of this figure, £5,170 was in respect of zero rated sales with the balance being in respect of standard rated sales. Standard rated sales are inclusive of VAT.

(3) On 10 January 2011, Sandy received a payment on account of £5,000 in respect of a contract that was completed on 28 April 2011. The total value of the contract is £10,000. Both of these figures are inclusive of VAT at the standard rate.

(4) Standard rated materials amounted to £11,200 of which £800 were used in work on Sandy's private residence.

(5) Since 1 December 2005, Sandy has paid £120 per month for the lease of office equipment. This expense is standard rated.

(6) During the quarter ended 31 March 2011, £400 was spent on mobile telephone calls, of which 30% relates to private calls. This expense is standard rated.

(7) On 20 February 2011, £920 was spent on repairs to a motor car. The motor car is used by Sandy in his business, although 20% of the mileage is for private journeys. This expense is standard rated.

(8) On 15 March 2011, equipment was purchased for £6,000. The purchase was partly financed by a bank loan of £5,000. This purchase is standard rated.

Unless otherwise stated, all of the above figures are exclusive of VAT.

Required:
Calculate the amount of VAT payable by Sandy for the quarter ended 31 March 2011.

(Note: answer available via lecturer's website)

Question 4   (based on ACCA December 1993).

Alison Able, a senior employee in Able, Keane and Ready Ltd., is planning to set up a new business venture in 2011 that she will run herself, rather than as part of this existing company. None of the existing business' assets or staff will be involved in the new business. The income from the new business is expected to be £60,000 p.a., net of VAT. All the income will come from standard rated supplies, 80% of which will be made to VAT-registered persons. Because of the highly competitive nature of the business, it will not be possible to pass on the additional cost of VAT to the 20% of customers who are not VAT registered.

The business is to be run from Alison's home, so the only expenses of the new business will be:

	£
Leased office equipment	2,820 p.a.
Telephone (40% private)	3,625 p.a.
Entertaining clients	4,910 p.a.
Insurance	1,000 p.a.

Alison also plans to spend £7,000 on a pre-launch advertising campaign. All the above figures include VAT where applicable.

Alison asks you to advise her on the VAT aspects of her new business. Specifically she asks the following questions. Draft a written reply to her.

(i)   Will she automatically have to account for VAT on the income of her new business as a result of her current business being registered for VAT? Explain the reason for your answer.

(ii) If the answer to (i) is that she does not automatically have to account for VAT on her income, would it be beneficial for her to register voluntarily for VAT in any case?

(iii) Would it be beneficial for her to defer the pre-launch advertising expenditure until after she has commenced trading? Your answer should consider both the VAT and the income tax implications.

(Note: answer available via lecturer's website)

Further test questions for this chapter to test your knowledge can be found in the student section of the website at:

http://www.taxstudent.com/uk

Further reading

For more details on the UK's VAT system use the HMRC website at http://www.hmrc.gov.uk. You can also refer to the detailed professional guides such as Tolley's VAT Guide.

For a discussion of VAT systems generally see S. Cnossen, 'Issues in Adapting and Designing a Value Added Tax' in C. Sandford ed. (1993) *Key Issues in Tax Reform*, Fiscal Publications, Birmingham 1993.

For an advanced examination of VAT on supplies of services, see I. Roxan, (2000), 'The Nature of VAT supplies in the Twenty First Century' *British Tax Review* 2000 (6): 603-623.

On the way in which VAT interacts with other taxes, see R.S. Nock, (1998), 'Value Added Tax and other Taxes: The Interaction' *British Tax Review*, 1998 (6):547-551.

Combs, A., Dixon, S. & Rowes, P. (2010), *Taxation: incorporating the 2010 Finance Acts*, Fiscal Publications: Birmingham.
– use this book for many other examples to further develop and test your knowledge of this chapter's contents. See http://www.fiscalpublications.com/rowes/2010

 **Tax planning**

Introduction

In Chapter 2 we discussed the concept of tax avoidance and the difference between avoidance and evasion. In this chapter we will consider tax planning, which involves strategic use of available tax concessions in order to minimise your tax liability. The distinction between the three types of activity is by no means straightforward, and you might like to think of it as a continuum:

Tax planning   *Tax avoidance*   *Tax evasion*

We saw in Chapter 2 that tax planning, availing yourself of legitimate tax concessions, is quite legal and acceptable. Tax evasion, at the other extreme, involves at least an element of fraud or non-disclosure including, for example, failing to declare income which is taxable. This is illegal activity.

It is the grey area of tax avoidance in between, however, which is particularly problematic, as exactly where the boundary exists between acceptable tax avoidance and unacceptable tax avoidance is difficult to determine. We will come back to this question later in the chapter, using the illustration of personal service companies to demonstrate the problems associated with this grey area, but we will start by considering tax planning, in the white zone.

At the end of this chapter you will be able to:
- identify some ways in which transactions can be structured so as to minimise income or corporation tax liabilities;
- discuss the advantages and disadvantages of being an employee as compared to being self-employed;
- compare the tax and national insurance differences of operating a business as a sole trader or a company;
- understand how the law related to tax avoidance operates at present in the UK; and
- discuss the concept of tax evasion.

Basic tax planning issues

A number of earlier chapters covered specific issues of tax planning and you may want to review these at this time. Chapter 4 looked at some basic income tax planning points for couples including shifting income from a high rate taxpayer to his or her basic rate paying spouse. In Chapter 8 we considered some basic capital gains tax planning issues which relate to controlling the timing of disposals and making sure that any available reliefs and exemptions are used. Chapter 9 looked at basic tax planning for UK resident companies, including avoiding having profits taxed in the marginal rate band. In Chapter 10 we considered VAT planning including the use of voluntary registration.

Note that if your course of study requires you to be aware of the loss provisions and/or company groups, there are other planning opportunities relating to those provisions which we will not be discussing further here. Instead you will need to visit the website to review these issues in detail.

We can now consider some other basic planning issues before considering broader structural issues.

Remuneration packages

A number of tax planning options are available to employees which will have the effect of reducing their income tax and NIC liabilities. Benefits in kind can be tax effective, even if they do not reduce the amount of income tax payable compared to a salary or bonus. Remember that employee (primary class 1) NICs are not payable on most benefits in kind (only class 1A – paid by the employer only), making them a relatively cheaper way to receive extra remuneration – at least as far as the recipient is concerned.

In addition, pension plans allow for tax savings, you may like to review Chapter 5 for more details of these.

Salary sacrifice

Salary sacrifice is a technique that can be used to reduce tax liabilities for both employers (secondary Class 1 NICs) and employees (both income tax and NICs). A salary sacrifice is where the employee gives up the right to receive some of his or her cash salary in return for an agreement from the employer to provide some kind of benefit in kind. To be effective for tax purposes, any arrangement to substitute benefits in kind for cash salary must be a genuine contractual arrangement. There are some potential pitfalls for employees, however, and the 'package' needs to be worked out carefully. For example, reducing the amount of cash payment entitlement under an employment contract may affect pension scheme contributions or even entitlement to working tax credit, child tax credit or state pension and other government benefits.

Typically, a salary sacrifice will involve a benefit that is not taxable such as pension contributions, childcare vouchers or mobile phones. The arrangement must be such that it is not possible for the employee to go back to the original salary whenever he or she wishes. This was established in a 1969 tax case *Heaton v Bell* where it was decided that because the taxpayer, who had the use of a car, could give up the benefit at any time, then it had a 'money's worth' that was taxable.

Capital allowances

Capital allowances provide scope for some tax planning for both incorporated and unincorporated businesses. You will recall from Chapter 7 that it is not compulsory to claim capital allowances in any given year. The choice of whether, or how much, to claim is the taxpayer's. This will have the effect of increasing the profit for that year, but also increasing the capital allowance claim that can be made the next year. This may be beneficial where a business has losses to be absorbed in the current period.

Timing is also important when considering capital allowances. Remember that first year allowances (when they applied) and writing down allowances are not pro-rated if an asset is purchased part way through the period. This means that even if you purchase an asset on the last day of the capital allowance period you still get a full period's allowance for that asset. Also, remember to classify the capital allowances you want to claim carefully to ensure the allocation you decide on gives you the option to claim the maximum allowances.

Finally, where assets qualify for treatment as short life assets, businesses should consider de-pooling them so as to crystallise a balancing allowance if it is sold at a loss within four years.

See if you can identify any other planning opportunities that arise in other chapters of the book. Remember these can include making sure that you meet the criteria for special tax treatment such as the special deduction for research and development expenditure that we considered in Chapter 9. In the remainder of this chapter, we will be looking at some structural issues, specifically the tax differences that arise between being an employee, self-employed and incorporated.

Employee or self-employed

There are a number of tax planning considerations that apply to the classification of employment status. To illustrate these we will use the following activity to provide a context for discussion.

Activity

Andrea is a management consultant who has recently taken up long-term residence in the UK having lived most of her life in the United States. In planning her future career options, she seeks your advice about the tax implications of being an employee compared to being self-employed. Discuss the issues that you would raise in the course of providing Andrea with advice.

Feedback

There are significant differences in how an individual is assessed for income tax as an employee or as a self-employed taxpayer. Self-employed persons generally enjoy tax advantages including:

- Payment of income tax later, through the payment on account system, than employees who are locked into payment through the PAYE system on a weekly or monthly basis;
- A wider range of deductible expenses. You will recall that to be deductible under earnings from employment rules, expenses generally must be *wholly, exclusively and necessarily* incurred in the performance of the duties of the employment. Under the trading income rules, expenses need only be *wholly and exclusively* for the purposes of the trade or profession, the *necessarily* requirement does not apply. In practice this means that some items of expenditure may be deductible to someone who is self-employed, but not to someone doing the same work but as an employee.
- Lower national insurance contributions under classes 2 and 4, although this must be weighed against reduced social security benefit entitlements that may then result.

Activity

Andrea (from the previous activity) expects to earn approximately £70,000 for a consultancy project she is to undertake. She will spend £2,000 on furniture for her home office, £1,000 on a computer, and it will cost her £500 travelling from her home to her client. She has asked you to provide some estimates of the different income tax and national insurance contribution liabilities arising if she is an employee or self employed.

Feedback

If Andrea is an employee of the client business, she will be taxed under employment income rules. While she may do some of her work at home, that in itself is not sufficient to make more than a very small amount of her household expenses deductible. The cost of travel between home and work is also not deductible for an employee. Andrea will be taxed as an employee on the full £40,000 salary as follows (assuming she has no other income and is entitled to just the basic personal allowance):

	£
Taxable income (£70,000 – £6,475)	63,525
Non savings income 37,400 @ 20%	7,480.00
26,125 @ 40%	10,450.00
Tax liability	17,930.00

As an employee, Andrea will also be liable for class 1 national insurance contributions; primary contributions will need to be paid by Andrea herself, and secondary contributions will be paid by her employer. We will assume that Andrea is not contracted out. These contributions are normally calculated on a periodical basis (see Chapter 4), however for simplicity we will calculate it on an annual basis by multiplying the weekly primary and secondary class 1 threshold of £110 x 52 weeks (i.e. £5,720), as follows:

Primary Class 1		
£38,155 (43,875 – £5,720) @ 11%	4,197.05	
£26,125 (£70,000 – £43,875) @ 1%)	261.25	£4,458.30
Secondary Class 1		
£64,280 (£70,000 – £5,720) @ 12.8%		£8,227.84

(Although secondary class 1 contributions are the legal responsibility of the employer, they can be considered part of the employee's effective tax liability. Remember our discussion of this idea when we discussed the question of tax incidence in Chapter 3) Therefore, earning the £70,000 as an employee will cost Andrea £22,388.30 (£17,930.00 + £4,458.30) in income tax and NICs, and her employer £8,227.84 in NICs.

If instead of becoming an employee Andrea becomes self-employed, she will be taxed under the trading income rules. If she can establish that her home is a place of business, there is a case for capital allowances to be claimed for her office furniture and computer. In addition, the cost of travel to the client's premises will probably also then be deductible.

Her tax adjusted trading profits will therefore be:

	£	£
Gross fees		70,000
Expenses:		
Capital allowances:		
AIA: computer	1,000	
furniture	2,000	
Travel expenses	500	(3,500)
Net profit from business		66,500
Less personal allowance		(6,475)
Taxable income		60,025
Income tax due:		
Non savings income		
37,400 @ 20%		7,480.00
22,625 @ 40%		9,050.00
Tax liability		16,530.00
National Insurance Contributions:		
Class 2		
£2.40 per week x 52 weeks		124.80
Class 4		
£38,160 (£43,875 – £5,715) @ 8%	3,052.80	
£22,625 (£66,500 – £43,875) @ 1%	226.25	3,279.05
Total		3,403.85

Therefore Andrea's total income tax and NIC liability is £19,933.85 (£10,682.29 lower than the total she and her employer would pay if she were an employee).

Of course, this is an over-simplified example and in reality other considerations will come into play. For example, Andrea's remuneration as an employee does not need to be salary only. A range of benefits in kind may be available which could help to reduce her total tax liability. Andrea may well decide to start a pension scheme of one or other type which will give her tax relief. It must also be remembered that the question of whether someone is an employee or self-employed is not a simple one (see Chapter 5) and care must be taken to ensure that the new rules relating to personal service income are not invoked. These are referred to as the IR35 rules and will be discussed later in this chapter. As we will see later, Andrea may well have a problem with these rules if she operates as proposed above.

Sole trader or company?

A taxpayer wanting to carry on business on his or her own account, has to make a decision about how to operate that business, as a sole trader or as a company. It is also possible to operate a business as a partnership, but for the purposes of this chapter we will only be considering the first two options.

Activity

Andrea (from previous examples in this chapter) has decided that she would rather have the independence of being self-employed, and wants to set up her own management consultancy business. She now seeks your advice on the tax implications of operating her business as a sole trader or as a company.

Feedback

As a sole trader, Andrea will be liable for income tax on her business profits under trading income rules as well as class 2 and class 4 national insurance contributions, as we saw in the previous activity.

If Andrea incorporates a company, with herself as sole director/shareholder, the company will be liable for corporation tax on the profits, which can then be distributed to Andrea in a number of ways. As a director/shareholder, Andrea can decide how much of the profits should be distributed to her as employment earnings, to be taxed under employment income rules, or as dividends to be taxed under dividend rules. Remember, the profits do not have to be distributed at all, they can be retained in the company which gives Andrea control over whether and when the higher rate of tax will apply.

The dates on which payments to HMRC are due differ between self-employed taxpayers and companies. As we noted earlier (in Chapter 6), for self-employed taxpayers income tax and class 4 national insurance contributions are payable by payments on account. Class 2 national insurance contributions are paid monthly by direct debit. Corporation tax, for companies paying less than the full rate of corporation tax, is payable nine months and one day after the end of the accounting period. Income tax and class 1 NICs must be deducted from any director's remuneration and remitted to HMRC on a monthly basis. Tax on dividends in the hands of shareholders will be taxed under self-assessment.

For a company, the choice of accounting date is not important for tax purposes, however for a sole trader, the current year basis rules may operate in the early years to create overlap profits. If you need to know about the current year basis period rules for unincorporated businesses, you may want to visit the website to refresh your memory of how these rules work in the early years of a new business.

There are also capital gains tax differences between sole traders and companies which you will recall from Chapters 8 & 9. For a sole trader, a flat rate of tax of 18% (28% for some taxpayers after 22 June 2010) applies and an annual exemption is available, currently of £10,100. Some specific capital gains tax reliefs and exemptions are only available to individual taxpayers, for example, the principle residence exemption, gift relief, and entrepreneurs' relief. For companies allowable costs are indexed to remove the inflation element and chargeable gains form part of the company's profits chargeable to corporation tax (PCTCT).

It should be noted that capital gains retained within the company will increase the value of the company's shares. If the shareholder sells the shares, he or she may be subject to further capital gains tax, which means that there is effectively double taxation of the gain.

Activity

Given that Andrea is expecting to earn £70,000, and incur expenses as noted in previous activities, how much corporation tax will be payable if she decides to incorporate her business? How will this change if the company pays her:
(a) £30,000 as a salary or
(b) £30,000 as a dividend?

Feedback

With PCTCT of £66,500 (the same net profit will apply whether she is trading as self-employed or incorporated in this case), the company is in the small company rate band:

	£
Corporation tax on £66,500 @ 21%	13,965.00

Compare this with the income tax and NICs payable as a sole trader on the same amount of profit in the earlier activity.

(a) If £30,000 is paid as a salary, this, together with the secondary Class 1 NICs, will be deductible for the company as follows:

	£
Net profit before salary and NIC	66,500
Less:	

Salary to Andrea	30,000	
Secondary class 1 NICs		
(£30,000 – £5,720) x 12.8%	3,108	33,108
PCTCT		33,392

The corporation tax then becomes:

$$£33,392 \times 21\% = £7,012.32$$

There will also be income tax and primary class 1 national insurance to pay by Andrea on the salary of £30,000 as follows:

	£
Taxable income (£30,000 – £6,475)	23,525

Non savings income	
£23,525 @ 20%	4,705.00
Tax liability	4,705.00

Primary Class 1:	
£24,280 (£30,000 – £5,720) @ 11%	2,670.80
Secondary Class 1:	
£24,280 @ 12.8%	3,107.84

Total tax and NICs payable by Andrea is therefore £7,375.80, with £10,120.16 payable by the company.

(b) If £30,000 is payable to Andrea as a dividend, and not a salary, the picture is a little different. The dividend will not be deductible for the company, and so the corporation tax will still be the same as we calculated earlier, i.e. £13,965.00.

In Andrea's hands, the dividend will then be taxed using the dividend income rules. Assuming she has no other income, her income tax liability will be nil as dividends paid to basic rate taxpayers (which she will therefore be) are taxed at the rate of 10% and then they receive a 10% credit which cancels out the tax liability. Dividends are also not subject to NICs, and so the result is the same as if no dividend payment were made to Andrea, because of the operation of the dividend imputation system.

Therefore, in this particular case, it will be more tax efficient for Andrea to have her income paid as a dividend not as a salary as the total tax cost to her and her company combined is lower this way (i.e. £13,965.00 compared to £17,495.96).

It can be seen that the advantages of operating a business through a company depend, to some extent, on the amount of profit extracted from the company and the form that the extraction takes. Dividends are tax free to basic and starting rate taxpayers, but are not deductible for the company and the corporation tax rate will be at least 21% on these dividends. Salary is deductible for the company, but taxable on the director under employment income rules.

It must also be remembered that the decision whether or not to incorporate a business, like all commercial decisions, should not be made with only tax in mind, there are many other non-tax issues that need to be considered. This includes quite considerable extra-legal reporting requirements that exist for companies that are not present for unincorporated businesses. This extra administrative burden needs to be considered when making the decision whether or not to incorporate as its cost could easily outweigh the tax advantages.

Constraints on the use of companies

Earlier in this chapter we mentioned some rules that may influence the decision whether to use a company as a vehicle through which to provide personal services to clients. Personal services in this context includes any work a taxpayer may perform for a specific client in return for payment of some kind. As we have seen in this chapter so far, being able to work as an employee, self-employed person or through a company you own can make a significant difference to the amounts of tax you have to pay. We have discussed in previous chapters how the timing of when tax must be paid is also different between these three ways of structuring your business activity. HMRC is concerned that these tax planning strategies are not used to avoid tax.

The use of personal service companies in the UK to avoid employment related tax obligations is by no means a new issue. Indeed, the 1981 Finance Bill contained provisions described by the Revenue then as being introduced to ensure that agency workers were taxed as employees even if they operated through a company. In April 1982, however, the then Financial Secretary announced that the Government had decided not to proceed with the legislation.

The IR35 rules

IR35, dated 9 March, 1999, was an Inland Revenue press release. In it Gordon Brown, the then Chancellor's 1999 Budget announcement of changes to counter avoidance 'in the area of personal service provision' was amplified. Clearly the Government sees this as an area of unacceptable tax avoidance, in the grey zone of the continuum we considered earlier.

The stated aim of the changes was "to ensure that people working in what is, in effect, disguised employment will, in practice, pay the same tax and national insurance as someone employed directly". This is an attempt by the Government to increase equity in the tax system so that all "employees" are taxed the same whether or not they consider themselves to be an employee. Following a period of consultation after the initial press release, where many expressed concern about the proposed rules, a new set of rules was introduced with effect from the 2001/02 fiscal year.

The rules look at whether a worker, who wants to be taxed as a self-employed person, would have been considered to be an employee of a client, using the usual tests of an employment relationship for tax purposes (which we looked at in Chapter 5). This will be clear in many cases by looking at the terms and conditions of the particular engagement. So, if a taxpayer "pretends" to be in self-employment to benefit from the kinds of tax advantages we discussed earlier in this chapter, and particularly if they offer their services through an intermediary (usually a company) to disguise the fact that they are really an employee under the usual rules to test for this, IR35 will be applied.

The IR35 rules operate so that the fee received by the intermediary for duties a taxpayer performs and to which the rules apply (net of specified deductions) is treated as having been paid to the taxpayer in the form of salary and wages subject to PAYE and NICs. Before 10 April, 2003 these rules only applied to business relationships, but after this date all services are potentially subject to these rules. Corporate intermediaries account for PAYE deductions and NICs as usual for any salary paid to the worker throughout the year and reconciliation is then required at the year end. Any shortfall between the actual salary paid and the amount to which the rules apply is then deemed to be paid to the worker on the last day of the year. The personal services company then has to remit PAYE and NICs to HMRC to cover this deemed payment.

Because the aim of the new rules is to make sure that taxpayers do not avoid tax by disguising an employment relationship, the intermediary can deduct expenses otherwise deductible under employment income rules as well as employer pension contributions, when working out the amount of the year end deemed payment to the worker. In addition, because the Government recognises that running a company involves extra administration costs, the company can deduct a further flat five per cent of the gross payment in working out the deemed payment. If the interposed personal services entity fails to deduct and account for PAYE and NICs, the normal penalties for employer default apply.

HMRC has made available on its website detailed information on IR35 including a page entitled "Supplying Services through a Limited Company or Partnership". This page provides a guide to determine whether the IR35 rules apply and, if so, what to do. More detailed information which specifically deals with how to compute the deemed payment and pay any resulting income tax and NICs can also be found on HMRC's website under the IR35 section.

This means that taxpayers like Andrea need to be careful about the nature of the contracts their companies enter into with clients. If they are really contracts *of* service, rather than contracts *for* services, IR35 may come into play so that extra tax and NICs are payable.

The introduction of the IR35 rules has led to some further developments in recent years. One response was for groups of taxpayers to get together, with the help of professional advisers, and form 'composite' companies, to provide their services to clients. It was possible to argue that the IR35 rules did not apply to these arrangements because the intermediaries were now acting for a number of different taxpayers, not just the one as is the case with a personal service company. Out of concern that this new form of arrangement was also unacceptable tax avoidance, the Government introduced, following consultation, some more rules in 2008, described as the Managed Service Company rules. These rules now sit beside the IR35 rules and aim to remove the tax advantage of providing personal services through a company rather than directly as an employee.

Since early 2009 there have been increasing calls from tax practitioners for the repeal of the IR35 rules. The Professional Contractors' Group, formed in 1999 to lobby against the initial rules, has reported recently that IR35 has raised only £9.2million between 2002/3 and 2007/8, compared to initial forecasts of additional revenue £220million in NICs alone.

Settlements and income splitting

Another potential problem area from a tax planning perspective is the settlement legislation. This was first introduced in the 1920s as a tax avoidance rule, but for many years had not been invoked by HMRC. Just recently, however, the rule has been used to attack husband and wife companies. The rules require that if income from property arises under a 'settlement', and the settlor has an interest in the property, then the income is taxed as income of the settlor. In one recent case, *Arctic Systems* (2007), Mr and Mrs Jones each owned one share in a company which earned fees by providing Mr Jones' services to clients. After drawing a small salary, the remaining profits were distributed as dividends to Mr and Mrs Jones. HMRC argued that this was an arrangement which came under the settlement rules and attempted to tax Mr Jones on the dividends distributed to Mrs Jones On 27 April 2005, the High Court found in favour of HMRC. The Court of Appeal overturned the High Court decision, however, in December 2005 but in July 2007, the House of Lords finally found in favour of the taxpayers.

Following the lack of success in the *Arctic Systems* case, Her Majesty's Treasury issued a consultation document suggesting alternative ways of dealing with the general problem of 'income shifting', that is using arrangements, including setting up family companies and partnerships, to split the income of one person between a number of taxpayers in order to reduce the overall tax liability. After consultation and discussion, it now seems that no action is to be taken at this stage to develop new ways of dealing with this issue; indeed the Chancellor announced in the 2008 pre Budget Report that HMRC will delay indefinitely bringing in the proposed new income shifting law.

IR35, the settlements legislation and proposed income splitting rules all deal with the tension in the tax system between acceptable tax planning and unacceptable tax avoidance. In the next section we will consider some of the court decisions dealing with the question of whether an activity constitutes unacceptable tax avoidance.

Tax avoidance

Over the past 75 years there has been a shift in the attitudes of the courts in relation to the question of what constitutes tax avoidance. Earlier in the twentieth century the courts adopted a strict interpretation of taxation laws: they looked at what the words of the legislation said and only considered the legal nature of any avoidance scheme, not any underlying issues. This has now evolved into a wider review beyond just the legal form of transactions and arrangements. In this section we will look at some of the more significant cases involving tax avoidance and trace the development of the courts' attitudes. Note, however, that we present here only a very simplified discussion of the case law to illustrate the developments over time.

Tax Avoidance Case Law

IRC v Duke of Westminster (1936)

The early, strict, interpretation is illustrated by the case of *IRC v Duke of Westminster* (1936). In this case an arrangement was entered into so that domestic servants were not paid wages but instead received an income under a deed of covenant. A deed of covenant produced a tax deduction for the person executing the deed and was valid only if no valuable consideration was provided by the recipient in return. However, the Duke of Westminster and his servants had an understanding, that so long as the deed of covenant operated the servants would not claim the wages due to them. The scheme enabled the Duke to claim tax relief for the amounts paid to his servants whereas payment of wages to servants would not have been an allowable deduction Today such a scheme could not be used because payments made under deeds of covenant are no longer tax effective when paid to individuals. However, at the time, the House of Lords found for the Duke, declaring that they would only consider the legal nature of the transaction, that is, they were more concerned with the form of the transaction than its substance. Until the mid-1980s this case remained an important precedent and the Inland Revenue were rarely successful in challenging tax avoidance schemes in the courts.

WT Ramsay Ltd. V IRC (1981)

In *WT Ramsay Ltd v IRC* (1981) the House of Lords took a completely different view of an avoidance scheme. The case involved an artificial scheme which was used to create a large capital loss. The company had realised a capital gain and intended to set the artificially generated loss against the capital gain to avoid paying tax on the gain. The scheme was artificial because it was made up of a series of preordained steps which were to be carried out in rapid succession. The scheme required that all steps be completed once the first one had been made. At the end of the series of steps the taxpayers would be in the same position as they had been at the beginning and any loss created would not be a real financial loss – just a paper loss. In fact the only real losses which had been suffered were the professional fees which were paid for the scheme's operation. The House of Lords decided that although each step in the scheme was a separate legal transaction, it was possible to view the scheme not as a series of separate legal transactions, but as a whole, by comparing the position of the taxpayer in real terms at the start and finish of the scheme.

When this was done no real loss was incurred and the scheme was self- cancelling.

Lord Wilberforce explained the decision as follows:

'While obliging the court to accept documents or transactions, found to be genuine, as such, it does not compel the court to look at a document or a transaction in blinkers, isolated from any context to which it properly belongs. If it can be seen that a document or transaction was intended to have effect as part of a nexus or series of transactions, or as an ingredient of a wider transaction intended as a whole, there is nothing in the doctrine to prevent it being so regarded; to do so is not to prefer form to substance, or substance to form. It is the task of the court to ascertain the legal nature of any transaction to which it is sought to attach a tax, or a tax consequence, and if that emerges from a series, or combination of transactions, intended to operate as such, it is that series or combination which may be regarded.'

Furniss v Dawson (1984)

The *Ramsay principle* established in the previous case was extended in *Furniss v Dawson* (1984). This time the objective was to defer capital gains tax by using an intermediary company based in the Isle of Man. The scheme was not circular or self-cancelling. However, the House of Lords decided that the scheme should still be set aside for tax purposes because once again the scheme required a series of artificial steps to be carried out in quick succession just to save tax rather than with a real business purpose in mind.

Craven v White (1989)

Later the case of *Craven v White* (1989) was used by the House of Lords to limit the application of the *Ramsay* principle somewhat. Once again an intermediary company in the Isle of Man was used to defer a capital gains tax liability. The key difference between *Craven v White* and *Furniss v Dawson* was that when the shares were transferred to the Isle of Man based company, their final disposal had not been agreed. Hence no preordained series of steps existed at the time that the first transaction was undertaken. Consequently the House of Lords refused to view the series of transactions as a whole and the scheme was successful this time in reducing the tax liability. This case has great significance for anti-avoidance schemes generally. It makes planning well in advance critical. If transactions are undertaken before the final step is known with certainty, there is a greater likelihood of the scheme being successful if challenged by HMRC as tax avoidance activity – although of course, not being certain of the full outcome makes such schemes inherently more risky.

IRC v McGuckian (1997)

IRC *v McGuckian* (1997) dealt with an issue in which there was a transfer of company shares to a non-resident trustee of a settlement, followed by the rights to a dividend being assigned to a resident company for consideration. The UK resident company then paid an amount of dividend less commission to the trustee. The question was whether this constituted a tax avoidance scheme, and the House of Lords were of the view that it did. This case raised some important issues, not so much because *Furniss v Dawson* was again applied, but from comments made by their Lordships in the course of the decision. They appeared to adopt a more purposive approach to interpretation which means the courts will look at what the legislation is designed to achieve, rather than just what it says.

McNiven v Westmoreland Investments Ltd (2001)

In *McNiven v Westmoreland Investments Ltd* (2001) the House of Lords had to consider whether steps inserted into a transaction had any commercial purpose or were present simply to affect the tax outcome. The case involved a company with accrued unpaid interest. In order to be deductible for corporation tax at the time, the interest had to be paid. The lender, which was the parent company, made a loan to Westmoreland that was then repaid in discharge of the outstanding interest. It was a preordained, circular, arrangement, designed purely so as to secure a tax deduction. The House of Lords found, however, that the company had incurred a real economic outlay and that this was tax mitigation to take advantage of a statutory tax relief. It was therefore legitimate tax avoidance.

Barclays Mercantile Business Finance Ltd. v Mawson (2005)

In 2005, the House of Lords delivered its decision in *Barclays Mercantile Business Finance Ltd v Mawson* [2005] STC 1. In this case, the Barclays group purchased a gas pipeline from the Irish Gas Board for £91million and leased it back to them. By a series of transactions, the £91million found its way back into the group as a deposit. The bank claimed capital allowances on the pipeline, however the Revenue was of the view that the money was spent on "financial engineering" rather than plant and machinery qualifying for capital allowances. The House of Lords affirmed the decision of the Court of Appeal that whether or not an expense is incurred is a legal question and so the arrangement did not constitute unacceptable tax avoidance.

Astall v Revenue and Customs Commissioners (2008)

More recently, in 2008, the High Court delivered its decision in the Astall case [2008] EWHC 1471 (Ch), in which the taxpayer sought to deduct a loss arising from the transfer of discounted securities. The Special Commissioners had earlier found in favour of HMRC that the loss was not deductible, taking a purposive approach to interpreting the relevant legislation. Their decision was upheld by the High Court.

The question of where the boundary between acceptable and unacceptable tax avoidance is will continue to be debated, and be subject to further subtle shifts, as a result of a number of forces. These will include the constitution of the courts and prevailing attitudes in HMRC, government and of society at large.

Tackling tax avoidance in the UK

The UK currently has a multifaceted approach to tackling tax avoidance that has been developing over a number of years. In the previous section we saw how the judiciary play a role in changing their approach to interpretation and are now looking to the purpose of the legislation and not just its strict wording. Another facet is to deal with specific transactions by specific legislation introduced to curtail new schemes. These are increasingly being referred to as Targeted Anti Avoidance Rules (TAARs). The difficulty that arises with this approach is that there is an ongoing incentive for the creation of new schemes not covered by existing legislation. It is also often the case that specific measures leave room for further tax planning opportunities.

Disclosure of tax avoidance schemes

The Finance Act 2004 introduced radical new rules as part of HMRC's attempt to modernise its approach to managing the risk from fraud, evasion, avoidance and error. The new rules require those who sell tax avoidance schemes, and those who use them, to disclose them to HMRC. According to the regulatory impact assessment issued by the Treasury, "they will help to maintain the integrity of the tax system and ensure that everyone pays their fair share of tax and so contributes to the UK's needs". The rules were initially confined to tax avoidance products that were either financial or employment related. In Finance Act 2006, this was extended to a broader range of tax avoidance schemes with wider tests as to when disclosure is required. The rules have caused quite a lot of controversy and there remains some doubt about what their impact will be in the long term. There is some anecdotal evidence, however, that the disclosure rules have put a brake on the mass marketing of generic tax avoidance schemes. Many of the TAARs referred to in the previous section have been introduced as a result of disclosure of tax avoidance schemes, and their introduction is adding significantly to the length and complexity of the tax legislation in the UK.

A general anti avoidance rule

In the UK there is currently no general anti-avoidance rule (GAAR), as there is in some other countries, such as Canada and Australia. There is an argument that not having a general anti-avoidance rule causes uncertainty in the operation of the tax system. The Inland Revenue proposed a draft GAAR in 1998, however it was rejected on the basis that it was too detailed, and so its application was uncertain. One commentator, Freedman (2003) has suggested that we need a GANTIP – a general anti avoidance principle, rather than a rule. She suggests that a legislative, principles based framework would give guidance to both taxpayers and HMRC.

The new coalition government has announced in 2010 that it intends to re-visit the question of whether the UK should introduce a GAAR, and so the issue is now being debated once again.

Tax evasion

At the extreme right of the diagram that we introduced the chapter with is the activity of tax evasion. As we noted, tax evasion is illegal activity, and in recent years it has become an important area of academic research, particularly in the field of economics. Researchers around the world are trying to work out what factors affect people's decisions to evade payment of taxes, including attitudes and norms, both personal and social. This research has led tax authorities to develop new strategies for dealing with taxpayers who evade taxes. For a list of references, see the end of this Chapter.

One recent example of tax evasion on a very large scale is referred to as 'missing trader' fraud where huge amounts of VAT have effectively been stolen. A version of this fraud, referred to as 'carousel' fraud, involves evasion of VAT in trade within the European Union taking advantage of the zero rating of cross border transactions within the EU. Importers of goods are able to receive them without paying VAT, but charge VAT on their resale without remitting it to the revenue authority.

Fiscal Fact

In a press release dated 5 July 2010, HMRC announced that two members of a 21-strong criminal tax fraud gang have been ordered to pay £92.3m in the biggest ever confiscation order secured by HMRC. The gang stole £37.5m in VAT tax fraud involving import and export of computer processing units through a chain of companies using sham invoices. They used the cash to invest in luxury properties.

Summary

We opened this chapter with a brief look at the difference between tax planning, tax avoidance and tax evasion. We then considered a limited number of different basic tax planning strategies for both employees and businesses. From a structural viewpoint, we considered the differences in the tax system for employees, self-employed taxpayers and incorporated taxpayers. We found that there are some clear differences, with employees generally paying more tax than self-employed taxpayers and unincorporated businesses paying more than incorporated businesses on the same amount of profits. We noted, however, that the decision of how to structure an income earning activity is not just a tax issue, there are other commercial considerations involved.

We also considered how the attitudes of the courts towards tax avoidance have changed over time and looked at some current developments in this area.

Project areas

The issue of tax planning provides lots of opportunities for projects as it is a subject that can be approached from a number of different directions. The boundary between tax planning and unacceptable tax avoidance for example raises questions about the different attitudes of the revenue authorities, taxpayers and their professional advisers and can also raise some interesting moral and ethical questions.

The incorporation of tax considerations into strategic management decision making is another area of potential project topics as is considering the tax policy questions of providing opportunities for tax planning in the first instance.

Discussion questions

1. The treatment of corporations separately from their shareholders for tax purposes can lead to tax avoidance, particularly where there is a significant difference between the rate of tax applicable to corporations and that applying to high income individuals. What measures can the government put in place to prevent high income taxpayers from sheltering profits behind the corporate form?

2. How can a government fairly determine the difference between employment and self-employment to ensure legitimate tax planning is allowed to continue but abuses of the system are minimised?

3. Discuss how tax planning can occur for other taxes, such as inheritance tax, stamp duty or VAT. Does the interaction of these taxes and income tax provide any opportunities for tax planning?

4. Do you think the decision in *WT Ramsay v IRC* was the right one?

5. Will a General Anti Avoidance Rule ever be enacted in the UK?

6. Is the new approach of HMRC – requiring tax avoidance schemes to be registered – an effective way to limit tax loss to the Government or an 'over-the-top' solution that prevents acceptable tax planning which would otherwise be allowed by the law?

Questions

Question 1 Zainab is employed by a company that does not currently contribute to her pension scheme, and she pays £80 per month to a pension scheme from her net (after tax) pay. What would be the effect of entering into a salary sacrifice arrangement so that the company pays pension contributions on her behalf?

Question 2 List the main differences between the taxation of trading income and employment income. Who do you think enjoys the more advantageous treatment, a sole trader or an employee?

Question 3 (based on CIMA Business Taxation November 1997)

Mr C, a single man, is about to start a business which will be engaged in the repair of domestic appliances. His starting date is 1 April, 2010 and he will make up accounts to 31 March each year.

His business plan shows that he is likely to make a taxable profit in the first few years, before any salary for himself, of approximately £60,000 per annum.

He is uncertain whether he should set up the business as a sole trader or as a limited company and seeks your advice. He has advised you that, if the business is run as a company, he will require a gross salary of £30,000 per annum.

Required: Draft a report for Mr C, indicating the important differences from a tax and NIC point of view, of the two alternative methods of running the business. Your answer should contain, as an appendix, computations showing the overall tax and NIC burden which will arise in each case.

(*Note: answer available via the lecturer's website*)

Question 4 (based on ACCA Tax Planning December 1995)

Basil Nadir is a computer programmer. Until 5 April, 2010, Basil was employed by Ace Computers Ltd, but since then has worked independently from home. Basil's income for his first 12 months of trading to 5 April, 2011 is forecast to be £65,000, of which 50% will be in respect of work done for Ace Computers Ltd.

His expenditure for the year will be as follows:
(1) Computer equipment costing £4,700 (inclusive of VAT) was purchased on 6 April, 2010
(2) Basil uses two rooms of his eight room private residence exclusively for business purposes. The cost of light, heat and insurance of the house for the year will amount to £1,800 (inclusive of VAT of £100).

(3) Basil's telephone bills currently amount to £250 per quarter. They were £100 per quarter up to 5 April, 2010. Both figures are inclusive of VAT.

(4) Basil owns a two year old motor car which originally cost £15,000. It was worth £10,000 on 6 April, 2010. His motor expenses for the year will amount to £3,500 (inclusive of VAT of £400). Although Basil works from home, he has to visit his clients on a regular basis. His mileage for the year ended 5 April, 2011 will be as follows:

Visiting Ace Computers Ltd	10,000 miles
Visiting other clients	10,000 miles
Private use	5,000 miles

Basil spends 50% of his time working for Ace Computers Ltd, and since 6 April, 2010 has been working for them on a 12 month contract to develop a taxation program for accountants. He visits the company's offices twice a week in respect of this contract. Apart from Ace Computers Ltd, Basil presently has five other clients.

On 8 August, 2010, Ace Computers Ltd was the subject of an HMRC PAYE compliance visit, and Basil's self employed status in respect of his contract with the company was queried. HMRC have stated that they consider Basil to be an employee of Ace Computers Ltd for the purposes of both income tax and National Insurance contribution.

Basil has not yet registered for VAT. He is single, and has no other income or outgoings.

Required:

(a) Briefly discuss the criteria that will be used in deciding whether Basil will be classified as employed or self-employed in respect of his contract with Ace Computers Ltd. Your answer should include:

    (i) an explanation as to the likely reasons why HMRC have queried Basil's self-employed status; and

    (ii) advice to Basil and Ace Computers Ltd as to the criteria that they could put forward in order to justify Basil's self- employed status;

(b) Calculate Basil's liability to income tax for 2010/11 if he is treated as self-employed in respect of his contract with Ace Computers Ltd, and advise him of by how much this liability will increase if he is instead treated as employed. You should ignore the implications of National Insurance and VAT, and should note that Basil's self-employed status in respect of his contracts with his other five clients is not in dispute.

(c) Assuming that Basil is classified as self-employed in respect of his contract with Ace Computers Ltd, state when he will have to compulsorily register for VAT, explain the implications of being so registered, and advise him of whether or not it would be beneficial to voluntarily register before that date. You should assume that Basil's income accrues evenly throughout the year and in the interest of simplicity, assume a 20% VAT rate throughout.

(*Note: answer available via lecturer's website*)

Further test questions for this chapter to test your knowledge can be found in the student section of the website at:

http://www.taxstudent.com/uk

Further reading and examples

Bowler, T. *Countering Tax Avoidance in the UK: Which Way Forward?* (2009) Institute for Fiscal Studies, Tax Law Review Committee Discussion Paper No. 7

Freedman, J. (2003) Tax and Corporate Responsibility *The Tax Journal* Issue 695. 2; 2 June 2003.

Kirchler, E. (2007) *The Economic Psychology of Tax Behaviour* Cambridge University Press.

Braithwaite, V. (2009) *Defiance in Taxation and Governance*, Edward Elgar Publishing.

Combs, A., Dixon, S. & Rowes, P. (2010), *Taxation: incorporating the 2010 Finance Acts*, Fiscal Publications: Birmingham.
– use this book for many other examples to further develop and test your knowledge of this chapter's contents. See http://www.fiscalpublications.com/rowes/2010

12 International tax

Introduction

The UK tax paid by an individual or company is influenced by the residence or domicile of the taxpayer.

As a general rule, an individual who is closely connected with the UK will pay tax in the UK on his or her income no matter where in the world it comes from. If an individual only has a vague connection with the UK, however, he or she will be taxed in the UK only on income arising in the UK. A similar principle applies to companies.

With increased globalisation, more and more UK-based individuals and companies are conducting business or earning income outside of the UK. It is important to know how the returns from these activities will be taxed. Overseas investments also allow scope for tax planning, particularly as there are a number of countries with much lower tax rates than the UK.

International tax is an extremely complex area and in this chapter we will only cover some of these issues at a level that will give you an overview of the key issues involved. We will also have a brief look at how some of the special tax rules work that are related to international activity.

At the end of this chapter you will be able to:

- explain the terms residence, ordinary residence and domicile;
- outline the general rules concerning whether an individual or company is liable to UK income and corporation tax;
- explain how payment of tax overseas can affect a UK tax liability and the measures available to prevent double taxation; and
- identify some international tax avoidance practices and the legislation which seeks to prevent them.

Residence of individuals

There are three connecting factors that are used to determine UK tax liability for individuals; *domicile*, *residence* and *ordinary residence*.

A person's domicile is generally either where he or she is born, or the place where the person intends to settle permanently. An individual has a domicile of origin from the moment of birth. Once the individual is aged 16 or over they may choose their domicile. To do this the individual must maintain a physical presence in the country concerned and must have evidence that he or she has an intention to remain there indefinitely. You can only have one domicile at any one time, although it may be possible to be tax resident of more than one country.

The terms *residence* and *ordinary residence* are not defined in the UK's legislation at present but can be determined from various court rulings. They are important rules, however, as they determine a taxpayer's likely exposure to UK tax legislation; UK residents have to pay UK tax.

An individual is deemed to be resident in the UK if he or she:

- Spends more than *183 days* in the UK in the tax year.
- Having been a resident has left the UK for permanent residence abroad but returns to the UK for periods which equal an average (*over a period of four consecutive tax years*) of *91 days or more* in the tax year..

HMRC has published a guidance booklet to help with this topic entitled *Residents Domicile and the Remittance Basis* (HMRC6). In general, a person cannot be a UK resident for only part of a tax year. He or she is either resident or not resident for the entire year of assessment. The only exception occurs when an individual either leaves the UK for permanent residence abroad or comes to the UK in order to take up permanent residence. Under these circumstances, the tax year is split and the UK tax liability will only apply to the part of the year for which they were a UK resident. Once considered a resident, this status is not usually lost for temporary absences from the UK. A taxpayer remains a UK resident unless they are absent from the country for a whole tax year.

You should note that residence status depends on your tax year dates, not the length of time lived out of the UK. You have to be absent for a whole tax year (i.e. 6 April one year to the 5 April the next year) to escape UK residence status, not just be away for 12 months. For example, if you left the UK in August 2009 and returned in December 2010 you would still be considered a UK resident for tax purposes for the whole period as your absence covered part of two tax years, but did not fully cover either one.

A taxpayer is *ordinarily resident* if the UK is normally their country of residence (where you are habitually resident). A taxpayer may therefore be resident but not ordinarily resident, or ordinarily resident but not resident (although this is rare), or both resident and ordinarily resident in any tax year. A British citizen who has been ordinarily resident in the UK but who leaves to live abroad is deemed to be resident during his or her absence unless they can prove otherwise.

Your residency status will determine how much of your income will be taxed in the UK and also when it will be taxed. Some income is taxed on an *arising basis*, that is the amount that is earned during the tax year, even if it is not brought over to the UK. Other income is taxed on a *remittance basis*, that is so long as it remains overseas it will not be taxed in the UK, but will attract tax as soon as it is remitted, or brought in to the UK.

Non-domiciles

Since 2002, the rules relating to residence and domicile have been under review. In 2008 a controversial change was brought in.

With effect from 6 April 2008, an annual charge of £30,000 1 applies to non-UK domiciled adults resident in the UK for the year and also at least seven of the previous ten years (the charge does not apply to children). It applies when a non-domicile claims the right to be taxed on their foreign income and gains on a remittance basis, that is, not as they are earned, but when the income or gains are brought into the UK (which they may never be, of course). This charge is in addition to whatever UK tax is also due but the charge will not apply if the unremitted foreign income is £2,000 or less.

Non-domiciled adult residents in the UK in the tax year who continue to claim the remittance basis do not have the right (from 6 April 2008 also) to UK income tax personal allowances against their remitted income (including the personal allowance itself, age-related allowances, blind person allowance and tax reductions for married couples or civil partners). They also cannot use the capital gains tax AEA against capital gains remitted to the UK. However, a £2,000 de minimus rule also applies so that if unremitted income does not exceed this sum, non-domiciles will be allowed to keep their allowances to offset their remitted income for both income and capital gains taxes.

As part of the new regime the Finance Act 2008 also included rules to stop non domiciles bringing certain income and gains into the UK free of tax as was previously possible in some cases.

Employment income

As we saw in Chapter 5, earnings from employment or pensions are assessed on an arising (taxed in the year it is received) basis. This applies to any employment earnings for any year of assessment in which the person holding the office or employment is both resident and ordinarily resident in the UK.

These rules also detail how to tax income, also on the arising basis, for UK-based duties performed by a person who is not a resident. In this circumstance the taxpayer is charged tax only on income generated in the UK.

A person who is resident but not domiciled or not ordinarily resident in the UK, will pay UK income tax on a remittance basis. This means they only have to pay income tax if they bring their income into the UK, subject to payment of the £30,000 fee if necessary.

Capital taxes

Capital gains tax is charged on individuals if they are resident or ordinarily resident in the UK. If they are also domiciled in the UK, this charge is on gains made anywhere in the world and tax due is reported and collected via the usual processes, as we studied in Chapter 8. If individuals are not domiciled in the UK then only gains arising in the UK, or remitted here, are taxed in the UK. Use of the remittance basis is subject to payment of the £30,000 fee.

Resident status does not affect inheritance tax. If you are domiciled in the UK, when you die you pay UK inheritance tax on your worldwide property. If you are not domiciled here you only pay inheritance tax on your UK property.

Rates of tax

For residents of the UK any foreign income earned is simply added to the other, UK-sourced, income as part of the tax computation. It is then taxed at the same rates as if it had arisen in the UK like other income. If tax has been paid overseas on this income already however, a reduction may be available in their UK tax computation to compensate for the tax already deducted by another Government. We will look at when this might apply later in this chapter.

Individuals who are only charged tax on amounts they remit in the UK, pay tax on all foreign sourced income (including foreign savings and dividend income) at UK rates for non-savings income (i.e., 20% 40% or 50% based on the usual bands).

Residence of companies

Companies do not have a domicile, only a residence status. UK resident companies are liable to corporation tax on their total worldwide profits arising in an accounting period regardless of whether those profits are remitted to the UK – the same rule as applies to resident individuals.

A company is deemed to be a UK resident if it is either incorporated in the UK or, if it is not incorporated here, its central management and control is exercised in the UK. This is generally where the key operational decisions are made, often the place where directors' board meetings are held.

Non-resident companies are liable to UK corporation tax if they trade in the UK through a UK based *permanent establishment* which usually involves staff, and often premises of some kind, based in the UK but owned by the non-resident company. The trading profits arising, directly or indirectly, from the UK-based permanent establishment are liable to UK tax, whether or not they are fully earned in the UK. Income from property or rights either used by, or held by, the permanent establishment is chargeable to corporation tax as are any chargeable gains on the disposal of assets situated in the UK.

Double taxation relief

It is possible, because of the way international rights to tax operate, that a UK resident can pay tax in two countries on the same income source; in their country of residence and the country in which the income or profit arises. A UK resident (individual or company) is taxed on worldwide income and so may have to pay tax on foreign business profits in both the UK and the country where the business is being carried on. This situation is called *double taxation*. Fortunately the problem of double taxation is well recognised by tax authorities around the world and, in most cases, the full effects of double tax can be avoided.

There are two main methods for reducing double taxation on overseas income. One is a credit system, where the home government taxes the overseas income but then allows a credit, or reduction in tax payable, for the tax paid overseas. The second is the exemption system where the home government chooses not to tax foreign income at all, i.e. it is treated as exempt from home country taxation.

In the UK, double tax is reduced by a system of double tax reliefs. These reliefs are outlined in a series of agreements between countries on how they will each handle this problem. These agreements are called *double tax treaties.*

The UK has a large number of double tax treaties with other countries that contain provisions explaining exactly how double tax is to be relieved and how taxable activities between their countries are to be reported. As a general rule, the UK tax is calculated on gross worldwide income and then double tax relief is deducted from that liability.

What if the country you pay tax to does not have a treaty with the UK? Fortunately this does not mean that you will have to suffer double taxation. The UK tax rules also contain provisions which allow for unilateral (one sided) relief for at least some of this double tax for such cases. These provisions require that the foreign income is first included in the taxable income of an individual (or PCTCT of a company), grossed up for any foreign tax suffered.

The double tax relief under these relief provisions is usually the lower of the foreign tax suffered on the overseas income or profits, and the UK tax liability on that overseas income. More relief can be available where a double tax treaty exists, but this basic rule is true in most circumstances.

Fiscal Fact

The cost to the government of providing double taxation relief under both income tax and corporation tax is estimated to be £15,000 million for 2009/10.

Activity

Aristotle Ltd is a UK resident company with no associated companies. During the year ended 31 March 2011, Aristotle had the following income:

	£
Tax adjusted trading profits from UK business	2,500,000
Tax adjusted trading profits from overseas branch office (net of 35% foreign tax)	208,000

Calculate Aristotle Ltd's UK corporation tax liability for the year.

Feedback

Firstly, in calculating Aristotle's PCTCT, it is necessary to gross up the foreign profits by the amount of foreign tax paid to determine the total overseas income.

	Total £	UK Income £	Overseas Income £
Tax adjusted UK profit	2,500,000	2,500,000	
Foreign profit (£208,000 × 100/65)	320,000		320,000
PCTCT	2,820,000	2,500,000	320,000
Corporation tax @ 28%	789,600	700,000	89,600
Less double tax relief:			
Foreign tax paid:			
£320,000 @ 35% 112,000			
UK tax on foreign income			
£320,000 @ 28% 89,600			
Relief is the lower of the two	(89,600)		(89,600)
Corporation tax payable	700,000	700,000	nil

Note: In this case £22,400 (£112,000 – £89,600) of foreign taxes payable cannot be offset against Aristotle's UK tax bill. FA2000 introduced a provision which allows eligible unrelieved foreign tax to be either:

- Carried back to accounting periods beginning not more than 3 years before the period in which the unrelieved tax arises; or
- Carried forward.

In both cases the unrelieved foreign tax is treated as if it was paid in respect of the same source of income and may be relieved against corporation tax payable on that source of income, in the earlier or later accounting period.

A review is currently underway of the UK system of double tax relief. As part of this review, consideration is being given to exempting from UK tax the profits of foreign branches, rather than using the credit system just described.

Dividend income from foreign companies

Up until 30 June 2009, the UK tax position was slightly more complicated if the foreign income of a company consists of dividends from foreign companies. There will generally be two types of foreign tax payable on dividends. The country where the foreign company is located is likely to levy what is called *withholding tax*, which is a tax at a fixed rate on dividends leaving that country to go to foreign shareholders. The other type of tax which foreign dividends may be subject to is the tax on the profits of the foreign company that is paying the dividends. This is referred to as *underlying tax*, since it is a tax on the profits out of which the dividends are paid.

UK resident companies receiving dividends from foreign companies will usually be entitled to double tax relief for withholding tax paid. Whether or not they are also entitled to double tax relief for the underlying tax will depend on how large the shareholding is in the foreign company. To be entitled to additional relief for underlying tax, the UK resident shareholder must control at least 10% of the foreign company's shares.

The amount of underlying tax is calculated using this formula:

$$\text{Gross dividend received} \times \frac{\text{Overseas tax actually paid}}{\text{Overseas profit available for distribution}}$$

With effect from 1 July 2009, however, the UK has switched from the credit system of double tax relief to an exemption system, for companies which receive dividends from foreign companies in which they own more than 10% of the shares. This means that the often complicated calculation of underlying tax is no longer required.

You will find a worked example of the application of the rules that applied until 30 June 2009 on the website.

Branch or subsidiary?

When a company is considering expanding overseas, a decision must be made about how best to establish its foreign activities. The most common options are to either set up the foreign business as a branch of the existing business, or to incorporate a separate subsidiary company in the foreign country. This is a complex decision and, of course, does not only involve tax considerations. However from a tax point of view, we can note the following that must be considered at the minimum:

- A branch office of a UK business is not a separate taxpaying entity. The profits of a branch will need to be included in the UK head office's trading income and so will be liable for UK corporation tax in the year in which they are earned in the same way as the profits of a UK based business are.
- A subsidiary company is a separate legal entity and for tax purposes there is no consolidation of profits required as there is for accounting reporting to stakeholders. This means that the UK parent company will only be taxed on the profits of the foreign subsidiary when they are remitted to the UK, usually in the form of dividends or interest on loans made to the subsidiary (taxed under loan relationship rules). With effect from 1 July 2009, as noted earlier, an exemption system will apply to dividend income received from overseas subsidiaries.

This meant that operating a foreign business through a subsidiary offered tax planning opportunities by enabling the parent to delay when the profits will be remitted to the UK and therefore be exposed to UK corporation tax. An important distinction between operating through a branch and through a subsidiary is that in the latter case, if the foreign business operates at a loss, that loss will be trapped within the foreign company and cannot be used by the UK parent company to reduce its own UK corporation tax liability.

International tax avoidance

Double taxation of profits by two different countries is an added cost of doing business overseas. Minimising taxes paid and, where possible, eliminating double taxation has led to the development of a large international tax planning community. This is of some concern to governments who want to protect their taxing rights and so the grey area between tax planning and tax evasion, that we discussed in Chapter 11, also arises in the international context. Some tax avoidance practices of multinational enterprises entail the use of tax havens, countries where little or no tax is imposed on the profits of organisations doing business there.

In the UK, there are some specific anti-avoidance provisions which aim to protect the Government's tax revenue from what they consider to be unacceptable international tax avoidance. Here we will consider two common avoidance practices and see how the UK provisions operate to prevent their inappropriate use to artificially affect taxes due to the UK Government. Specifically they are the transfer pricing rules and the rules dealing with controlled foreign companies.

Transfer pricing

Transfer pricing refers to the process of determining the price to be charged for goods or services flowing between related or associated enterprises. Where goods or services are bought or sold between unrelated enterprises, the parties will agree what is known as an *arm's length price*, which is the market price for the particular item being traded where both parties seek to get the best price they can from their perspective. Where the two enterprises are related to one another, perhaps through common shareholding or some other arrangement, it is possible to agree to set a price for trades between them which is not the same as an arm's length bargain. The way in which transactions are structured can then allow for some tax planning, particularly where the parties are in different countries and there is a difference in the tax rates in force in those two countries.

To illustrate how transfer pricing can be used to affect tax bills, take the case where a company resident in the UK sells goods to a subsidiary company resident in France, which then sells the product to French customers. The product cost £1,000 to manufacture, £100 to ship to France and retails for £2,100 in France.

Depending on how the parties wish to price the transaction, the profit can appear to be made in either the UK or France or partly in both. For example, the UK company can sell the product to the French associate for £2,000 leaving a £900 profit in UK and a £100 profit in France. Alternatively, it can sell the product for £1,100 leaving £100 profit in UK and £900 profit in France.

The companies could also introduce a third party through which to trade to place the profits somewhere else again. For example, the company could create a wholly owned subsidiary, perhaps in a tax haven where there are no taxes on business profits. If this new company then charge say £900 to arrange the transport of the goods, £800 of the profit is shifted from either UK or France to the tax haven.

Given the flexibility transfer pricing across tax borders offers to companies, HMRC has been given the power under UK law to substitute an arm's length price for any prices they consider to be artificial, in situations where:

- Sales are made by a UK company to an overseas company at what they consider to be an undervalue; or
- Purchases are made by a UK company from an overseas company at an over-value.

The legislation gives HMRC wide powers to enter premises and examine documents to obtain information relating to transfer prices.

The legislation applies not only to trading activities but also to:

- Sales or purchase of fixed assets
- Letting or hiring of property
- Loan interest
- Patent royalties
- Management charges

It should be noted that these rules did not used to apply to transactions between associated companies who are both UK residents for tax purposes. As HMRC is the relevant tax authority in both cases then they were less concerned about the use of transfer prices to artificially adjust inter-group profits in this way as the total tax paid across the groups was the same and was all paid to the same tax authority, however it is sliced up between the associates. With effect from 1 April, 2004, however, new rules mean that transactions between related companies will have to be at arm's length prices even when they are both residents of the UK. There are, however, some exceptions to these rules for small and medium companies.

Thin capitalisation

Thin capitalisation refers to a company's gearing; a thinly capitalised company is one which has a high proportion of debt financing compared to equity. The fact that dividends paid to holders of equity are not tax deductible, whereas interest payments to creditors are, means that there is a tax induced incentive for companies to finance operations through debt. The UK government, along with others, is concerned that companies may artificially inflate the amount of debt, and therefore interest payable, in order to get an extra tax advantage, which is viewed as a form of tax avoidance.

To counteract this, the UK government introduced a 'worldwide debt cap' that operates to restrict the deductibility of interest payments by a group of companies. The debt cap applies to periods of account beginning on or after 1 January 2010. Amendments to the rules were announced in the 22 June 2010 Emergency Budget following consultation with businesses and advisers about their practical application. The rules are complex and beyond this scope of this introductory chapter so we provide no further information here, but if you are interested, the HMRC website has useful details on these rules with further discussion in the June 2010 Budget document.

Controlled foreign companies

We saw earlier that differences in the tax situation result from the choice of earning foreign profits through a branch office as compared to a separately incorporated subsidiary. Having a subsidiary company, where the UK parent company has a controlling interest, presents opportunities for at least the deferral of some tax, and maybe some tax savings. Remember that the profits of a subsidiary will not attract UK corporation tax until such time as they are remitted to the UK. If that overseas subsidiary is also located in a country where the tax rate is low, considerable overall tax savings can be made, so long as the profits are left in the hands of the overseas subsidiary.

When taken to extremes, this is viewed by the UK Government as being unacceptable tax avoidance, and so provisions are contained in the UK legislation to make deferring tax by leaving profits in the hands of some foreign companies less attractive. These rules specifically refer to what are called *Controlled Foreign Companies* (or CFCs). If the controlled foreign company rules are applied, then HMRC has the power to apportion the profits of the CFC between its corporate shareholders and charge those profits to corporation tax in the UK even though they have not yet been actually remitted to the UK as either dividends or in another form.

A CFC is a company which is:

- resident overseas but is controlled by UK residents, and
- is subject to taxation in its country of residence where the tax rate applicable is less than 75% of the corresponding UK tax rate.

In deciding whether or not an overseas company is controlled by UK residents, the rules look at shareholdings, voting power and other rights which give control. The foreign company does not need to be controlled by just one UK resident, a combination of UK residents can cause the foreign company to be classified as a CFC.

You will find a worked example of these control rules on the website.

Even where the control test is met, there are some exceptions to the CFC rules. In the following situations, the foreign company will not be treated as a CFC:

- Where the profits of the CFC for the accounting period are not more than £50,000;

- Where the CFC is engaged in an exempt activity, for example, a business which is effectively managed in the country where the foreign company is resident that does not consist of investment or delivery of goods to or from the UK; or
- HMRC is of the view that the main reason for setting up the foreign company was not to reduce the overall UK tax liability.

Prior to 1 July 2009, it was possible for a company to be excluded from the CFC rules if it met the acceptable distribution policy test. To meet this test the CFC had to distribute 90% of its profits as a dividend within 18 months of the end of its accounting period. This exemption no longer applies.

Where a company has been identified as being a CFC through the control test, and does not fall within any of the exceptions listed above, then the rules potentially apply to attribute a proportion of the CFC's profits to the UK companies that control it. Only those companies with at least a 25% interest in the CFC will have profits attributed to it in this way. Those with smaller shareholdings will still be able to benefit from deferment of UK tax until these profits are remitted to the UK.

Activity

The voting shares of Forco, a company resident in a country with a corporation tax rate of 10%, are owned by three businesses, 12% by Alto, 37% by Baritone and 42% by Contralto (the remaining shares are held by unrelated individuals). Alto, Baritone and Contralto are UK resident companies. For the year ended 30 September Forco has profits of £200,000 on which tax of £20,000 has been paid in its country of residence. If Forco is deemed to be a controlled foreign company, how will the corporation tax positions of Alto, Baritone and Contralto be affected?

Feedback

Alto will not be subject to an apportionment of Forco's profits since it does not have at least a 25% interest.

Baritone will be assessed on 37% of Forco's profit i.e. £74,000, and will be entitled to double tax relief for a portion of the tax paid by Forco i.e. £7,400.

Contralto will be assessed on 42% of Forco's profit i.e. £84,000 and will be entitled to double tax relief for a portion of the tax paid by Forco i.e. £8,400.

The CFC provisions are very complicated and here we have provided only a very brief overview of their operation. There are also further changes expected in 2010 as a result of continued consultation in relation to the taxation of foreign profits in the UK.

Under self assessment, UK companies are required to calculate their own liability to tax on the profits of CFC's. This is an onerous requirement, especially given the need to compute the CFC's profits as if they had been liable to UK corporation tax. Given, however, that the provisions only apply to UK companies with at least a 25% interest in the CFC, and then only if one of the exemption provisions does not apply, the rules do not have wide application.

Information access and exchange

A further anti-avoidance tool HMRC regularly uses is information access rights and information exchange agreements. HMRC has the power to obtain information from taxpayers to determine the extent to which they are telling the truth about their taxable activity overseas. The information can be supplemented by information from those with whom the UK has a tax treaty or tax information exchange agreement. Although such agreements do not exist with all countries, these agreements do cover a large number of the major trading countries where individuals or companies are likely to invest their wealth.

Summary

In this chapter you have read an introduction to how the UK taxation system works in an international setting. The application of the UK income and corporation tax rules depends on whether the taxpayer concerned is a resident of the UK for tax purposes. In some cases, taxpayers may be subject to tax in more than one country on the same income or profits. When this happens, the UK tax laws provide for a credit to be allowed for the foreign tax paid in order to mitigate, if not eliminate the double taxation.

For companies setting up an overseas business, there are different tax consequences depending on whether it is established as a branch operation or a subsidiary company.

The existence of countries with considerably lower tax rates than the UK allows scope for tax planning, and HMRC is concerned about the boundary between tax planning and unacceptable tax avoidance this opportunity offers. In this chapter we have considered two examples of special rules that allow HMRC to combat international tax avoidance, the transfer pricing rules and the controlled foreign company rules.

Project areas

This area of tax study is complex, but provides plenty of opportunity for projects. You may wish to explore some of the issues we have touched on in more depth, for example, the decision whether to adopt a branch or subsidiary structure for a new foreign operation.

The UK offers a tax credit for foreign taxes paid (under treaty agreements or unilaterally) as we have discussed. However, other countries offer double tax relief in other ways. You might like to explore how these other methods work and compare the use of these different methods to the use of credits.

The UK Government is not the only one to tackle issues like transfer pricing and controlled foreign corporations, you could compare the approaches taken by governments in other jurisdictions to the question of international tax avoidance.

You might also like to review the work of the OECD in the area of co-ordinating international activity in this area.

Questions

Question 1   Which of the following individuals will be considered to be resident or ordinarily resident in the UK for 2009/10?

(a) William was born in Texas and lived in the USA until he moved to the UK on 12 June, 2010 where he remained until 18 April, 2011 when he moved to Canada.

(b) Patrick was born in New Zealand and moved to the UK in 1996. He went to Australia on 12 June, 2010 and returned to the UK, where he intends to live permanently, on 18 April, 2011.

(c) John was born in the UK and lived in the UK until 10 January, 2010 when he moved to Germany. He returned to live permanently in the UK on 18 April 2011.

Question 2   Petra is both resident and ordinarily resident of the UK, but is non-domiciled and has claimed to be taxed on a remittance basis. In the year ended 5 April 2011, she had income from the following sources:

i.   Bank interest paid on an account held in Jersey and not remitted to the UK

ii.   Salary paid by a UK employer for work performed in the UK, but paid directly into an Australian bank account.

Required:
Explain how Petra's income will be taxed in the UK

Question 3   (based on CIMA November 2000)

The UK taxing statutes contain important anti-avoidance provisions relating to Controlled Foreign Companies (CFCs).

Required:
(a) State the conditions which must be satisfied for a company to be deemed a CFC
(b) State the circumstances where a company satisfying the above conditions would be exempt from the CFC provisions.
(c) State the UK taxation consequence when a company is a CFC.

(Note: answer available via lecturer's website)

Further reading and examples

Lymer, A. & Hasseldine, J. (2002), *The International Tax System*, Springer: Boston;

James, S. & Nobes, C. (2010), *The Economics of Taxation (10th edition 2010/11)*, Fiscal Publications: Birmingham; or

Miller, A. & Oats, L. (2009), *Principles of International Taxation (2nd edition)*, Tottel: Haywards Heath, UK.

– all three books provide further explanation of international taxation issues.

Appendix A: Tables of tax rates and allowances

The current rates and allowances for income tax, corporation tax, capital gains tax, inheritance tax and other taxes are set out below.

Personal Income Tax Rates

	2010/11 £	2009/10 £	Increase £
Income tax allowances			
Personal allowance	6,475	6,475	nil
Personal allowance – age 65–74	9,490	9,490	nil
Personal allowance – age 75 and over	9,640	9,640	nil
Income limit: personal allowances	100,000	n/a	
Married couple's allowance – age 75 or more	6,965	6,965	nil
Married couple's allowance – minimum amount	2,670	2,670	nil
Income limit for age-related allowances	22,900	22,900	nil
Blind person's allowance	1,890	1,890	nil
Capital gains tax annual exempt amount			
Individuals, etc.	10,100	10,100	nil
Capital gains tax standard rate	18%	18%	
Capital gains tax higher rate	28%	n/a	
Entrepreneurs' Relief to 22/6/10	2 million	1 million	1 million
Entrepreneurs' Relief > 22/6/10	5 million	1 million	4 million
Inheritance tax threshold (each if couple/partner)	325,000	325,000	nil
Inheritance tax rate	40%	40%	0
Pension scheme allowances			
Annual allowance	255,000	245,000	10,000
Lifetime allowance	1,800,000	1,750,000	50,000

Taxable bands 2010/11

	Non-savings	Savings	Dividends
£0 – £2,440	–*	10%*	–*
£0 (or £2,441) – £37,400	20%	20%	10%
£37,400 – £150,000	40%	40%	32.5%
Over £150,000	50%	50%	42.5%

*10% rate on savings only available up to £2,440 of taxable income if non-savings income does not exceed this sum

National Insurance Contributions

Item	2010/11	2009/10
Class 1:		
Lower Earnings Limit (per week)	£97	£95
Upper Earnings Limit		
(per week – employees only)	£844	£844
Upper Accrual Point	£770	770
Primary (employees) Threshold (per week)	£110	£110
Secondary (employers) Threshold (per week)	£110	£110
Employee's contributions	11%	11%
(£110–£844pw +1% over £844)		
Employee's Contracted-out Rebate	1.6%	1.6%
(£110–£770pw)		
Employer's Contribution Rates	12.8%	12.8%
(all earnings over £110pw)		
Employer's Contracted-out Rebate		
Salary Related (£110–£770pw)	3.7%	3.7%
Money Purchase (£110–£770pw)	1.4%	1.4%
Class 1A and 1B	12.8%	12.8%
Class 2: Self employed Contribution (per week)	£2.40	£2.40
Small Earnings Exception (per annum)	£5,075	£5,075
Class 3: (voluntary) Contribution (per week)	£12.05	£12.05
Class 4: Contributions – Upper Profits Limit	£43,875	£43,875
Contributions – Lower Profits Limit	£5,715	£5,715
Contribution Rate	8.0%	8.0%
(£5,715 – £43,875 pa then 1% over £43,875 pa)		

Tax Credits:

Working Tax Credit

	£ per year
Basic element	1,920.00
Second adult and lone parent element	1,890.00
30 hour element	790.00
Disability element	2,570.00
Severe disability element	1,095.00
50+ return to work payment (16–29 hours)	1,320.00
(30+ hours)	1,965.00

	£ per week
Childcare element:	
Maximum eligible cost for 2 or more children	300.00
Maximum eligible cost for 1 child	175.00
Max. percent of eligible costs covered	80%

Child Tax Credit

	£ per year/per week
Family element	545.00/10.48
Family element, baby addition (first year only)	545.00/10.48
Child element (each child)	2,300.00/44.23
Disabled child element	2,715.00/52.21
Severe disabled child element	1,095.00/21.05

Tapering

	£
Income thresholds & withdrawal rates	
First income threshold	6,420.00
First withdrawal rate	39%
Second income threshold	50,000.00
Second withdrawal rate	6.67%
First threshold for child tax credit	16,190.00
entitlement only (where no WTC claimed)	
Income disregard	25,000.00

Pension Credit

	£
Standard Minimum income guarantee credit: (per week)	
Single	132.60
Couple	202.40
Capital:	
Amount disregard	10,000.00
Amount disregard – care homes	10,000.00
Deemed income:	
£1 per week for every £500 (or part thereof) in excess of these amounts	

Car and Fuel Benefits in kind

CO$_2$ g/km	Taxable % Petrol	Diesel	CO$_2$ g/km	Taxable % Petrol	Diesel	CO$_2$ g/km	Taxable % Petrol	Diesel
120	10	13	160	21	24	200	29	32
125	15	18	165	22	25	205	30	33
130	15	28	170	23	26	210	31	34
135	16	19	175	24	27	215	32	35
140	17	20	180	25	28	220	33	35
145	18	21	185	26	29	225	34	35
150	19	22	190	27	30	230	35	35
155	20	23	195	28	31	235	35	35

Round down to find the correct percentage.
For QUALECs where the CO$_2$ level is exactly 120g/km or lower = 10%
(petrol) and 13% (diesel).

Authorised private car mileage rates

Business Miles	Allowance rate per mile
0 – 10,000	40p
10,000+	25p

Excess payments over these rates are taxable. Shortfalls can be claimed as tax
relief by the employee.

Corporation tax 2010/11

Band	Rate	Marginal rate	Marginal relief fraction
0 – 300,000*	21%**		
300,000 – 1,500,000*	21% – 28%	29.75%	7/400
1,500,000+*	28%		

*reduced for associated companies and/or for short accounting periods

Marginal relief formula: Fraction $\times$ (M – P) $\times$ I $\div$ P

VAT

	after 1 April 2009	after 1 April 2009
Standard Rate	17.5%*	17.5%
Annual Registration Limit	£70,000	£68,000
De-registration Limit	£68,000	£66,000
VAT Fraction- standard rate	7/47*	7/47
Cash Accounting Scheme		
– max. turnover to join	£1,350,000	£1,350,000
Annual Accounting Scheme		
– max. turnover to join	£1,350,000	£1,350,000
Optional Flat Rate Scheme		
– max. taxable turnover (ex VAT)	£150,000	£150,000

*increases to 20% on 4 Jan 2011 (VAT fraction returns to 1/6)

Landfill Tax & Aggregates Levy

	£ (2009/10)
Standard rate (per tonne)	48.00 (40.00)
Lower rate (inactive waste per tonne)	2.50 (2.50)
Aggregates levy (per tonne)	2.00 (2.00)

HMRC Interest Rates

(from 06/4/10)	Late Payment (%)	Repayment (%)
Income tax, NIC, CGT, SDRT	3.00	0
Corporation tax (CTSA)	3.00	0
Inheritance tax	3.00	0
(These rates change occasionally – see the HMRC website for details)		
Average Official rate for 2010/11	4.00% (provisional)	

Capital gains tax (Corporations only)

Retail prices index (January 1987 = 100.0)

	Jan	Feb	Mar	Apr	May	Jun	Jul	Aug	Sep	Oct	Nov	Dec
1982	–	–	79.44	81.04	81.62	81.85	81.90	81.90	81.85	82.26	82.66	82.51
1983	82.61	82.97	83.12	84.28	84.64	84.84	85.30	85.68	86.06	86.36	86.67	86.89
1984	86.84	87.20	87.48	88.64	88.97	89.20	89.10	89.94	90.11	90.67	90.95	90.87
1985	91.20	91.94	92.80	94.78	95.21	95.41	95.23	95.49	95.44	95.59	95.92	96.05
1986	96.25	96.60	96.73	97.67	97.85	97.79	97.52	97.82	98.30	98.45	99.29	99.62
1987	100.0	100.4	100.6	101.8	101.9	101.9	101.8	102.1	102.4	102.9	103.4	103.3
1988	103.3	103.7	104.1	105.8	106.2	106.6	106.7	107.9	108.4	109.5	110.0	110.3
1989	111.0	111.8	112.3	114.3	115.0	115.4	115.5	115.8	116.6	117.5	118.5	118.8
1990	119.5	120.2	121.4	125.1	126.2	126.7	126.8	128.1	129.3	130.3	130.0	129.9
1991	130.2	130.9	131.4	133.1	133.5	134.1	133.8	134.1	134.6	135.1	135.6	135.7
1992	135.6	136.3	136.7	138.8	139.3	139.3	138.8	138.9	139.4	139.9	139.7	139.2
1993	137.9	138.8	139.3	140.6	141.1	141.0	140.7	141.3	141.9	141.8	141.6	141.9
1994	141.3	142.1	142.5	144.2	144.7	144.7	144.0	144.7	145.0	145.2	145.3	146.0
1995	146.0	146.9	147.5	149.0	149.6	149.8	149.1	149.9	150.6	149.8	149.8	150.7
1996	150.2	150.9	151.5	152.6	152.9	153.0	152.4	153.1	153.8	153.8	153.9	154.4
1997	154.4	155.0	155.4	156.3	156.9	157.5	157.5	158.5	159.3	159.5	159.6	160.0
1998	159.5	160.3	160.8	**162.6**	163.5	163.4	163.0	163.7	164.4	164.5	164.4	164.4
1999	163.4	163.7	164.1	165.2	165.5	165.6	165.1	165.5	166.2	166.5	166.7	167.3
2000	166.6	167.5	168.4	170.1	170.7	171.1	170.5	170.5	171.7	171.6	172.1	172.2
2001	171.1	172.0	172.2	173.1	174.2	174.4	173.3	174.0	174.6	174.3	173.6	173.4
2002	173.3	173.8	174.5	175.7	176.2	176.2	175.9	176.4	177.6	177.9	178.2	178.5
2003	178.4	179.3	179.9	181.2	181.5	181.3	181.3	181.6	182.5	182.6	182.7	183.5
2004	183.1	183.8	184.6	185.7	186.5	186.8	186.8	187.4	188.1	188.6	189.0	189.9
2005	188.9	189.6	190.5	191.6	192.0	192.2	192.2	192.6	193.1	193.3	193.6	194.1
2006	193.4	194.2	195.0	196.5	197.7	198.5	198.5	199.2	200.1	200.4	201.1	202.7
2007	201.6	203.1	204.4	205.4	206.2	207.3	206.1	207.3	208.0	208.9	209.7	210.9
2008	209.8	211.4	212.1	214.0	215.1	216.8	216.5	217.2	218.4	217.7	216.0	212.9
2009	210.1	211.4	211.3	211.5	212.8	213.4	213.4	214.4	215.3	216.0	216.6	218.0
2010	217.9	219.2	220.7	222.8	223.6							

Personal Benefit Rates

Item	2010/11 £	2009/10 £
Basic Retirement Pension (per week):		
– Single Person (based on own NIC)	97.65	95.25
– Single Person (based on spouse's NIC)	58.50	57.05
– Non-contributory (over 80 pension)	58.50	57.05
Child Benefit (per week):		
– First Eligible Child	20.30	20.00
– Each Extra Child	13.40	13.20
– Guardian allowance	14.30	14.10
Statutory Sick Pay:		
normally receive £97 per week or more	79.15	79.15
Statutory Maternity Pay		
Average Weekly Earnings of £97 or over		
– Higher Weekly Rate (first 6 weeks)	90% of weekly earnings	
– Standard Rate (remaining 33 weeks)	124.88	123.06
Statutory Paternity/Adoption Pay	124.88	123.06
Job Seekers Allowance (income based):		
– Single Person (over 25)	65.45	64.30
– Married Couple (both over 18)	102.75	100.95
National Minimum Wage:		
aged 22 and over	From October 2010 – £5.93 per hour	
	From October 2009 – £5.80 per hour	
Youth rate		
– ages 18 to 21	From October 2010 – £4.83 per hour	
– ages 16 to 17	From October 2010 – £3.64 per hour	
Employment & Support Allowance (replaced Incapacity Benefit Oct 08)		
Assessment phase (first 13 weeks):		
– under 25	51.85	50.95
– 25 and over	65.45	64.30
Main phase		
– Work related Activity Group	up to 91.40	up to 89.80
– Support Group	up to 96.85	up to 95.15

These rates are selected from a complex list of benefits available based on personal circumstances and therefore are provided in basic outline only. For a full list of work and pensions related benefits see the Direct.gov website at http://www.direct.gov.uk/en/MoneyTaxAndBenefits/index.htm

Duty rates

	Duty	Change in tax from 24/3/2010 on typical item	Typical Item
Cigarettes	24% of retail price + £119.03 per thousand	7p	packet of 20
Cigars	£180.28/kg	3p	packet of 5
Hand rolling tobacco	£129.59/kg	7p	25g
Beer	17.32p/litre	1p	pint
Wine			
15%–22%abv	£2.9997/litre	4p	75cl bottle
5.5%–15%abv	£2.2500/litre		
4%–5.5%abv	95.33p/litre		
1.2%–4%abv	69.32p/litre		
Sparkling wine			
5.5%–8.5%abv	£2.1783/litre	5p	75cl bottle
8.5%–15%abv	£2.8820/litre		
Cider/Perry			
Still			
1.2%–7.5%abv	36.01p/litre	1p	litre
7.5%–8.5%abv	54.04p/litre		
Sparkling			
1.2%–5.5%abv	33.46p/litre	5p	75cl bottle
5.5%–8.5%abv	£2.17.83/litre		
Spirits	£23.80/litre of pure alcohol	13p	70cl bottle

Fuel Duties (from 1 Apr. 2010)*:

Sulphur free petrol/diesel (SFP)	57.19p/litre
Ultra-low sulphur petrol/diesel (ULSP)	57.19p/litre
Bio-diesel & bioethanol	57.19p/litre
LPG	27.67p/kg
Other Natural gas	22.16p/kg
Aviation gasoline	37.12p/litre

*rates are due to rise again on 1 Oct. 10 and again 1 Jan. 11

B Appendix B

This appendix reviews recent UK budgets, and their associated Finance Bills and Acts to provide a summary of recent changes to the UK tax system.

The 2010 Budgets and 2010 Finance Acts

2010 was an unusual year in which there were two budgets and potentially three Finance Acts as a result of the change of government. The first Budget and Finance Act was fairly uncontroversial, in the run-up to the election. Key changes include the increase of the annual investment allowance for capital allowances from £50,000 to £100,000 and an increase in the lifetime limit for CGT entrepreneurs' relief from £1m to £2m. Most tax bands and thresholds were frozen, although the VAT registration threshold was increased to £70,000 from £68,000.

On 22 June 2010, the new Conservative/Liberal Democrat coalition government brought down a second budget for the year, dubbed an 'emergency budget'. This contained much more controversial measures to tackle the deficit including the following:

- Reduction in tax credit eligibility from April 2011 and removal of a number of elements of the tax credits system;
- Introduction of a new levy on banks based on their balance sheets from 1 January 2011, to encourage them to be more risk averse;
- Changes to corporation tax rates in an attempt to make the UK more competitive internationally, although the rates remain unchanged for 2010/11. The main rate of corporation tax will be reduced to 27% and the small profits rate to 20% from 1 April 2011 with further cuts foreshadowed.
- The rate of writing down allowance for capital allowances will reduce from 20% to 18% for main pool items and from 10% to 8% for special rate pool items, but not until 2012.

This change will be accompanied by a reduction in AIA down to £25,000.

- Planned changes to the furnished holiday letting rules have been put on-hold and will now be subject to further consultation.
- For capital gains tax, a new 28% rate was introduced for higher and additional rate taxpayers, reinstating the link between capital gains tax rates and income tax rates. The entrepreneurs' relief limit was increased to £5m. Both of these changes take effect from 23 June 2010.
- VAT will increase from 4 January 2011 from its current rate of 17.5% to 20%.

The Finance Bill 2010 containing draft legislation for these proposals was published on 1 July 2010.

On 12 July 2010, the Government published draft legislation that contains technical tax measures inherited from the previous Government that are to be legislated in Finance Bill (No 2) 2010, to be introduced to Parliament in the autumn. The consultation process will close on 2 September 2010.

Previous Budgets: changes to the UK's tax system

2009 Budget and Finance Act

The 2009 Budget did not introduce any radical changes, although it was the latest budget on record to that point.

Several modest measures were introduced to ease the impact of the recession on business, including a new loss carry back provision and reintroduction of 40% first year allowances for plant and machinery. A new regime for capital allowances for cars, now based on CO_2 emissions, completed the Government's review of the treatment of cars under the tax system.

The new dividend exemption system for taxing foreign profits of companies was announced and took effect from July 2009

The new 45% personal tax rate announced in the November 2008 Pre Budget Report was lifted to 50% effective from April 2010. For corporation tax, the planned increase of the small companies' rate to 22% was deferred.

2008 Budget and Finance Act

The 2008 Budget contained a number of controversial measures. The abolition of the 10% starting rate of income tax for non-savings caused an outcry, despite being announced in the 2007 Budget. Another controversial issue was the new additional charge of £30,000 for non-domiciles who wish to continue to use the remittance basis for their UK tax liabilities.

Other key changes introduced by the 2008 Budget included the simplification of capital allowances and of capital gains tax. For capital allowances, in addition to the reforms previously announced in 2007 (for example, the introduction of the new Annual Investment Allowance), Finance Act 2008 provided for the write off of small pools of expenditure of £1,000 or less.

Radical overhaul this year of capital gains tax for individuals (although not for companies) mean that taper relief and indexation were abolished and capital gains were taxed at a flat rate of 18%, from April 2008. Following concerns that this would adversely affect those whose retirement savings are tied up in businesses, a new Entrepreneurs' Relief has been introduced to reduce the capital gains tax rate to 10% where taxpayers dispose of all or part of their business.

For corporation tax, the changes announced in 2007 came into effect so that the small companies' rate increased to 21% and the full rate of corporation tax fell to 28%, a lower rate than most of the UK's competitors.

2007 Budget and Finance Act

The 2007 Budget was interesting, not so much for the changes coming into effect for 2007/08, but because of the changes it announced that would come into effect in 2008/09, some of which were quite controversial. Thresholds for income tax and national insurance and the VAT registration threshold were increased in line with inflation as was the capital gains tax annual amount. The budget in this year was a continuation of the Government's long term aim to reform the tax and benefits system. A number of specific measures were introduced to make sure that all individuals and companies pay their fair share of tax, including strengthening the disclosure of tax avoidance rules and some new targeted anti avoidance measures (TAARs). Finance Act 2007 also introduced rules to deal with Managed Service Companies, along the lines of the IR35 rules.

2006 Budget and Finance Act

The 2006 Budget was relatively uneventful from a tax point of view, although the pattern of announcing most changes in the pre Budget Report continued. Once again, rates for income tax and national insurance contributions were unchanged but rate bands increased in line with inflation. Somewhat controversially, the starting rate band for corporation tax was removed, finalising the Government's U-turn in respect of tax rate incentives for micro companies. No key changes were made to other taxes, simply rate band changes as usual.

2005 Budget and Finance Acts

The 2005 Budget was delivered on 16 March, 2005. Income tax and national insurance contribution rates were unchanged from the previous year, although inflation adjustments were made to the rate bands. Corporation tax remained unchanged from 2004 and VAT registration and deregistration thresholds were increased modestly as usual. A reasonably large increase was made to the zero rate band for stamp duty land tax, from £60,000 to £120,000 to remove a considerable number of cheaper houses from the burden of stamp duty.

As a result of the general election, two Finance Acts were introduced, the Finance Act (2005) and Finance Act (No 2) 2005.

Summary of main reforms, 1979–2004

Personal income taxes	Basic rate 33% down to 22%
	Top rate 98% (unearned income), 83% (earnings) down to 40% Lower rate 25% down to 10%
	Independent taxation introduced
	Married couple's allowance abolished, Children's Tax Credit introduced
	Mortgage interest tax relief abolished Life assurance premium relief abolished PEP, TESSA and ISA introduced Capital gains tax at income tax rates
	Car benefits in kind switched to a CO_2 emissions base rather than mileage.
	Childrens' tax credit introduced
National Insurance	Rate for employee increased from 6.5% to 11%
	Rate for employer reduced from 13.5% to 12.8%
	Ceiling abolished for employers
	Cuts for low earners
	Alignment of floor with income tax allowance
	Imposition of NI on benefits in kind

	1% increase in rates and removal of the zero rate beyond the UEL – 1% applies without limit.
VAT	Standard rate increased from 8% to 17.5% Higher rate of 12.5% abolished
	Reduced rate introduced on domestic fuel and other selected items
	Thresholds for various schemes (e.g. cash accounting) increased.
	Flat rate scheme introduced for small business.
Excises	Large real rise in duties on road fuels
	Smaller increase in tobacco duties
	Slight real decrease in duties on beer, larger decline for spirits
	Small increase in real duties on wine
Corporate income taxes	Rate cut from 52% to 30%
	General 100% first-year allowance replaced by 25% writing- down allowance
	Reintroduction of FYA for small businesses on selected other capital expenditure
	100% FYA for energy saving plant and machinery.
	R&D credit introduced for SMEs, then extended to large business and the rate of credit increased.
	Advance corporation tax and refundable dividend tax credit abolished
Local tax	Domestic rates replaced by council tax (via poll tax)
	Locally varying non-domestic rates abolished, replaced by national non-domestic rates

(Source: originally based on 'A Survey of the UK Tax System',
IFS Briefing Notes No 9 by L. Chennells, A.Dilnot and N. Roback)

G Glossary

Ability to pay
> A system of taxation under which tax is levied on a taxpayer according to his economic ability to pay tax, or 'taxable capacity'. *See also* Benefit principle.

Accounting period
> The interval for which corporation tax is assessed and charged on the profits arising during the interval.

Accruals basis
> Under the accruals basis profits for an accounting period equal revenue earned in the period less expenses incurred in earning that revenue. This can be contrasted with a cash receipts basis which looks at the amount of cash received and paid during a period.

Accumulation and maintenance trust
> A trust in which income is accumulated for minor children until they reach a specified age.

Ad valorem
> varying according to value or price

Additional personal allowance (APA)
> An allowance that was given to any single person with a child living with them (not available from 6 April 2000).

Additional voluntary contributions
> Payments made by an employee to increase retirement benefits due from the approved pension scheme run by his or her employer.

Advance corporation tax
> A payment which was made to the Inland Revenue whenever a UK company paid a dividend (no longer part of the UK tax system).

AESP
> All employee share-ownership plans that enable share ownership in their own companies to employees with tax advantages.

Age allowance
> An allowance available to individuals over 65 years of age instead of the ordinary personal allowance.

Agricultural buildings allowance
> An allowance, for income tax and corporation tax purposes, available for capital expenditure on farmhouses, farm buildings cottages, fences, drainage and similar works.

Agricultural property relief
> Relief from inheritance tax available on the agricultural value of agricultural property in the UK, the Channel Islands or the Isle of Man.

Annual accounting scheme

A method of accounting for VAT which only requires the registered trader to complete one VAT return each year.

Annual exemption

The amount of capital gains that an individual may make each year that is not subjected to capital gains tax. Also the amount which an individual may transfer each year which is not subjected to inheritance tax.

Annual Investment Allowances

A special capital allowance that effectively relieves 100% of the first £50,000 of qualifying expenditure per annum.

Annuity

An amount of money paid annually or at other regular intervals.

Arising basis

Income which is taxed as it arises regardless of whether or when it is remitted to the UK.

Arms length price

A price that would be struck between two unrelated parties, i.e. an open market price. Used in income and corporation tax where transactions are made between related individuals or companies.

Associated companies

Companies which are under common control or where one company controls the other. Used in corporation tax when deciding which rate of tax is applicable.

Associated disposal

One of a series of linked disposals of related assets to connected persons for capital gains tax purposes.

Associated operations

Two or more operations which are related are deemed to take place at the time of the last of the operations for inheritance tax purposes.

Average rate of tax

Equal to the total tax paid in the tax period, usually one year, divided by the value of the tax base.

Avoidance

The legal manipulation of a taxpayer's affairs in order to reduce the taxpayer's tax liability, although often against the sprit of the legislation.

Bad debt relief

Relief for VAT paid on a taxable supply made by a registered trader who has subsequently written off all or part of the debt in his accounts.

Badges of trade

The six elements which the Royal Commission identified as helping to determine whether or not trading is taking place for income tax and corporation tax purposes.

Balancing allowances and charges

For capital allowance purposes, relief for capital expenditure, or the claw back of relief already given, given in the year in which an asset is disposed of or the business ceases to trade.

Basic rate of tax

The main rate at which income and capital gains taxes are levied (see Rates and Allowances for current rate).

Basis period

The time period that determines which income or profits are taxed in a particular tax year.

Beneficial loan

A loan given to an employee who derived the benefit of the loan because of their employment.

Beneficiary

Individual who may derive benefit from a trust.

Benefit principle

In contrast to the ability to pay principle, under the benefit principle tax is raised by reference to the amount of benefit a taxpayer is deemed to receive from the public sector. *See also* Ability to pay.

Benefits in kind

A benefit received by an employee or members of his or her family or household due to their employment.

Blind person's allowance

An allowance given to taxpayers that are registered blind.

Bonus issue

An issue of additional shares in proportion to existing holdings to shareholders.

Budget

An annual statement by the Chancellor of the Exchequer setting out proposals for taxation and government expenditure in the following tax year.

Burden of tax

The amount by which a taxpayer's income or wealth is reduced because of taxation.

Business property relief

Relief from inheritance tax on transfers of relevant business property.

Capital allowances

Relief from income tax and corporation tax on capital expenditure on eligible assets. Similar to depreciation for accounting purposes.

Capital distribution

A repayment of capital by a company to its shareholders.

Capital gain

The increase in the value of an asset on its disposal by an individual or company.

Capital gains tax

The tax levied on capital gains. The liability to tax only arises when the asset is disposed of.

Capital transfer tax

A tax on the transfer of wealth between individuals. It was imposed in the UK between 1975 and 1986.

Capitalisation of future tax benefits

Future tax benefits are capitalised when the current value of an asset includes an allowance for the increased expected yield from the asset due to future tax benefits.

Cash accounting scheme

A method of accounting for VAT which depends on payments and receipts rather than invoices for identifying tax points.

Cash basis

Income and expenditure recognition basis which allows for inclusion in tax computation when each flow occurs.

Cash voucher

A voucher, stamp or similar document capable of being exchanged for a sum of money.

Cash-flow tax base

Under a cash-flow tax based system, cash flows rather than profits are taxed.

Chargeable asset

All assets are chargeable assets unless they are specifically exempted from capital gains tax.

Chargeable business asset

The whole or part of a business or assets used in a business until it ceases to trade, or shares or securities of a company.

Chargeable lifetime transfer

Under inheritance tax, a transfer of value made by an individual during their lifetime that is not an exempt or potentially exempt transfer. In practice, only transfers into a discretionary trust are chargeable lifetime transfers.

Chargeable transfer

A transfer of value made by an individual who intended to confer a gratuitous benefit that is not an exempt transfer.

Chattel

Tangible movable property, for example furniture.

Child Tax Credit

Tax credit introduced in April 2003 (replacing Children's tax credit). Sums paid based on core family element payment with additional payments based on the number of children in a family unit.

Class 1 national insurance contribution

Payments made by employees, primary contributions, and employers, secondary contributions.

Class 1A national insurance contribution

Payments made by employers when employees are provided with most benefits in kind.

Class 2 national insurance contribution

Flat rate payments made by the self- employed.

Class 3 national insurance contribution

Voluntary payments made to individuals in order to maintain rights to some state benefits.

Class 4 national insurance contribution

Payments made by the self-employed based on a percentage of taxable profits.

Close company

A UK resident company which is under the control of five or fewer participators or of participators who are directors.

Close investment-holding company

A close company which is a non-trading company.

Collector of taxes

Civil servants appointed by the former Board of Inland Revenue to collect the tax which is assessed to be payable.

Commissioners for Her Majesty's Revenue and Customs

Civil servants appointed by the Crown who are responsible for collecting and accounting for, and otherwise managing, the UK's Revenue and Customs laws and regulations. They appoint all the officers for Revenue and Customs who run HMRC on a day to day basis. Established by the Commissioners for Revenue and Customs Act 2005. They are responsible for all the tasks previously performed by the Commissioners of Inland Revenue and Commissioners of Customs and Excise.

Compliance costs

Costs which are incurred by taxpayers in order to enable them to comply with a specific tax or more generally with the tax system.

Components of income

The name given to the various sources of incomes that need to be aggregated together at step 1 of a personal tax computation – introduced by ITA 2007.

Composite supply

A taxable supply for VAT purposes made up of a mix of standard rated, zero rated or exempt supplies where it is not possible to apportion the value of the supply to each of the rates. One rate is applied to the whole of the supply.

Comprehensive income tax

A tax which is levied on an individual's comprehensive income. An individual's comprehensive income is the amount which an individual could consume without diminishing the value of their wealth. *See also* Economic income.

Connected persons

Persons who are defined as having a special relationship for tax purposes and transactions between them are sometimes accorded special treatment (see Chapter 8: *Gross proceeds on disposal* for list of connected persons).

Consortium

A group of companies in which one company is at least 75% owned by UK resident companies who are called members of the consortium.

Consortium relief

Allows trading losses to be surrendered from a member of a consortium to a consortium held company and vice versa for corporation tax purposes.

Consumption taxes

Also called expenditure taxes, a consumption tax taxes the resources which an individual has consumed during a set period of time.

Contracting out

When employees leave the additional state pension and join a contracted out occupational pension or stakeholder pension instead, They eventually receive payments from the scheme rather than the State, and pay reduced national insurance contributions as a result..

Corporation tax

The tax that is levied on the profits of companies and unincorporated associations such as clubs and political associations but not partnerships.

Corrective taxes

A tax which is intended to affect the behaviour of taxpayers. Tax relief on pension contributions is intended to encourage individuals to provide for a private pension.

Crowding out

This is the effect which may occur when public expenditure increases and causes a reduction in size of the private sector, thus reducing the tax base.

Cum div

A quoted security which carries the right to an imminent dividend.

Cum int

A quoted security which carries the right to an imminent interest payment.

De minimis limit

Various taxes use a minimum value rule below which different rules to usual often apply. For example, expenditure on long life assets for single companies below £100,000 will not be subject to a writing down allowance of only 10%. They continue to receive allowances at 20%.

De-pooling

For capital allowance purposes, an election made by taxpayers for nominated items of plant and machinery with a short life to be maintained outside the pool so that balancing allowances may be claimed on their disposal.

Deed of covenant

A promise to pay over a number of years relating to the old system of relief for charitable payments.

Depreciating asset

For capital allowances purposes, an asset which is, or within the next ten years will become, a wasting asset. Wasting assets have a useful life of 50 years or less thus a depreciating asset has a useful life of less than 60 years.

Deregistration

The process by which a registered trader voluntarily or otherwise ceases to be registered for VAT.

Diminution in value

The loss in value of an item, for example, of the donor's estate when a transfer of value for inheritance tax purposes occurs.

Direct tax

A tax which is levied on the taxpayer who is intended to bear the final burden of paying it. Examples include income tax and employee national insurance contributions.

Disabled person's tax credit

Benefit paid to person with illness or disability.

Discovery assessment

An assessment made by HMRC based on evidence they discover after a self-assessment return became final.

Discretionary trust

A trust in which no beneficiary has an absolute right to the income. The income is distributed at the discretion of the trustee.

Disincentive effect of taxation

Where a transaction, such as employment, is subject to tax there is a gap between the selling price and the purchase price which is equal to the tax levied. This gap may act as a disincentive to the transaction. For example an employee may be unwilling to undertake overtime at the rate offered if he is subject to a high marginal rate of tax.

Dispensation

Usually refers to an agreement between an employer and HMRC over expense reimbursements that results in them not needing to be separately disclosed to HMRC by both employer and employee.

Divisional registration

Registration by a company so that each division is registered separately for VAT purposes.

Domicile

The place that an individual thinks of as home. He or she may not live in the place of domicile but is likely to retain some links with it.

Duality test

When expenditure has both a business and a private purpose the expenditure is likely to fail the 'wholly and exclusively' test and be disallowable for tax purposes because of a duality of purpose.

Earnings basis

Income and expenditure recognition basis which allows for inclusion in tax computation on normal accounting accrual and realisation concepts.

Earnings cap

The upper limit on the earnings on which an approved pension scheme can be based.

Economic efficiency

A tax is economically efficient if it does not distort the economic decisions which are made by individuals or companies *See also* Fiscal Neutrality.

Economic income

The maximum value which an individual can consume during a period and still expect to be as well off at the end of the period as at the beginning. *See also* Comprehensive income tax.

Economic rent

The amount that a factor of production, such as land, earns over and above what could be earned if it was put to its next best use.

Effective incidence of tax

The effective incidence of tax falls on those individuals whose wealth is reduced by the tax. This may not be the same as the formal incidence of tax.

Eligible interest

Interest paid on loans to purchase annuities, or other qualifying loan interest payments. Used in Income Tax.

Emoluments

Income (not necessarily just money) from an office or employment.

Employee

An individual with a contract of services.

Employee share ownership plan (ESOP)

A trust into which a UK resident company transfers funds for the benefit of some or all of its employees.

Enhanced Capital Allowance Scheme

Government Scheme under which extra capital allowances are given to certain types of environmentally friendly plant and machinery.

Enhancement expenditure

Capital expenditure incurred to enhance the value of an asset.

Enterprise zone

An area designated as benefiting from tax and other incentives in order to encourage investment.

Entrepreneurs Relief

Introduced in 2008 to allow certain capital gains to be taxed at 10% instead of 18%.

Error or mistake relief

Relief for tax overstated due to some error or mistake on the part of the taxpayer.

Estate at death

The value of all the assets owned on the date of death together with any interest held as a joint tenant and capital held by a trust in which the deceased had an interest in possession.

Estate Duty

A wealth tax imposed on the transfer of property on death. In the UK estate duty was abolished in 1975 and replaced with Capital Transfer Tax

Evasion

The illegal manipulation of a taxpayer's affairs so as to reduce the taxpayer's tax liability.

Ex div

A quoted security which does not carry a right to the imminent dividend.

Ex Gratia

Done or given as a favour and not under any compulsion.

Ex int

A quoted security which does not carry a right to the imminent interest payment.

Excepted estate

An estate in respect of which it is not necessary to deliver an account of the property for inheritance tax purposes.

Excess burden of tax

Where a tax is not economically efficient the loss to the economy caused by the distortion is termed the excess burden of tax.

Excluded property

Property which is specifically excluded from an estate at death for the purposes of inheritance tax.

Exempt income

Income which is specifically exempt from income tax.

Exempt supply

A supply of goods or services which is specifically exempt from VAT.

Expenditure tax

A tax on the amount consumed by an individual in a given period of time.

Extra-statutory concession

A series of statements made by HMRC which give concessions to taxpayers over and above those allowed by legislation.

Factor of production

Resources used as inputs into a production activity to produce outputs such as goods and services. Typically include land, labour and capital. Some argue entrepreneurship should also be included in this list.

Fall in value relief

An inheritance tax relief available if assets are disposed of within a given period after death for less than their value at the date of death.

Finance Act

Usually an annual Act of Parliament which contains the fiscal legislation needed to implement the budget.

Financial year

The rate of corporation tax is set for financial years, which runs from 1st April to the following 31st March.

First year allowance

A special capital allowance which may be available in the year in which an asset is acquired and is at a higher rate than the normal writing down allowance..

Fiscal drag

An increase in tax revenues generated when a tax threshold is not increased in line with inflation

Fiscal neutrality

A fiscally neutral tax system does not discriminate between economic choices.

Fixed profit car scheme

Maximum allowance available to an employee for use of their own car on their employer's business. Expense payments in excess of this amount is a taxable benefit in kind. Scheme ceased to exist April 2002 when new approved rate scheme commenced.

Flat tax

An income tax system with only one rate of tax for all income levels and in which an income is taxed once and only once.

Foreign emoluments

The emoluments of a person, not domiciled in the UK, from an office or employment with an employer not resident in the UK.

Franked investment income (FII)

Dividends together with the related tax credit received by a UK company from another UK company which are not treated as group income.

Franked payment (FP)

Dividends together with the related tax credit paid by a UK company to another UK company which are not treated as group income.

Free estate

The value of all the assets owned outright by an individual at his death.

Free-standing additional voluntary contributions

Payments made by an employee who is a member of an occupational pension scheme in order to increase retirement benefits.

Functional test

A test to identify assets which are actively used in the business and thus are eligible for capital allowances as opposed to those which form part of the setting in which the business was carried on.

Furnished holiday lettings

Holiday lettings taxed under Property Income using the regulations for Trading Income. The income is treated as earned income for tax purposes.

Furnished letting

A letting of furnished property which is taxed under Property Income.

General Commissioners

Part time and unpaid individuals who used to hear taxpayers' appeals against the assessments of the inspectors before the introduction of the Tribunal System in April 2009.

Gift relief

A relief from capital gains tax when a qualifying asset is disposed of and both the transferor and transferee elect for the transferor's gain to be reduced to nil.

Gift with reservation

A gift which the donor is not able to benefit from to the exclusion of the donor during the period.

Gratuitous disposition

A disposal of an asset which was intended to confer some benefit to the recipient.

Gross amount of tax

The aggregate of the input tax and output tax included in the VAT return for a period.

Grossing up

The conversion of net receipts to gross receipts such as in tax computations. Use the formula 100/ (100 – tax rate).

Group charge

A charge paid under an election by one member of a 51% group to another without deduction of income tax.

Group

Two or more companies which are related for either corporation tax or capital gains tax purposes for transfer of losses and other payments.

Group income

Dividends paid under an election by one member of a 51% group to another member of the same group.

Group interest

Interest paid under an election by one member of a 51% group to another without deduction of income tax.

Group registration

Registration for VAT purposes by a group of companies under common control.

Group relief

Trading losses incurred by one member of a 75% group can be surrendered to another member of the same group.

Her Majesty's Revenue and Customs (HMRC)

Government department responsible for administering and collection of all UK revenue and customs laws and regulations. The combined responsibilities of the Inland Revenue and HM Customs & Excise were vested in this new body from 2005.

Higher rate tax

Taxable income of an individual in excess of a specified threshold is taxed at the higher rate of tax.

HM Customs and Excise

The Government department, responsible to the Treasury, which once administered VAT and all customs and duties. These tasks are now undertaken by HMRC.

Holdover relief

Relief from capital gains tax which can be claimed when a business asset is replaced by a depreciable asset.

Horizontal equity

A tax system displaying horizontal equity treats similar individuals, companies or situations in similar ways.

Hypothecated taxes

Taxes raised to fund specified benefits or Government spending.

Imputation system

A system under which shareholders in receipt of dividends are given a tax credit for the corporation tax paid by a company.

Incidence of taxation

The formal incidence of tax falls on those who must actually pay the tax while the effective incidence of tax falls on those whose wealth is reduced by the tax. *See also* Indirect taxes; Regressive taxes.

Incidental costs of acquisition

Specified costs incurred when an asset was acquired which are allowed when calculating a chargeable gain for capital gains tax purposes.

Incidental costs of disposal

Specified costs incurred when an asset was disposed of which are allowed when calculating a chargeable gain for capital gains tax purposes.

Incidental expenses

Small payments to employees to cover expenses.

Income tax

A tax levied on all income, earned and unearned, attributed to an individual in a given period.

Income taxed at source

Income paid net of tax, usually at the basic rate of income tax.

Income taxed by assessment

Income paid gross on which income tax is levied for example rental income.

Income

Valuable consideration received in exchange for the provision of goods or services.

Incorporation

Creation of a company to conduct an income earning activity, for example to operate a business previously run by a sole trader or partnership.

Independent taxation

The taxation of spouses as individuals rather than as a family unit.

Indexation allowance

An allowance intended to compensate for the effect of inflation on the value of capital assets when determining a capital gains tax liability.

Indirect tax

A tax which is ultimately borne by someone other than the taxpayer on whom it is levied. It is not always possible to identify the effective incidence of an indirect tax. VAT is an example of an indirect tax which is intended to be suffered by the final consumer. However, market forces might lead to manufacturers absorbing some of the VAT themselves, rather than passing it on to the final consumer. *See also* Incidence of taxation.

Individual Savings Account (ISA)

Savings product providing tax free income. Used to replace TESSAs and PEPs.

Industrial buildings allowances (IBA)

Capital allowance available on expenditure on industrial buildings and hotels. To be phased out by 2011.

Inheritance tax

Tax levied on certain lifetime transfers and estates on the death of individuals.

Inland Revenue

The government department that was, until 2005, responsible for income tax, corporation tax, capital gains tax and inheritance tax. Its responsibilities are now undertaken by HMRC.

Input VAT

VAT levied on the purchases of goods and services by a registered trader.

Inspector of taxes

Civil Servants who assessed individuals, companies and other organisations liability to tax in the former Inland Revenue.

Instalment option

Facility which allows some capital, gains tax and inheritance tax to be paid in instalments.

Intending trader registration

Registration for VAT by an individual or organisation which has not yet begun to trade.

Interest in possession trust

A trust in which the beneficiaries, the life tenants, have a right to receive the income from the trust for a period of time.

Interim payments

Payments of income tax on account on 31st January in the tax year and 31st July following the end of the tax year.

Intra-group transfer

A transfer of assets between two members of a company group which would in other circumstances give rise to a capital gains tax charge.

Irrecoverable VAT

VAT levied on the purchases of goods or services that cannot be recovered as input tax.

ISA

Savings product providing tax free income. Used to replace TESSAs and PEPs.

Job-related accommodation

Accommodation provided to an employee which is eligible for relief from being taxed as a benefit in kind.

Landlord repairing lease

A lease of property at a full rent. That is the rent paid under the lease is sufficient taking one year with another, to defray the cost to the lessor of any expenses subject to the lease which fall to be borne by him.

Large business

For tax purposes a large business would be one that exceeds two or more of the conditions necessary to be a medium sized business.

Lease

The granting of a right to the use of an asset for a specified period.

Lease premium

An initial payment made to the lessor (owner of the property) in return granting of a right to the use of an asset for a specified period.

Less detailed VAT invoice

May be issued by retailers when the VAT inclusive total is less than £100.

Letting exemption

Relief from capital gains tax available when part or all of a property, which was at some time the taxpayer's principal private residence, is let.

Life interest trust

A trust in which beneficiaries have an interest in possession throughout their life.

Life tenant

An individual who has a right to receive the income from a trust for a period of time.

Linked transactions

A series of transactions to connected persons where the disposal proceeds of each disposal are taken to be a proportion of the value of the aggregate of the assets transferred for capital gains tax purposes.

Long-life assets

For capital allowance purposes assets with useful lives of more than 25 years receive writing down allowances of 10% per annum.

Loss relief

Tax relief for trading or capital losses given by setting losses against taxable income or chargeable gains.

Lower rate of tax

The rate of tax which was levied on savings income and capital gains that fell into the basic rate band but was lower than the basic rate of tax.

Lump sum taxes

A fixed amount of tax paid by an individual regardless of his or her income.

Maintenance payments

Payments to a spouse, former spouse or children.

Management expenses

Expenses incurred in managing an investment company.

Marginal rate of tax

This is the rate at which a taxpayer would be taxed on the next unit of the tax base.

Marginal relief

Relief given to companies with taxable profits lying within given limits.

Marriage exemption

Relief from inheritance tax on gifts made in consideration of marriage.

Married couple's allowance

An allowance available to a married man whose wife lives with him (not available from 6th April 2000 unless aged over 65 as at that date).

Matching rules

The rules used to match acquisitions and disposals of quoted securities for capital gains tax purposes.

Medium-sized business

To be classed as medium-sized for tax purposes the business must be larger than a small business and satisfy at least two of the following conditions (pre-April 08 levels in brackets): turnover not more than £25.9 million (£22.9 million), balance sheet total of not more than £12.9 million (£11.4 million) and not more than 250 employees (unchanged).

Minor

An unmarried child under the age of 18.

MIRAS

The mechanism used to give individuals tax relief on the interest paid on their mortgages called Mortgage Interest Relief at Source (not available from 6th April 2000).

Mixed supply

A supply of goods and services by a registered trader which is made up of a separable mix of elements. The appropriate VAT rate to be applied to each part.

National insurance contributions

A tax paid by individuals and employers to secure certain benefits such as a state pension.

National Savings & Investments

A government owned bank in which individuals can invest in order to obtain interest.

National Savings Certificates

Certificates issued by the Government which offer tax-free returns.

Negligible value claim

A capital gains tax relief that can be claimed by a taxpayer when an asset becomes effectively worthless.

Net income

Line item in the personal tax computation resulting from deduction of tax reliefs from total income (before personal allowances are deducted to produce taxable income). Introduced by ITA 2007.

Net Relevant Earnings

Trading profits, employment income and income from furnished holiday lettings net of loss relief and excess of trade charges over other income.

Nil rate band

The band of transfers for which the rate of inheritance tax is nil.

No gain/no loss transfer

Disposal of an asset without a gain or loss for capital gains tax purposes regardless of the actual costs and the value of any proceeds.

Nominal rent lease

A lease which is not expected to generate a profit over a number of years.

Non-cash voucher

A voucher which can only be exchanged for goods or services.

Non-savings income

Income other than interest and dividends. Includes employment income, business income and property income.

Normal expenditure out of income exemption

Exemption from inheritance tax where the gift or gifts are not so large that the donor's residual income is inadequate to maintain his or her usual standard of living.

Occupational pension scheme

Pension schemes available for employees set up by their employers.

OECD

Organisation for Economic Co-operation and Development. A grouping of the major economic world powers part of whose remit is to provide an international forum for tax issues (see http//www.oecd.org).

Ordinary residence

A taxpayer is ordinarily resident if the UK is a regular choice of abode which forms part of the regular order of an individual's life.

Output VAT

The VAT on supplies made by a registered trader or on the acquisition by a registered trader of goods from another member state.

Overlap losses

Losses incurred by a trader in a period which forms all or part of the basis period of more than one tax year.

Overlap profits

Profits earned by a trader in a period which forms all or part of the basis period of more than one tax year.

Part disposal

The disposal of part of an asset for capital gains tax purposes.

Partial exemption

Where a VAT registered trader makes some taxable supplies and some exempt supplies he or she may be unable to recover all of his input tax.

Participator

A person who has a share or interest in the capital or income of a close company.

Partnership

Two or more individuals carrying on a business together.

Pay and file

The system used to collect corporation tax before the introduction of corporation tax self assessment (CTSA).

Pay As You Earn (PAYE)

The system used to collect income tax and national insurance contributions from employees.

Payment basis

Charges are recognised for tax purposes when they are paid.

Payroll deduction scheme

Payments to charity from an employee's gross income under the PAYE scheme.

Period of account

The period for which a business prepares accounts.

Personal allowance

An amount of income that can be received tax free by an individual.

Personal company

A company is an individual's personal company if he exercises at least 5% of the voting rights in the company.

Personal equity plan (PEP)

A plan which enables individuals to invest in equities either directly or using unit trusts free of income tax or capital gains tax.

Personal pension scheme

A pension scheme which employees can invest in provided that they are not a member of their employer's occupational pension scheme.

Plant and machinery

Apparatus used by a business person for carrying on business not their own stock-in-trade which they buy or make for resale. Capital expenditure on plant and machinery may qualify for capital allowances.

Political accountability

Tax raising bodies should be accountable to those they raise taxes from. This usually takes the form of requirement to obtain a mandate from the electorate in regular elections.

Potentially exempt transfer (PET)

A transfer of assets which may become liable to Inheritance Tax if the transferor dies with seven years of the transfer.

Premium

A payment in return for the granting of a lease on land or property.

Principal charge

A charge of 15% of the inheritance scale rate on the value of a discretionary trust every ten years.

Principal private residence

The main residence of an individual or a married couple, generally exempt from capital gains tax. An individual who owns more than one residence may nominate one as his or her main residence.

Profit sharing scheme

A scheme for employees which enables shares in their employer company to be distributed to them.

Profits chargeable to corporation tax (PCTCT)

Tax adjusted profits of a company excluding franked investment income after deducting charges and loss relief.

Profits for small companies rate purposes

Profits chargeable to corporation tax plus franked investment income.

Progressive tax

A tax is progressive if individuals with a larger taxable capacity pay proportionately more of their income in tax than individuals with a lower taxable capacity.

Proportional tax

A tax is proportional if tax paid is a fixed proportion of taxable capacity.

Qualifying corporate bond

A sterling bond which is a normal commercial loan which is exempt from capital gains tax for individuals (but not for companies).

Quarter days

25th March, 24th June, 29th September and 25th December. Often rents are due on the quarter days.

Quarter up rule

A valuation rule for quoted securities for capital gains tax purposes. The valuation is equal to the lower of the two prices quoted in the Daily Official List plus a quarter of the difference between the two prices.

Quarterly accounting

The system used by large companies to account for corporation tax under self-assessment.

Quick succession relief

Relief from inheritance tax when a chargeable transfer increased the value of a person's estate within the previous five years.

Ramsay principle

If an artificial scheme is used to avoid or delay a tax liability the courts can set aside the scheme and instead compare the position of the taxpayer in real terms at the start and finish of the scheme.

Rate applicable to trusts

The 40% (32.5% for dividends) rate for income tax and capital gains tax applied to discretionary trusts.

Rebasing

The procedure under which capital gains are calculated by assuming that assets owned on 31st March 1982 were bought on that date at their market value on that date.

Receipts basis

A way of allocating income to tax years on the basis of when it is received. Also known as cash basis.

Receivable basis

A way of allocating income to tax years on the basis of when it was due to be received. Also known as accruals basis.

Regressive taxes

A tax is regressive if the proportion of tax paid increases as income falls. *See also* Incidence of tax.

Reinvestment relief

Relief from capital gains tax available to individuals or trustees, but not companies, when some or all of the proceeds from the disposal of an asset or a material disposal of shares in a qualifying company are reinvested in a qualifying investment.

Relief

A reduction in tax allowed to a taxpayer.

Relevant supplies

Supplies to a non-taxable person in the UK from another EU member state. The supplier may be liable to register for VAT in the UK.

Remittance basis

A way of determining taxable income on the basis of amounts remitted to the UK.

Remoteness test

A test for determining whether an expense is deductible. An expense which is considered to be too remote from activities of the trade will generally not be deductible.

Renewals basis

An allowable deduction from income from furnished letting for the replacement of furniture.

Rent a room scheme

A scheme under which if an individual lets one or more furnished rooms in their main residence rents received up to £4,250 a year are exempt from tax under Schedule A.

Residence

An individual is deemed to be resident in the UK for a tax year if he or she spends more than 183 days in the UK during the tax year.

Retail prices index (RPI)

An index measuring inflation that is used to calculate the indexation allowance for capital gains tax purposes.

Retail schemes

Special schemes for accounting for VAT which are available to some retailers.

Retirement relief

Relief from capital gains tax is given in any case where a material disposal of business assets is made by an individual who, at the time of the disposal, has attained the age of 50 or has retired on the grounds of ill-health below the age of 50. This no longer applies for tax years after 2000/01.

Reverse charge

A system of accounting for VAT on supplies made to a UK resident registered trader by a person resident overseas.

Reversionary interest

An interest in a trust which will depend on the termination of another interest in the trust.

Rollover relief

Relief from capital gains tax available if the proceeds from the disposal of certain classes of assets are reinvested in other qualifying assets within a specified period.

Royalty

Payments made in consideration for the use of, or right to use, intellectual property (e.g. patents, copyrights, design plans, trademarks, business processes etc).

Savings income

Income source, primarily interest from banks and building societies.

Schedular system of taxation

All income was taxed under the schedular system in the UK until 2005/6 when a new scheme was introduced for individual taxpayers. Companies continued to use the schedular system until April 2009.

Secondhand goods scheme

A VAT scheme available to traders who buy second- hand goods from individuals who are not registered traders.

Self assessment

A system of administration of taxation in which taxpayers are responsible for assessing their own liability to tax. Applies to most UK taxes.

Self-employed person

An individual who has a contract for services. As compared to an employee who has a contract of service.

Self-supply

A supply of goods or services by a registered person which is used by themselves in the course of their business.

Settled property

Assets held within a trust.

Settlement

A trust.

Seven year cumulation

An inheritance tax computation depends on the transfers of value which have occurred in the seven years prior to the most recent transfer.

Share option scheme

A scheme open to employees and directors which grants them share options.

Short-life asset

Plant or machinery which is kept separate from the general pool for the purposes of calculating capital allowances.

Small Business

To be classed as a small company requires at least two of the following conditions to be true (pre-April 08 levels in brackets): turnover not more than £6.5 million (£5.6 million), balance sheet total of not more than £3.26 million (£2.8 million), not more than 50 employees (unchanged).

Small profits (previously companies') rate

The rate at which profits chargeable to corporation tax are taxed provided the profits for small companies rate purposes lie below a given limit.

Small gifts exemption

An inheritance tax exemption for gifts to the same person provided that they have a total value of less than £250 in the tax year.

Special Commissioners

Full-time paid individuals who had been legally qualified for at least ten years who used to hear complex appeals of taxpayers against the assessment of the inspectors before the introduction of the Tribunal System in April 2009.

Stakeholder Pension

Pension scheme available from 6 April 2001 to widen provision for own retirement income. Not tied to earnings and low cost.

Stamp duty

A tax on documents usually involving transfers of property (e.g. houses or shares).

Standard rated supply

Supply by a registered trader of goods or services which are not VAT exempt or zero rated.

Starting rate

Introductory rate of income and corporation taxation.

Statement of practice

A statement issued by HMRC in order to clarify the application of some aspect of the legislation.

Statutory total income

An individual's total income before deduction of allowances.

Structural reliefs

Tax allowances or reliefs considered to be integral to the design of the tax system (i.e. likely to last multiple years rather than undergo substantial changes year on ear).

Substitution effect of tax

A substitution distortion occurs when individuals consume one item rather than another because of the effect of taxation.

Surplus ACT

Used to arise when ACT was paid by a company that could not be set against its corporation tax liability for the period in which the ACT was paid (no longer a core part of the current UK tax system).

TAARS

Targeted anti-avoidance rules – used post Pre-Budget 2005 in relation to corporate tax avoidance.

Taper relief

Relief given to companies with taxable profits lying within given limits. Also called *marginal* relief. Also used to refer to relief given for capital gains from ownership of assets after April 1998 by individuals.

Tax additions

Relating to extra tax that might be included in personal tax computations at step 7 (introduced by ITA 2007).

Tax avoidance

The use of legal means to reduce tax liabilities, although often against the spirit of the legislation.

Tax base

The subject matter on which a tax is based. Tax may be levied on income, wealth or expenditure, making these the primary tax bases.

Tax borne

The tax on an individual's taxable income less tax relief on tax reducers other than those paid net.

Tax credit

A credit received with dividends from UK companies which is equal to the amount of tax deemed to have been suffered by the taxpayer. Also various schemes by which transfers are made to the needy such as working tax credit.

Tax evasion

The use of illegal means to reduce tax liabilities.

Tax exempt special savings account (TESSA)

Savings accounts which give tax free returns provided that they are held for five years. No longer available (replaced by ISAs)

Tax expenditures

Tax allowances or reliefs given in place of direct Government subsidies; effectively tax foregone by the Government

Tax liability

Tax borne plus income tax retained on charges paid net.

Tax life

The deemed life of an industrial or agricultural building for the purposes of capital allowances.

Tax payable

Tax liability less tax already suffered and tax credits.

Tax point

The date on which a supply of goods or services is treated as taking place for VAT purposes.

Tax reducer

An allowance or relief which has the effect of reducing the tax due on taxable income. In the case of income tax these specifically relate to step 6 of the personal tax computation (ITA 2007).

Tax relief

The deduction allowed to reduce the amount that must be paid of a specific tax. In the case of income tax, these specifically refer to deductions allowable at step 2 of a personal tax computation to turn total income into net income (ITA 2007).

Tax system

The collection of specific taxes and tax rules that together describe how revenue is raised for a Government.

Tax wedges

In the case of an indirect tax the tax wedge is the difference between the marginal cost of producing a good or service and the marginal benefit of consumption.

Tax year

An income tax year for individuals which runs from 6th April until the following 5th April. A particular tax year is described using the two calendar years crossed by the tax year, e.g. tax year 2005/06 is the tax year starting 6th April 2005 and ending 5th April 2006. Used to be known as fiscal year.

Taxable capacity

This is the capacity of an individual to pay tax and may be measured by reference to the individual's income, expenditure, wealth or even ability to generate income. Not easy to compute with certainty.

Taxable income

Total income less allowances and reliefs.

Taxable person

A person who is, or should be, registered for VAT.

Taxable supply

A supply of goods or services by a registered trader which is not an exempt supply.

Taxable turnover

The turnover of a business which is subject to VAT at any rate.

Taxed income

Income received net of basic rate or lower rate tax.

Taxpayer's Charter

A statement setting out what a taxpayer is entitled to expect from HMRC.

Tenant's repairing lease

A lease where the tenant is obliged to maintain or repair the whole or substantially the whole, of the premises which are the subject of the lease.

Terminal loss relief

An income tax relief available to individuals for losses incurred in the final 12 months of trading.

Transfer of value

A disposition by an individual which reduces the value of their estate for inheritance tax purposes.

Treasury

The Government department responsible to the Chancellor of the Exchequer for the development of tax policy.

Trust

A trust is created when a settlor transfers assets to trustees who hold the assets for the benefit of one or more persons (beneficiaries).

Trustees

Hold assets within a trust for the benefit of one or more persons (beneficiaries).

Unfranked investment income (UFII)

Dividend income received by a UK resident company plus the associated tax credit.

Upper Accruals Point

Upper threshold level at which entitlement to state basic pension is capped. Affects national insurance contribution payments for contracted out employees.

Upper Earnings Limit (UEL)

A point at which the tax rate changes for national insurance contributions for employees and their employers.

Upper Profits Limit

A point at which the tax rate changes for national insurance contributions for business profits.

Value Added Tax Act 1994 (VATA 1994)

The Act containing the principal legislation for VAT.

Value added tax (VAT)

An indirect or expenditure tax borne by the final consumer which is charged whenever a taxable person makes a taxable supply of goods or services in the course of his or her business.

VAT invoice

An invoice which must be supplied by registered traders to other registered traders.

VAT period

The period of time, usually three months, that is covered by a VAT return.

VAT return

Form VAT 199 which must be submitted to HM Customs and Excise together with any VAT payable within one month of the end of the VAT period.

Vertical equity

A tax system has vertical equity if those in differing economic circumstances are taxed differently, e.g. those on higher incomes pay more tax than those on lower incomes.

Vertical fiscal imbalance

Occurs when there is an imbalance between two levels of government in terms of revenue raising and spending obligations. For example in the UK, local government does not raise enough of its own revenue to fund its spending obligations and must rely on central government grants for funding.

Void period

A period in which there is no tenant leasing property and the property is not occupied by the owner.

Wasting asset

Assets with an estimated remaining useful life of 50 years or less.

Wealth taxes

A wealth tax is levied on a taxpayer's assets at a particular date. The primary difficulty with a wealth tax comes from valuing assets, especially intangibles like pension funds.

Wear and tear allowance

A deduction from the income from furnished lettings to give relief for the wear and tear of furniture and equipment provided.

Withholding taxes

Some income, such as debenture interest, has tax deducted at source regardless of the personal circumstances of the recipient. The tax so deducted is termed a withholding tax.

Work effort and taxes

There is a potentially complicated relationship between work effort and taxes. If marginal rates of tax are too high they may act as a disincentive to work.

Worldwide Debt Cap

Places a limit on the deductibility of interest payments under corporation tax for groups of companies with world wide operations.

Working Tax Credit

Benefit available to families in which the parent (or parents) are currently working.

Writing down allowance

A capital allowance which is given as a deduction from profits to determine tax adjusted trading income for income tax or corporation tax..

Year of assessment

For income tax, a fiscal or tax year which runs from 6th April to the following 5th April.

Zero rated supply

A supply of goods or services made by a registered trader which is subjected to a nil rate of VAT

Suggested solutions to questions

Chapter 4

Quick quiz answers

1. Benson is entitled to an age allowance of £9,490 reduced by ½ of the excess of his income (£24,300) over £22,900, i.e. reduced by £700. His taxable income is £24,300 – £8,790 = £15,510.

Tax due:	£
Non-savings	
15,510 @ 20%	3,102.00

2. Candice has a taxable income comprising savings income of £15,000 × 100/80 = £18,750; dividend income of £2,500 × 100/90 = £2,777 less a personal allowance of £6,475 i.e. a total taxable income of £15,052. Remember the personal allowance is offset first against saving income ahead of dividend income as she has no non-savings income to use it on. Her taxable income is therefore (£18,750 – £6,475) + £2,777 = £15,052.

Tax due:	£
Savings	
2,440 @ 10%	244.00
9,835 @ 20%	1,967.00
Dividends	
2,777 @ 10%	277.70
Tax liability	2,488.70
Less: Tax credits	
2,777 @ 10%	(277.70)
18,750 @ 20%	(3,750.00)
Tax repayment	(1,539.00)

Candice can get back this overpaid tax that was withheld at source by simply writing to HRMC.

3. Taxable income comprises non-saving income of £22,500 less personal allowance of £6,475 and less the patent royalty (grossed up) of £250 i.e. £15,775.

Tax due:	£
Non-savings:	
15,775 @ 20%	3,155.00
Add: Tax withheld patent royalty	
250 @ 20%	50.00
Tax liability	3,205.00

4. Dominic's taxable income comprises employment earnings of £20,000 less the personal allowance of £6,475 i.e. £13,525.

Tax due:	£
Non-savings:	
13,525 @ 20%	2,705.00

The charitable gift does not affect Dominic's calculation as he has paid sufficient basic rate tax to cover the repayment to the charity and is not a high rate taxpayer. Dominic has probably paid this tax payable fully through the PAYE system as he is an employee.

5. Erica is entitled to an age allowance of £9,640 which is not reduced as her income does not exceed £22,900. Her taxable income is £10,500 plus savings income of £500 × 100/80 = £625 less age allowance of £9,640 i.e. £1,485. Remember the age allowance comes off the non-savings income first in the computation.

Tax due:	£
Non-savings	
860 @ 20%	172.00
Savings	
625 @ 10%	62.50
Tax liability	234.50
Less: Tax credits	
625 @ 20%	(125.00)
Tax payable	109.50

6. Frank's taxable income comprises non-savings income of £32,500 plus dividends of £3,000 × 100/90 = £3,333 less a personal allowance of £6,475 i.e. a total taxable income of £29,358.

Tax due:	£
Non-savings	
26,025 @ 20%	5,205.00
Dividends	
3,333 @ 10%	333.30
Tax liability	5,538.30
Less: Tax credits	
3,333 @ 10%	(333.30)
Tax payable	5,205.00

National Insurance contributions: this is only due on his trading income (not dividend income) at Class 2 and Class 4:

Class 2:	£2.40 x 52 =	£124.80
Class 4:	(32,500 – 5,715) x 8% =	£2,142.80

Full questions

Question 1

Personal tax computation for Sam for 2010/11

	Non-savings £	Savings £	Dividends £	Total £
Employment earnings	26,000			26,000
Savings income:				
Building society interest				
(1,600 × 100/80)		2,000		2,000
Dividend income				
(2,700 × 100/90)			3,000	3,000
Net Income	26,000	2,000	3,000	31,000
Less personal allowance	(6,475)			(6,475)
Taxable income	19,525	2,000	3,000	24,525

Income tax due:	£
Non-savings income	
19,525 @ 20%	3,905.00
Savings	
2,000 @ 20%	400.00
Dividend income	
3,000 @ 10%	300.00
Tax liability	4,605.00
Less: tax credits:	
PAYE	(3,905.00)
Building Society interest	(400.00)
Tax credit on dividends	(300.00)
Tax payable/repayable	0

Note: As Sam is a basic rate tax payer, the combination of his PAYE deducted by his employer, the tax withheld at source on his Building Society account and the tax credit he can claim on his dividends amounts to the exact amount of tax he is liable to pay on his various income sources for the tax year. This is a common situation for the many basic rate UK taxpayers and is the reason many taxpayers do not have to file a tax return each year. The charitable donation does not affect the calculation as Sam has paid sufficient basic rate tax and is not a high rate taxpayer.

Question 2

Personal tax computation for Janet for 2010/11

	Non-Savings £	Savings £	Dividends £	Total £
Income:				
Employment earnings	35,000			35,000
Bonus	3,000			3,000
Savings income:				
Building society interest				
£3,500 × 100/80		4,375		4,375
Property income				
6/12 × £8,000	4,000			4,000
Less expenses	(1,000)			(1,000)
Net income	41,000	4,375	0	45,375
Less personal allowance	(6,475)			(6,475)
Taxable income	34,525	4,375	0	38,900

Tax due:

Non-savings income	
34,525 @ 20%	6,905.00
Savings income	
2,875 @ 20%	575.00
1,500 @ 40%	600.00
38,900	
Tax liability	8,080.00
Less: tax credits	
Building society interest	(875.00)
PAYE	(6,500.00)
Tax payable	705.00

Note: The premium bond winnings are tax free and therefore do not need to form part of Janet's tax computation. Do not forget that the property was only rented for half the year and that building society interest needs to be grossed up.

Personal tax computation for Dave for 2010/11

	Non-Savings £	Savings £	Dividends £	Total £
Income:				
Employment earnings	34,500			34,500
Savings income:				
Bank deposit account				
£3,000 × 100/80		3,750		3,750
Dividend income:				
£6,760 × 100/90			7,511	7,511
Net income	34,500	3,750	7,511	45,761
Less personal allowances	(6,475)			(6,475)
Taxable income	28,025	3,750	7,511	39,286

Tax due:	£
Non-savings	
28,025 @ 20%	5,605.00
Savings	
3,750 @ 20%	750.00
Dividends	
5,625 @ 10%	562.50
1,886 @ 32.5%	612.95
39,286	
Tax liability	7,530.45
Less: tax credits	
Bank £3,750 @ 20%	(750.00)
Dividends £7,511 @ 10%	(751.10)
PAYE	(5,725.00)
Tax payable	304.35

Chapter 5

Quick quiz answers

1. Iain will be taxed on £2.85 per day, the remaining 15p being exempt by concession.

2. Julia's mileage allowance is exempt as it is less than 40p for the first 10,000 miles. She will actually be able to claim a deduction from her employment earnings for the shortfall of 3,000 miles @ (40p – 30p) = £300.

3. Assuming the house is not job related, Keith will be taxed on the annual value of the house of £10,200, plus the extra charge which arises because it is an expensive house of 5%× (£250,000 – £75,000) plus the value of the running costs of £2,500 i.e. a total of £21,450.

4. With this emission rating, Lorna will be taxed on £27,000 at the rate of 35% i.e. £9,450.

Full questions

Question 1

Employment income assessment for Martin

	£
Salary £30,000×9/12	22,500
Commission (none paid in fiscal year)	–
Car [(£30,000×35%)×9/12] – (£50×9)	7,425
Fuel (Note 1)	–
Clothing allowance £600×10/12	500
Flat (£1,200×9/12) + [(£120,000 – £75,000) ×9/12×5%]	2,587
Furniture £10,000×9/12×20%	1,500
Employment income	34,512

Note 1: The cost of private fuel is chargeable as a benefit if any of it is provided by the employer after taking any employee contributions into account. A calculation is necessary to find out if this benefit therefore exists. The actual cost of his private fuel is £190.00 (1,000/5×95p) but the minimum guidance amount Martin should have repaid is £130 (13p×1000 miles). This is less than the amount reimbursed by Martin of £180 (£20×9) and hence no benefit is deemed to exist.

Question 2

Personal tax computation for Mr Thistlethwaite for 2010/11

	Non-Savings £	Savings £	Dividends £	Total £
Earnings from employment	33,500			33,500
Benefits in kind				
Car £14,500×23%×5/12	1,389			1,389
Fuel £18,000×23%×5/12	1,725			1,725
Less professional subscriptions	(100)			(100)
Trading income	3,000			3,000
Savings income				
Bank interest (£300×100/80)		375		375
Building Society Interest				
(2,000×100/80)		2,500		2,500
Dividends				
(1,750×100/90)			1,944	1,944
Net Income	39,514	2,875	1,944	44,333
Less personal allowance	(6,475)			(6,475)
Taxable income	33,039	2,875	1,944	37,858

Mr Thistlethwaite paid his contributions to pension funds under a relief at source arrangement which provides basic rate but not higher rate relief. To provide higher rate relief we need to adjust his basic rate band. The top of the basic rate band is increased by the gross amount of pension contributions, i.e. £2,800 (5%×£33,500) + (£900×100/80) and is therefore extended from £37,400 to £40,200.

Income tax due:	£
Non-savings	
33,039 @ 20%	6,607.80
Savings	
2,875 @ 20%	575.00
Dividends	
1,944 @ 10%	194.40
37,858	
Tax liability	7,377.20
Less Tax credits	
Savings 2,875 @ 20%	(575.00)
Dividend 1,944 @ 10%	(194.40)
PAYE	(5,986.00)
Tax payable	621.80

Personal tax computation for Mrs Thistlethwaite for 2010/11

	Non-savings £	Savings £	Dividends £	Total £
Earnings from employment	19,000			
Less: professional subscriptions	(60)			
	18,940			18,940
Savings income:				
Bank interest (300×100/80)		375		375
Building Society Interest				
(2,000×100/80)		2,500		2,500
Dividend income				
(1,750×100/90)			1,944	1,944
Total income	18,940	2,875	1,944	23,759
Less personal allowance	(6,475)			(6,475)
Taxable income	12,465	2,875	1,944	17,284

Income tax due:	£
Non-savings	
12,465 @ 20%	2,493.00
Savings	
2,875 @ 20%	575.00
Dividends	
1,944 @ 10%	194.40
17,284	
Tax liability	3,262.40
Less:	
Tax at source on savings 2,875 @ 20%	(575.00)
Tax credit on dividend 1,944 @ 10%	(194.40)
PAYE	(2,530.00)
Tax repayable	(37.00)

Note: In the case of Mrs Thistlethwaite, it is unlikely that the academic gown will be tax deductible under the wholly, exclusively and necessary rule, despite her employer requesting it. In addition, Mrs Thistlethwaite's contribution to her pension fund was made under a net pay arrangement, which means that she has already received relief and no further adjustments are necessary in her tax computation.

Chapter 6

Quick quiz answers

1. The staff loan written off and the increase in general provision are not deductible for tax purposes and so Matthew must add back £400 in his adjustment of profits.

2. As Nola's car is an expensive car, £4,200 × ((£12,000 + (½ (£25,000 – £12,000)) ÷ £25,000 only is deductible, i.e. £3,108; and so £1,092 of her £4,200 lease charges must be added back in her adjustment of profits. If the lease was entered into on or after 6 April 2009, we need to know the CO_2 emission levels. If they are more than 160g/km, then only 85% of the lease payments will be deductible, i.e. £3,570.

3. Both the T shirts and the Christmas party are fully deductible for tax purposes. Note, however, that as the cost of the Christmas party exceeds £150 per head, a benefit in kind may arise for Orlando's employees.

4. Pauline must add £115 to her profit for tax purposes (i.e. sales value not cost price must be added back).

5. Quentin's landlord will be taxed under the property income rules on £10,000 – (£10,000 × 14 × 2%) i.e. £7,200. Quentin can therefore deduct this amount over the term of the lease i.e. £480 (£7,200 ÷ 15) per annum.

6. The cost of debt collection is deductible. Both the acquisition of new premises and the patent registration are capital transactions and so on face value the fees associated with these are not deductible. However special provision allows the cost of patent registration to be deducted and so Rachel can claim £230.

7. Rental income is taxed on an accruals basis so Gerald will be assessed on 6/12×£8,400 + 6/12×£8,600 = £8,500.

8. Using the formula for short lease premiums, Heather will be assessed on: £48,000 – (48,000× (40 – 1) ×2%) = £10,560

Full questions

Question 1

The treatment of each of the items, for tax purposes, is as follows:

(a) *Reconstruction of the roof*

The expenditure was incurred to renovate an asset soon after it was acquired and the asset, a building, was not in a usable condition immediately after acquisition. Following the decision in *Law Shipping* the expenditure will be deemed to be capital and hence will be disallowable for tax purposes. (If the use of the warehouse qualifies the building for an industrial buildings allowance the expenditure will qualify for capital allowances which we will learn more about in Chapter 7).

The expenditure on the roof should be added back to the net profit in order to determine the tax adjusted trading profit.

(b) *Embezzlement by the director*

Defalcations by directors are not allowable deductions for trading income purposes. Hence the expense should be added back to the net profit in order to determine the tax adjusted trading profit. (Embezzlement by a staff member (not a partner or director), however, is an allowable tax expense). All payments in connection with criminal offences (e.g. fines or bribes) are explicitly excluded as deductions.

(c) *Redundancy payment to a works manager*

Redundancy payments made wholly and exclusively for the purpose of trade are allowed without limit, provided that the business continues to trade. If Jones ceases to trade there is a limit on the amount of any redundancy payment of the statutory amount plus up to three times the statutory amount. In the case of the works manager the maximum deductible is £48,000 (£12,000 × 3 + £12,000). Since the actual payment is lower than this it will be an allowable expense even if Jones ceases to trade. Hence no adjustment needs to be made in order to determine the tax adjusted trading profit.

(d) *Salary of senior manager seconded to a charity*

Such a payment is specifically allowable for tax purposes and hence no adjustment needs to be made in order to determine the trading profit.

(e) *Costs of the crèche*

The construction costs are capital expenditure and as such are not allowable for tax purposes (although if Jones' trade is a qualifying trade, he may be eligible for industrial buildings allowance, which we will learn more about in Chapter 7).

The running costs of the crèche are incurred in order to provide a benefit in kind for employees and as such are allowable deductions for tax purposes. Hence the construction costs should be added back to the net profit in order to determine the tax adjusted trading profit while no adjustment is required for the running costs.

(f) *Receipt from insurance company*

The cost of repairing the asset is an allowable expense. The receipt from the insurance company will reduce the allowable expenditure by £18,000 because the business has been reimbursed for its costs.

The receipt of £6,000 in compensation for loss of profits is taxable. Since the business has already reduced the balance on the repairs account by £18,000 and increased the balance on the profits and loss account by £6,000 no adjustments in respect of these items are necessary.

(g) *Gain on the sale of investments*

Capital gains are not taxed under trading income rules. Hence the gain of £30,000 should be deducted in order to calculate the tax adjusted trading profits. We will see in Chapter 8 how capital gains are dealt with.

(h) *Sales to X Ltd*

Drawings in the form of goods or services made by sole traders or partners have to be dealt with at market prices. This includes selling goods to an associate for less than market value. The sales figure should therefore be increased by £30,000.

Chapter 7

Quick quiz answers

1. The car is a high emissions car and must go into the special rate pool where it will receive a 10% writing down allowance. It does not qualify for either the AIA or FYA. There is no apportionment for the length of ownership within the accounting period and no private use reduction as it is used solely for business purposes.

2. Theresa can claim full 100% of £15,000 as this is a low emission car.

3. Umut will be entitled to claim AIA of up to a maximum of £79,167. This is computed using the transitional basis rules i.e.

$$(5/12 \times £50,000) + (7/12 \times £100,000)$$

4. Vivian will be able to get 100% allowance using the AIA for this tax year - assuming she hasn't purchased other assets totally more than the AIA limit for the year i.e. £100,000. If Vivian has used up all her AIA for the year and she expects to sell the computer within four years and realise a loss (i.e. if it is expected to fall in value faster than the 20% tax allowances it will receive in the main pool) then it will be worth de-pooling the asset and keeping it separate as a short life asset so as to get the benefit of the balancing allowance that is expected as soon as possible.

5. Walter has sold the car for less than its tax written down value and so for tax purposes has a balancing allowance of £5,000. He can only claim 75% of this (£3,750), however, as he uses the car 75% for business purposes. Note that even though throughout its life for tax purposes the writing down allowance has been restricted to a maximum of £3,000 (under the pre April 2009 rules), no maximum restriction applies to the calculation of the balancing allowance when the asset is sold.

6. The cost of land does not qualify for industrial building allowances, however the cost of site preparation, and the other costs do.

Full questions

Question 1
For each new asset, we need to think about whether it qualifies for the AIA (in operation for the whole period but increasing from £50,000 to £100,000 on 6 April 2010) and or the 2009/10 FYA (which started on 6 April 2009 and ended on 5 April 2010). Luke's AIA for this year will be (3/12 x £50,000) + (9/12 x £100,000) i.e. £87,500. Remember also the rules for newly purchased expensive cars ceased to apply from 6 April 2009.
Looking at the new assets acquired by Luke we can say:
- The new van (29/7/09) qualifies for AIA and 40% FYA because it was purchased after 5 April 2009 (remember vans are not treated the same as cars).
- Cars don't qualify for AIA and so the first new car (25/10/09) is dealt with under the new rules that put cars into either the main or special (10%) rate pools depending on their CO_2 emission levels. Here the car is 190g/km, and so must go into the special rate pool.
- The new plant (1/05/10) qualifies for AIA but not FYA as it was purchased after 5 April 2010.

- The second new car (15/05/10) is also a high emissions car and must go into the special (10%) rate pool.
- The new lift (30/5/10) qualifies for AIA but not FYA as again it was acquired after the end date for the FYA rules.

Luke has a choice as to how he applies the AIA as he has both the new lift and new plant that qualify. His AIA covers both items, however.

y/e 30/6/10	£	Main £	Sp rate £	CAs £
AIA:				
New van	14,000			
New lift	58,000			
AIA	(max 87,500)			72,000
Writing down allowance:				
Opening balance		10,000		
Additions				
1st new car			16,000	
2nd new car			20,000	
Disposals				
Plant		(7,000)		
		3,000	36,000	
WDA (20%)		(600)		600
WDA (10%)			(3,600)	3,600
WDV c/f		2,400	32,400	
Total allowances				76,200

Question 2

(a) The land does not qualify for IBA, although site preparation costs do. The non-qualifying part of the building, the general office space, is less than 25% of the cost of the building can also be included in the calculation. For 2010/11 the IBA available will be 1% of £218,000 or £2,180.

(b) Buildings in enterprise zones are generally entitled to 100% initial IBA, and if less than this is claimed, the remainder is written off at 25% per annum on a straight line basis. Here Jack only claimed 50% in the first year of ownership, and so he is now entitled to £50,000 (25% of £200,000) this year.

Chapter 8

Quick quiz answers

1. Andrew will have a chargeable gain as follows:

	£
Disposal proceeds	5,000
Cost	(1,700)
Chargeable gain	3,300

He will have to add this gain to any others in the year to see if he has to pay any CGT on this transaction. If he has no other gains he'll not have to pay CGT on this as it comes under his AEA for 2010/11.

2. A hearse may be exempt from capital gains tax as a motor vehicle, however, the exemption is for passenger vehicles and arguably a hearse is not constructed to carry passengers (of the kind implied by the rule anyway). However, assuming Barbara is not carrying on a business as an undertaker, the hearse will be exempt as a wasting chattel and so Barbara will not pay capital gains tax on the profit.

3. A painting is a chattel and since it was sold for less than £6,000, it will be exempt from capital gains tax.

4. As Davina's gain of £450,000 is fully available for entrepreneurs' relief, it will simply be subject to a 10% charge (i.e. £45,000) under the new rules for disposals after 22 June 2010. Had she disposed of it on or before 22 June 2010 however, the resulting CGT liability would have been the same as it would still have fallen within the entrepreneurs' relief limit, but instead of a simple 10% flat charge, the gain would instead have reduced by 4/9ths (i.e. £200,000) and so £250,000 would have been liable for capital gains tax in 2010/11. She has no other gains or losses for the year so the gain would have been calculated to be £250,000 @ 18% = £45,000.

5. Eddie will be able to claim a loss of £6,950 based on deemed disposal proceeds of £50.

6. When part of an asset is sold, the formula A ÷ (A+B) is used to determine how much of the cost is attributable to the part of the asset that has been sold. In this case 200,000 ÷ (860,000 + 200,000) of the original cost is attributed to the part sold i.e. £94,340 and so the gain is £105,660.

Full questions

Question 1

Dates	Notes	Exempt months	Chargeable months
Jul 92–Dec 92	(i)	6	
Jan 93–Jun 94	(ii)	30	
Jul 94–Jun 95	(iii)		12
Jul 95–Jun 06	(iv)		132
Jul 06–Jun 10	(v)	36	
Total		72	144

Notes

(i)   The property was occupied as a principal private residence.

(ii)   James was working overseas. It was not necessary for James to return to the property on his return to the UK because he was required by his employers to live elsewhere in the UK.

(iii)   James did not return to the property after working elsewhere in the UK although not required to live elsewhere by his employers. Hence the period is chargeable.

(iv)   James did not occupy the property as his principal private residence.

(v)   The final 36 months of ownership are exempt.

Capital gains tax computation	£
Proceeds	200,000
Less cost	(50,000)
Gain	150,000
Less exempt proportion [72 ÷ (72 + 144)]	(50,000)
Chargeable gain	100,000

Question 2

(a) Arthur

Capital gains tax computation:	£
Proceeds	40,000
Less allowable cost	
$\dfrac{120,000}{40,000 + 187,500} \times 40,000$	(21,099)
Chargeable gain	18,901

(b) Margaret

	£	£
Proceeds		65,000
Less allowable costs		
Purchase	25,000	
Enhancement expenditure		
October 1985	1,000	
May 1995	4,000	(30,000)
Chargeable gain		35,000

(c) Anne

Gift relief can be claimed when business assets are transferred provided that both the transferor and the transferee make an election. Once the election has been made the transferor's gain is reduced to nil and the base cost to the transferee will be taken to be the market value on the date of transfer less the amount of the gift relief.

Question 3:

a)   Holiday Cottage:

	£
Disposal proceeds	225,000
Less: Incidental costs of disposal	(1,500)
Deemed cost	(20,000)
Conservatory	(3,500)
Chargeable gain	200,000

b)   Vacant Land:

	£
Gross sale proceeds	52,800
Incidental sale costs	(1,300)
Net sale proceeds	51,500
Less: Cost	
$31,700 \times \dfrac{52,800}{(52,800 + 22,000)}$	(22,376)
Chargeable gain	29,124

Chargeable gains:	
Holiday Cottage	200,000
Vacant land	29,124
	229,124
Less: Annual exemption	(10,100)
Chargeable gain	219,024
Capital gains tax payable @ 28%	61,326.72

490

Chapter 9

Quick quiz answers

1. Grotius Ltd will have two accounting periods for tax purposes, the year ended 31 August, 2010 and the four months ended 31 December, 2010.

2. The dividends received by Helvetius Ltd must be converted to FII by grossing them up by 10% - i.e. they become £146,667. This is added to the company's PCTCT to determine which tax band the company is in, but the dividends do not form part of PCTCT and so are not taxed again as part of Helveticus' income.

3. Isocrates Ltd can claim 4% per annum as a deduction in calculating trade profits, as this exceeds the rate used for accounting purposes which is 3%.

4. Justinian Ltd must include £4,875 in its PCTCT under trade profits (£3,900 × 100 ÷80). The income tax withheld on the patent royalties by the payer of £1,100 (£5,000 − £3,900) can be offset against any income tax withheld on payments made by the company, and any surplus can be reclaimed against the corporation tax liability.

5. Knox Ltd's corporation tax liability is:

	£
PCTCT	1,000,000
FII	50,000
'Profits'	1,050,000
Tax on 1,000,000 @ 28%	280,000
Less marginal relief:	
$\frac{7}{400} \times (1{,}500{,}000 - 1{,}050{,}000) \times \frac{1{,}000{,}000}{1{,}050{,}000}$	(7,500)
Corporation tax liability	272,500

6. Lychophron Ltd will have instalments due on 14 July, 2010 and 14 September, 2010.

Full questions

Question 1

Ultimate Upholsterers Ltd, Corporation Tax computation for the 12 months to 30 September, 2010

		£
Trade Profit (Note 1)		324,960
Non-trade loan relationships		
Loan interest accrued	12,000	
Less Debenture Interest accrued	(10,000)	
		2,000
Chargeable gain (Note 2)		21,040
Profits chargeable to corporation tax		348,000
Franked investment income		
(£18,000 × 100/90)		20,000
'Profits'		368,000
Corporation tax: £348,000 × 28%		97,440.00
Less marginal relief		

$$\frac{7}{400} \times (1,500000 - 368000) \times \frac{348000}{368000} \qquad 18,733.37$$

	78,706.63

Note 1: calculation of trade profits

In order to calculate the trade profits we need to calculate the capital allowances. The writing down allowance is given in the question. Ultimate Upholsterers cannot claim capital allowances on the factory because the right to capital allowances on a lease of less than 50 years rests with the lessor. However, tax relief will be available on the lease premium paid. The landlord will be assessed on £26,000 i.e.

£50,000 – [£24,000 (£50,000(25 – 1) × 2%)].

Ultimate Upholsterers will be able to claim relief of £1,040 (£26,000 ÷ 25).

Adjustment of Profits:	£
Trading profit	375,000
Less Capital Allowances:	
Plant and machinery	(49,000)
Less relief on lease premium paid	(1,040)
Adjusted trade profits	324,960

Note 2: calculation of chargeable gain on land

	£
Proceeds	47,410
Less cost	(10,000)
Un-indexed gain	37,410
Less indexation allowance	
£10,000 × 1.637	16,370
Indexed gain	21,040

Question 2

ABC Ltd has a corporate tax liability of more than £1.5 million so is required to make instalment payments of their tax liability.

a)   Instalment dates will be

1st instalment	31 Oct 2009+ 6 months + 14 days	14 May 2010
2nd instalment	14 May 2010+ 3 months	14 Aug 2010
3rd instalment	14 Aug 2010 + 3 months	14 Nov 2010
Final instalment	14 Nov 2010+ 3 months	14 Feb 2011

Amounts due on each date above:

$$\frac{3 \times 1,800,000}{12} = £450,000$$

b)   Instalment dates

1st instalment	31 Oct 2009 + 6 months+ 14 days	14 May 2010
2nd instalment	14 May 2010 + 3 months	14 Aug 2010
3rd instalment	(not due as falls beyond final instalment date)	
Final instalment	30 Jun 2010+ 3 months + 14 days	14 Oct 2010

Amounts due each instalment

$$\frac{3 \times 1,800,000}{8} = £675,000$$

Chapter 10

Quick quiz answers

1.   Yes, Kieran will have to register for VAT as his turnover exceeds the threshold which is £70,000 with effect from 1 April 2010.

2.   The value of the supply is £475 i.e. £500 less 5% so the VAT is £83.12. Even though the customer does not take up the discount, the VAT remains £83.12 and so the customer actually pays £583.12.

3.   Maurice does not have to register as his taxable supplies are less than the threshold. He could, however, register voluntarily so that he can reclaim his input tax.

4.   The input tax attributable to taxable supplies is £50,000. Nigella can also recover a portion of the unattributable input tax i.e. 80%, since 80% of her supplies are taxable. This means that a total of £53,200 is recoverable and the balance of £5,800 is not recoverable. Do not forget the de minimus test though, £5,800 spread over the whole year is £483 per month which is less than the de minimus of £625 and so Nigella can in fact recover all of her input tax.

5.   The basic tax point is 20 August as this is when the goods are made available to the customer. Do not forget though that this basic tax point can be altered if an invoice has been issued within 14 days of the basic tax point. That is the case here, and so the actual tax point will be 30 August, the date of issue of the invoice, even though the customer did not pay until 13 September.

6.   Under cash accounting we are only concerned about cash received and paid, not invoices issued. Portia has received £5,525 from her debtors, so we can use the VAT fraction of 7/47 to work out the VAT i.e. £822.87. She has paid £4,000 to suppliers before VAT and so the tax on that is @17.5% i.e. £700.00. Portia must therefore pay HMRC the difference between these two figures i.e. £822.87 minus £700.00 which is £122.87.

Full questions

Question 1

A person who makes taxable supplies becomes liable to be registered for VAT:

- at the end of any month, if the value of his or her taxable supplies in the period of one year then ending has exceeded £70,000, or
- at any time, if there are reasonable grounds for believing that the value of his or her taxable supplies in the period of thirty days then beginning will exceed £70,000.

Taxable supplies are made up of both standard rated and zero rated supplies. Since the trader's taxable supplies of £73,000 (£65,000 + £8,000) exceeds the annual limit of £70,000, the trader is liable to register for VAT. The trader must notify HMRC within 30 days of the end of the month in which the limits were exceeded. The trader will then be registered from the first day of the following month.

Had the trader voluntarily registered from the beginning of the accounting period his VAT position would have been:

	£
Output tax:	
Standard-rated supplies £8,000 × 17.5%	1,400
Less input tax:	
(9,000 + 4,000) × 7/47	(1,936)
VAT recoverable	(536)

Question 2

Deductible input tax – quarter ended 31 October, 2010

	£
Input tax attributable to taxable supplies	18,000
Proportion of remaining input tax	
88,400 ÷ 100,000 = 89% (rounded)	
89% × (24,000 – 18,000 – 1,500)	4,005
	22,005

(Non deductible of £1,995 exceeds *de minimis* of £625 per month.)

Chapter 11

Question 1

Without a salary sacrifice, Zainab has a gross pension contribution of £100 per month, because the incentive system to encourage pension contributions adds basic rate tax (currently 20%) to the pension contribution, so her £80 net pay contribution becomes a gross contribution of £100. Zainab could sacrifice £115.94 of gross (before tax) pay each month, which would be worth £80 of net pay after deduction of basic rate tax and national insurance. The employer contributes this sacrificed salary of £115.94 to Zainab's pension, so pension contribution increases by £15.94 compared to the previous arrangement. Zainab's net (take home) pay is the same, but she has now put more each month into her pension. Her employer saves £14.84 in national insurance contributions (£115.94 x 12.8%).

Question 2

You might have written your answer using different headings but you should have noted most of the following points.

Basis of assessment
Employees are taxed on the basis of the income received in the current tax year while self-employed taxpayers are taxed on the taxable profits for the accounting period which ended in the tax year. This provides a small advantage for taxpayers with accounting dates which are early in the tax year, the end of April for instance, particularly in times of inflation or growth, because of the relatively long delay between earning the profits and paying tax on them.

Allowable deductions
The self-employed can claim relief for expenses which are incurred wholly and exclusively for the purpose of trade while the employed can only gain relief for expenses which are wholly, exclusively *and necessarily* incurred in the performance of their duties. It is likely therefore that the self-employed will be able to claim a larger total deduction from income than employees. For example, if an academic purchases a computer to enable him or her to produce teaching materials at home no deduction for the cost of the computer will be allowable. However, a freelance lecturer who takes the same action will be able to claim a capital allowance for the cost of the computer.

National insurance
The self-employed must pay both Class 2 and Class 4 national insurance contributions and yet receive fewer benefits in return for their contributions. Employees also pay national insurance contributions (under Class 1 rules) but in return become entitled to sickness benefit, maternity benefit and unemployment benefit none of which self-employed people can usually claim. The levels of national insurance contributions will usually be different for the same levels of income but these differences may not reflect the differences in benefit entitlement.

Administration
Most self-employed individuals use the services of an accountant and certainly find themselves spending some time maintaining records which are required by the tax authorities. Employees usually incur few expenses when dealing with tax matters. This difference is likely to remain despite the introduction of self-assessment. These costs are called the compliance costs of the tax system and can be heavy for self employed people with anything other than simple tax affairs.

Chapter 12

Question 1

(a) William spent at least 183 days in the UK during 2010/11 and hence is resident for the tax year but is not ordinarily resident as this is not his normal country of residence.

(b) Patrick does not spend 183 days in the UK during 2010/11. However, he is ordinarily resident in the UK and does spend part of the tax year in the UK and hence he will be considered to be both resident and ordinarily resident in the UK in 2010/11.

(c) John is absent from the UK for the whole of the fiscal year and hence cannot be resident in the UK for the tax year. However, he is ordinarily resident for 2010/11 as he was born in the UK and it is to be his normal country of residence.

Question 2

Petra's income will be subject to UK tax as follows:

i. Bank Interest – not taxable as not remitted to the UK;
ii. Employment interest – taxable, since it was paid by a UK employer for work performed in the UK.

Index

Index of cases

Subject index

Note:
- G = Defined in Glossary
- W = See Website for more details